Business and Sustainability

Business and Sustainability

Michael Blowfield

Senior Research Fellow
Smith School of Enterprise and the Environment
University of Oxford
Oxford, UK

OXFORD
UNIVERSITY PRESS

OXFORD
UNIVERSITY PRESS

Great Clarendon Street, Oxford OX2 6DP,
United Kingdom

Oxford University Press is a department of the University of Oxford.
It furthers the University's objective of excellence in research, scholarship,
and education by publishing worldwide. Oxford is a registered trade mark of
Oxford University Press in the UK and in certain other countries

British Library Cataloguing in Publication Data

Data available

ISBN 978-0-19-964298-4

Printed in Great Britain by
Ashford Colour Press Ltd, Gosport, Hampshire

How to use this book

Purpose

This book provides a comprehensive overview of how the world's sustainability challenges are affecting and are affected by business. It has been written to educate present and future managers of for-profit enterprises, and for anyone interested in the business–sustainability relationship.

It does not present a particular view of business and sustainability. Its aim is to offer different perspectives and examples from around the world so that readers can discuss, explore, and reach their own conclusions. The content is divided between three main themes:

- The context: exploring the evolution of the business–sustainability relationship, today's key sustainability challenges, and the position of business in a resource-constrained world.
- Management: examining the management challenges posed by sustainability, and how these are and will be dealt with.
- The external environment: looking at the ways other segments of society, from governments to consumers, are reacting to sustainability challenges.

The book does not pretend to be an encyclopaedia for any of these themes, but it provides its users with a structured, coherent, and thorough introduction that is useful in its own right, and offers a launch pad for anyone wanting to investigate in more detail the issues raised.

Audience

The primary audience is people studying business' relationship to social and environmental sustainability at graduate and undergraduate level. It has been written with the specific needs of management students in mind, but its content is relevant to anyone with an interest in the management and governance of sustainability, or the role of business in society.

Limits

The book provides an introduction to sustainability issues, but it does not provide an in-depth analysis of any particular aspect of sustainability. Likewise, it does not provide in-depth analyses of sustainability from any particular business studies discipline (e.g. finance, accounting, marketing). In both cases, it signposts sources for this more specialist knowledge, but its emphasis is on offering teachers and students a sufficiently detailed map of the full business–sustainability topography.

Structure

The content is divided into 12 chapters:

Section 1—The global context
   Ch 1. Business and sustainability overview
   Ch 2. Sustainability challenges confronting business
   Ch 3. Business in a resource-constrained world

Section 2—Managing sustainability
   Ch 4. Leadership, entrepreneurship, and change
   Ch 5. Strategy and execution
   Ch 6. Innovation, planning, and design
   Ch 7. Financing sustainability
   Ch 8. Cooperation, collaboration, and partnership
   Ch 9. Next-generation competencies

Section 3—The external environment
   Ch 10. Governance
   Ch 11. Sustainable consumption and production
   Ch 12. Looking to the future
Extended case studies

Using the materials

It should not matter which order the chapters are used in. The book can be read from start to finish, and is structured to take its users through the process of understanding why sustainability matters to business, how business can manage the issues that arise, and what management can expect in future.

Equally, the chapters are also written so that they can be used individually, or shuffled about to suit users' own needs. The chapters are comprehensively cross-linked so that, for example, a user could begin by looking at governance (Chapter 10), discuss how government policy relates to renewable energy (Chapter 3), and then explore technological innovations to reduce carbon emissions and intensity (Chapter 6). There is no right, wrong, or best way of using this book, and it is intended to be a flexible aid.

Acknowledgments

I am deeply indebted to the Smith School of Enterprise and the Environment at the University of Oxford which has not only paid my fellowship while writing this book, but has also provided the intellectual environment that stimulated my ideas. Sir David King, the School's first director and someone who helped make sense of the science to me, and Martin Smith, the School's benefactor, both deserve my particular thanks.

I am also grateful to the Cambridge Programme for Sustainability Leadership, the International Air Transport Association, Cary Krosinsky and Nick Robins, Marks & Spencer, PricewaterhouseCoopers LLP, Trillionthtonne.org, and the World Resources Institute for permission to use materials reproduced in this book. Francesca Griffin at Oxford University Press remains as patient and helpful an editor as one could hope for, and Catherine Dolan and Lucy Blowfield have been equally patient in tolerating the piles of books and papers scattered around our house.

Contents in brief

Detailed contents

SECTION 1 **The global context**

SECTION 2 **Managing sustainability**

· ·

List of figures

List of boxes

List of key concept boxes

List of snapshot cases

List of abbreviations

3BL	triple bottom-line
BEV	battery electric vehicle
CCS	carbon capture and storage
CDM	Clean Development Mechanism
CDP	Carbon Disclosure Project
CDR	carbon removal technologies
CEO	chief executive officer
CFC	chlorofluorocarbon
CFL	compact fluorescent light
CO_2	carbon dioxide
CO_2e	carbon dioxide and its equivalent greenhouse gases
COP	Conference of Parties
CPSL	Cambridge Programme for Sustainability Leadership
CSR	corporate social responsibility
DFID	Department for International Development (UK)
EABIS	European Academy of Business in Society
EMH	efficient markets hypothesis
E P&L	environmental profit and loss account
EPA	Environmental Protection Agency (USA)
ESG	environmental, social, and governance—a common abbreviation, sometimes synonymous with sustainability and corporate responsibility
ETI	Ethical Trading Initiative
ETS	emissions trading scheme
EU	European Union
FSC	Forest Stewardship Council
GDP	gross domestic product
GHG	greenhouse gas
GRI	Global Reporting Initiative
HEV	hybrid electric vehicle
ICEV	internal combustion engine vehicle
ICMM	International Commission on Mining and Metals
ICT	information and communications technology
IFOAM	International Federation of Organic Agriculture Movements
IPCC	Intergovernmental Panel on Climate Change

IPO	initial public offering
IRR	internal rate of return
LEED	Leadership in Energy and Environmental Design
LOHAS	lifestyles of health and sustainability (consumer category)
MDG	Millennium Development Goal
MSC	Marine Stewardship Council
mtoe	million tonnes of oil equivalent
NEF	New Economics Foundation
NGO	non-government organization
OECD	Organisation for Economic Co-operation and Development
ppm	parts per million
PRI	Principles for Responsible Investment
PRME	Principles for Responsible Management Education
PV	photovoltaic
R&D	research and development
RCE	resource-constrained economy
REDD	Reducing Carbon Emissions from Deforestation and Forest Degradation
RPIC	Responsible Property Investing Center
RSPO	Roundtable on Sustainable Palm Oil
SLEPT	social, legal, economic, political, and technological
SLF	sustainable livelihoods framework
SME	small and medium-sized enterprise
SRI	socially responsible investment
SRM	solar radiation management
TEEB	The Economics of Ecosystems and Biodiversity
UN	United Nations
UNCTAD	United Nations Conference on Trade and Development
UNEP	United Nations Environment Programme
UNFCCC	United Nations Framework Convention on Climate Change
UNGC	United Nations Global Compact
UNICEF	United Nations Children's Fund
UNPRI	United Nations Principles for Responsible Investment
USS	Universities Superannuation Scheme
VC	venture capital
WBCSD	World Business Council for Sustainable Development
WEF	World Economic Forum
WWF	World Wildlife Fund

About the book

Chapter in brief

In this chapter, we look at how sustainability shapes the world b
now and in the future. We examine the implications for conver
discuss some of the alternative roles companies will be expect
understand the historical role of business in society, and con
change in a resource-constrained society. It also requires u
business could play, not just to protect itself from sustainability
process of transformation to a prosperous resource-constraine

Chapter in brief

A concise overview can be found at the
beginning of each chapter to help guide you
through the different topics you will encounter
in this section of the book and enable you to
quickly navigate your way around specific
topics that will be addressed.

 Key terms

Resource-constrained economy   Interconnectednes
Energy   Water
Low carbon society   Health
Poverty   Social organizatior

Key terms

At the beginning of each chapter you will
find a list of key terms which have been
incorporated throughout that unit. You can
familiarise yourself with their definitions in the
glossary at the end of the book.

 Online resources

- Signposts to information on sustainability leadership.
- Resources on sustainable entrepreneurship.
- Suggestions for case studies on leadership.
  http://www.oxfordtextbooks.co.uk/orc/blowfield/

Online resource box

An Online resource box is featured at the
opening of each chapter and identifies a series
of related materials and activities that are
available on the Online Resource Centre.

 Key concept 4.1   Leadership

According to Peter Drucker, the only useful definition of a le
Sustainability leadership is about the skills, styles, competen
organizations take to build this followership. It is not necess
innovation from across the company can be an important e
is also no single approach, and quite different leadership ap
and win commitment from those whose lives will be affecte

Key concept boxes

This feature will offer you a brief explanation
of key concepts that are particularly pertinent
within that chapter and help you to become
familiar with essential sustainability concepts
in the context of business.

Discussion points

Sustainability is often portrayed as crucial to corporate

- What are the business-sustainability sweetspots for N
- Which companies do you think have done well at in
  strategy?
- Which companies have made sustainability their stra

Discussion points

Each chapter has a series of discussion points
posing questions that draw upon the
concepts and themes that have been covered.
These provide an opportunity for you to
demonstrate your understanding of core issues
as well as prompting further thought and
discussion on a particular topic.

Snapshot 9.1   Embedding sustainabi

The Tata Group comprises more than 90 operating compani
communications and information technology, engineering,
products, and chemicals. It has operations in over 80 countr
companies export products and services to 85 countries. Alt
India, most of its revenues now come from outside its histor
A challenge for a company of this size is how to enable th

Snapshot boxes

Snapshot boxes offer short, succinct examples
of real business and sustainability scenarios to
help illustrate an array of current issues that
organizations face. They are followed by
questions to prompt analysis and discussion.

Summary

The different challenges associated with sustainability a
we fail to establish a low carbon energy system, busines
global average temperatures. The cost of establishing su
and require significant investment of patient, risk tolera
generation plants, and new consumer products. There a
benefit and which ones will suffer from this change, but

Chapter summary

At the end of every chapter you will find a
concise summary, which reiterates the key
points that have been covered in the current
chapter and the most significant aspects to
take away from that section.

Further reading

Chang, H. 2010, *23 things they don't tell you about cap*
Not a book about business or about sustainability, but i
about why some countries prosper and the way capitali

Jackson, T. 2009, *Prosperity without growth: Economic:*
A well-constructed argument against the need for econ
perspective.

Further reading

If you are interested in a particular aspect of
a chapter, the author has provided a list of
further reading materials where you can find
out more about a specific topic, or read
further to extend your own development and
understanding of business and sustainability.

Case study 9   Sustainability dichoton

Professor Marquez had been dean of Maxwell School of Ma
made his name for his research into equity derivatives, altho
from trends he saw as confirming Warren Buffet's view that t
mass destruction'. He had also published a couple of papers
investors in social enterprises.
    That all seemed a long time ago; before he became more

End-of-chapter case study

At the end of each chapter, the author has
provided a longer case study, complete with
three themes for discussion and out-of-class
assignments, which consolidates the themes
and issues covered in the chapter as well as
helping to contextualise core sustainability
issues which have affected working business
environments.

The challenge

Plan A was launched in January 2007. It is retail giant Marks & S
to make itself the greenest multiple retailer, and comprises 100
as climate change, waste, human health, trading, and natural re
placed it amongst the most respected companies when it cor
challenges, and it has achieved this while lifting its share price a
    However, Plan A was due to end in 2012. It has decided to in
from 2012–2014 to ensure that Plan A commitments are emb

Extended case studies

In addition to the book's 36 snapshots and 12
chapter case studies, there are two Extended
case studies. These provide more comprehensive
material for analyzing the circumstances
companies find themselves in, the forks in the
road managers confront, and the decisions they
have to make. They are especially suited to
courses that use the Harvard case study
approach, but can be adapted to other teaching
techniques.

About the Online Resource Centre

www.oxfordtextbooks.co.uk/orc/blowfield/

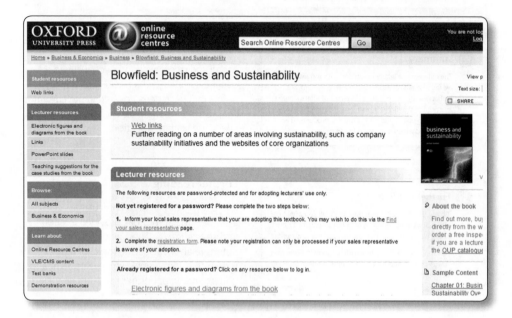

Free resources available to students include:

Web links

This feature of the site allows you to click through to a list of web links. These will take you to a collection of further reading on a number of areas involving sustainability such as company sustainability initiatives and the websites of core organizations.

Resources for registered adopters of the textbook include:

Teaching the case

The case is structured as follows:

a) An introduction to the Dean and the dichotomy he faces
b) A discussion of sustainability from the business management perspective
c) A discussion of the issues sustainability (and by implication other new topics) presents for business schools
d) Information on the market place for sustainability competencies
e) Exhibits

Depending on the context within which the case is being used, different degrees of emphasis can be applied to the different sections. For example, if you are teaching a course where

Teaching suggestions for the case studies from the book

This resource provides you with teaching tips and solutions from the case studies in the textbook to help you structure lectures and seminars.

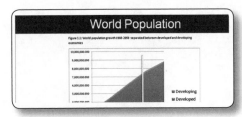

PowerPoint slides

Here you can click through to various sets of PowerPoint slides that align with selected chapters of the textbook and can be used as a basis for handouts and assist your teaching of that chapter.

Resource title: 'Just Good Business'
Description: Adnams, RiverSimple and Wilson James: sustainat
Source: ICAEW
Link (URL): http://www.icaew.com/en/about-icaew/what-we-do/su /just-good-business

Resource title: Blood in the Mobile
Description: Blood in the mobile : the social and environmental c

Audio-visual library

The author has provided a list of links to films, online videos, and other audio-visual resources relevant to business and sustainability complete with teaching notes.

Electronic figures and diagrams from the book

You can find electronic versions of the figures and illustrations from the textbook online, so that you can easily incorporate them into your own teaching materials and navigate to a particular figure of interest.

Section 1

The global context

Business and sustainability overview

Key terms

Sustainability	Demographic change
Ecosystem services	Scepticism
Climate change	Social capital
Natural capital	Scientific evidence

Online resources

- Links to key resources for understanding the scientific and social aspects of sustainability.
- More figures on demography, global warming, and ecosystems.
- Company sustainability initiatives.
  http://www.oxfordtextbooks.co.uk/orc/blowfield/

Chapter in brief

This chapter provides the basis for thinking about the relationship between sustainability and business. It introduces the concept of sustainability and some of the main arguments about why it matters to the private sector. It reviews scientific theories of sustainability, and how they have been interpreted. It identifies three main areas of sustainability—demography, ecosystems, and climate change—and provides the basis for thinking about their importance to business. It sets out the social and environmental nature of sustainability. It also discusses doubts about sustainability, and whether they are justified.

The sustainability transformation

Imagine. You have the chance to invest in a government-chartered monopoly giving you revenues from 45,000 kilometres of toll roads. The monopoly comes with a nationwide network of 8,000 vending outlets, and there are additional opportunities to establish restaurants, accommodation, and refreshment outlets for weary travellers.

Before you contact your broker, however, consider this other opportunity. You have the chance to team up with Shell and Unilever in investing in the largest supplier of lighting fuel in the world. The company also has patents on key fuel processing technologies, and its strategy of buying up natural resources means it is well hedged against fluctuations in supply.

These seem to be two great opportunities. And if you invested in either you would lose a fortune. The lighting industry opportunity was for raw material used in making candles, and the proposition landed on your desk on 26 January 1880, the day before Thomas Edison patented the electric light bulb. The roads in question were toll roads for horse-drawn carriages, and the share offer was made on 26 September 1825, the day before the first steam-hauled passenger train came into service. In both cases, incumbent industries were wiped out almost overnight, turned into historical curiosities just as Gutenberg's printing press had done to hand-copying centuries earlier, and the personal computer would do to typewriters a century further on.

REBOCADO

The steam age, harnessing electricity, printing, and the IT revolution are not simply examples of innovation: they demonstrate how business and society as a whole experience profound change because of radical innovation.

Sustainability can be seen as the latest example of profound change demanding transformation throughout society. Climate change in particular is inspiring radical ways of thinking about energy production and consumption, transportation, and consumerism that threaten to make incumbent technologies such as coal-fired power plants and the internal combustion engine redundant. During the financial crisis of the later 2000s, countries such as South Korea and China earmarked significant portions of their recovery packages for investment in the needs of a low carbon economy, i.e. one where emissions of carbon dioxide (CO_2) and other greenhouse gases would be much lower than today. The European Union has announced its 20–20–20 targets whereby it aims to reduce greenhouse gas emissions by 20 per cent, and produce 20 per cent of its energy from renewable sources by 2020.

Be it through investment, policy, or regulation, governments around the world are anticipating a major shift in their economies, and these shifts will have a significant impact on business. Industries from aviation to oil palm to coal have come under attack because of their environmental impacts. Away from climate change, the practices of companies such as Coca-Cola, Findus, and IKEA have come under the spotlight because of responsible water, fisheries, and forestry management respectively. Moreover, new industries are emerging to meet the challenges, and companies such as Suzlon (wind power), Sindicatum Carbon Capital (finance), and d.light (solar lighting) all view sustainability challenges as an innovation opportunity.

A variety of frameworks have been developed to help managers incorporate sustainability into management practice. The 'triple bottom-line was originally the brainchild of John Elkington and offers the basis to allow companies to account equally for the social, economic, and environmental performance (Chapter 9). It reflects some of the thinking behind the Five Capitals model which identifies five types of capital that a company needs to nurture and manage if it is to be sustainable, and this in turn has been used to help companies identify their social and environmental footprints (Chapter 2). The Natural Step sets out principles for managing companies' social and environmental impact (Snapshot 9.2). Companies have developed increasingly sophisticated methods for assessing product lifecycles to understand the environmental impact goods and services have at all stages of their existence. These types of framework and method are discussed in different contexts throughout this book (e.g. Chapters 6 and 9).

However, as with any period of change and innovation, there is much tension, conflict, confusion, and disruption associated with sustainability. As we will see, there is dispute surrounding sustainability itself, and whether some phenomena are more hype than fact. Even if we believe the scientific evidence, the scope of sustainability—ranging from global warming to aquifer depletion to deforestation to conservation to human poverty and more—seems too great and complex, and is it the responsibility of private companies, with their legally prescribed fiduciary duty towards investors, to get involved in issues of human and environmental justice, or the management of the planet?

However, we can turn this question around and ask whether business can ignore sustainability given how resource scarcity, social shifts, and ecosystem change will fundamentally alter the world in which business operates. Whether we are talking about accounting, marketing, organizational behaviour, finance, or strategy, sustainability challenges conventional business thinking: what is accounted for, what is produced, and the very nature of prosperity and success.

Section Two of this book deals with these matters in detail, but we are already touching on different interpretations of business' sustainability challenge. On the one hand, there are many people who see sustainability as essentially an investment play: their interest is in substituting one set of technologies—those associated with high degrees of carbon emissions—with an alternative set. Thus, oil and coal, for example, could be replaced with nuclear and solar. The change would cause disruption, and has significant implications in terms of investment, regulation, and the introduction of new technology and infrastructure. But theoretically, if sufficient funding could be found and there was adequate political will and technological expertise, the energy power house of our current economic system could be replaced with another one, and little else would change.

However, other people see that sustainability challenges are more profound than switching technologies: they question not only if the switch-over is achievable, but whether it is desirable. They wonder if economic growth—the heart of private sector innovation—might be the enemy of sustainability, and question whether it is conducive to a prosperous society in the future.[1]

Therefore, as we look in more depth at business' relationship to sustainability, we should ask ourselves not only whether business will need to change and how, but whether sustainability represents a paradigm shift where the old is replaced by the new for the good of economic growth, a simpler transition akin to replacing worn-out tyres on a car, or a more radical transformation wherein the very nature of business and the definition of business success is open to question.

Dimensions of sustainability

The Brundtland Commission's definition of sustainability—'meeting the needs of the present generation without compromising the ability of future generations to meet their own needs'—is the one most widely used today (see Key concept 1.1). It is not without

Key concept **1.1**   Sustainability

Sustainability is a relatively new term: its first recorded use in an environmental context was as recent as 1980,[2] but the concept of the environment as the sum total of the external conditions needed to maintain life goes back to the nineteenth century, perhaps replacing 'economy of nature' which had been used since the seventeenth century to refer to the natural world as a whole.

The notion of a oneness of nature predates even this, and various faiths have been eager to demonstrate humanity's role as custodian of planet earth. However, it is also the case that humans have treated natural resources as an infinite source of capital that can be exploited with impunity. To a degree this was acceptable so long as populations were low, technologies were limited, and financial systems were basic. Nowadays, an unprecedented combination of population density, technological innovation, wealth creation, and capital has enabled humanity to exploit nature as never before, and made us more aware of the finite nature of our environment. In turn, this has led us to think of natural resources not only as something to be exploited or preserved, but as something in need of management.

This change in thinking became noticeable in the 1960s following the publication of *The Silent Spring* (Carson, Darling, & Darling 1962) that highlighted the damage caused by pesticides, and played a major role in kick-starting the environmental movement. In 1987, the World Commission on Economic Development (WCED), more commonly known as the 'Brundtland Commission', focusing on 'environmental strategies for achieving sustainable development by the year 2000 and beyond', agreed a definition of 'sustainable development':

> Humanity has the ability to make development sustainable—to ensure that it meets the needs of the present generation without compromising the ability of future generations to meet their own needs. The concept of sustainable development does imply limits—not absolute limits, but limitations imposed by the present state of technology and social organization on environmental resources and by the ability of the biosphere to absorb the effect of human activities.
>
> (World Commission on Environment and Development & Brundtland 1987, p. 8)

This definition of sustainable development—commonly paraphrased as 'meeting the needs of the present generation without compromising the ability of future generations to meet their own needs'—lay at the heart of the United Nations' (UN) 1992 Conference on Environment and Development, normally called the Earth Summit, which resulted in the first international agreement to tackle environmental management issues. Although aimed at governments, it carries various implications for business, and requires companies to think and act in 'three time zones' in order to:

1. deal with historical liabilities from times when it was acceptable to externalize part of their costs onto the environment, people, or future generations;

2. meet the increased expectations of today's citizens and consumers;

3. take into account the interests and rights of future generations.

The definition implies not only that business can no longer regard the environment as a limitless pool of natural capital that can be drawn down upon without liability, but that it should also play a part in efforts to manage that capital in ways that might well go against the interests of its owners. It also highlights that in acting as a custodian of natural capital, it has special responsibilities towards people, and cannot discount their legitimate interests.

☐ Discussion points

We all have ideas about companies that are green and ones that are not.

- Is sustainability of material interest to companies?
- What companies would you put on your list of 'green leaders'? Why?
- Do consumers factor sustainability into their buying decisions?

controversy because when used as a starting point for action it raises all manner of awkward questions. For instance, how are we to value the rights of future generations against those of present ones? Is it better to conserve natural capital now or to spend it so that there is a larger pool of wealth for our descendants? How can we constrain rights to exploit resources across the world when some regions continue to reap the benefits of unfettered exploitation in the past? Sustainability is not just about natural resources and ecosystems; there are strong ethical, political, social, and economic aspects that affect what has and will occur.

Furthermore, this definition of sustainability has been altered in the context of business. The Dow Jones Sustainability Indices define corporate sustainability as a 'business approach that creates long-term shareholder value by embracing opportunities and managing risks deriving from economic, environmental and social developments',[3] while consultancy firm Accenture calls it 'the way an organization increases its positive – and reduces its negative – effects on society, the environment and the economy'.[4] Such definitions are not alternatives to the Brundtland Commission's, but reflect how that generic vision has been made more actionable in the business environment.

The Brundtland definition has been altered in other ways as well, notably the scope of what sustainability includes or does not. For instance, is there a fundamental difference between an environmental catastrophe such as the grounding of the *Exxon Valdez* or the Montara oil spill off East Timor, and systemic issues of contamination and degradation such as the Gulf of Mexico 'dead zone' or the conversion of forests to pasture in the Amazon Basin? This book is not intended to be an Introduction to Sustainability—other resources serving that purpose are listed at the end of this chapter. However, to make sense of the business-sustainability relationship, we need to have an indication of sustainability's scope.

In this book, sustainability is limited to those issues where systemic changes rather than individual events seem likely to affect the well-being of the Earth and in particular human life. Incidents such as the Montara spill when an Australian-owned oil rig caused widespread damage to wildlife and livelihoods in the Timor Sea are rightly thought of as disasters, but they are not the consistent anticipated or predictable outcome of human activity. Management practices might be to blame for incidents such as the explosion at BP's Texas refinery, and understanding the pressures that lead to them is important in its own right as part of corporate responsibility or wider management practice. However, they are of a different order to an issue such as the legally sanctioned, investor endorsed, technologically-assisted conversion of high-value forests to palm oil plantations which is linked to endangering wildlife and the release of CO_2 from peat swamps. Environmental disasters are an important part of corporate responsibility, but sustainability is about long-term systemic relationships, including both the use of natural capital and its contamination. With that in mind, sustainability has been divided into three main areas that will recur throughout this book:

1. **Demographic change**—shifts in size and patterns of population over time, including the distribution of wealth and poverty.
2. **Ecosystem change**—variations over time in the Earth's natural capital affecting the planet's ability to sustain future generations.
3. **Climate change**—changes in the Earth's climate over time due to natural variability and human activity.

Demographic change

Sustainability is often depicted from a natural environment perspective, downplaying the wants and needs of human beings. In reality, human behaviour is a major element of sustainability as we shall see throughout this book. Some people go further and argue that tackling poverty and inequality are essential to the sustainable management of our planet (Chapter 2); some believe that sustainability is a moral problem that brings into focus issues of fairness, avarice, justice, alienation, and so on. Setting aside the more complex aspects of the human–sustainability relationship for the time being, we will begin by highlighting the undisputed fact of demographic change.

Demographic change—shifts in size and patterns of population over time—is one of the main ways people affect the Earth's capacity to sustain current and future generations. A time traveller who stopped off in the Bronze Age (2000 BC) and then during the European Black Death (1500 AD) would notice very little change in total population (less than 500 million people). But if she landed 500 years later, she would find herself on a planet of 6.5 billion people—a 13-fold increase. Even if she landed in 1950 and then 50 years later, she would see an historically unprecedented increase of four billion, and it is estimated that if she reappeared in 2050, she would be in a world of over nine billion people (Figure 1.1).

Population is a key factor in the 'environmental burden' we place on our planet. Malthus famously recognized this at the turn of the eighteenth century when he predicted that the Earth's capacity to sustain human life was limited. Subsequently, technological innovation and advances in environmental management extended the Earth's carrying capacity beyond anything Malthus could have imagined—and this in spite of vastly increased lifespans and natural exploitation. Moreover, counterintuitively given the laws of supply and demand, increases in population and resource exploitation have been achieved during periods of cheaper prices and greater material well-being (Chapter 11). There is plenty of disagreement about what a prosperous society looks like, but for well over a century an ever-increasing number of people have associated it with needs and aspirations met through the increased deployment of human, natural, and financial capital.

Around the world, people are having longer and healthier lives than ever before. Overall, they are more literate and have higher incomes: but the picture is complex. About 1.2 billion people, or one-fifth of the world's population, still live in 'extreme poverty' (less than US$1 a day). Half of the world's people live on less than US$2 a day. If we remove China from the equation, the total number of extremely poor increased by 28 million in the 1990s, and gross domestic product (GDP) in sub-Saharan Africa has fallen by 17% since 1975. Life

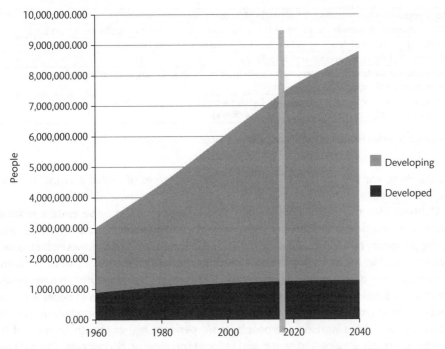

Figure 1.1 World population growth 1960–2050 separated between developed and developing economies.
Source: adapted from United Nations Population Division (2009); Bloom, Canning, & Sevilla (2003).

expectancy, maternal health, child mortality, malnutrition, and disease not surprisingly reflect degrees of wealth and poverty. A woman has a 1-in-16 lifetime risk of dying from pregnancy-related illness in sub-Saharan Africa compared to 1 in 3,500 in North America. While life expectancy has increased from 47 to 65 years overall since 1950, in richer countries it is now 82 years.

Demographic dividends

However, poverty does not mean population growth is less in the developing world. On the contrary, developing economies account for 95 per cent of population growth, and the population of the 50 least developed nations is set to double by 2050 at the same time as what the UN calls developed nations is expected to remain steady at 1.2 billion (Figure 1.2). This is because, while infant and child mortality is high in poor countries compared to richer ones, it has nonetheless fallen by two-thirds since 1950, faster than declines in the fertility rate. Policy-makers have long argued about the relationship between rising populations and economic prosperity. China with its one-child policy was only one country that pursued birth control policies and still grew its economy, but it can be argued that to lift people out of poverty requires more capital deployment: natural and human. Nowadays, however, many believe sustainable development requires us to reduce or stabilize the environmental burden of human activity, but the world's population is not only increasing, it is changing in other ways too (Figure 1.2). According to some sustainability theory (e.g. the aforementioned triple bottom-line and the

Total population has gone from 2.5 billion in 1950, to 7.1 billion today
76 million new inhabitants are added each year because births outnumber deaths more than 2:1
3 billion people live on less than US$2 a day—half of the world's population
Nearly half of the world's population is under 25
Population in the least developed countries will triple by 2050, and change little (even decline) in more developed regions
Emerging economies such as China and India have increasingly large proportions of elderly people (31% and 21% of total population by 2050 respectively)

Figure 1.2 Selected features of global demographic change.

Natural Step; see Key concept 1.1), balancing different types of capital is crucial to future prosperity, but in each case the implication is that we should do more with less.

Malthus's idea that population growth hinders development may be evident in family planning programmes but some demographers say rapid population growth promotes economic prosperity by adding human capital and increasing market size. However, that ignores a critical variable: the way a population is distributed across different age groups. Economic behaviour varies depending on a person's age, and a nation's age structure can have a major effect on its development. For example, a high proportion of young or old dependents can limit economic growth because of the resources devoted to their care (especially by women). Countries with more working age people can experience higher growth because of the number of people earning and saving, and reduced spending on dependents. This has been called the 'demographic dividend' (Bloom, Canning, & Sevilla 2003), and some developing countries are experiencing the kind of boom generation that stimulated economic growth in the USA after the Second World War.

As Europe, Japan, and the USA are finding, population booms present different challenges as the boom generation moves through its lifecycle. Early on in the boom, the key concerns are health care and education; later they are job creation and capital accumulation; later still social security and retirement provision. The current debate about pension funds—should the younger generation support an increasingly elderly population through higher pension fund contributions? Should the retirement age be raised? How can individuals take more responsibility for their retirement?—is an inevitable result of demographic change and its economic consequences. Some predict that growth in household financial wealth in the richest nations will fall by more than two-thirds compared to historical rates, with knock-on effects around the world.[5] Even if that does not transpire, there is still a major question whether the type of economic growth open to earlier baby boomers is an option today given how some believe degraded ecosystems and climate change are becoming barriers to prosperity.

Nonetheless, there is much enthusiasm—not least from parts of the business community—that poverty can be solved by private enterprise, and that the poor are an attractive market for companies. Prahalad and Hart were early protagonists of the 'bottom of the pyramid' business model[6] where the large number of poor people is held to represent a vast, untapped market that can profitably be served by the private sector. Companies such as Vodafone have found that poor people in developing countries can be a viable market but need different approaches to product development and marketing (see Chapter 2, Case study 2). The 2006 Nobel Prize for Economics went to the Grameen Bank whose micro-finance brought capital to the poor, and has now been taken up by major banks such as Citigroup.

In developed countries, migration from poor to rich countries such as Italy and the USA is part of demographic change involving 2.2 million migrants each year, although it should also be noted that international migration is often between poor nations because of events such as war, political unrest, and food or water shortages. Migrants also flock to urban centres, and today 44 per cent of people in developing countries and 75 per cent in developed ones live in cities. The emergence of mega cities with over ten million people, and the enormous rise in populations near the coast both bring new challenges with regards to pollution, transportation, housing, and waste management. Such trends in themselves have been encouraged by economic globalization, especially the use of low-cost labour in typically coastal, urban-sited economic development zones in developing countries, and this in turn has consequences for ecosystem change.

 Discussion points

Demographic change is an issue worldwide, but with different features in developing, emerging, and developed economies.

- Why might population growth be a boost to economic growth in poorer countries?
- Why might it be a threat to poorer and richer countries?
- Do you agree with Prahalad and Hart that there is a fortune at the bottom of the pyramid?

Ecosystem change

Ecosystem refers to systems created by the dynamic interrelationship of living and non-living things. An ecosystem can be as large as a desert or as small as a puddle, but a sustainable ecosystem cannot contain more organisms than it can feed, water, and shelter. If that is not the case, the ecosystem is imbalanced, and it is the imbalances—particularly through human activity—that have attracted concern in recent years.

Ecosystems contain different elements, but the major ones are soil, atmosphere, heat and light from the sun, water, and living organisms. Research, most notably the Millennium Ecosystem Assessment completed in 2005,[7] has shown how humanity's 'ecological footprint'—its pressure on global ecosystems—has affected ecosystems through demographic change, economic growth, global warming, and other activities, and there are various signs associated with an historically unprecedented footprint (Figure 1.3).

Over the past 50 years, ecosystems have changed more rapidly and extensively than in any comparable period of time in human history, largely to meet rapidly growing demands for food, fresh water, timber, fibre, and fuel. The changes made to ecosystems have contributed to substantial net gains in human well-being and economic development (Figure 1.4). For instance, increases in land under cultivation and agricultural yields have meant that food production has risen threefold since 1961, resulting in lower food prices and a fall in the number of undernourished people.[8] Some of these improvements have been criticized: Have indigenous populations lost out because of the expansion of agricultural lands? Are we now seeing the end of low food prices as competition for land and population size increase? Will the dietary demands of the rich world make the poor more vulnerable to malnutrition? More generally, the Millennium Ecosystem Assessment, which is the most comprehensive review of the health of the world's ecosystems conducted by natural and social scientists, concluded that human actions are

Rising greenhouse gas emissions
Overexploitation of many surface and ground water resources
Continuing threats to biodiversity associated with habitat destruction and invasive species
Intense exploitation and depletion of wild fish stocks
Fragmentation of many forest ecosystems
Increasing air pollution in expanding urban areas of developing countries
Build-up of toxic chemicals in infants and the natural environment

Figure 1.3 Selected features of global ecosystem change.

Source: Millennium Ecosystem Assessment Reports, http://www.maweb.org.

Food production increased 2½ times
Water use doubled
Wood harvests for pulp and paper production tripled
Timber production increased by more than half
Installed hydropower capacity doubled

Figure 1.4 Changes in ecosystem services 1960–2000.

Source: Millennium Ecosystem Assessment Reports, http://www.maweb.org.

depleting the Earth's natural capital to the extent that we can no longer take for granted its ability to sustain future generations. This is not to say that with appropriate actions it is impossible to reverse the degradation of many ecosystem services, but it is claimed the changes in policy and practice this would involve are substantial and not currently underway.

The Assessment paid special attention to the consequences of ecosystem change for human well-being and the scientific basis for future action. It provides ample evidence of how the ways we manage ecosystems affect the Earth's capacity to sustain human life, and can ultimately impact economic prosperity, health, security, social relations, and freedom of choice and action. This does not imply that all ecosystems are in decline, and part of the sustainability challenge is understanding what can and cannot be exploited without causing lasting damage. However, if one looks at the full range of services ecosystems provide, it seems that more are being degraded than improved (Figure 1.5). Moreover, the complex interrelationship of services means that losses in one area cannot be easily offset by gains in another. For instance, increases in aquaculture in some coastal areas have been achieved at the cost of degrading mangroves, wetlands, and other natural defences meaning that the impact of hurricanes and similar extreme weather events can be greater than before.

Land use

There are numerous industries directly dependent upon particular ecosystems (Figure 1.6), and there is clear evidence that some aspects of ecosystem degradation are already having a tangible impact on people's lives and livelihoods. Take, for example, land use: population growth is increasing the demand for food, and is rising faster than agricultural productivity; economic growth is increasing the demand for high-value food crops, and also biofuels; urbanization and demand for housing is eating away at farmland (e.g. the UK's demand for 120,000 new homes a year could swallow up 8,000 hectares of rural land). The upshot of

Provisioning Services			
Food	crops	▲	substantial production increase
	livestock	▲	substantial production increase
	capture fisheries	▼	declining production due to overharvest
	aquaculture	▲	substantial production increase
	wild foods	▼	declining production
Fiber	timber	+/–	forest loss in some regions, growth in others
	cotton, hemp, silk	+/–	declining production of some fibers, growth in others
	wood fuel	▼	declining production
Genetic resources		▼	lost through extinction and crop genetic resource loss
Biochemicals, natural medicines, pharmaceuticals		▼	lost through extinction, overharvest
Fresh water		▼	unsustainable use for drinking, industry, and irrigation; amount of hydro energy unchanged, but dams increase ability to use that energy
Regulating Services			
Air quality regulation		▼	decline in ability of atmosphere to cleanse itself
Climate regulation	global	▲	net source of carbon sequestration since mid-century
	regional and local	▼	preponderance of negative impacts
Water regulation		+/–	varies depending on ecosystem change and location
Erosion regulation		▼	increased soil degradation
Water purification and waste treatment		▼	declining water quality
Disease regulation		+/–	varies depending on ecosystem change
Pest regulation		▼	natural control degraded through pesticide use
Pollination		▼[2]	apparent global decline in abundance of pollinators
Natural hazard regulation		▼	loss of natural buffers (wetlands, mangroves)
Cultural Services			
Spiritual and religious values		▼	rapid decline in sacred groves and species
Aesthetic values		▼	decline in quantity and quality of natural lands
Recreation and ecotourism		+/–	more areas accessible but many degraded

Figure 1.5 Changes in ecosystem services.

Source: Adapted from Maweb Synthesis Report.

Food production: US$980 billion per year
Timber industry: US$400 billion per year
Marine fisheries: US$80 billion per year
Marine aquaculture: US$57 billion per year
Recreational hunting and fishing: >US$75 billion per year in the USA alone

Figure 1.6 Worldwide market value of ecosystem-service industries.

Sources: WWF 2010; Millennium Ecosystem Assessment Reports, http://www.maweb.org.

these competing pressures is that agricultural land is expanding in about 70 per cent of countries, declining in about 25 per cent, and is roughly stable elsewhere. This in turn is causing deforestation, soil erosion, overuse, and desertification in some parts of the world.

Water

Water is an aspect of ecosystems that has come to prominence in recent years, and is considered by some experts to be a bigger problem than climate change. About 30 per cent of the world's population lives in countries suffering from moderate-to-high water stress, and GE's investments in desalination technologies, for instance, are based on calculations that about two-thirds of the world's population will live in water-stress by 2025. Although the absolute quantities of freshwater are fairly constant, population growth, industrial development, irrigated agriculture, and uneven water distribution mean that there are concerns about the availability of and access to water. Companies such as Unilever and Diageo have put water reduction and reuse at the top of their environmental agendas. Major utilities companies such as Suez have found themselves embroiled in the politics of water, not least in poor countries where one of the greatest environmental threats to health remains the continued use of untreated water, accounting for hundreds of millions of cases of water-related diseases, and more than five million deaths every year.

Forests

Forests play multiple roles in sustainable development, from nourishing the natural systems underpinning agriculture and supporting important economic activities, to helping regulate climate change and freshwater. Forests are recognized as the largest, most complex, and self-perpetuating of all ecosystems, and sections of industry such as the DIY retailers B&Q and Home Depot take seriously the need to promote sustainable forest management. However, deforestation, though not new, has accelerated, and in the 1990s was three times greater than reforestation. In countries such as Indonesia, the area of production forest has been halved since 1992, and although forested areas are on the increase in some parts of the world, overall they are in decline. Seventy per cent of deforested areas have been converted to agricultural land, and population increases combined with growing per capita consumption mean this trend is likely to continue.

Oceans and fisheries

Over 70 per cent of world fisheries are estimated to be at or near the point where yields decline, and ocean ecosystems are under further pressure because of sewage discharge, coastal urbanization, industrialization, and tourism. It has been estimated that in 1994, 37 per cent of the global population lived within 60 kilometres of the coast which is more people than inhabited the entire planet in 1950. Marine and coastal eutrophication—where high levels of plant growth reduce the amount of oxygen in water—is a relatively new and growing phenomenon related to human activity that causes dead zones in water bodies, and has occurred in several enclosed or semi-enclosed seas, including the Black Sea. Oceans are at risk of further degradation because of how global warming causes bleaching of coral reefs: the 1997 El Niño, for example, caused considerable reef damage in the Indian Ocean, Southeast Asia, the far western Pacific, and the Caribbean.

Biodiversity

Biodiversity is an important part of functioning ecosystems, and is the result of millions of years of evolution. Although extinction is part of evolution, biodiversity is being lost at rates far higher than that of natural extinction due to land conversion, pollution, climate change, and the introduction of exotic species. Although insufficient information is available to determine precisely how many species have become extinct in the past three decades, worldwide about 24 per cent (1,130) of mammal species and 12 per cent (1,183) of bird species are currently regarded as threatened. In what are called the 'environmental hotspots'– the 25 areas of the world identified as having the richest reservoirs of plant and animal life– over 70 per cent of original vegetation has been lost.

Interpreting the implications of change

For all the evidence that ecosystems are changing, there is much debate about the implications. There are innumerable examples of unexpected and unwanted local-level changes, but when do more macro changes become unsustainable, and can human ingenuity not be trusted to enable us to adapt? The frog in a pot of boiling water is an analogy widely used by environmentalists for describing humanity's perceived sluggish response to

 Snapshot 1.1   TEEB–putting a value on nature

The Economics of Ecosystems and Biodiversity (TEEB) is an international initiative to study the economics of biodiversity loss. Its first major report was entitled *Mainstreaming the Economics of Nature*, and one of its goals is to establish global standards for accounting for natural capital. TEEB was set up by the European Commission and is now hosted by the UN Environment Programme. It is run by Pavan Sukhdev, a banker with Deutsche Bank.

TEEB has identified the economic size and welfare impact of ecosystem and biodiversity loss, and the links between biodiversity conservation and poverty elimination, as well as drawing attention to the ethical dimensions of selecting discount rates in an ecosystem and biodiversity context. For example, TEEB estimates that investing US$45 billion a year in protected areas would secure the delivery of ecosystem services valued at US$5 trillion per annum. Conversely, natural capital loss, particularly due to deforestation, costs more than US$2 trillion a year.

TEEB is now in its second phase, and one of its main objectives is to develop an alternative national accounting system to GDP that would incorporate the welfare benefits provided by biodiversity and ecosystem services. It is also engaging with business to highlight the value of biodiversity and ecosystems. For instance, it points to the threefold increase in global sales of organic food and drink since 1999, and the 50 per cent increase in the market for eco-labelled fish from 2008 to 2009. It also highlights the value of ecosystem services such as the US$190 billion insect pollinators effectively contribute to agriculture each year, or the US$150 billion plus genetic resources provide to the pharmaceutical market.

Sources: http://www.teebweb.org–accessed 11 July 2011; http://teebforbusiness.earthmind.net–accessed 11 July 2011.

Questions

TEEB has been heralded as doing for biodiversity what the Stern Report (see 'Climate change consequences') did for climate change.

1. What is the significance of TEEB?

2. What are the advantages of putting an economic value on biodiversity and ecosystem services?

3. Why do some people object to the TEEB approach?

sustainability challenges, but others would claim that as a species humans have a track record of surviving and thriving in hot waters. They argue that we have or will develop the knowledge and wealth to protect ourselves against any long-term consequences of ecosystem change, and that it makes little sense to forego short-term economic gains for the sake of uncertain long-term benefits.

As we shall see in the next section, this is an argument prevalent in the debate over climate change. One of the forms it takes is that economic resources should not be used to mitigate climate change or other ecosystem changes because that is taking resources from the poor. Instead, we should concentrate on making the poor wealthy enough so that they have the economic resources themselves to respond to damaging changes. This is the argument made by Lomberg,[9] and is one that complements that of certain economists who believe that a combination of resources, technology, and free markets will lead to prosperity and sensible environmental decisions.[10] But, as Collier points out, the playing field is very skewed to begin with (e.g. 80 per cent of the world's wealth is in the OECD (Organisation for Economic Co-operation and Development) countries that occupy a quarter of the land, while the poorest 'bottom billion' live in about the same total area but own just one per cent of total wealth), and a combination of natural resources and technology in the immediate future is more likely to lead to plunder rather than sustainable exploitation because of immediate economic needs and weak regulatory systems.[11]

For Collier, neither the worldview of economists nor that of environmentalists is satisfactory when it comes to understanding ecosystem change. The latter tend to see the environment as a good in itself, and the cliché view of the tree hugger is someone who rejects any human exploitation of natural resources. Economists, on the other hand, ignore what is unique about nature, and treat it as any other asset that can be valued and allocated.

> . . . mainstream economics has blundered into [ecosystem] change guided only by an ethical framework that is simply inadequate to deal with nature because it ignores rights. Rights are central to the ethics of the natural world: the rights of the present versus the future, and my rights versus yours . . . Nature is *special*: our rights over the natural world are not the same as our rights over the man-made world.
>
> (Collier 2010, p. 10)

Both views at their extreme underpin many of the disputes, delays, and dogma that are often evident in grappling with sustainability challenges. However, the different rights humans have over man-made assets compared to natural ones may help narrow certain gaps. For example, a man-made asset whether it be a car, a factory, or a spaceship might justifiably be exploited by its current owner and user who might feel an ethical duty to future generations (cf. a father to his children) but is under no legal obligation; whereas a natural asset such as an ecosystem might only be exploited if all those affected by its exploitation are properly involved in the decision (e.g. a neighbouring country or community affected by the damming of a river), and if a portion of the benefits of depleting the natural asset are set aside for future generations, as has happened, for example, with Kuwait's use of oil revenues to establish investment funds for when the oil runs out. In other words, the current generation of users of a natural resource can be argued to have clear responsibilities not to harm the present, and to share any benefits with the future.

In reality, these kinds of principle are not widely applied in managing ecosystems, and most policies revolve around humanity's duty as curators of the environment and our rights as exploiters. Companies can be both instigators and victims of these policies, and at times can be found on both sides. For example, in the 1970s, car manufacturers lobbied vigorously to prevent anti-pollution legislation in smog-affected California, arguing that the technologies were neither affordable nor effective. Other companies such as Johnson-Matthey argued that technological solutions existed, and eventually the legislature made catalytic converters mandatory throughout the state, improving emissions by over 70 per cent, and enabling Los Angeles to continue its love affair with the car. It is this kind of technology-enabled win–win that many people hope will help us tackle climate change.

 ## Discussion points

Many significant changes appear to be happening to ecosystems around the world, each with its own implications for business.

● Why do you think climate change has attracted more attention than biodiversity?
● Which ecosystem changes seem to pose the biggest threat to companies?
● Do you think sustainability is a fad or a lasting issue?

Climate change

Climate change is the most talked about type of ecosystem change. There is a lot of public debate about its causes, its severity, its consequences, and the role of human beings. This book is not intended to be an introduction to the science of sustainability, but it needs to be emphasized that there is an overwhelming scientific consensus that (a) greenhouse gases (GHGs) have reached unprecedented levels, (b) this rise is essential to explaining the global warming seen in the past few decades, and (c) the GHG increase can only be explained with reference to human activity. (See Key concept 1.2 for an overview of the science.) 'Human activity is to blame for the rise in temperature over recent decades . . . There are plenty of areas for debate in the global warming story but this is not one of them' (Walker & King 2008, p. 37).

Carbon dioxide, the most often mentioned GHG, is found at higher levels in the atmosphere than at any time in the last 650,000 years (*Homo sapiens* have inhabited the Earth for 50,000 years). Its effects are exacerbated by rises in another GHG, methane, linked largely to agriculture and oil exploration. A decline in mountain glaciers and snow cover, a rise in sea levels, loss of ice sheets, changes in wind patterns, and extreme weather are all part of what the UN Intergovernmental Panel on Climate Change's (IPCC's) fourth assessment (2007) report calls 'unequivocal evidence' that the climate system is warming. It is predicted that by 2020 agriculture yields could be halved in some African countries, 30 per cent of Asian coral reefs could be lost, the heatwaves that killed over 30,000 people in 2003 in Europe will become the norm by 2030, over 40 per cent of southern California's water supply will be at risk due to loss of snowpack, and South American forests will be further at risk because of increased wildfires. Some academics (and indeed climate change sceptics) point out that warming will bring benefits as well, such as higher crop yields in northern Europe, New Zealand, and southern Australia, or lower cold-related mortality in Siberia.[12] However, acting on claims that the benefits will outweigh the negative and above all unpredictable impacts of change is a very risky gamble that does not reflect the overall predictions about what will happen.

Moreover, different predictions about the impacts do nothing to undermine current changes. 2010 was the warmest year on record, and prior to that 11 of the warmest years since 1850 occurred in the previous 12 years. This current burst of warming has been evident since the 1970s, and global temperature is now at its hottest for a thousand years. Indeed, the average global temperature is 0.75°C higher than a century ago, and rises are found on every continent. What might seem a relatively small change in the global average can reflect a huge shift in climate because only a few degrees separates us today from the last ice age.[13]

 Key concept 1.2 Climate change

Global warming is a good thing. Without the greenhouse gas effect, the warmth of the planet would pour into space, the UK would be in the grip of frost, and the Earth would have the climate of Mars or Venus. In a greenhouse, sun shines through the glass and heats the inside. Whatever is inside the glass glows with warmth, and pours out infrared light. Some of that light remains inside, however, and overall the light and heat inside is more than that which pours out.

The greenhouse effect central to our understanding of climate change is similar to a real greenhouse. Greenhouse gases such as CO_2, water, and methane act as the glass, and they trap enough infrared light to stop the world freezing or boiling. Water is the largest GHG but it is not important in the climate change context because it is already so plentiful that any changes would be like a bucket tossed into the ocean. CO_2 and methane comprise less than 0.1 per cent of the atmosphere, and any changes in that amount are akin to pouring buckets into a bath. In other words, human activity can affect these particular GHGs in significant ways.

The greenhouse effect was discovered by Joseph Fourier in 1827, but we can understand previous climate changes by looking at ice cores, tree rings, coral, the pollen in lake mud, and at least since 1659 through temperature records. These different sources of evidence reveal that the Earth's climate changes, but that for the past 10,000 years (i.e. since the start of the Neolithic era) there has been a period of relative steadiness. That appears to be changing, quickly. For the last 400,000 years according to ice core data the amount of CO_2 in the atmosphere varied in cycles between about 175 parts per million (ppm) and about 300 ppm. Now it is 389 ppm, well above the 350 ppm figure that many scientists feel is the safe upper limit for CO_2. Today, climate change experts tend to accept that we will not achieve that figure, and instead talk about stabilizing at 450 ppm, equivalent to a 2°C rise in global average temperature.

To achieve this, the use of coal, natural gas, and oil (what have been called the 'three wicked witches' of the climate change story) needs to be seriously curtailed. Although burning wood and crops also emits CO_2, the real danger lies in unlocking ancient stores of CO_2 as this leads to a drastic change in the balance of the air. Volcanoes may erupt and naturally occurring wildfires are part of sustainable ecosystems, but only the release of CO_2 through the use of hydrocarbons can realistically explain what has happened with the Earth's atmosphere since the industrial revolution. This is the overwhelming conclusion of global climate models, and while there is disagreement about what will happen (e.g. articles published by the Royal Society in 2010 predict a 4°C rise in temperature by 2060), there is no scientifically robust evidence that the causes are anything other than man-made.

Climate change consequences

One reason climate change has attracted a lot of attention, not least from business, is that the UN IPCC was able to show ways that it would affect the planet, and subsequent authors such as Stern and Jaeger[14] have shown the costs of action and inaction (Figure 1.7). The Stern Review for the British government stated that failure to mitigate climate change as an immediate priority would cost the economy at least five per cent and up to 20 per cent of GDP for the foreseeable future, whereas mitigation would cost one per cent. This led Stern to conclude that 'Tackling climate change is the pro-growth strategy for the longer-term, and it can be done in a way that does not cap the aspirations for growth of rich or poor countries' (Stern 2008, p. viii). Moreover, this view was endorsed by some in business such as Blackstone's Steve Schwarzman who said of climate change, 'It's not a green issue, it's not a pink issue, it's not a red issue. It's *the* issue'.[15]

Stern's analysis of risk tackled the gorilla in the room: can we address climate change without sacrificing economic growth? His conclusions proved controversial because although he argued for climate change mitigation as a pro-growth strategy, for some his cost–benefit analysis was unconvincing. Would it not be better, for instance, if we did not sacrifice any growth, and used the resultant wealth to tackle climate change further down the line, or to address human needs that ultimately stifle growth and make people more vulnerable to climate change's impacts? This is especially true if it turns out that the costs of tackling climate change are higher than Stern estimates, something that Lomborg argued by dissecting Stern's calculations (although his own analysis was subsequently held to be deeply flawed).[16] Nordhaus and Dasgupta[17] have also queried Stern's findings, and argue that there are rational economic arguments for limiting up-front investments in climate change mitigation. At times the argument has taken a nationalist tone (Nordhaus accused Stern of 'stoking the dying embers of the British Empire' because of his prescriptive, as opposed to free market, approach (Nordhaus 2006, 148), but at its core the dispute is about the discount rate used by Stern. Stern's opponents say that it is ethically unacceptable not to value the cost of disaster to our grandchildren at less than the costs

1°C (50 years' time according to IPCC)	Crop yields rise in high-latitude developed countries Crop yields fall in lower-latitude developing countries Small glaciers disappear, threatening some water supplies Coral reef systems extensively damaged
2°C	Rising number of people at risk of hunger (20–60% by 2080) Increase in hurricane intensity doubling costs of damage in USA Onset of irreversible melting of Greenland ice sheet
3°C	Significant changes in water availability More than 50 per cent of species face extinction Increased risk of abrupt, large-scale shifts in climate system (e.g. collapse of Gulf Stream)
4°C	Major regional declines in crop yields Major world cities threatened by sea level rises (e.g. London, New York, Tokyo, Hong Kong)

Figure 1.7 Economic consequences of temperature rises.

Source: IPCC Fourth Assessment Report 2007; Stern 2008.

of the same disaster to ourselves, and that a higher discount rate as used in most economic analysis would make the costs of global warming in 100 years' time appear small or even negligible in present-day terms. Such critics raise important questions, not only about methodology, but about: How much should we invest and in what? Should the costs be evaluated as an investment or as insurance? Is adaptation (adapting to changes in temperature) a better long-term option than mitigation (preventing changes happening in the first place)? These are likely to be important issues for business and policy-makers in the coming years.

The discussed disputes are not simply an economists' parlour game: they have a number of genuine implications. As I will show in the next section, the economic arguments for essentially allowing business to carry on as usual have been taken on board by climate change sceptics, even if these economists do not refute the science of climate change. Second, the difference between Stern and Nordhaus is not so much about economics as it is about ethics, and the distinction between prescriptive and descriptive viewpoints. Stern argues in the tradition of Ramsey and Pigou,[18] and echoing the definition of sustainability set out earlier (see 'The sustainability transformation'), that future generations need to be given equal consideration as the present one, whereas Nordhaus focuses entirely on observable economic trends and how these will affect future well-being. The Nordhaus/descriptive viewpoint is attractive because it is in line with the kind of economic reasoning used in short/medium-term project appraisal where decisions are based on observable rates of return and other available market information. However, for all its familiarity, one can question the usefulness of a descriptive approach when dealing with what according to scientists will be events without precedent in human history and with a good chance of unforeseen consequences. In other words, the value of a descriptive model seems very questionable if the universe which it is describing and basing its predictions on might no longer apply.

Doubts about climate change

Economists may disagree but not about climate change as a phenomenon caused by human activity. However, there are still many who are sceptical about climate change and its likely impacts, and in countries such as the UK and the USA opinion polls show a rise in the proportion of the public who are not concerned about climate change.[19] There are various reasons for this scepticism (Figure 1.8). There are some who dispute the science, although sceptical scientists themselves are now focused on questioning individual elements of the body of evidence, and nobody claiming to disprove the central claims about the link between climate change and human activity is publishing their work in the peer-reviewed journals that are central to the scientific verification process.[20] Non-scientists such as Monckton and Delingpole (both journalists) now put less emphasis on disputing the climate change phenomenon, and more on arguing that the amount of warming has been exaggerated, saying that the global temperature average will change much less than the IPCC figures. These views are welcomed by those who see climate change as a threat to both maintaining and achieving prosperity. Climate change has been called an attack on personal liberty,[21] and the hostility towards policies connected to climate change mitigation (e.g. cap

| **The science is faulty**: there may have been equally high levels of CO_2 in the past, implying that this is not disastrous but part of a natural cycle |
| **Human activity is not the cause**: climate change is the consequence of natural phenomena such as volcanoes and water vapour |
| **Climate change is real**, but we are not in a position to predict what will happen in the future |
| **Climate change is a hoax** concocted to spread fear and raise funds for environmental causes |
| **Adaptation is better than mitigation**: human influence on climate change is a fact, but the best way to tackle it may be to adapt to the new conditions rather than alter our current socio-economic models |

Figure 1.8 Reasons for scepticism about climate change.

and trade initiatives, taxation, government energy policies) seems to stem in part from a fear about the ways tackling climate change will undermine people's lifestyles in wealthier economies. Politicians who were once keen to burnish their green credentials are now nervous about public attitudes. None of the 2010 Republican candidates for USA national election believed in anthropogenic climate change, and the Tea Party, which is credited with influencing an important part of the post-financial crisis political agenda, has declared in its ten-point Contract From America that it rejects measures to combat climate change because they will damage the USA's competitiveness, and demands an oil-based energy policy.[22] In Australia, Prime Minister Rudd, who was voted in because of concerns about the climate, was forced to shelve an emissions trading scheme, and was eventually ousted from office in part because of concerns about how his environmental policies would hurt the country's mining industry.

For anyone who believes the scientific evidence, claims that climate change is an attack on liberty is like claiming that gravity is an assault on our freedom to leap tall buildings. There are several basic scientific assertions that would need disproving in order to establish a claim that climate change theory is wrong, and these are set out in Figure 1.9. Science is all about testing and disproving theories, and anyone who could do so in this case would probably be in line for a Nobel Prize. However, while scientists may assert that attacks on

| Increases in atmospheric CO_2 and in oceanic acidity have no consequences that are of concern to the human race. They do not cause an increase in atmospheric energy and a rise in overall temperature |
| The energy from emissions is going somewhere other than into the atmosphere, and is not causing warming |
| Raising the overall temperature isn't a cause for concern: changing patterns of weather do not affect agriculture, water supply, or sea levels |
| There are no convincing trends about changes to polar ice caps, Antarctic ice sheets, montane ice-caps and glaciers, or sea-levels |
| There is no evidence of an increase in the global average temperature over the period since industrialization |
| The observed recent increase in global average temperature has now reversed, and the planet is getting detectably cooler |
| Changes in planetary temperature due to exterior or interior physical processes (e.g. volcanic eruptions) are so huge that humans can do nothing to increase or prevent increases in temperatures |

Figure 1.9 Theories that need proving in order to discredit climate change science.

their profession do not change the truth of their theories, they have also added to scepticism to some degree. For example, the event known as 'Climategate' when prominent climate scientists at the UK's University of East Anglia were forced to disclose emails and other materials about their work, prompting a frenzy of activity in the media and blogosphere that they were distorting the evidence, was a public relations disaster, especially coming before a major international climate change meeting in Copenhagen in 2009. Handling of the event by the academics involved fuelled prejudices that scientists are elitist and secretive, and reignited interest, not least from business, in funding research that would undermine climate change theory.

However, there are plenty of other reasons for the scepticism, and often it is tinged with a strong ideological, nationalist, or political hue. Large companies and wealthy businessmen have put money into campaigns and research to discredit climate change theory and policy. Echoing a strategy seen in the tobacco industry's attempts to fight allegations about the damage caused by smoking, there has been a swathe of initiatives to turn the scientific consensus into a major scientific debate, and to use this to influence public, media, and government opinion. Companies such as ExxonMobil, wealthy businessmen such as the Koch brothers, and business groups such as the US Chamber of Commerce have all been linked to climate change scepticism activities.[23] (See Snapshot 1.2.)

An entirely separate strand of scepticism comes from those who wholeheartedly embrace global warming as a human-related phenomenon, but believe that the consequences will be much greater than predicted. Some proponents of the Gaia hypothesis of the Earth as a life force[24] are pessimistic that humanity can control climate change, and Lovelock, for example, has said, 'I don't think we're yet evolved to the point where we're clever enough to handle a complex a situation as climate change. The inertia of humans is so huge that you can't really do anything meaningful.'[25] Such thinkers are focusing on the consequences of what climate change modellers say are unlikely events, but if those events did transpire their impact would be much greater than mainstream climate change theorists imagine.[26]

These very disparate sceptical viewpoints cannot be explained just by different interpretations of the data: they are often about interpreting the data from the perspective of the individual's or group's established worldview. For example, to claim climate change is an assault on liberty (see earlier in this section) is to interpret the data in ways that position global warming as a threat to one's deeply held beliefs about less regulation, wealth creation, and incursions on freedom. This interpretation of climate change through the lens of pre-existing ideologies is not unique to sceptics: there are leftwing, rightwing, and of course environmentalist interpretations. Hulme calls this 'framing' and argues that one of the reasons society has done so poorly at tackling climate change despite the overwhelming scientific consensus is that we persist in approaching it from vantage points that may be highly inappropriate. '[D]epending on who one is or where one stands . . . the idea of climate change carries quite different meanings and seems to imply quite different courses of action' (Hulme 2009, p. xxxvi). Thus climate change—and sustainability more broadly—is not just a scientific phenomenon; it is a social, psychological, and political one as well, and this fact becomes very apparent when we look at the challenges sustainability presents for business in Chapter 2.

Snapshot 1.2 Quest for truth or sower of doubt?—Applying the tobacco strategy to global warming

Since the 1950s, the tobacco industry has been criticized for marketing a product that is harmful, often fatal, to its consumers. But for much of this time, the industry defended itself against the efforts of medical professionals, government, consumers, and lawyers. It was only in the 1990s, when state governments alleged that companies had long known about the addictive risk of nicotine and had not only lied about this in public enquiries, but had artificially boosted the nicotine content of cigarettes, that the industry finally agreed to multi-billion-dollar settlements.

One of the reasons the industry successfully fought off its critics for so long is that it appeared to develop a strategy that has since been imitated by others whose reputation has come into question. In recent years, that strategy has been evident in the frenzy of climate change scepticism. It involves funding research that questions the scientific consensus. In the case of tobacco, that consensus said tobacco caused cancer, something first identified by doctors in Nazi Germany. In the case of climate change, the consensus says that global warming is a result of human activity. The anti-consensus research is part of a four-pronged strategy that incorporates challenging the scientific evidence, generating alternative evidence, monitoring public opinion about the issue, and disseminating information to influence government, media, and public opinion. In neither case does the aim appear to be overthrowing the consensus; only to undermine its certainty, and to turn it into a subject for heated scientific debate. The research that questions the consensus can then be used as leverage to be heard at public forums such as news programmes that feel obliged to be fair and balanced in their coverage, and therefore give equal weight to all sides. At this point, what began as a debate about scientific evidence becomes a discussion of different opinions in which all views are treated as valid. This in turn creates public uncertainty and eventually scepticism about the science, a situation that benefits whoever sponsored the strategy in the first place.

Sources: National Conference of State Legislatures: http://www.ncsl.orgs, accessed 8 June 2010; Oreskes & Conway 2010; Palazzo & Richter 2005.

Questions

Climate change has fomented a lot of scepticism: public scepticism about the science, and scepticism about the role of companies in fostering doubt.

1. Why have companies and individual business leaders been accused of fostering doubts about climate change?

2. Are the parallels between the tobacco industry and climate change valid?

3. How effective do you think this strategy is, and why?

 Summary

Sustainability includes some of the greatest challenges of the present age such as demographic change, and ecosystem change including the phenomenon of climate change. These are social and economic challenges as much as ecological ones, and sustainability is about social as well as environmental change. Moreover, these are challenges as much for business as for wider society as they have implications not only for innovation, strategy, and markets, but also for the entire economic environment within which business operates.

The science of sustainability is developing continually, although in areas such as climate change there is a very strong consensus that is difficult to dispute. The evidence shows that human activity is having an historically unprecedented impact on aspects of sustainability, and although the story is not unrelentingly bad, there are elements such as the rise in average global temperatures and increases in flooding and drought that are causes of serious concern. These are also elements which will have serious implications for business, and which business is increasingly expected to take a role in addressing.

However, it is mistaken to think of sustainability as simply a scientific issue. Conceptualizing sustainability has required us to rethink theories of ethics, justice, and economics, not least the responsibilities of the current generation to future ones and for the actions of previous ones. The most widely accepted definition of sustainability makes it clear that meeting the needs of the present generation should not compromise the ability of future generations to meet their needs. This is hugely challenging for business which—even when it accepts responsibility to a wider group of stakeholders than shareholders—has not had to think about people as yet unborn.

Not surprisingly given the challenges raised by sustainability, there is a lot of disagreement and contention. Nowhere is this more apparent than in the context of climate change, which is the aspect of sustainability receiving most attention because its implications seem so enormous. Scientific agreement about the core principles of climate change has not prevented political, economic, and ideological disagreement about what to do, how to do it, and whether responses are justified in the first place. This has created an environment of great uncertainty for business, and considerable disagreement amongst the business community itself with prominent individuals speaking out on all sides of the debate.

 ## Further reading

Bloom, D.E., Canning, D., & Sevilla, J. 2003, *The demographic dividend: A new perspective on the economic consequences of population change* Rand, Santa Monica, CA.
An intriguing perspective on how to understand the advantages of demographic change in different countries.

Collier, P. 2010, *The plundered planet: How to reconcile prosperity with nature*, Allen Lane, London.
A comparison of economists' and environmentalists' perspectives on sustainability, and the errors in their analysis.

Helm, D. & Hepburn, C. 2009, *The economics and politics of climate change*, Oxford University Press, Oxford.
Comprehensive collection of articles on the economic aspects of climate change.

Hulme, M. 2009, *Why we disagree about climate change: Understanding controversy, inaction and opportunity*, Cambridge University Press, Cambridge.
Fascinating and well-argued overview of why climate change is a social phenomenon that is proving difficult to address despite the scientific consensus.

Millennium Ecosystem Assessment, 2005, *Ecosystems and human well-being: Our human planet: summary for decision-makers*, Island Press, Washington, DC.
Concise summary of the findings of the Millennium Ecosystem Assessment and their implications for human society.

Case study 1   GE's ecomagination—is sustainability material to business?

Thomas Edison once said, 'Vision without execution is hallucination'. Many people have a vision of what business could do to address sustainability, but they fall short when it comes to execution because they fail to pull together the why, the what, and the how of transformation management, i.e. the rationale, the expected results, and the way in which these will be achieved.

GE, founded by Edison, and which has owned businesses in industries as diverse as aviation, film and television, transportation, energy, and healthcare, is trying to make this connection. In developing its 'ecomagination' initiative, managers consulted across the company and with what were sometimes hostile external groups, and came up with a list of social and environmental issues in relation to which it could employ the corporation's assets to bring about change. For GE, ecomagination is a commitment 'to imagine and build innovative solutions to today's environmental challenges while driving economic growth'. Based on the early consultations, senior managers created a business plan that committed company resources to, set output targets for, and not least promised to double company revenues to US$2,000 million by 2010 by developing products offering environmental advantage to customers.

The company promised to double its annual investment in ecomagination-related R&D by 2010, and achieved this a year ahead of schedule when it invested US$1.5 billion. It has now committed to invest an additional US$10 billion in ecomagination R&D by 2015. By 2009, ecomagination revenues had grown six per cent to $18 billion despite what seemed to be an unfavourable global environment. It now expects that ecomagination revenue will grow at twice the rate of total company revenue by 2015, making ecomagination an even larger proportion of total company sales. In the process, the company has reduced its GHG emissions by 22 per cent compared to 2004, and improved its energy intensity by 34 per cent (ahead of its projected 30 per cent). It has also reduced its water consumption by 30 per cent compared to 2006. GE now aims to improve the energy intensity of its operations by 50 per cent, and reduce its absolute GHG emissions by 25 per cent.

Sources: GE 2005; Stewart & Immelt 2006; http://www.ecomagination.com.

Questions

1. Under long-time chief executive officer (CEO) Jack Welch, GE was widely admired by investors, but repeatedly criticized for its environmental performance.

   a. What evidence is there that GE has acted on the ecomagination promise of putting sustainability issues at the core of business strategy?

   b. Are the reasons that GE gives for integrating sustainability convincing from a shareholder's perspective?

   c. What is the business case for ecomagination?

2. One of GE's ecomagination commitments is to keep the public informed about what it is doing.

   a. How useful is the information GE provides about ecomagination on its websites?

   b. Does the information convince you that GE has a genuine commitment to tackling environmental challenges?

   c. What other information would you like to see GE provide?

   (continued)

3. Part of GE's strategy with ecomagination is to expand into what it calls underserved markets.

  a. Which of its current products could help tackle sustainability issues in developing economies?

  b. Do any of its products pose a threat to poor countries?

  c. What products would you like to see GE develop in order to meet the needs of developing economies?

Endnotes

1. See, for instance, Collier (2010), Daly (1996), and Jackson (2009).

2. The *Oxford English Dictionary* records its use in the July 1980 edition of the *Journal of the Royal Society of Arts*.

3. http://www.sustainability-index.com/07_htmle/sustainability/corpsustainability.html, accessed 5 May 2011.

4. http://careers.accenture.com/gb-en/about/Pages/sustainability.aspx, accessed 5 May 2011.

5. (McKinsey & Co 2005)

6. (Prahalad 2002)

7. The Assessment's website is http://www.maweb.org.

8. Data for 1960–2003 from http://faostat.fao.org, accessed 6 May 2011.

9. (Lomberg 2001, 2007, 2010)

10. (Nordhaus 2007)

11. (Collier 2010)

12. (Tol 2009)

13. (Walker 2008)

14. (Jaeger et al. 2011; Stern 2008)

15. (Fildes 2007)

16. (Friel 2011; Lomborg 2007)

17. (Dasgupta 2008, Nordhaus 2006)

18. See, for instance, studies of intertemporal social welfare.

19. See, for instance, http://news.bbc.co.uk/1/hi/8500443.stm; http://www.independent.co.uk/environment/fewer-americans-worry-about-climate-change-poll-2243087.html, accessed 9 May 2011.

20. For an overview of disputed areas of climate change science see Carter et al. (2006). For an individual view of why the science is still contentious see the writings of Richard Lindzen, e.g. http://online.wsj.com/article/SB10001424052748703939404574567423917025400.html, accessed 9 May 2011.

21. This is a theme in James Delingpole's *Daily Telegraph* blog, http://blogs.telegraph.co.uk/news/jamesdelingpole/.

22. See coverage of 'Contract From America', for instance at http://abcnews.go.com/Politics/tea-party-activists-unveil-contract-america/story?id=10376437, accessed 3 May 2011.

23. Greenpeace's research on the Koch brothers and climate change is available at http://www.greenpeace.org/usa/campaigns/global-warming-and-energy/polluterwatch/koch-industries/, accessed 3 May 2011. Myron Ebell's work on climate change denial is carried out as Director of Global Warming and International Environmental Policy at the Competitive Enterprise Institute which is part-funded by ExxonMobil. Several members of the US Chamber of Commerce such as Nike left because of the organization's stance on climate change in 2009 when it called for climate change 'to be put on trial'.

24. E.g. Margulis and Lovelock (1976)

25. (Hickman 2010)

26. (Weitzman 2007)

Sustainability challenges confronting business

 Key terms

Resource-constrained economy	Interconnectedness
Energy	Water
Low carbon society	Health
Poverty	Social organization

 Online resources

- Ideas for water-related case studies.
- Signposts to material on challenges relating to urbanization and the built environment.
- Country examples of transforming to a low carbon economy.
- Links to resources for thinking about resource-constrained economies.

  http://www.oxfordtextbooks.co.uk/orc/blowfield/

Chapter in brief

This chapter examines specific challenges affecting business as a result of the sustainability challenges outlined in Chapter 1. It starts with an historical look at how our attitudes to the environment have changed over time, and how the ways we manage sustainability have shifted as a result. It then sets out the idea of a resource-constrained economy (RCE) as something unique since the onset of industrialization, and something that has profound implications for economic prosperity and business success.

The chapter then examines what life in a RCE looks like with reference to energy, water, food, and poverty. It concludes by discussing how organization of a RCE could differ in terms of politics, the law, consumer behaviour, and the role of companies.

The changing nature of sustainability

The industrial revolution was a resource revolution. Since its beginning, we have viewed nature as a resource to be exploited for mankind's benefit. The technologies of the industrial revolution allowed us to make use of the Earth's natural assets in ways never imagined previously. They also gave us much greater access to those resources, and created unprecedented demand. Alongside technology, capital markets and colonialism allowed resources that had previously only been available on local markets or imported as exotic rarities to be produced and traded as international commodities. Prior to the industrial revolution, resources were used and sometimes used up (e.g. the forests of Easter Island),[1] but the impact was local. The international nature of the industrial revolution removed such limits on exploitation, changing the dynamic of economic and political power in the process.

The industrial revolution created economies where resources were not a constraint to prosperity and economic growth. It also raised fears that nature would be damaged in some way; for instance, the ivory trade in nineteenth-century Africa, the decline in fish species in the Rhine first noted in 1890, and the extinction of the Tasmanian Wolf in 1930 due to the expansion of ranching.

Conservation—the idea that large areas were to be protected from human economic activity—had become an increasingly important part of environmental management by the late 1800s, and figures such as President Theodore Roosevelt and John Muir, founder of the Sierra Club, were making a case that free markets could not be relied on to manage the environment effectively. This was controversial then and is controversial today, at least in some parts of the world. Hardin's ecological theory, 'The tragedy of the commons',[2] has been widely used to justify the private ownership of natural resources on the grounds of better management and conservation. Put briefly, the theory says that where resources are limited, people with shared access to them will deplete the resource by acting out of self-interest. Others, including anthropologists and economists, have argued against Hardin, citing numerous cases under which common access and good management go hand in hand.[3] However, his theories have been used to support market-based solutions to natural resource management, arguing that the market is best placed to value environmental services (see Key concept 2.1). This reasoning is more influential in countries such as the USA than it is in ones with a different historical legacy. Nonetheless, market-based approaches have become an important part of contemporary environmental management. For instance, the Forest Stewardship Council has created a shadow market applying the leverage of the private and non-government sectors to promote responsible forest management. Likewise, the Marine Stewardship Council, the Rainforest Alliance, and the International Federation of Organic Agriculture Movements have adopted popular market-based approaches to encourage sustainable fisheries and agricultural practices.

As noted in Chapter 1, sustainability is not simply an ecological issue: it is something with social, economic, and environmental dimensions. Poverty, for instance, can be seen as a cause and a consequence of poor environmental management (see 'Poverty'), while political-economic policies such as global free trade have led to the de facto management of human and natural resources by economic entities such as companies through new governance constructs such as value chains.[4] Business initiatives such as voluntary regulation of supply chains have emerged over the last 20 years to tackle these issues, and are typically

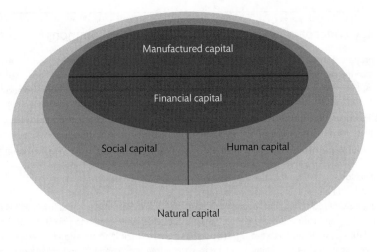

Figure 2.1 The Five Capitals.

categorized as 'corporate responsibility'.[5] The Five Capitals model of sustainability tries to capture these different dimensions by setting out the different types of capital any organization needs to function (Figure 2.1). It is argued that a 'sustainable organization' is one that maintains—and, where possible, enhances—these stocks of capital assets.

The emergence of private sector initiatives has come about after a long period when sustainability was the preserve of government and civil society, and business was typically portrayed as the opposition. Pea soupers in 1950s London, the smog of 1970s Tokyo, and the heavy metals contaminating the River Hudson in the 1980s were all blamed on business. Environmentally-oriented non-government organizations (NGOs) such as Greenpeace and Friends of the Earth arose in the early 1970s out of discontent with what many felt were outdated government policies, and politicians' obsequiousness to business. Government was not unaware of this: the Green Party in Germany, for example, made inroads into the main political system, eventually becoming part of the governing coalition in the late 1990s. Even where the environmental movement did not make inroads, government took a tougher regulatory stance as, for instance, in the USA which established the Environmental Protection Agency (EPA) in 1970, in response to what by then had become a widespread view that not only did nature need to be conserved, but human—especially commercial—activity had to be tightly regulated.

Agencies such as the EPA learned over time to adopt a combination of carrot and stick approaches, not simply fining and naming and shaming environmental offenders, but encouraging better practices through tax incentives, encouraging self-policing, and reducing fines when non-compliances are owned up to. Today, issues of sustainability around much of the world are governed by a combination of market mechanisms, business self-regulation, conservation policies, and legislation. (See Chapter 10 for a more detailed discussion.) However, as we start to examine the sustainability challenges facing business, four points are worth noting.

First, as we have seen, not only have the goals of environmental management changed over time, but so too has the influence of different sectors. Today, influence rests with the

Key concept 2.1   Private property versus the commons

Not all property is privately owned. In many parts of the world, for much of history land, water bodies, and the produce of both have been controlled by communities, families, and other social groups. At times this control can look like ownership (e.g. a group can give access rights to another group), but often the arrangement is best seen as custodianship (a duty to guard the resource) not ownership (the right to use and dispose of the resource). Some ecologists and economists have argued that common property is less likely to be well managed than that which is privately owned. The basic laissez-faire position is that land should be the private property of an identifiable body, and that an individual or organization has the sole right to determine how the resources attached to the land are exploited. As it is not in the owner's interest to destroy the value of the land, privately-owned land will be better, more sustainably managed.

There are numerous arguments against this position ranging from the spiritual (the Earth is the creation of God and cannot be owned; humans are custodians with a duty to pass it on for the benefit of future generations) to the legal (a person's rights to their land are curtailed by the rights of others to enjoy the benefits to their own land [e.g. to be free from chemical and visual pollution]); from the political (to what extent can an owner exploit resources such as water that pass across their land on to others'?) to the idea of communal good that legitimately limits what an individual owner can do to their land (e.g. conversion of land from one use to another may be objected to by other stakeholders; there may be multiple usage rights to land that have accrued over time [e.g. footpaths in the UK]).

This might seem an arcane dispute, but many sustainability challenges involve resources that are commons. These include water (particularly rivers and aquifers that cross private property and national boundaries), marine fisheries, forest lands, the Arctic and Antarctic, and the atmosphere. The rush to assert private ownership and sovereignty over such resources is a cause of conflict. Similarly, getting states to agree on managing the commons (e.g. the atmosphere) in ways that appear to conflict with national self-interest has been a major obstacle in tackling climate change and biodiversity.

state, civil society, and the private sector, and there is increasing pressure on business not just to comply with the law, but to go beyond legal requirements in being a good environmental custodian. This is especially the case in countries where government environmental agencies or civil society are weak.

Second, the mechanisms we have to manage the environment have evolved to address specific types of problem, and none of them was intended to address the complexities of sustainability. Although ambitious in their own way, wilderness and wildlife conservation, or legislation to prevent environmental damage were relatively narrow in scope: they are quite different in terms of goals and implementation to a global commons problem such as climate change. Some argue that the use of mechanisms appropriate to a previous problem but not the danger at hand is something that hampers attempts to address sustainability challenges.[6] At the very least, it can be difficult for a company to know who to talk to when an issue such as climate change appears to be the shared responsibility of different government departments such as the departments for the environment, for industry, for agriculture, for international development, and for climate change itself. As we will examine further in the section on 'Organizing a resource-constrained economy', one of the challenges of sustainability is how to manage complex, interlinked problems defined as much by uncertainty as predictability.

Third, for much of modern history the environment has been managed separately from society as a whole, building and reinforcing a view that nature and humanity are separate and, indeed, in conflict. Many groups associated with sustainable living draw on ideas from pre-industrial society or non-capitalist cultures to construct a more holistic vision of a sustainable society. However, for the most part, contemporary society is characterized by social and economic policies that run counter to the needs of sustainable ecosystem management (e.g. fostering carbon-intensive production and consumption; encouraging economic growth as the sine qua non).

Fourth, there is something fundamentally distinctive about the sustainability challenges society faces today. Whether one is considering peak oil, water depletion, competition for land, or caps on carbon emissions, what we confront is a global resource-constrained economy: the opposite of the resource-abundant economy created by the industrial revolution. It is the features of that economy that are central to the challenges for business.

Implications of a resource-constrained world

Climate change is the clearest example of how sustainability challenges will result in RCEs. Dating back to Malthus (Chapter 1), population growth has been predicted to destabilize economies, but so far technological innovation, migration, and the stimulus provided by demographic change itself have prevented the worst scenarios from happening. Likewise, the consequences of most ecosystem change, its irreversibility, and its ultimate costs, are still widely debated, and issues such as biodiversity are not widely seen as a threat to the global economy.

Climate change is different because there is a scientific consensus about its causes, and unusually strong agreement about its consequences (Chapter 1). The effort put in to understanding the implications of climate change by natural and social scientists make it a particularly strong vantage point for viewing what we mean by a RCE.

Physicist David MacKay (2009) calculates, based on an estimate of the current world population of approximately six billion people,[7] that in order to keep emissions at year 2000 levels, each individual has an annual carbon budget of 5.5 tons of CO_2 or its equivalent. As Figure 2.2 demonstrates, industrialized countries far exceed this average, and even emerging economies such as China are only under budget by a relatively small amount. In fact, if the world's emissions budget were distributed evenly, Indonesia and India's populations have little more than two tons of carbon dioxide and its equivalent greenhouse gases (CO_2e) per person to spend on all of the improvements they expect from economic growth.

At the other end of the budget scale, countries such as Australia and the USA have to slash their budgets in ways that would decimate their lifestyles. In the United Arab Emirates and Kuwait—the world's biggest per capita emitters—emissions would need to be reduced more than sixfold. In Europe and Japan, emissions would need to be halved.

MacKay does not expect any country to slash its emissions fivefold or limit its growth to stay inside the 5.5 tons per capita emissions cap. His aim is to provide a baseline for calculating how much alternative energy we will need to achieve a prosperous, low carbon society, and to ask the vital question of whether we can realistically achieve non-fossil energy targets (see 'Energy'). Moreover, staying inside a 5.5 tons budget would not actually help because to prevent global average temperature from rising more than 2°C above pre-industrial

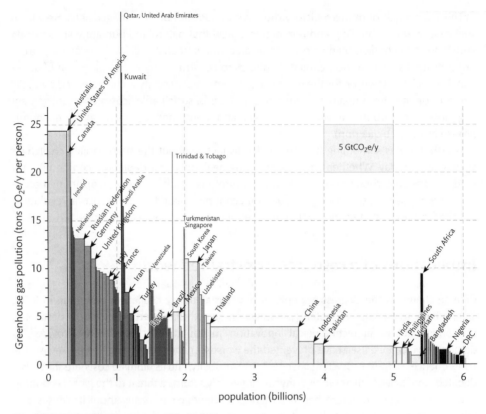

Figure 2.2 Per capita CO$_2$e emissions for individual countries.
Source: MacKay 2009.

revolution levels—a level unknown in the history of *Homo sapiens*—we would probably need to live off an annual budget as low as one ton of CO$_2$e emissions per person by 2050 due to projected population growth.[8]

This introduces the second element of any sustainable challenge: the amount of time available to achieve a transformation. The Kyoto Protocol—the first international agreement to set binding targets on climate change (Chapter 10)—established the principle that climate change action needed to be timebound. Since then, depending on the intended goals and not least the political will, 2020, 2030, and 2050 have all been used as key dates by which emissions reductions must be achieved. For example, the European Union (EU) has committed itself to reduce GHG emissions by 20 per cent by 2020; and the California Air Resources Board requires regions in the state to set reduction targets for 2020 and 2035. All such targets estimate emissions based on the historical record and economic growth, and seek to prevent the amount of CO$_2$e in the atmosphere exceeding 450 ppm, a figure associated with a temperature rise of 2°C. As discussed in Chapter 1, there is debate about whether this is an appropriate figure, with some wanting a much lower one. But assuming it is, achieving it is a major challenge that will have significant implications whether one is talking about energy use, consumer behaviour, or even the viability of certain industries closely associated with GHGs.

It is also argued that rather than think in terms of timeframes, we should think about cumulative emissions.[9] Targets based on emission rates or carbon concentration give the impression that we can stabilize warming by meeting certain deadlines, but this is meaningless if it is not related to cumulative emissions. It has been estimated that the total carbon emissions budget the world can afford is one trillion tonnes, half of which has already been emitted since the onset of the industrial revolution.[10] Therefore, our remaining budget is half a trillion tons, and if we go beyond that the temperature rise is highly likely to exceed 2°C. From a climate change perspective, it is less important when we make these emissions (*pace* timebound targets) than that we stay strictly within this budget for eternity. Thus, to give an extreme case, it might be more effective to emit high amounts of carbon for 20 years to establish the infrastructure of a low carbon economy and then to implement draconian reductions, than to reduce emissions year on year over a prolonged period.

Whatever pathway is adopted (and at present incremental reduction targets dominate), what will emerge is a RCE that will constitute a very different environment for business to operate in compared to what it has experienced previously. Figure 2.3 gives a number of features of the RCE. For instance, there is a high likelihood that without astonishing advances in geoengineering or power generation innovation, energy will be more expensive, and emissions will be a major cost to producers and consumers alike. This era of energy austerity will take place against a backdrop of rising expectations from emerging economies, eager to maintain their levels of growth and demanding the right to prosperity that developed economies have enjoyed.

How this affects business will depend on the industry, the region, negotiations between companies and governments, public attitude, and numerous other factors that firms may or may not have control over. Figure 2.4 gives an idea of which industries might be winners and losers as resource constraint becomes a determinant of business success. For example, companies involved in energy efficiency are likely to prosper, while those locked into fossil fuels will be under growing pressure in terms of costs, liabilities, and overall licence to operate. Equally, the situation with water and agriculture means that beer producers could find themselves in a volatile situation, while the automotive industry's success will depend on how well it adapts to providing low carbon mobility solutions. In the following section, I discuss how different facets—from energy to food, from water to health, etc.—will form parts of the RCE puzzle.

Economic, political and social uncertainty as societies shift from resource-rich to resource-constrained economies
Natural resources treated as finite rather than infinite
Depletion of natural resources treated as a business cost rather than an externality
Conventional energy sources less abundant, and all energy more expensive
Caps on emissions at national, individual, and individual level much lower than at present
Pressure to distribute rights to emit carbon on an equity basis
Public pressure to maintain and improve standards of living
Public, political, and investor pressure to increase levels of economic growth
Increasing trends towards national isolationism in the interests of energy security
Investor, innovator, and entrepreneurial opportunity to create breakthrough technologies

Figure 2.3 Features of a resource-constrained economy.

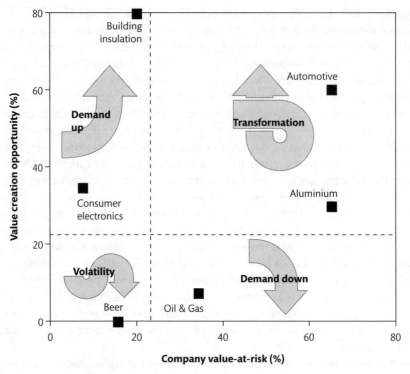

Figure 2.4 Industry winners and losers in a low carbon economy.

Source: Carbon Trust and McKinsey & Company analysis.

◉ Discussion points

A RCE will look very different to anything we have experienced since industrialization.

- What are the main actions society can take to shift to a RCE?
- Look at http://trillionthtonne.org and compare what you see with Figure 2.5. What do differences in the numbers tell you?
- Should carbon budgets be distributed equally between countries?

Life in a resource-constrained economy

A RCE wherein nature is treated as a finite resource rather than in terms of abundance has important implications for the way that we live and equally the way we organize society. In this section, we will focus on living in a RCE; in the following one we will look at organizing a RCE.

Energy

Climate change has been described as an energy problem because 74 per cent of GHG emissions come from the generation and consumption of energy in the human economy. If we can reduce our dependence on fossil fuels, replace them with alternative, low carbon

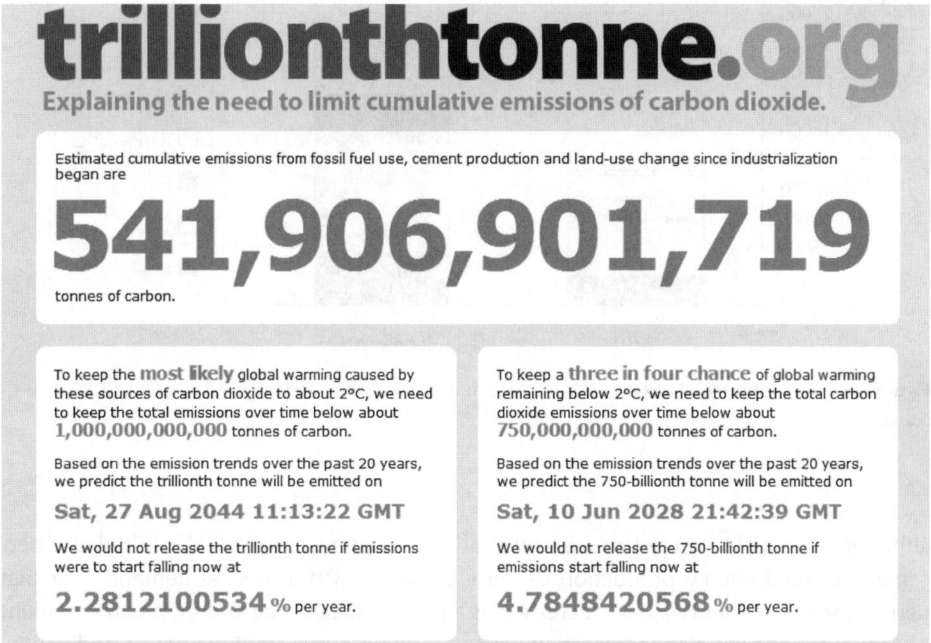

trillionthtonne.org

Explaining the need to limit cumulative emissions of carbon dioxide.

Estimated cumulative emissions from fossil fuel use, cement production and land-use change since industrialization began are

541,906,901,719

tonnes of carbon.

To keep the **most likely** global warming caused by these sources of carbon dioxide to about 2°C, we need to keep the total emissions over time below about **1,000,000,000,000** tonnes of carbon.

Based on the emission trends over the past 20 years, we predict the trillionth tonne will be emitted on

Sat, 27 Aug 2044 11:13:22 GMT

We would not release the trillionth tonne if emissions were to start falling now at

2.2812100534 % per year.

To keep a **three in four chance** of global warming remaining below 2°C, we need to keep the total carbon dioxide emissions over time below about **750,000,000,000** tonnes of carbon.

Based on the emission trends over the past 20 years, we predict the 750-billionth tonne will be emitted on

Sat, 10 Jun 2028 21:42:39 GMT

We would not release the 750-billionth tonne if emissions start falling now at

4.7848420568 % per year.

Figure 2.5 Screenshot from http://Trillionthtonne.org, October 2010.

Source: http://trillionthtonne.org.

sources of energy, and use energy more sensibly, then the rise in the global average temperature (Chapter 1) can be stopped. Consequently, for many, life in a RCE is about tackling low carbon energy.

This will be neither easy nor cheap, but theoretically at least, it is possible. Individual industries have significantly improved their energy efficiency in recent years. New power plants are up to ten per cent more efficient than earlier models. The steel industry has reduced its energy consumption per unit by 29 per cent since 1990, and advanced economies such as Germany and Japan have demonstrated that manufacturing sectors with relatively low carbon intensities can compete with ones such as those in Indonesia and China that are much less energy efficient.[11] Overall, however, the world has only slightly reduced its dependence on fossil fuels, from 85 per cent in 1980 to 81 per cent today.[12] Moreover, comparing total energy production in 1973 with that in 2008 (Figure 2.6), we see that

	Total energy production	Renewable energy (including hydro)	Renewable as % of total
1973	6,115.21	762.32	12.46%
2008	12,267.38	1,610.77	13.13%

Figure 2.6 Comparison of fossil fuel and renewable energy production in 1973 and 2008 (million tonnes of oil equivalent).

Sources: HSBC 2011; IEA 2010a.

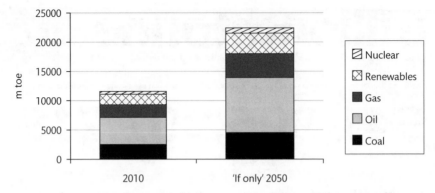

Figure 2.7 Projections of fuel mix necessary to meet future energy demand (million tonnes of oil equivalent).

Source: HSBC 2011.

although renewable energy has risen by nearly 50 per cent, it has barely shifted as a percentage of total energy production because of the growth in overall demand over that period. Indeed, gas and oil have increased as a percentage of total energy, and the amount of coal produced has also increased. If we continue on our current economic and energy trajectories, it is possible that the demand for gas, coal, and oil will double by 2050, despite efforts at increasing energy efficiency and renewable supplies (see the 'if only' scenario in Figure 2.7).

Balancing production and consumption

The energy challenge would be difficult but relatively straightforward if old, high carbon forms of energy could simply be replaced with low carbon ones. But this is not the case. Theoretically, it is possible to reshape the future of energy supply. The 'stabilization wedges' (Pacala & Socolow 2004) were developed to show how we could transform from a high carbon to a low carbon economy using the scientific, technical, and industrial know-how already at hand (e.g. greater energy efficiency, more nuclear energy, more wind, solar and biomass energy, introducing carbon capture and storage, and stopping deforestation).[13] This juggling of different energy pathways has been taken up by individual countries, so that, for example, the British government's Department for Energy and Climate Change has published *Carbon 2050*, a scenario planning tool available from its website.[14] What such tools claim and seek to explain is that we can live sustainably provided we balance our *consumption* of energy with the *production* of energy from sustainable sources.

The need for balance stems from the fact that most forecasts about alternative energy lead to the conclusion that we will be unable to substitute renewable energy for fossil-based energy for the foreseeable future. The original stabilization wedges proposed how we could stabilize emissions at end of twentieth-century levels, but even with major increases in renewable energy and the use of carbon capture and storage and nuclear, this would still require 20 per cent efficiency savings on current energy use.[15] Moreover, stabilizing emissions at 2000 levels may not be enough to prevent temperatures rising by more than 2°C,

Stabilizing CO_2 emissions at 2000 levels by 2050	$50 per tonne of CO_2 saved $17 trillion total energy sector investment $400 billion per year, equivalent to GDP of Holland
Reducing CO_2 emissions at 50% below 2000 levels by 2050	$38–117 per tonne of CO_2 saved depending on technological progress $45 trillion total energy sector investment $1.1 trillion per year, equivalent to GDP of Italy

Figure 2.8 Estimates of costs and investment to achieve different types of low carbon economy (USD).

Source: data from IEA 2008, 2010, 2011; OECD 2008;

and at the Heiligendamm Summit of 2007, G8 political leaders agreed to seriously consider a 50 per cent reduction in CO_2 levels by 2050.

This would require not only huge investments (Figure 2.8), but significant changes in our energy consumption. For example, it has been estimated that even in a windy country such as Britain, wind-derived energy would barely meet half the demand for energy to power cars, never mind other energy uses such as flights, heating, agriculture, and powering our gadgets.[16] Furthermore, different types of energy are not always interchangeable. For example, energy generated through photovoltaic cells is difficult to store compared to the energy contained in petrol, so even assuming that internal combustion engine cars vanished from the streets, it would be a huge challenge to power the electric vehicles that might replace them (see 'Mobility').

A major cost associated with low carbon energy is building the infrastructure. This includes replacing or supplementing the oil and gas supply networks used in transport with ones for electric powered vehicles; more costly still, it includes investing in transmission systems suited to new sources of energy. Some estimate that about half of the US$22 trillion it could cost the world for energy investment between now and 2030 will go on transmission,[17] and a country's readiness for a low carbon economy, as measured, for instance, in the Ernst & Young *Renewable Energy Country Attractiveness Indices*, is to a large extent dependent on how readily its energy grid can be linked up to the sites where energy will be generated. Unlike in the past, these sites will be ones where production takes place and not in sites convenient for transmission. Moreover, because much of the supply of clean energy will come from 'intermittent sources' (i.e. ones where supply fluctuates due to changes in wind or sunlight, for example), there will need to be a base-load of power from non-intermittent sources (e.g. conventional power plants, coal-fired plants fitted with carbon capture and storage technology, nuclear power). The new transmission grid will also need to deal with 'distributed energy' (energy fed in from small generating facilities such as rooftop solar panels) and the flow of energy in more than one direction. The grid will need to be 'smarter' than in the past at managing energy flows through load measurement and control; this in turn enables utility companies to increase energy efficiency, and to manage supply and demand using stored power from distributed energy sources.

Once one considers not only generation but distribution, not only the substitution of one form of energy with another but the different qualities of each form, the size of the energy challenge in creating a prosperous resource-constrained society becomes increasingly apparent. Creating 'smart grids' will add to the cost, and it is unclear who will pay. Such a grid is probably essential to spur investment in renewable energy, and is creating all manner of opportunities for start-ups such as Grid Point which focuses on information and communi-cation technology (ICT) solutions for smart grids. However, the scale of investment required is beyond the reach of venture capital, or even private investment in general. Historical examples show that similar challenges have been met with government intervention (e.g. 1.1 million miles of electricity distribution cable were laid in the USA between 1935 and 1950), but nowadays many governments in rich economies are hesitant to invest public money for ideological reasons, and even if they were not, the state purchase of private sector debt dur-ing the financial crisis of the late 2000s means governments are cash-strapped. Awareness of the dangers inherent in this kind of situation have led companies such as GE and Google to team up and lobby government for more rapid investment in electricity transmission infra-structure on top of their joint ventures in alternative energy projects.[18]

Emerging economies sometimes offer a more optimistic picture. In 2006, for example, China added 100,000 megawatts of electricity generating capacity, equivalent to the total capacity of the UK and the Netherlands. However, such economies face very different energy challenges. While China has done well at linking much of its population to the grid, in India over 40 per cent of people are not on the grid, and investment in improving and broadening the infrastructure is hampered because up to a third of electricity is lost on transmission and distribution, including through theft. In countries such as South Africa, access to energy is an important part of the political agenda because previous regimes have literally disempow-ered the poor. Indeed, if it is a choice between carbon power and no power, politicians will typically have to favour the former or be voted out of office. All told, there are 1.6 billion people who currently lack access to a reliable supply of electricity, and who will either need to be supplied through new grids or localized power generation from solar, wind, and mini-hydro facilities if they are not to rely on high carbon alternatives such as oil or biomass products (e.g. paraffin and firewood).

The clean energy race

Following the stabilization wedges idea proposed by Pacala and Socolow (see 'Balancing production and consumption'), there have been various attempts to understand what needs to be achieved through clean energy. Essentially, this boils down to how much clean energy do we need to substitute for fossil fuels, and how soon do we need to bring this online in order to prevent different global warming scenarios from materializing? An example of this is the BLUE Map Scenario developed by the International Energy Agency (IEA) which shows the emissions reduction potential and the related costs for the power sector, fuel switching, clean technologies, and alternative fuels for transport.[19] The implications of these measures are discussed in the following sections.

Efficiency

The cleanest energy is arguably the energy that isn't consumed in the first place, and various low carbon energy scenarios stress the importance of using energy more efficiently. For instance, the US$22,000 billion needed to invest in energy infrastructure by 2030 gets reduced by 12 per cent once efficiency savings are introduced. Many governments including the EU prefer to encourage energy efficiency instead of introducing new energy sources as demonstrated by their increasingly stringent targets for CO_2 emissions at the exhaust pipe.

Table 2.1 Current and projected demand for hydro, biomass, solar, and wind energy

	Current demand (mtoe)[20]	2020 demand	2035 demand
Hydro	276	383	519
Biomass	1225	1539	2316
Other renewables	89	325	1112

Buildings account for 38 per cent of global energy use, and increasingly buildings are required to be energy efficient (e.g. the EU requires all new buildings to be zero energy by 2020), although this is a challenge due to the vast number of old stock buildings that at present rates will not be replaced until the next century.

Given efficiency's significance, therefore, it is important to note that it is attracting relatively little investment. While investment in wind and solar is rising sharply, efficiency seems unattractive. Most investment in this area is coming from government (e.g. US$33.5 billion of the US$94.8 billion green stimulus funding went into efficiency), but government has not proved a reliable or trusted player when it comes to energy.

Hydro, biomass, solar, and wind (Table 2.1)

Current clean energy power generating capacity is 388 GW and accounts for about 13 per cent of energy supply.[21] Hydro in the form of both large-scale and small schemes, offshore and onshore wind, biomass including biofuels but also waste-to-energy schemes, and solar are the most common forms of clean energy at the present time (Figure 2.9). Although clear progress is being made in bringing clean energy generation capacity online, fossil fuels continue to grow more rapidly still (e.g. in the 2000s, coal was the fastest growing energy source, accounting for 47 per cent of new electricity supply).[22] Furthermore, in some parts of the world, important types of clean technology are problematic in their own right. For example, China is aiming to triple its hydroelectric capacity to 300 GW by 2020, and this may well be a much more important part of its much vaunted drive to a clean energy economy than wind power which could equal just ten per cent of hydro-generated power.[23] Yet, large-scale hydro including the development of dams is highly contentious in terms of human rights and long-term environmental consequences. In some analyses of clean energy, large-scale hydro is dismissed along with nuclear power because of its potential social and environmental impact.

Biofuels have also proved problematic for similar reasons. The first generation of biofuels (e.g. grains, sugar, beets, oilseeds) were welcomed as ways of reducing oil consumption

TYPE	Gigawatts (GW)
Wind	193
Small hydro	80
Biomass	65
Solar	43
Geothermal	7
Marine	0.27

Figure 2.9 Installed clean energy capacity worldwide, 2010.

Sources: data from IEA 2010a; IEA & OECD 2011; Pew Charitable Trusts 2010.

(e.g. by mixing petrol with ethanol) but they became controversial once biofuel crops were seen as competing with food crops, and their impact on overall emissions proved relatively small.[24] A few countries, such as Brazil with its promotion of flex-fuel vehicles able to run off different fuels, have made good use of the biofuel opportunity, but overall investment in biofuels has declined. A second generation of biofuels using agricultural and forest waste to make cellulosic ethanol does not compete with food crops, but there are as yet few commercial-scale processing plants and the production costs are high. By some estimates biofuels will only become competitive once oil reaches US$150 per barrel,[25] at which point the price elasticity of energy demand will become seriously tested.

Solar photovoltaic cells and wind turbines are now treated as the most significant forms of clean energy, and finance and overall investment have risen sharply, reaching US$243 billion in 2010. Solar energy, especially small and residential projects, is the fastest growing technology attracting US$79 billion in private investment in 2010, and reaching 17 GW generating capacity. However, wind remains larger overall, accounting for 48 per cent of private investment (US$95 billion).[26] The EU is the largest recipient of finance and investment with most of this going into small-scale distribution, notably solar installations in Germany and Italy. Therefore, much of the investment is from private individuals, and there is little asset finance compared to China and the USA.

Europe's leadership position is being challenged as Asia attracts more and more private investment, and China in particular is being touted as the first 'clean energy superpower'. How and indeed whether this promise will be realized depends not on the technology, but on the cost, the market price, and competition for land. Europe has so far played to its strengths in encouraging small-scale distributed generation, but such densely populated, democratic countries are already proving resistant to large-scale wind or solar farms that put further pressure on land needed for housing, agriculture, industry, and leisure. Costs, on the other hand, are falling, and wind power is already competitive with gas. Solar is becoming more cost competitive in areas where either electricity is costly or sun is plentiful (e.g. Italy, California), but it remains the most costly of the current range of renewable energy largely due to the cost of existing photovoltaic material, and the short lifespan of alternatives such as polymer. Wind is also problematic because while the energy generated may be carbon free, there is a lot of embedded carbon in each facility. For example, seven times as much concrete and steel are needed to create an offshore wind farm than a similar capacity nuclear power plant. Moreover, it is not simply the emissions associated with such construction that are at issue; it is also the amount of material that would be required. To build onshore and offshore wind farms sufficient to meet Britain's projected needs would require 60 million tons of concrete and steel, or five per cent of global steel production.[27] Historically, this level of production was achieved for the manufacture of Liberty ships during the Second World War, but currently this level of effort and urgency is not reflected in private or public sector actions.

Alternative energy solutions

Scientists are trying to develop other technologies that will directly or indirectly help meet the energy challenge. Some of these go beyond the incremental improvements being achieved by harnessing renewable energy sources, and while the likelihood of success is slim, the potential impact is enormous. For instance, using nuclear fusion (the process used in H-bombs) to trigger nuclear fission (the atom-splitting process in current nuclear reactors) would allow more recycling of nuclear waste, reducing fears about uranium disposal. Turning solar energy into liquid fuels would provide a direct competitor for oil with all of its portability and energy return on energy invested advantages. New generations of semi-conductor crystals could bring a sixfold increase in the conversion of solar energy to electricity. These and other energy technologies are at the laboratory stage, and the failure rate for such innovations is 90 per cent. Nonetheless, some believe that changes of this magnitude are the only way to tackle sustainability challenges in the long term,[28] and this thinking has led to the creation of initiatives focused on high-impact solutions such as the 'Carbon War Room' founded by a group of international entrepreneurs.

A similar belief in the significance of revolutionary technologies is evident in the area of geoengineering. This includes techniques to remove CO_2 from the atmosphere, and solar radiation management techniques to reflect a small percentage of the sun's light and heat back into space. If either were successful, the global warming element of sustainability could be resolved far more easily, but geoengineering methods do not offer an immediate solution to the problem of climate change, or reduce the need for continued emissions reductions (Chapter 6).[29]

Table 2.2 Current and projected demand for carbon capture and storage

	Current demand (%)[30]	2020 demand	2035 demand
CCS	0	n.a.	1.5%

Carbon capture and storage (Table 2.2)

The proliferation of coal and its accessibility continue to make it attractive, but while coal accounts for 41 per cent of total generation, it accounts for 71 per cent of power-related GHG emissions.[31] Continuing to use coal but without these emissions is therefore very appealing, and lies at the centre of carbon capture and storage (CCS) whereby GHG emissions are captured at power plants, and then stored underground (e.g. in disued oil wells) so that they do not affect the atmosphere. The technology for this is not fully developed but there are plants in operation such as Vattenfall's Schwarze Pumpe in Germany. As older, inefficient coal plants are phased out, government regulations encourage both the retrofitting of existing plants and the construction of far more efficient new ones. China is rapidly replacing its old plants with new technologies.

Nonetheless, the IEA estimates that there will need to be 100 large-scale CCS plants world-wide by 2020, and 3,000 by 2050 if clean coal is to play a meaningful part in powering a low carbon economy. At present there are only five such plants, and developing new ones has been highly problematic. The aforementioned Vattenfall plant has been unable to get per-mission from local residents to store the captured CO_2, and the company had to abandon its pilot project in Denmark for financial reasons.[32] In Britain, E.ON shelved its plans for a high-efficiency, CCS-ready plant at Kingsnorth after prolonged protest. There are plans for 77 operational and demonstration plants worldwide, but except for five in China, none of these are in emerging economies even though countries such as India and South Africa are highly dependent on coal-fired power stations. Moreover, even some of these plants may not be built because of the widening gap between funding needs and current commitments.[33]

Table 2.3 Current and projected demand for nuclear energy

	Current demand (mtoe)[34]	2020 demand	2035 demand
Nuclear	712	1003	1676

Nuclear (Table 2.3)

Nuclear power is highly contentious. After years of being marginalized from energy debates because of issues about safety and environmental hazard, the need for low carbon sources of energy drove it to prominence once more. Today, not only prominent scientists, but also some environmental activists have concluded that nuclear power is essential to meeting the energy challenge. However, at present total electricity generation from nuclear power plants is still flat, with the retirement of older plants in richer economies only being offset by new plants in emerging economies.

Nuclear power is an exemplar of the type of 'wicked problem' that characterizes much of sustainability: it is a solution that poses as many threats and complications as it appears to resolve. For many who favour the technology, it is also an example of the communication problems that dog sustainability issues: the public and the media seem to concentrate on nuclear disasters (actual and prevented) from the past such as Chernobyl and Long Island, and this prevents the news getting across that the current generation of nuclear plants are much safer and efficient. What is more—and this is an argument heard from some pro-nuclear environmentalists—increasing nuclear generation capacity would reduce the stress on the environment by, for instance, removing the need to drill in the Arctic.

There are many compelling aspects to nuclear power in the sustainability context. Although it is not a form of renewable energy because it uses uranium, uranium itself will be recyclable in future generations of reactors. Although it is considered dangerous, aside from the Chernobyl disaster, nuclear power has proved less dangerous than mining or offshore drilling, and climate change itself is already a bigger cause of deaths than nuclear power plants. In recent years, Sweden, Germany, and the UK have relaxed their anti-nuclear power policies as they come to realize that it offers one of the most reliable ways of ensuring a low carbon contribution to a stable electricity base-load.

Yet, just when this message starts to receive a wider audience, an event occurs such as the impact of a tsunami and earthquake on the Fukushima Daiichi nuclear plant in 2011. Nearby communities were evacuated; reactors in units at the plant were close to meltdown; and three months after the event the International Atomic Energy Agency said the situation remained 'very serious'.[35] Subsequently, Germany announced in June 2011 that it would close down all of its reactors by 2022, and focus instead on renewable energy. Although nuclear advocates were keen to point out that Fukushima had been handled well, and rather than being seen as a nuclear disaster should be treated as an example of how well nuclear can deal with natural events, it revived people's uncertainties once more. Not only were there safety fears, but the lack of transparency about the incident reminded people that government had often hidden the truth about nuclear power in the past. There were also renewed fears about cost overruns and delays with the state of the art, third-generation Olkiluoto 3 plant built by Siemens and Areva being three years behind schedule and approaching €2 billion over budget.[36] Given how long it can take to get permits for such plants, and the subsequent time to construct them, new power stations would need to be approved by 2012 and construction begun by 2015 if nuclear capacity is to reach 512 GW by 2020 as anticipated in scenarios such as the aforementioned BLUE Map (see 'The clean energy race'). These plus other realities such as the shortage of nuclear engineers and a policy environment that makes nuclear engineering an unappealing career choice mean that while for some nuclear is essential in a RCE, it may not make the contribution many hope for.

 Discussion points

Solving global warming is often described in terms of an energy challenge.

● What will we need to do to reduce GHG emissions caused by energy generation?

● What are the consequences for business if demand for fossil-based fuel does not come down?

● What are the implications for business of reducing energy consumption?

 Snapshot 2.1   Kickstarting the electric car—TH!NK

Automotive companies have been on a long search for battery electric vehicles (BEVs). Automotive giants, notably General Motors, tried unsuccessfully to introduce BEVs to the mass market, but this did not stifle innovation by smaller players. TH!NK began developing BEVs in Norway in the early 1990s, and was eventually bought out by Ford. However, after six years, Ford decided to exit the BEV market, and TH!NK was bought by Norwegian investors in 2006.

TH!NK's City car is one of a new generation of BEVs seeking to exploit the need for zero emissions transportation. Originally a two-seater, a four-seater version is now marketed in Europe along with a delivery van. It has a corrosion-free, thermoplastic body, and an aluminium frame that meets European safety standards. The city car has a top speed of 110 kph, and a range of about 160 real world kilometres between charges. It can be charged from a normal electrical outlet in four or six hours.

But the TH!NK story also shows the difficulties involved in introducing new technologies to an established market. Ford launched an early version of City at the Detroit Auto Show in 2000, but in 2003, faced with growing company-wide financial problems, it decided to sell off TH!NK. Ford sold the firm to a Swiss company that then went bankrupt in 2006. A group of Norwegian investors took TH!NK out of liquidation, and injected US$25 million of new capital. In March 2008, TH!NK launched the latest of its electric car models in Oslo hoping that an innovative sales, marketing, and partnership approach will help it crack the elusive mainstream market. It focuses on markets with conducive regulatory environments and an eco-aware public; and it enters into partnerships with mainstream players such as electric utilities and alternative, non-traditional automotive distribution networks that can help the vehicles penetrate beyond a niche market. The company has targeted eco-friendly cities and countries where congestion charges, free parking and other related incentives for low emission vehicles are already in place. 'TH!NK City owners who drove into Central London every day would save close to £8,000 a year due principally to the combination of the congestion charge waiver and free parking for electric vehicles', says business development vice president, Richard Blundell. However, an earlier plan to retain ownership of the batteries in order to reduce the purchase price, and the high cost of battery replacement appears to have been abandoned, making the price before tax about US$25,000.

Sources: Automotive World 2010; http://www.greenpeace.org.uk/climate/electric-vehicles; http://money.cnn.com/magazines/business2/business2_archive/2007/08/01/100138830/index.htm, accessed 31 July 2007.

(continued)

> **Questions**
>
> TH!NK is one of a number of BEV manufacturers hoping to profit from rising demand for non-petrol vehicles.
>
> 1. What are the most significant differences between the BEV market today and the past?
> 2. How would you improve on TH!NK's strategy?
> 3. Do newcomers such as TH!NK have advantages in the BEV market compared to automotive industry incumbents?

Water

There is no valid reason why there should be a shortage of water on Earth, or why there should not be enough to meet the anticipated 30 per cent rise in demand by 2030.[37] Nonetheless, it is increasingly common to talk of a water crisis. This relates to (a) the spatial and temporal misalignment of supply and demand; (b) the consequent scarcity of freshwater around the world compared to increasing demand, and (c) the lack of clean water and sanitation in many developing economies. The main causes of the former are population growth, the concentration of demand as a result of urbanization, rising per capita consumption due to economic growth, and the impact of climate change on water distribution.

There is no clear definition of water scarcity, but it is usually measured by comparing the total renewable supply compared with the total water withdrawals (i.e. the water extracted from a freshwater source for human usage). Withdrawals of 20–40 per cent of supply are considered to be medium to high water stress. Thus, for instance, a bottling plant such as PepsiCo's in Sevilla, southern Spain, is situated in an area of very high stress, and although this is not due to the plant itself, it poses various material risks for the company (see 'Water as a business risk').

Developing economies account for 71 per cent of global water withdrawal, and include important regions of medium to high stress such as the Ganges (54 per cent withdrawals), the Indus (81 per cent), and Haihe (China) (147 per cent). India, China, Pakistan, the Philippines, South Korea, Mexico, and Egypt all have serious and worsening water stress. This is not currently a threat to economic development worldwide, unlike climate change, but it is starting to hamper growth in specific areas where water shortages are affecting agriculture or industry.[38] Unlike climate change, too, offsetting one's water use has to take place locally (i.e. in the same river basin), in contrast to carbon where offsetting can take place anywhere in the world. Water depletion in one river basin cannot be neutralized by savings or pollution control in another basin: it must take place in the hydrological unit where the impacts occur.[39]

This is not to say, however, that water is a purely local issue. In agricultural or industrial areas, water extracted locally finds its way around the world in the form of commodities and finished products. Thus, for instance, a kilogram of beef requires 15,000 litres of water; 2,500 litres of water are needed for a one-kilogram serving of rice; and 10,000 litres are required to produce a kilogram of cotton.[40] This water embedded in products is often called virtual water, and much of it is used far away from where the product is consumed. For example, ten per cent of China's water consumption and 77 per cent of Japan's is virtual water from overseas.

Social dimensions of water

Freshwater shortages are a looming threat at a global level, although companies such as Nestlé and Coca-Cola have already made it a prominent element of their sustainability programmes. Absence of clean water and sanitation is already a major problem for many, although the fact that the people worst affected are the poor means awareness is limited compared to some other challenges. Seven hundred million people across 43 developing economies are said to live in conditions of water stress, i.e. less than 1,700 cubic metres per person (about half the amount of water needed to raise a cow). It is not just that the poor have insufficient water; the cost of water is five to ten times more per unit compared to developed economies. The poorest people in Jamaica, for instance, spend ten per cent of their household income on water, and those in Dar es Salaam pay thirty times more per litre than richer inhabitants.[41]

In poor communities, water is especially a problem for women who are typically charged with collecting it, often considerable distances from their homes. In Darfur (Sudan), for instance, women are subject to assault and rape by militias in the region, something that has led to the introduction of large cylindrical containers that can be rolled, reducing the number of trips to the water source.[42] All told, it is estimated that about a half of people in developing countries have experienced health problems related to unclean water and poor sanitation, and 443 million school days are lost a year.

As ever, it is easy to get lost in large numbers that are intended to open our eyes to a problem but have the effect of blurring our vision. Furthermore, particularly if water is a problem for the poor in developing economies, can a compelling case be made that water is a sustainability challenge for business? There is evidence that business is becoming more engaged in poverty alleviation efforts, whether that be for reasons of reputation, supply chain risk, market opportunity, operational efficiency, and in some cases moral values.[43] Water is a key part of the Millennium Development Goals—the internationally agreed targets set to reduce global poverty by 2015—including, for instance, halving the proportion of people without sustainable access to safe drinking water and sanitation. Some regions such as Latin America, South Asia, and the Caribbean have already met the drinking water target, but overall it is estimated that $10 billion a year or one per cent of developing country GDP is needed to achieve the goal. Companies such as Procter & Gamble (P&G) with its PuR water purifiers (Snapshot 2.2) and start ups such as WSUP (Water and Sanitation for the Urban Poor) are already involved in this, and the benefits in terms of lives saved, additional school days, and increased household income due to a reduction in illness and health costs, are well documented (e.g. World Health Organization [WHO] 2008). Moreover, because water is already a high-cost item for the poor, making clean water available on a sustainable basis could represent a genuine commercial opportunity as seen, for example, in Manaus, Brazil.

Water as a business risk

Water stress worldwide is seen as a business risk whether that be because of higher prices and direct water shortages, or the knock-on effects of water depletion such as local and transboundary conflict. A strong case has been made for some time that a reform of pricing policies is critical to improve water services, and that better water management is best achieved through market-based instruments to enable not only clean water supply, but also stream flow modification, sewage treatment, and water quality management. However, the sensitive nature of water as a basic need and indeed a human right, together with what some in the water industry now admit were ham-fisted efforts at 'water privatization' have made it difficult to develop such market-based instruments in certain regions. On top of this, parts of the private sector are viewed as causes of water stress, as witnessed, for example, in the prolonged struggle between Coca-Cola and farmers in India who blame the company for water scarcity.[44] PespsiCo is a relatively small water user in Sevilla, Spain, but like many firms is still at risk from poor water management because of absolute scarcity, increased costs, regulation, and reputational risk. Moreover, once the use of crops such as potatoes for crisps is taken into consideration, the company's water footprint increases considerably. However, ironically the reputational risk is most closely associated with bottling. This creates a dilemma affecting various companies tackling sustainability challenges: public and regulatory pressure can push companies to focus on aspects of their operations that, from a pure sustainability perspective, are not the number one issue.[45]

 Snapshot 2.2   Clean water for poor communities—P&G PUR

Procter & Gamble is the largest consumer goods manufacturer in the world with a turnover of US$79 billion. In 1995, in association with the US Centers for Disease Control and Prevention, it developed PUR packets which purify dirty water. It invested more than US$10 million in R&D, and a similar amount on market testing for bottom-of-the-pyramid markets. However, it eventually shifted the product to its charitable foundation because testing in 2000–2003 found the product take-up to be commercially non-viable. This was because PUR required too much investment in public health education to be profitable despite its undoubted benefits for consumers, employees, and society. Seeing the social returns on investment, the company shelved plans to end the product, and chose instead to explore non-conventional marketing approaches.

Instead of using normal outlets, PUR was sold to NGOs for about 3.5 US cents per sachet. Through P&G's Corporate Sustainable Development unit, the company launched its Live, Learn and Thrive programme, and PUR became an important element in partnerships with community development NGOs such as World Vision, Care, and Save the Children. The alliances cost P&G about $3.5 million to fund donations of product, technical expertise, and marketing expertise. Operating around the world, including in disaster zones such as Haiti, P&G aims to provide four billion litres of clean water by 2012, and two billion litres a year by 2020. This would save an estimated 10,000 lives, and prevent about 80 million days lost due to diarrhoea annually. PUR sachet sales have increased as a result of the partnership model. Between 2004 and 2006, 50 million sachets were sold at cost to emergency relief organizations (social model), compared to three million previously.

Questions

PUR is a market approach to delivering clean water to poor communities, but it was almost dismissed as a commercial failure.

1. Is the current partnership model a genuine, viable business model?

2. Why does P&G continue to market PUR despite selling the product at cost?

3. Are there other bottom of the pyramid situations where this type of marketing approach could work?

Food

Galbraith famously said that a symptom of a wealthy economy is not starvation but obesity. Although there is still chronic malnutrition in some parts of the world, and severe obesity in others, the situation is no longer as black and white. Poor people can spend half of their income on food, and food prices today are the highest since the 1990s. But economic growth in emerging economies is changing the nature of diets to more closely mirror those of the richest countries (e.g. animal protein, fats, sugar). The current food situation is not just about who has or has not, but about the way we produce and consume food. There have long been concerns about the poor conditions for agricultural workers, the use of harmful chemicals to boost yields, and the impact of intensive farming on the environment. Some of these issues are exacerbated by facets of sustainability: as noted, agriculture is a major user of water, and a major contributor to greenhouse gas emissions. Yet population growth and poverty alleviation are issues that many argue can only be dealt with if there are higher yields, more food, and low retail prices, implying greater oil and water usage, and more intensive production.[46]

Social dimensions of food

The food challenge, therefore, is how to produce sufficient food in ways that do not have reprisals for other sustainability challenges such as energy, water, and poverty. Already, there are indications that climate change, while it might increase yields in some areas, will result in lower overall yields than hitherto, and even in northern climate zones it has been shown that corn and soyabean yields fall 17 per cent for every degree rise in temperature.[47] There are additional challenges as well such as the safety of the food value chain given the frequently reported health incidents caused by food-borne pathogens such as *Escherichia coli* and *Salmonella*, or the demands for higher animal welfare standards. Moreover, there is the changing nature of our relationship with food that appears connected with the lifestyles of a modern economy. For example, in the USA people spend less than 31 minutes a day preparing food, and in France 25 per cent of meals are taken outside of the home.[48] As leisure time decreases and more members of the household go out to work, the opportunity for meals to be a family or social event are reduced, even though, ironically, there are unprecedented numbers of cook books and TV shows. More seriously in health terms, time poverty and financial poverty mean that in wealthy nations nutrition problems amongst the poor are on the rise because of the low-cost, calorie-rich diet of meals from McDonald's, KFC, and other fast-food chains.[49]

This situation is to a large account testament to the undoubted success of the agri-food industry. Despite a rapidly growing population, it has succeeded in producing more food at less cost per capita than ever before. In the last 50 years, world output of corn, wheat, and cereal crops has more than doubled. Food costs are half what they were after the Second World War, and the global food supply exceeds per capita caloric needs by about 20 per cent.[50] This is made possible by a high-volume, low-cost production system that has not only made food more affordable and readily available, it has meant that a family that in Europe or North America spent half its household income on food in 1900, by 1980 spent under 15 per cent.[51] This in turn meant people could spend money on other things, from cars to bigger houses to fashion, that have become the hallmark of prosperity and conspicuous consumption.

For some, lifestyles built on consumption are something that will have to change in a RCE. Others argue that if people's need for low-cost, nutritious food is to carry on being met, then the combination of sustainability challenges mean that the agri-food production system will need to change. At the heart of the current system is the belief that more food would result in greater health and happiness by driving down prices, increasing availability, and feeding more mouths. Yet this system appears to foster and rely on paradoxes. As noted, obesity exists together with malnutrition; climate change threatens farming with flood and drought, but maintaining current levels of production requires inputs from oil; increased production will exacerbate water stress, but without it there is an increasing risk of food shortages and social inequality. In each case, the challenge of food seems to put one aspect of sustainability at loggerheads with another.[52] Furthermore, even when the difficulties of the food challenge are recognized, the solutions seem inadequate. There is a lot of discussion of local food production and the strengthening of local economies, not just amongst the traditional environmental movement but also amongst libertarians and other right-wing groups.[53] The rapid spread of farmers' markets, and the emergence of movements such as 'Slow Food' are indicative of this. But such movements are a reaction to industrial food production and the wider pathologies of modern life; they do nothing to address the persistent problem of hunger, and the fact that there are 36 million hunger-related deaths worldwide annually. A challenge for any new, more sustainable food industry is that it will not only meet the needs of the relatively wealthy, it will help achieve a balance between the problems of the 20 per cent of the world's population who have too many calories, and the 20 per cent who are malnourished.[54]

Companies such as Dow and Monsanto argue that the food challenge can be met through genetic manipulation, but they will need to achieve this without the advantages enjoyed in previous eras such as cheap energy, abundant land, cheap and ample water, and a stable climate. The wildly fluctuating commodity prices of recent years are in part because of these new uncertainties. Starbucks founder, Howard Schultz, has spoken of a 'seismic change in the cost of commodities',[55] and a combination of rising demand plus the impact of extreme weather is seen by some as meaning they are likely to be volatile for the foreseeable future.[56] For instance, droughts in China in 2010 led to that country importing grain for the first time in three decades, and a combination of poor harvests, the diversion of grains to make biofuels, and just in time management systems means that world grain surpluses are down to less than 70 days.[57] In 2010, a combination of too much rain in Saskatchewa and not enough in Russia led to a worldwide surge in wheat prices that helped stir political unrest in countries such as Tunisia and Egypt in 2011.

Poverty

We have seen how sustainability challenges affect poor people differently to others (see 'Social dimensions of food'). In affluent societies, the energy challenge is about the type and amount of energy consumed, but for the poor it is about getting access to more reliable, affordable, safer forms of energy. In the richest countries, the mobility challenge is about reducing the impact of transport; for the poor it is about experiencing the benefits of mobility in the first place. Similarly, in poor regions overuse of water is much less of an issue than access to clean water. The sustainability challenges of the poor also differ depending on where one lives, so that in richer countries the poor are confronted by obesity due to their diet whereas in poorer ones the issue is one of hunger. For many, the challenge of sustainability is how to address these various facets while narrowing the gap between rich and poor.[58]

We have also noted that there are critical social dimensions to sustainability alongside any economic and environmental ones. The Five Capitals model that explains the different asset types needed for a sustainable organization (Figure 2.1) draws heavily on the 'sustainable livelihoods framework' (SLF) developed in the 1990s. SLF was designed to explain the different types of capital needed to lift people out of poverty.[59] For some people, sustainable livelihoods for all people is a key sustainability challenge in its own right.

This gives rise to all manner of ethical questions about how we address sustainability challenges. Should poor countries be given special treatment because of 'ecological debt', i.e. the poor should not suffer today because of the historical behaviour of the wealthy in the past? Is it fair that the poorest billion people who account for about three per cent of GHG emissions should be amongst the ones most affected by climate change?[60] Do the poor have the right to rapid economic growth even if that leads to increased GHG emissions and exacerbates food and water challenges? Is it acceptable for wealthy economies to 'outsource' their emissions to poorer ones by encouraging manufacturing overseas? Do all people have the right to a comparable standard of living?

It is a fact that global society is highly inequitable with about half of the world living in extreme poverty, and it is estimated that even as emerging economies such as South Africa and the Philippines reach middle-income status, they will still have ten per cent of their populations living on less than two dollars a day.[61] Ethicists such as Sen, Rawls, and Singer[62] agree that poverty represents an injustice, and if sustainability were simply an ethical issue, addressing poverty would clearly be amongst the challenges. Furthermore, from both a moral and instrumental perspective, there can be good reasons for business to engage in tackling poverty as has been well documented in corporate responsibility literature.[63]

However, the conclusion drawn by some that poverty is a sustainability challenge because sustainability and poverty alleviation are inextricably linked[64] deserves to be questioned. Poverty is ultimately an ethical issue (Is it right that wealth is distributed inequitably?), whereas sustainability is viewed by some as an existential issue concerning the maintenance of the Earth in ways that allow society to exist. Environmental and human ethicists do not agree with this, but one does not need to take a particular ethical stance to make a compelling case for sustainability, even though, as noted, there are clear ethical dimensions to sustainability. Poverty has been a feature of the human condition since time immemorial, and hence one can argue that it is quite sustainable. It is quite possible to imagine scenarios where sustainability challenges are met, and the rich benefit while the poor do not. There may be even be a business case for taking this direction, mirroring Ajay Kapur's idea of 'plutonomy' where companies are encouraged to target the rich as a market because 40 per cent of household wealth lies with one per cent of the world's population.[65] Unmitigated climate change may be incompatible with sustainable development for the poor as it is currently defined (World Bank 2010, p. 39), but how viable is that development model in the context of a RCE? From a sustainability perspective, it is valid to ask if and under what conditions the accepted model of sustainable development (including the central role given to economic growth) is compatible with mitigating or adapting to climate change? Indeed, some of the objections to tackling climate change (Chapter 1) are rooted in the express or implicit belief that the means of doing this would infringe upon individuals' moral right to choose and achieve their own level of well-being.

Again, this is not to deny that there are ethical questions relating to sustainability challenges as outlined earlier. However, none of these questions leads us to conclude that in the sustainability context tackling poverty is an ethical imperative. Indeed, it might be argued that an insistence on treating poverty as a moral dimension to what are otherwise the instrumental crises of sustainability is hindering our effectiveness in dealing with either.[66] A major World Bank report on poverty and climate change makes only three mentions of population growth, and the USA, the largest international development donor, does not fund family planning.[67] Both cases highlight how aspects of poverty are treated as ethical issues, something that prevents their consequences for sustainability being addressed adequately. Yet it is exactly this kind of issue that constrains how we tackle sustainability challenges such as water, food, and energy.

In the context of business and sustainability, therefore, the question is not whether poverty is a moral issue, but to what degree a failure to address poverty will exacerbate other sustainability challenges. As discussed in Chapter 1, population growth is a major factor in natural resource exploitation, and most of this growth is happening in poorer countries. Companies could benefit from this growth if it leads to new markets, a better workforce, and more investment. They will equally be at risk if the growth is unequal, and the new markets come to be characterized as exploitative as happened, for instance, in the 1990s with labour rights in Asian factories. Absence of growth could also present a threat if it leads to more migration to richer countries and the accompanying political instability as citizens fear for their jobs and call for protectionism. More likely, though less discussed, it will lead to migration into neighbouring countries with similar political consequences.

With mass migration comes increased health problems as health services, social services, and sanitation providers struggle to meet unanticipated demand. The health risks to the poor of climate change could also be material to business. Climate change is already associated with ill health and mortality due to increased incidents of malaria, flood-related accidents, diarrhoea, and food shortages. It is reckoned that relatively slight changes in the risk for climate-sensitive health conditions such as diarrhoea and malnutrition will significantly increase the overall disease burden.[68] Changes in food availability and yields will affect nutrition amongst the poor, and inland flooding will bring its own fatalities unless the vulnerable are equipped to deal with water run-off and landslides. All told, insofar as poverty is an obstacle to business prosperity as the likes of Hart and Easterly claim,[69] sustainability issues worsen that situation. However, it remains debatable how and in what ways poverty has to be addressed to resolve those challenges.

Organizing a resource-constrained economy

A RCE will be significantly different to anything experienced since the industrial revolution. Unless there is a vast leap in geoengineering that allows us to continue to emit GHGs with impunity, we will have to reduce our carbon intensity at unprecedented rates. Even if there is such a leap—something we have seen is highly unlikely (see 'Implications of a resource-constrained world')—it may compound other parts of the sustainability riddle such as the water crisis, poverty, and biodiversity. Until now, industrialized society has been organized to enable the exploitation of natural resources for humanity's benefit. Our laws, economic systems, and political institutions reflect this: we may put limits on who benefits from exploitation and who suffers, but we rarely limit exploitation itself. Governments in liberal economies, for example, prefer demand side policies intended to influence price rather than supply side ones that would require governments to interfere with individual choice or the availability of certain types of resource. Worldwide, many governments currently promote demand for oil through subsidies estimated to be worth US$312 billion, or more than five times the government support for renewable energy.[70] Such policies encourage oil demand and the use of oil in transport, and thereby limit the possibility of higher prices that would stimulate investment in alternative energy. This leaves alternative energy having to demonstrate its cost and energy security advantages over conventional resources if it is going to be more attractive from an economic perspective than exploiting new fossil fuel resources such as the oil and gas in the Caspian region.

A RCE is, therefore, something quite different to what we currently know because, barring the kind of innovation and dissemination miracle that is not supported by the evidence presented in this chapter, a prosperous society will need to discover new ways of organizing itself. Governments will need to exercise more political will in interfering with supply side factors, as well as stimulating demand that is sustainability oriented. This was the hope of the 'green investment packages' that were part of several countries' economic stimulus packages in 2008–2009. This is discussed more in Chapter 10, but while countries such as South Korea, China, and the USA made significant sums available, the projects were overwhelmingly focused on demand (e.g. mass transit, smart grid, renewable energy), and moreover important economies such as Brazil, India, and Russia made no commitments towards a green stimulus.[71]

According to Barbier, a global green new deal worthy of the name 'must encourage the widespread adoption by national government of fiscal measures and other policies in the short-term that will expedite economic recovery and create jobs while being consistent with the medium-term objectives of reducing carbon dependency, environmental deterioration and extreme world poverty' (Barbier & United Nations Environment Programme 2010, p. 32). However, for all of the talk about the link between a green new deal and growth, governments have proved more vexed about the latter, and shown a lack of consistency or thoroughness in linking economic recovery with sustainability.

This may change: for instance, Germany's rejection of nuclear power at least in part seems to have been supported by a willingness to take seriously a green growth strategy.[72] However, government is only one element of organizing society, and the idea that companies fulfil their obligations to society if they abide by the law is not only outmoded but was probably never true (pace Friedman). Many of the social and environmental issues raised in this chapter were initially championed by NGOs, and as the P&G PUR example shows (Snapshot 2.2), many companies now choose to partner with civil society to tackle sustainability challenges. But NGOs have traditionally been focused on single issues such as conservation, poverty alleviation, and water, and do not have a track record of dealing with the kind of complex, multidimensional problems characteristic of sustainability. These problems often require trade-offs between the vital issues of particular NGOs as mentioned in the section on

'Poverty', and organizing a RCE will present as many challenges for the established model of NGOs as it does for government (Chapter 10).

Companies will typically look to the law in deciding how to act. Governments have been reluctant to enact sustainability-related legislation that would put industries in their jurisdiction at a disadvantage, or that might reduce the private sector's ability to generate economic growth. This has not been universally welcomed by business, and, for example, led to the creation of the 'Corporate Leaders Group on Climate Change' through which major companies worldwide are lobbying for new, long-term policies for tackling climate change.[73] Yet, fundamental legislation pertaining to corporate governance limit how companies can respond to sustainability challenges. Although countries such as the USA and the UK require companies to report on climate change-related risks, there are no requirements on other facets of sustainability. More importantly, company law almost without exception gives paramountcy to the interests of the company's shareholders, and these are measured in terms of share price and dividend payments that are lagging indicators of short-term performance. Time and again in debates about business and sustainability a key barrier to more aggressive corporate action is said to be the clash between this short-term focus and the long-term perspective needed to address issues such as climate change. (See Chapters 3 and 7.)

Whether one is referring to government, civil society, or corporate law, there are questions to be asked about whether our current means for organizing society are fit for purpose in tackling sustainability challenges. This is a potential risk for business because in the current climate of high expectation that business should and can do something about these challenges, inadequacies on the part of others may not be an acceptable excuse for private sector inaction, and may well ramp up the demand for more corporate engagement. This is already evident in the retail sector where companies are expected to mediate in the area of consumer behaviour. For example, Home Depot, IKEA, Walmart, and Woolworth have all introduced policies to influence customers in areas of sustainability, and as the cases in Chapters 5 and 6 demonstrate, company responsibility for consumer behaviour is part of maintaining a firm's licence to operate. Yet, this poses all manner of risks for companies that need simultaneously to demonstrate bottom-line growth to maintain their legitimacy with shareholders, to meet the consumption demands of customers, and to maintain their licence to operate with wider society by managing multiple, interconnected sustainability challenges that other social organizations are struggling to address. When Drucker called business the 'representative institution' of modern society,[74] he was talking about companies having a prominent role in creating wealth in a society that was organized to allow this. Now business retains that image of being the representative institution, but in a society that is not organized to meet the challenges of sustainability, and that in many ways is looking to business to reorganize it in ways congruent with being a prosperous RCE.

Discussion points

A prosperous RCE will need to be organized differently to industrial society.

● What does Drucker mean when he calls business the 'representative institution' of society?
● Will business continue to be the representative institution in a RCE?
● What are the main constraints to business taking a leadership role in organizing society?

Summary

The different challenges associated with sustainability all have important implications for business. If we fail to establish a low carbon energy system, business will be faced with less energy or higher global average temperatures. The cost of establishing such a system will drive up the price of energy, and require significant investment of patient, risk tolerant capital in new electricity grids, new generation plants, and new consumer products. There are no fixed rules about what companies will benefit and which ones will suffer from this change, but it will have far-reaching effects on any company that relies on energy, which basically means every company.

Already companies are adapting to resource constraint as emissions trading schemes are rolled out into more and more industries, and oil subsidies are removed. Climate change is affecting the agri-food industry, creating new uncertainties and speculation. Water stress is also a threat to the industry, not just in terms of production but also the impact on its reputation as it is accused of being the cause of water depletion and high food prices. In industries from aviation to automotives, utilities to fast-food there is awareness of how different sustainability challenges affect business success, and in many cases this is leading companies to participate in sustainability-related initiatives such as the Sustainable Agriculture Initiative Platform and the Global Environmental Management Initiative's work on water. However, the evidence shows that we are a long way from transforming to a prosperous RCE, and are facing enormous problems in decoupling economic prosperity from unsustainable increases in water and fossil fuel usage.

The situation is complicated by pressure to tackle sustainability while improving the lives of those who have not enjoyed economic prosperity. For many, poverty alleviation is an inextricable part of the sustainability challenge. The situation is also complicated by the interconnectedness of the challenges so that, for example, attempts to address the energy challenge can exacerbate the food or the water challenge. Companies have been innovative in meeting particular challenges, but like other organizations they fall short when tackling multidimensional complexity. They are not alone in this, and a look at the situation regarding governments, the law, economics, and civil society shows that while awareness of the meaning of a resource-constrained economy has grown enormously, our knowledge of how to organize such an economy is very poor.

 Further reading

Costello, A., Abbas, M., Allen, A., Ball, S., Bell, S., Bellamy, R., Friel, S., Groce, N., Johnson, A., & Kett, M. 2009, 'Managing the health effects of climate change', *Lancet*, 373(9676), 1693–1733.
An overview of the health and poverty problems associated with other sustainability challenges, notably climate change.

IEA 2010a, *Key world energy statistics 2010*. International Energy Agency, Paris. Accessed 6 March 2011 at: http://www.iea.org/textbase/nppdf/free/2010/key_stats_2010.pdf.
Every year the IEA publishes an update on the world energy situation. These reports are increasingly important in understanding how well we are meeting the energy challenge.

Lang, T. 2009, *Food policy: Integrating health, environment and society*, Oxford University Press, Oxford.
Insights from agriculture, food industry, and health specialists on the food challenge and how to address it.

MacKay, D.J.C. 2009, *Sustainable energy – without the hot air*, UIT, Cambridge.
A highly readable, informative approach to understanding what it would take to replace our current energy systems with alternative ones.

Singer, P. 1972, 'Famine, affluence, and morality', *Philosophy and Public Affairs*, 1(3), 229–43.
Fascinating, controversial essay on the moral imperative of tackling poverty.

Case study 2 Poverty as a business opportunity—M-Pesa

Mobile telephony is having a huge impact in Africa where the relatively cheap infrastructure is helping bridge the gap caused by poor transport and communications infrastructure. In Kenya, for example, one in three adults carries a mobile phone, and in five years the number of mobiles in Kenya has grown from one million to 6.5 million, compared to 300,000 landlines. One driver of the boom is the large population of economic migrants eager to stay in touch with their home communities. Migrant workers are a main source of income in many rural areas, but one challenge is how to remit money home given the lack of banks, and unsafe roads.

Vodafone is the world's second largest wireless phone services carrier with more than 200 million customers, and sales of $50 billion. Although most of its business is in Europe, it has interests in companies worldwide including Safaricom in Kenya, and is increasingly looking to penetrate developing markets. In Africa, there are only 16 mobile phones for every 100 people, compared to Europe where there is more than one phone per head. Recognition of this market potential, and the unique contribution mobile phones could play in meeting consumer needs led to the introduction of M-PESA.

At first glance, there is nothing spectacular about M-PESA. For the user, it is simply an extra line on their mobile phone menu that says 'Send Money'. The subscriber goes to a shop, adds funds to their phone account, and then sends them to friends, family, or anyone else with a mobile. The recipient goes to a similar shop, shows the code on the mobile and some ID, and collects the money.

Yet in Kenya where bank accounts and plastic money are scarce, and carrying cash on journeys can leave you prey to robbers, the M-PESA money transfer system is a genuine innovation. It is not the brainchild of the conventional banking system, but an entirely new product, developed by Vodafone and Safaricom, part-funded by the British government's Department for International Development (DFID), and piloted with the help of Kenyan microfinance institution, Faulu.

M-Pesa was launched commercially in March 2007 after a two-year trial period, and Safaricom CEO, Michael Joseph, says there are over two million active users. 'We also know that it channels over Kenyan Shillings (KSh) 100 million in a day. . . . I see it getting to three or four million customers very soon.'

According to M-PESA pioneer, Nick Hughes, the idea came about at the 2002 World Summit on Sustainable Development in a conversation with someone from DFID about what Vodafone could do to address the Millennium Development Goals. One area where he thought Vodafone could play a role was making it easier to move money around so that entrepreneurs and others had better access to finance. Returns on investment would not be great, and it was likely that as with many ideas linked to social development, this one would lose out to others in the internal competition to allocate project funding. However, DFID ran a challenge fund offering capital to help ideas that were useful to developing countries circumvent the constraints of company product development processes. With the government offering 50% matching funding, what would otherwise have been seen as a low-yield, low-priority project, started to look like an interesting idea. However, making the idea a reality presented a variety of challenges ranging from new software to the systems and capabilities of Safaricom, introducing the product to Safaricom's staff and distributors, and working with Faulu savings groups to on product testing.

None of these hurdles has proved insurmountable, and overcoming them may have put M-PESA in a stronger position in the long run because the internal support and external relations are that much stronger than before. Soon after its launch, M-PESA was being talked about as a serious competitor to existing money transfer agencies, and Safaricom has started an aggressive campaign to extend the number of subscribers by partnering with established financial institutions such as Equity Bank and Post Bank.

An unintended consequence of M-PESA is how it has spawned new enterprises. M-PESA is no longer just about sending money: the brand has grown organically, taking on a life of its own. Account-holders now deposit money in their virtual accounts, and withdraw it at dealers all over the country whenever they want. Long-distance traders put money in their accounts before coming to Nairobi, and take it out when they arrive in the city. Long-distance travellers use their accounts like travellers cheques, and some contractors even pay workers through their M-PESA accounts. The service is being expanded beyond Kenya. Vodafone is running a pilot project in Afghanistan, and its subsidiary Vodacom was due to launch M-PESA to its 4.1 million subscribers in Tanzania in April 2008. Safaricom has also joined forces with a mobile phone service operator in Uganda to expand the service there.

Sources: Akumu 2008; Hughes & Lonie 2007; original research.

Questions

1. M-PESA is a product aimed at poor and marginalized consumers.

   a. Is it a good example of a company identifying commercial opportunities at the 'bottom of the pyramid'?

   b. Is it a financially viable business model?

   c. What impacts has it had on poor consumers?

2. There are strong arguments as to why poverty should be treated as a sustainability challenge.

   a. How does M-PESA help poor people enjoy more sustainable livelihoods?

   b. How can poor people have a negative impact on other aspects of sustainability?

   c. Do you agree poverty alleviation is a sustainability challenge?

3. M-PESA's funding model allowed it to compete for internal resources.

   a. Do you think the service's success will have a significant impact on either Vodafone or Safaricom in the future?

   b. How might their behaviour change?

   c. How might Safaricom build on this success as it attempts to expand its services in East Africa?

 Endnotes

1. Deforestation due to overexploitation is said by writers such as Heyerdahl (1996) to have been at the root of conflict and the society's subsequent demise.

2. (Hardin 1968)

3. (See, e.g. Fairhead 1996; Ostrom 1990).

4. (Gereffi 2005; Humphrey 2001)

5. (Blowfield 2011)

6. (Hulme 2009)

7. MacKay's analysis is based on an estimated global population of 6.1 billion people. In 2011, this estimate was raised to seven billion.

8. (Baer & Mastrandrea 2006)

9. (Allen et al. 2009)

10. One trillion tonnes of carbon is equivalent to 3.67 trillion tonnes of CO_2. Tonnes and tons are used interchangeably in this book except where a particular source applies a specific meaning.

11. (HSBC 2011)

12. (HSBC 2011)

13. The wedges scenarios can be found at http://ngm.nationalgeographic.com/2007/10/carbon-crisis/img/stabilization_wedges.pdf.

14. Accessible at http://my2050.decc.gov.uk/?utm_source=isend&utm_medium=email&utm_campaign=issue%2045.

15. (IEA 2008)

16. (MacKay 2009)

17. (HSBC 2011; Murray 2011)

18. http://money.cnn.com/2008/09/26/technology/google_ge.fortune/index.htm, accessed 1 June 2011.

19. http://www.iea.org/textbase/nppdf/free/2008/etp2008.pdf, page 3.

20. IEA figures.

21. (IEA 2010a)

22. (IEA 2011)

23. http://www.buyusa.gov/china/en/clean_energy.html, accessed 3 June 2011.

24. (HSBC 2011)

25. (HSBC 2011)

26. (Pew Charitable Trusts 2010)

27. (MacKay 2009, p. 62)

28. (E.g. Prins et al. 2010).

29. (Royal Society 2009)

30. IEA figures.

31. (IEA 2011)

32. (Slavin & Jha 2009)

33. (IEA 2011)

34. IEA figures.

35. http://www.iaea.org/newscenter/news/tsunamiupdate01.html, accessed 3 June 2011.

36. (Thomas 2010)

37. (Institution of Mechanical Engineers 2010)

38. (Barbier & United Nations Environment Programme. 2010)

39. (Hoekstra 2011)

40. http://www.waterfootprint.org, accessed 24 May 2011.

41. (Barbier & United Nations Environment Programme 2010)

42. Actors George Clooney, Brad Pitt, and Don Cheadle founded the Not On Our Watch project (http://notonourwatchproject.org) which has tried to raise awareness of the environmental and human rights crises in Darfur.

43. (Blowfield 2010)

44. See, for instance, http://www.theecologist.org/News/news_analysis/373906/cocacola_just_part_of_indias_water_freeforall.html and http://www.pbs.org/newshour/bb/asia/july-dec08/waterwars_11-17.html, accessed 26 May 2011.

45. For more detail of the PepsiCo example, see the Online Resource Centre case study.

46. (Lang 2009)

47. Lobell and Asner cited in Costello et al. (2009, p. 1704).

48. (Barbier & United Nations Environment Programme 2010; Roberts 2008)

49. (Ehrenreich 2001)

50. (Roberts 2008)

51. (Roberts 2008)

52. (Lang 2009)

53. (E.g. Dreher 2006)

54. (Roberts 2008, Millstone 2008, Sen 2000)

55. http://www.channel4.com/news/starbucks-boss-schultz-attacks-high-coffee-prices, accessed 7 June 2011.

56. (Drzik 2011)

57. (Worldwatch Institute 2010)

58. (E.g. Blackburn 2007; Collier 2010)

59. (Scoones 1998)

60. (Costello et al. 2009)

61. (Medeiros 2007)

62. (See Rawls 1971; Sen 2000; Singer 1972)

63. (Blowfield 2010)

64. (E.g. DFID 2008; Stern 2008; World Bank Group 2003)

65. (Kapur 2005)

66. (Frame & Hepburn 2011)

67. (World Bank 2010)

68. (Costello et al. 2009)

69. (Easterly 2006; Hart 2010)

70. (IEA 2010b)

71. (Barbier & United Nations Environment Programme 2010)

72. (Jaeger et al. 2011)

73. http://www.cpsl.cam.ac.uk/Leaders-Groups/The-Prince-of-Wales-Corporate-Leaders-Group-on-Climate-Change.aspx, accessed 7 June 2011.

74. (Drucker 1946)

Business in a resource-constrained world

Key terms

Carrying capacity   Attitudes to business
Mobility   Decarbonization
Decoupling   Supply-side economics
Carbon footprint   Economic growth

Online resources

- Links to online sustainability decision-making tools.
- Signposts to company sustainability initiatives.
- The implications of a resource-constrained economy for small business.
- Vision2050 scenarios game.

  http://www.oxfordtextbooks.co.uk/orc/blowfield/

Chapter in brief

In this chapter, we look at how sustainability shapes the world business operates within, both now and in the future. We examine the implications for conventional ideas on business, and discuss some of the alternative roles companies will be expected to play. This requires us to understand the historical role of business in society, and consider if that relationship will change in a resource-constrained society. It also requires us to think about what roles business could play, not just to protect itself from sustainability challenges, but to guide the process of transformation to a prosperous resource-constrained world.

The chapter begins by looking at what business is being praised and criticized for, and where we stand today after the effort put in to meeting sustainability challenges. It describes the features of contemporary business that aid and hinder private sector action, and concludes with a discussion of how sustainability challenges perceived business wisdom.

Perceptions of business

Society has strong but often conflicted attitudes towards business in the sustainability context. They range from great anger to enormous hope about what business has done, could be doing, and will do. Public sentiment, expressed through the media, NGOs, trades unions, or direct protest is a significant part of the sustainability management challenge as discussed in other chapters; but in this section we will concentrate on the range of perspectives that sit somewhere on the perception spectrum in Figure 3.1.

Business as the enemy

Business is often portrayed as the villain in the sustainability story. This is especially true in wealthier economies where ironically the standard of living is due in significant part to commercial enterprise. Government policies may receive ample criticism, but government departments do not receive the same attention as companies. In emerging economies, business is held in relatively high esteem because of its association with prosperity and better goods and services. In wealthier economies, this is taken for granted, and the spotlight shifts to issues such as private sector waste and exploitation, the consequences of the profit motive and short-termism, and the power of big business. For some, the impact business has on the environment and society is an extension of the inherent injustice and destruction of capitalism.[1] Others would say that it is not business per se, but big business and large incumbent companies that are the cause because their size, their products, or their business models put them at odds with the demands of sustainability. The examples of energy where 80 per cent of our needs are met by fossil fuels, and deforestation to create agricultural land (Chapters 1 and 2) highlight how certain industries in particular are blamed for damaging ecosystems. The issue of greenhouse gases (Chapter 1) has drawn attention to high-emissions industries such as aviation, cement, steel, and oil and gas. But at times it is big industry per se that is criticized as the enemy of sustainability: the ideological notion that Walmart is worse than 'small-mart', and that a reversion to an economy of smaller firms with stronger relations to their stakeholders (including the natural environment) is essential.[2]

A further criticism is that business fosters consumption and what has been called 'affluenza'.[3] This criticism takes different forms. Some take a moral view that consumption beyond a certain degree is wrong because it is an expression of avarice and greed, and that it is unacceptable for the rich to spend money on themselves when spending it on the poor would improve overall well-being.[4] A different view, but similarly rooted in utilitarian ethics, draws on measurements of happiness and well-being, and argues that beyond a certain point wealth is not associated with genuine prosperity, and once that point is passed, government policy or business should focus on redistribution.[5] In other words, consumption and the associated right to choose is not to be treated as a uniform good (pace neo-liberal economic theory), but should be seen as bringing different marginal benefits related to the relative wealth and poverty of the people concerned.

Some take an ecological view which states that, irrespective of any ethical arguments, the Earth has a limited and knowable ecological carrying capacity. We are currently living beyond that capacity—perhaps by more than twofold[6]—and this is in no small measure because of business' inability to put limits on the throughput of materials irrespective of how this ulti-mately depletes the stock of natural capital.[7] Moreover, business success often appears to depend on discounting any cost to the natural environment from resource use, pollution, or waste, creating a picture of value that is distorted.[8] For example, a company will record the cost of a hazardous chemical bought for manufacturing, but not the actual and potential cost of the chemical in terms of environmental impact. Therefore, the company's decisions are based on a nominal price for the chemical, not its true cost.

Not everyone who takes this line of argument is anti-capitalism per se; but they object to capitalism in its current form. Eco-capitalism theory states that capitalist enterprise is benefi-cial if it recognizes and is accountable for the true value of the impacts and assets on which it depends (i.e. ecosystem services, human capital, social capital, natural capital, financial capital, manufactured capital). The Natural Step (Chapter 9) and 'prosperity without growth' (Chapter 10) are interpretations of eco-capitalism, or what is also called natural capitalism.

There are various other aspects of business where the link between non-sustainability and unfettered consumption are highlighted. Marketing in general, not least the marketing of desire, is blamed for encouraging behaviour that is good for business but not for sustainabil-ity.[9] As I will discuss in much more detail later, the very concept of production and consump-tion growth that is central to business success is seen by some as diametrically opposed to sustainability.[10] Furthermore, the way that success is measured, and in particular the increased frequency of its measurement, has been criticized from a sustainability perspective. The phe-nomena of short-termism evident in faster reporting cycles and rapid turnover of shares is held by some to be antithetic to effective management of sustainability challenges that seem to require a more patient, long-term outlook.[11] Even when companies are praised for their efforts at tackling sustainability issues, there is often criticism that their actions are curtailed because of the behaviour of the finance and investment communities.[12]

Business as a positive force

The criticisms of business each sit somewhere on a spectrum between those fundamentally opposed to private enterprise, those who want fundamental changes, and those who believe business could be doing more (Figure 3.1). We can extend that spectrum by including arguments for being a positive force in the sustainability context. At the extreme end are those who consider business as having the pre-eminent role in creating a new wave of global growth that is sustainable and fair.[13] For example, the 'shared value' concept has been posited as a way to reset the boundaries of capitalism by reconceiving products and markets so that they focus on social and environmental impact, redefining productivity, and embedding business activities more in local communities (e.g. through cluster development). Porter & Kramer (2011) argue that shared value is still driven by the profit motive, but claim that not all profit is equal, and commercial activities with a social purpose represent 'a higher form of capitalism'. Furthermore, this is not merely a theoretical concept, but one that is already evident in the fairtrade movement, and in the strategies of companies such as Nestlé (on coffee sourcing) and Coca-Cola (in its partnership with WWF on water management).

A claim made of shared value is that it does not just redistribute the wealth created through commercial activity—it expands the total pool of economic and societal value. This claim is similar to that made by some advocates of social entrepreneurship, and reflects a belief that

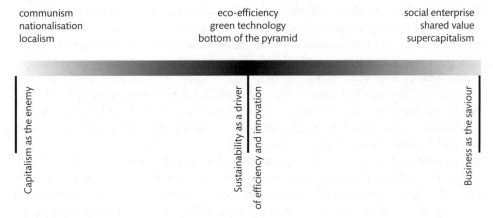

communism   eco-efficiency   social enterprise
nationalisation   green technology   shared value
localism   bottom of the pyramid   supercapitalism

Capitalism as the enemy   Sustainability as a driver of efficiency and innovation   Business as the saviour

Figure 3.1 Different perspectives of business in the sustainability context.

the application of elements of business management and principles can address socio-environmental challenges in ways that government or traditional civil society organizations cannot do successfully.[14] The actual evidence base for this is sporadic and weak, and where systematic research has been done, the findings have been unconvincing.[15] It may be that pitching sustainability challenges as something requiring business leadership is a ploy to capture the attention of corporate leaders, but it does also reflect the concerns of some executives and investors that business will need to pursue a different path than it has in the past.[16]

Those who would reset the boundaries of capitalism are at pains to distinguish themselves from those who feel business can best serve societal ends through some kind of redistribution. There is still considerable confusion about the meaning of corporate social responsibility (CSR), but in part at least it refers to voluntary actions taken with a view to achieving societal benefit. Friedman, in his critique of CSR (Chapter 2), interpreted this as redistributing the wealth of the company away from its owners to social causes often chosen by the CEO.[17] CSR policies today are much broader than this, and would include, for instance, HSBC's commitment to reduce its GHG emissions as much as possible, and where it cannot to buy carbon credits. Indeed, the embedding of societally beneficial outcomes into corporate strategy that Porter & Kramer claim is unique to shared value is an already well-established element of corporate responsibility thinking (e.g. Werther & Chandler 2011) (Chapter 5).

However, voluntary CSR is prone to criticism that a company's commitments can change with the whims of its leadership, that it has not proved robust during periods of economic downturn, and that it is too often housed in public relations departments rather than in operations. Consequently, some view the treatment of sustainability as a CSR issue with scepticism.[18] There seems to be a stronger case when companies can see the instrumental benefits of improved social or environmental performance. A reason retail companies such as J Sainsbury and Royal Ahold are focused on reducing fuel and electricity consumption is that, aside from any sustainability consequences, it will reduce costs. Likewise, a company such as BASF can justify its spending on less environmentally harmful concrete for construction by showing that it is the most economical to produce.[19]

Eco-efficiency is well documented and has been a driver of, but also a constraint on, companies' engagement with sustainability. Put simply, if good environmental management saves money, why wouldn't a company do it? But more challenging is getting companies to change when the costs are greater and there is not a legal imperative. One motivation is risk: the potential damage that sustainability issues could cause to business. At a meta level, it can be argued that serious sustainability challenges are an inherent risk to business because of the uncertainty they cause, their potential to destroy value, and their implications for long-term growth. However, the meta-risk horizon is often long, and even business leaders that understand the issues can be tempted to discount them. This is not always the case. Cadbury established its Sustainable Cocoa Partnership because of fears that its supply of cacao beans was under threat; the steel company Nucor has built its business around an understanding that conventional steel manufacturing is at risk because of sustainability pressures.

Parts of the financial services industry were amongst the earliest to recognize these risks. In the 1990s, changes in weather patterns increased insurers' exposure to hurricane and flooding-related claims, and the need to securitize this risk led to reinsurance companies developing sophisticated thinking about sustainability, especially climate change. It also led to the creation of catastrophe bonds and futures, a market worth US$5 billion in 2006.[20]

Sustainability and finance is discussed in detail in Chapter 7, but clearly capital can influence corporate behaviour. Investors have the option of withdrawing their capital, and companies have options to apply similar pressure by making sustainability part of their procurement and trading policies. The WRAP partnership for reducing waste helps companies remove waste from their supply chains, and Saab's development of a bio-ethanol engine was an example how a company can use its leverage over suppliers.

Where companies and their stakeholders sit on the spectrum between criticizing and praising private sector performance varies significantly by region, broadly reflecting the dominant political outlook and business–government environment. In Europe and Japan, for instance, business and government tend to have a collaborative approach in developing legislation, while in the USA companies have historically tended to oppose it. This can lead to peculiar situations amongst multinational firms: Shell in Europe and the USA, for instance, once held contradictory policies on climate change because of fundamentally different philosophies about regulation.[21] Equally, different industries respond quite specifically, and those facing the most pressure will often have the most options. For instance, industries with high emissions and levels of water demand can reap rewards from investing in innovation, whereas those with low direct environmental impacts are more focused on management programmes (e.g. energy efficiency in buildings). However, companies within the same industries have choices about whether to focus on process improvements, or compensation. For instance, a company may choose not to reduce its emissions, but transfer them to other parts of the business, through the supply chain, or by purchasing carbon credits.[22] These kinds of decision all have an impact on where the company places itself and where it is placed by others on the spectrum of sustainability leader and sustainability criminal.

Discussion points

Companies are criticized and praised because of how they seem to interact with sustainability issues.

- What do you think is the most stinging criticism of business today?
- What are the strongest motivations for companies to act on sustainability issues?
- Are Porter and Kramer right to call for more business leadership in tackling societal issues?

How well is business doing?

There have been various initiatives setting out what business will look like in what is typically called a sustainable world. The World Business Council on Sustainable Development launched its Vision 2050 initiative in 2010 which sets out a picture of a sustainable world by 2050, the measures of success for business in realizing that vision, and the transformations that would need to happen along the way. (A game based on Vision 2050 is at the Online Resource Centre: http://www.oxfordtextbooks.co.uk/orc/blowfield/.)

It would be helpful if we could readily measure business' progress towards such visions, but this is not possible. DuPont is a chemical giant that is addressing sustainability in some of its major product categories; for instance, it is shifting from petroleum to bio-based feed-stocks, and has become a leader in making soy-based polymer. Nike has cut its carbon foot-print by 75 per cent since 1988 by rethinking the design, production, and distribution of its products.[23] Although there are many examples like this and private sector initiatives outlined in the Snapshots throughout this book, it is hard to judge if they are enough or even headed in the right direction. P&G's PUR product (Chapter 2, Snapshot 2.2), for example, has helped a large number of people get access to cleaner water, but the drinking water situation in much of the world continues to worsen: should we expect PUR to end this problem? Would it be better to tax industries associated with water stress, and hypothecate those revenues for government or NGO programmes? Should we praise P&G for doing this much, or blame it for not doing more?

Starting in Kenya, but now spreading to other countries, Vodafone's M-Pesa mobile phone-based money transfer service has made remittances by migrant workers safer and more affordable, and helped improve the lives of people in poor countries (Chapter 2, Case study 2). But this is a small part of the company's global business, and does not shed light on what a company with a market capitalization of US$159 billion should be doing about sus-tainability. Various powerful corporations have endorsed the Forest Stewardship Council's certification programme to improve forest management, and the supply of certified timber has grown enormously since FSC began in 1992. But in the same period, Indonesia, home to the second largest stock of tropical forest in the world, has lost over half of its production forest.

Such stories are open to subjective interpretation, and can be used to make the case that the glass is half full or half empty. It is hard to evaluate whether business is doing enough or too little of the right thing in a sustainability context because often we do not know what is needed. For example, we are encouraged to turn off our televisions rather than leave them on standby because this will save energy, but leaving a TV set on standby for 20 hours uses less energy than ten seconds under a power shower. Do we know the relative carbon foot-prints of a bottle of water, a portion of rice, or a congested commute? (Box 3.1.) And if we do not, how can we make sensible decisions about how to achieve a prosperous resource-constrained economy?

This kind of basic knowledge is important not just to understand the relevance of particu-lar products to sustainability, but to build industry strategies for adapting to a resource-constrained world. The vast majority of business' sustainability-related investment today is focused on efficiency and innovation, and if we map that against the spectrum of public

> **Box 3.1   The carbon footprint of things**
>
> If we know the carbon footprint of different products and activities, then we have a basis for figuring out what actions will have the greatest impact. Here is the carbon footprint of some very different behaviours.
>
> - **Drinking a 500-ml bottle of water**: water is a low carbon resource, but by the time the polyethylene terephthalate balls have been melted and turned into bottles, the bottles moved to the bottling plant, and the heavy, water-filled bottles shipped to the stores, up to 215 grams of CO_2e have been emitted. That may not seem a lot per bottle, but if 200 billion litres of bottled water are sold, then bottled water accounts for 80 million tonnes of CO_2e each year. It also makes bottled water a thousand times more carbon intensive than tap water.
>
> - **A kilogram of rice**: what can be better than rice? Yet, by some measures, burning a litre of diesel fuel or manufacturing a kilo of cement leave less of a footprint than producing rice. The problem with rice is that most of it is produced in paddy fields which account for a large amount of methane, and to increase yields a tonne of nitrogen-based fertilizer could be used for every three tonnes of rice harvested. The carbon footprint of rice is much higher than that of wheat, which is nutritionally similar, but at present rice provides 20 per cent of our food energy and 3.5 per cent of our carbon emissions.
>
> - **A congested commute**: if you commute five miles each way in an average car, crawling most of the way, then your emissions will be 22 kg, three times more than if you drove the same distance on a clear road. If you did this every working day for a year, then your emissions would be 4.8 tonnes CO_2e, more than a return flight from Hong Kong to London. Even if you had a zero-tailpipe emissions hydrogen cell car, you could still be culpable for increased emissions because by being on the road during rush hour you slow others down and therefore increase their petrol consumption.
>
> *Sources:* Berners-Lee 2010; Smith School of Enterprise and the Environment (SSEE) 2009.

attitudes mentioned earlier (Figure 3.1), there is relatively little happening at those ends of the spectrum associated with the most radical change (Figure 3.2). We can see from the example of the energy sector (Chapter 2) that there are enormous challenges in terms of substitution, efficiency, innovation, and capitalization that need to be addressed, and how well certain industries do at meeting these challenges will have a knock-on effect for business as a whole. Similar challenges and complexities emerge if we look at particular industries such as retail or aviation.

Zero-carbon retail

Consumption, rising incomes, volatile food prices, and water stress are all elements of the sustainability challenge affecting companies. The retail industry—especially multiple retailers such as the supermarket chains—is particularly aware of these issues because it occupies a unique position as the mediator between consumers and producers, the driver of efficiency along the supply chain, a crucial factor in maintaining and improving standards of living, and not least as an icon in modern self-image. It may or may not be true that humans have an inherent instinct for acquisition,[24] but psychologists, marketers, and economists have all noted how consumer goods are not simply a good in their own right, but provide a symbolic language through which we communicate status, friendship, purpose, and affinity.[25] Retailers

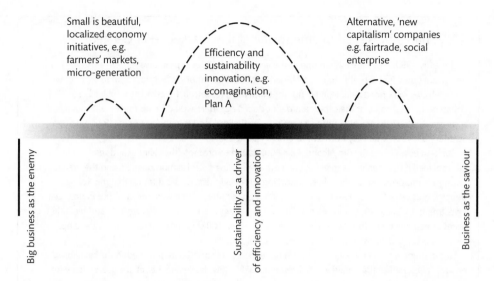

Small is beautiful, localized economy initiatives, e.g. farmers' markets, micro-generation

Efficiency and sustainability innovation, e.g. ecomagination, Plan A

Alternative, 'new capitalism' companies e.g. fairtrade, social enterprise

Big business as the enemy

Sustainability as a driver of efficiency and innovation

Business as the saviour

Figure 3.2 Areas of business investment in sustainability today.

are facilitators of this communication, and hence much is expected of them when it comes to sustaining this aspect of our lives.

The pressure that results from this has led retailers such as IKEA, Marks and Spencer, and Walmart to invest in sustainability initiatives. Tesco, the world's third largest retailer, has set itself the target of becoming a carbon neutral business which would mean radically reducing its carbon footprint and offsetting remaining emissions by generating clean energy, reducing CO_2, and other measures within its business (but notably without resorting to buying carbon credits). This means cutting absolute emissions from 38 million tonnes CO_2e in 2008, halving direct emissions by 2020, and being carbon neutral throughout its business (including the behaviour of consumers and suppliers) by 2050. This is not a trivial task given that the company tripled its direct emissions in 2000–2010, and plans to continue its aggressive growth strategy. However, there is ample evidence that the company is serious, and in 2011 it won *The Guardian* newspaper's Sustainable Business carbon award, not least because of its investment in zero carbon stores such as the one in Ramsey (UK).[26]

Zero-carbon stores could save 80 million tonnes of GHG emissions by 2050 in the UK alone, but stores are only a small part of Tesco-related emissions. Even if we include stores and the transport needed to supply them, that is only one-ninth of the emissions that come from customers getting to the stores and the manufacture of products on the shelves.[27] For example, two per cent of the emissions from a pair of jeans come from transport and retailing; 32 per cent are from production and manufacture; and 66 per cent are from use (e.g. washing and drying). In other chapters, I discuss how companies address this kind of issue, but this situation clearly poses questions in terms of how far a company's responsibilities stretch, and what are the consequences if it does not take them on. Zero carbon stores may appear to make a significant contribution, but the biggest challenges for companies such as Tesco will be cutting emissions from goods on sale and customer transport.

Snapshot 3.1   Building sustainability markets—Per Carstedt

In the early 1990s, Per Carstedt ran one of the largest Ford dealerships in Sweden. On a trip to Brazil, he saw that dual fuel cars able to run on bioethanol were commonplace, and began to wonder why such vehicles were not available in his home country. On his return, he asked around his Ford contacts, and learned that the cars could be produced but there would be no market without a supportive infrastructure. He found a champion inside Ford, and together they set about making Sweden ready for what they both saw as greener vehicles.

Carstedt established the Bio Alcohol Fuel Foundation to promote the refining and retailing of ethanol fuel. It took ten years to get the first ethanol-selling petrol station opened, and the first ethanol ready cars imported. After several years working with engineers, Carstedt found that marketing departments were the quickest to see the ethanol opportunity, and it was they who put in financial investment. By 2002, 40 stations were selling ethanol, two years later there were 100, and by 2006 the number had reached a thousand. Says Carstedt, 'The first 100 stations took ten years to develop. Nowadays we add 100 stations every three months'.

Not content with creating a market for ethanol powered cars, Carstedt turned to the retailing environment. Rather than build an environmentally friendly dealership, he set about working with neighbouring businesses such as a McDonald's franchise and a petrol station to create a Green Zone where companies worked together to reduce the footprint of their operations. For instance, by cooperating on energy distribution within the zone they were able to optimize their energy use and reduce consumption by 20 per cent. Now there are Green Zones across Sweden, examples of entrepreneurs collaborating together without government intervention or regulation.

Sources: Senge, Smith, & Kruschwitz 2008; http://makestuffhappen.com.au/?p=1158; http://www.baff.info, both accessed 26 June 2011.

....

Questions

Small and medium-sized enterprises (SMEs) often see sustainability as a threat more than an opportunity.

1. What are the key lessons for other SMEs from Per Carstedt's experiences?

2. Why was Carstedt able to create a new market?

3. Is the Green Zone idea replicable in other countries?

Low carbon aviation

Air travel accounts for up to three per cent of anthropogenic CO_2e. However, once consequences such as radiative forcing are also factored in, aviation could account for up to 15 per cent of anthropogenic CO_2, as well as having an impact on other GHGs including water. Nonetheless, modern aircraft are 70 per cent more fuel efficient than their forerunners 40 years ago. Moreover, the airline industry has various initiatives in place to further improve this situation including reducing fuel consumption per unit of thrust by 15 per cent, introducing biofuels, improving aerodynamic efficiency, and operational efficiencies such as better managed arrivals and flight paths. These could result in future planes having 28 per cent less emissions than today's, although replacing the current fleet with a new generation will not happen quickly. However, reducing the carbon intensity of flights by a projected one

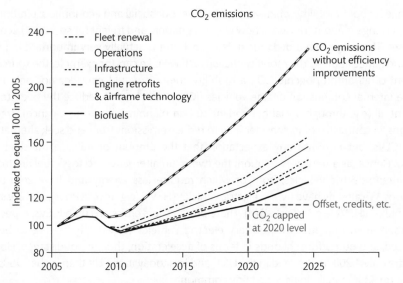

Figure 3.3 The aviation industry's path to carbon neutrality.
Source: IATA 2009.

per cent a year will not lead to a decrease in aviation's emissions if the industry continues to grow by five per cent per annum. The global air fleet has more than tripled since 1978, meaning that even with efficiency savings, the industry would have needed to cut emissions by more than 50 per cent in 30 years to avoid an absolute emissions increase.

In 2009, the industry announced its four-pillar climate protection strategy intended to deliver carbon neutral growth by 2020.[28] This would be achieved through fleet renewal, improvements in operations, the use of biofuels, and retrofitting existing aircraft. However, the industry's figures show that if all of these efforts are successful, its absolute emissions will be nearly 20 per cent higher in 2020 than they are today. Consequently, its pursuit of carbon neutrality will depend increasingly as the industry grows on offsets and purchasing carbon credits (Figure 3.3). Moreover, reflecting the situation with retailing, the industry's indirect impacts from freight and passenger transport before and after flights, the operation of airports, heating and cooling, the manufacture of planes, and so on are all relevant when considering what a genuine sustainable aviation business means.

Transport or mobility?

The examples of retail and aviation both point to transport as an area where sustainability challenges are likely to have a significant effect on business. There is much interest in alternative sources of energy (Chapter 2), but 94 per cent of transport is reliant on oil, and in Europe it accounts for 22 per cent of total GHG emissions. These emissions arise from fuel burnt to satisfy propulsion loads. The challenge is whether tackling climate change demands that we reduce those loads and the kind of freedom, prosperity, and identity associated with them, or whether we can reduce emissions while enhancing our mobility. The former challenge is about mobility: what we need to meet our social and economic aspirations. The latter challenge is about transport: how we move people and freight for social and economic purposes. This may seem a pedantic difference, but it is actually very important in how we view, and hence address, the mobility challenge. If we take cars for example, the source of six per cent of all anthropogenic CO_2, a mobility solution would consider not only how to replace internal combustion engine vehicles (ICEVs), but how to reduce the need to move about at all (e.g. through social networking, urban planning, work–life balance). Transport solutions, in contrast, would consider how to reduce emissions from and seek alternatives to using ICEVs, but not with any expectation that the amount of mileage travelled would change. Hence, as a transport solution, the two main alternatives to fossil fuel are fuel cells and battery electric vehicles, both of which require less energy and have zero-tailpipe emissions. We already have hybrid electric vehicles (HEVs) (e.g. Toyota Prius), and are starting to see plug-in HEVs (e.g. BYD's F3DM). These produce less emissions than ICEVs, especially in the urban environment. Now, battery electric vehicles (BEVs) are starting to be mass produced, and outperform hybrids in terms of acceleration, though not distance. However, there are only 4,200 on the road in the USA, and less today in the UK than in the 1950s when electric trucks and milk floats were fairly common.

From a transport perspective, battery size is a barrier in HEVs and BEVs, at least until a single-battery technology can deliver both acceleration and distance. HEVs could have a lower carbon footprint if biofuels were used instead of petrol, but as the clean energy race demonstrates (Chapter 2), biofuel itself presents sustainability challenges in terms of water use, land use, and the cost of processing. The footprint of BEVs depends on how much of the electricity comes from low carbon sources. With the right fuel mix, widespread adoption of BEVs using a decarbonized grid could ultimately reduce emissions by 90 per cent compared to today's vehicles,[29] but until that infrastructure is established, a car such as Nissan's Leaf or the Chevy Volt is insignificant in carbon terms.

Similar obstacles confront other technologies. Another alternative to ICEVs is fuel cells that produce electricity that change chemical energy into electrical energy by converting hydrogen and oxygen into water. They have been tested on buses in Perth, Vancouver, and Aichi, and although Riversimple is promising to have hydrogen powered cars on trial by 2012, the technology appears to be more suited to fleet rather than private vehicles for infrastructure reasons.[30]

The technological aspects raised earlier make clear that transport in a RCE is not simply a question of replacing one form of transport with another, and then expecting life to continue as before. None of the technologies in their present form are a substitute for oil-based, road, air, or water freight transport. Freight and passenger trains are often looked on favourably in the context of low carbon transport, and although the initial costs and carbon emitted during construction are high, once the rail network is in place emissions are low if the power comes from clean energy sources, and indirect emissions from generation can be reduced or contained. However, trains and other forms of 'public transport' fit uncomfortably with many people's vision of a prosperous society and are inconvenient given many people's present lifestyles. For example, even in the UK with a high population density, trains account for only one per cent of commuter traffic, whereas over 70 per cent of commuter journeys are by car.

High-speed rail is widely touted as a way of reducing short-haul air flights, and thereby cutting back on air travel emissions, which as discussed in the previous section could account for up to 15 per cent of anthropogenic CO_2e. Ultimately, blended wing bodies, biofuels, and the use of airships for long-haul freight could result in planes having up to 95 per cent less emissions than today's aircraft, but this is a long way off. Water transport offers a further way of reducing aviation emissions, but although there are opportunities associated with energy efficiency, renewable energy, and emission reducing technologies, any true advances are unlikely to happen for another 30 years when the current fleet is fully replaced.

Thus, the transport situation mirrors that of the energy challenge in general. Although there are many opportunities to replace high carbon technologies with lower carbon ones, and in doing so to have a measurable impact on emissions, ultimately the need for techno-logical advances, new infrastructure requirements, and cost all serve to limit what can be achieved. This means that transformation to a low carbon economy will not rest on innova-tion and finance alone, but will require significant changes in consumer behaviour in terms of much increased efficiency and finding alternatives to current mobility patterns. Indeed, just as the energy challenge described in Chapter 2 requires a balancing of production and consumption, the transport challenge requires us to revisit what we mean by mobility and how we can find alternatives to the ways we currently behave.

Complexity

Retail, aviation, and mobility have been chosen as examples of what business is currently doing and the challenges it faces in a resource-constrained world. We could, however, have chosen any number of other industries, each of which is being affected in specific ways. A feature of sustainability is that, although some industries are praised, criticized, or spotlighted more than others, all industries will be different than they have been in the past. According to Senge, in hindsight we should think of the industrial age as a prolonged bubble where—just as with subprime mortgages and the dot.com boom—the price of assets has outpaced their fundamental value.[31] Unlike many bubbles, the positive impacts have been enormous, but its overall costs in terms of toxicity, pollution, environmental stress, etc. make it ultimately unsustainable. To recover from this bubble, he argues, we will not only need to rethink cars, freight, energy, the urban environment, and so on, but fundamentally rethink our lives and work. This does not entail reverting to pre-industrial society (although as noted earlier, some would prefer this), but it does mean making choices based on different principles.

Another thing to consider is that not only is every industry affected in specific ways, but no industry can isolate itself from a cauldron of change within which sustainability is a major ingredient but not the only one. Cities, for example, are an area where facets of sustainability such as climate change, water stress, and ecosystem services are very important. But cities are also the sites of immigration, job creation, the changing nature of work, ageing, and social exclusion. Such factors will influence how sustainability can be addressed, and the speed at which any action will need to occur. At present, we have ancient cities such as Mumbai expanding at a rate of 42 people an hour. Some of these have implemented suc-cessful initiatives (e.g. the 100 per cent rise in middle-class bus ridership in London after introducing a congestion charge; Delhi's war on pollution by replacing petrol with natural gas for public transport), but despite such measures not all cities will meet the goal of becom-ing net carbon absorbers because they are too sprawling (e.g. Mexico), or were built around the needs of the car (e.g. Houston).[32]

Behavioural phenomena as much as physical ones are part of what confronts business. How cities evolve is important, but so too are human expectations. If we think, for example, about the future of choice, talk of sustainability might stir up public resistance if it seems to constrain choice at a time when there are other threats to choice from the use of sugar to tobacco, to the permissibility of speed, to conspicuous consumption.[33] As has happened in previous eras of globalization, attempts to tackle sustainability could be affected by a back-lash against other social phenomena such as declining wages in rich countries as jobs move overseas, and loss of purchasing power fires resentment leading to protectionism.

As with any aspect of sustainability, there are opportunities for business as well as risks. For example, while consumers seem to want more categories of goods than ever before, they seem to accept less choice within categories if that means items are more affordable. Thus, a retailer will stock far fewer detergent brands today than in the 1970s, but many more overall SKUs (stock-keeping units). What this means in sustainability terms is that it is possible in some product categories to focus on one or two companies producing the incumbent brands, something that in theory makes the change process simpler than if there was more competition. Oligopolies might not be healthy for market competition, but they could offer advantages from a sustainability perspective.

 Key concept 3.1   Decoupling

Historically, carbon emissions and resource usage have increased commensurate with economic growth. A major challenge in the sustainability context is decoupling these two phenomena so that economies can grow without increasing material throughput. The reductions in material and energy intensity in OECD countries in recent years have strengthened belief that decoupling can be achieved. This is an example of relative decoupling where resource intensity for every unit of production/output is reduced. However, the greater challenge is absolute decoupling, i.e. reducing the total carbon emissions or other resource use without affecting economic growth. According to the IPCC, absolute decoupling would need to reduce carbon emissions by 50–80 per cent by 2050 to avoid dangerous climate change. Changes of this magnitude are unlikely to be achieved by relative decoupling which can lead to greater efficiency but does not prevent a net increase in inputs to the overall economy.

Totalling the scores

As discussed, innumerable companies are factoring sustainability issues into their strategies, but despite this it is hard to assess whether the decisions being made are the right ones, and what their eventual impact will be. One way of answering such questions is to consider how well society as a whole is doing, on the assumption that because business is such an important part of global life, it is impossible that effective sustainability outcomes could have been achieved without significant private sector effort.

Progress on climate change is the easiest to measure because of the amount of work done not only on understanding climatic change over time, but also its costs. In order to keep the rise in global average temperature below 2°C, CO_2e emissions need to be kept below 450 ppm by 2050 (Chapter 1). In 2000, in order to achieve this we would have needed to reduce emissions by two per cent a year. Between 2000 and 2008, what we actually achieved were

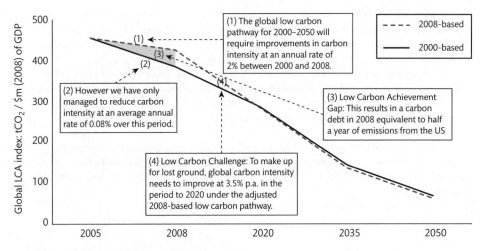

Figure 3.4 The low carbon achievement gap.

Source: PwC 2011.

reductions of 0.8 per cent; a shortfall equivalent to 13.4 gigatonnes of CO_2e which is roughly equal to the combined annual emissions of China and the USA. This meant that from 2008, we would have needed to decarbonize at an annual rate of 3.4 per cent, and the wide-reaching recession starting that year suggested that conditions to achieve this were favourable. However, despite the economic downturn, emissions continue to rise, and by 2010 we had left ourselves with a target of 3.8 per cent annual reductions in carbon intensity (Figure 3.4).[34] Indeed, in 2011, global carbon intensity increased for the first time in a decade, and as of 2012 we face a target of 4.8 per cent annual reductions until 2050.

This kind of shortfall between aspiration and performance has serious repercussions for the environment business will operate in, and also for what will be acceptable levels of achievement as judged by customers, investors, the media, and government. It will also affect the future economic environment. Stern's initial analysis led him to conclude that mitigating climate change would cost one per cent of GDP between 2008 and 2050.[35] This was based on keeping emissions to 550 ppm, and he minimized the costs during the early years (0.3 per cent by 2015), deferring them until nearer 2050 when the global economy was expected to be able to afford them. Since then, Stern has said we should focus on a target of 500 ppm, and this would increase the cost to two per cent of GDP. PricewaterhouseCoopers economists believe, however, that reducing

---

 Snapshot 3.2 Business leaders' influence on sustainability—Koch brothers

The billionaire brothers, David and Charles Koch, are well-known libertarians who over many years have sponsored political think tanks and campaigns aligned with their world view. They also own the second-largest privately owned conglomerate in the USA, Koch Industries, which has interests in paper, oil refineries, pipelines, and chemicals, and owns the company that created Lycra.

Koch Industries and its workforce are the largest oil and gas donor to members of the US congress who sit on the House Energy and Commerce Committee. The brothers founded Americans for

(continued)

Prosperity, an advocacy group that opposes plans to regulate GHGs. Nine of 12 new Republican members of the Committee in 2011 formally support Americans for Prosperity goals, including restricting the powers of the Environmental Protection Agency to regulate carbon emissions. The Committee's chairman, Fred Upton, released a draft bill to strip the EPA of its ability to curb carbon emissions. This kind of policy is in line with the Koch brothers' ideological commitment to minimize government's regulation of business, but if passed it would help Koch Industries' oil and chemical operations which would face multi-million dollar payments if new air pollution regulation were enacted.

Opponents of the Koch brothers' worldview say that they are using their wealth to corrupt the democratic process in order to protect their business interests. Supporters say that the EPA needs to be reined in to protect jobs, and that rich donors on the left such as George Soros are just as active as the Kochs.

Sources: Greenwald 2011; Hamburger, Hennessey, & Banerjee 2011; NPR 2011.

Questions

Companies and business leaders are often accused of influencing governments about sustainability policies.

1. Is sustainability a political issue?

2. Are the Koch brothers exerting the same right to free speech enjoyed by anyone in a democracy?

3. Should companies be allowed to spend money on championing aspects of sustainability?

emissions by 50 per cent would cost three per cent of GDP, or as Jackson puts it, the difference between a growing and non-growing economy.[36] While of course this will create opportunities for some companies, it means a significant portion of global wealth will be diverted to mitigating or adapting to climate change. Moreover, this will be in addition to the wealth spent on other facets of sustainability such as ageing, health care, and biodiversity conservation.

 Discussion points

A crucial part of addressing sustainability is the need to deal with complexity, and the contradictions this throws up for companies.

● Is Jackson right to say that the cost of climate change will be the difference between a growing and a stagnant economy?

● Can industries that depend on offsetting and carbon credits truly claim to be carbon neutral?

● Why is there so much more evidence about the implications of climate change than other facets of sustainability such as demographic change and biodiversity?

Barriers to progress

Many people would say that business is one of the largest barriers to making progress on sustainability issues. For every environmentalist such as Krupp who has embraced business as an ally, there are others who remain sceptical, not to mention organizations such as Greenpeace that are publicly hostile but regularly engage with companies behind closed doors.[37] Corporate leaders may sully their image in this respect when they use their individual and corporate wealth to try to influence political agendas and sustainability-related policy (Snapshot 3.2). However, executives also point out that they are not free to act as they want when it comes to sustainability. When they talk about the emphasis on short-term performance, earnings, and balancing the diverse—often competing—interests of stakeholders, they are highlighting some of the many ways that business is managed by society. SLEPT (social, legal, economic, political, and technological) is a framework for analysing how key external factors affect business, and in this section it is used to examine the barriers business faces in the sustainability context.[38] We have already discussed some of the technological obstacles in relation to mobility (see 'Transport or mobility?'), and in this section will focus primarily on the remaining types of barrier.

Legal factors

Companies are social institutions that evolve over time to serve the needs of society. Companies may share features in common, and influential countries have certainly imposed their particular ideas of enterprise on others over the years. But the laws pertaining to companies even today reflect a strong national flavour, and a company incorporated in Delaware (USA) will be quite different to ones from South Korea, Germany, or even Hawaii. It has been argued that company law in some countries promotes more responsible or sustainable practices,[39] although it is hard to discern any genuine trends. However, the main point here is that companies are legal not natural entities, and their practices are ultimately permitted or prohibited by society.

In the sustainability context, this is an important point for two reasons. First, it is contentious, not least in the wider political debate about tackling sustainability issues. There is a long history, particularly in the USA, of treating private enterprise as a natural phenomenon that has evolved with freedom and liberty, and should not be fettered by government. Rand, for example, is part of a libertarian tradition and her ideas are prominent in contemporary libertarian critiques of both central government (e.g. opposition to climate change regulation, and cap and trade) and big business (e.g. opposition to the rescuing of banks and automotive companies).[40] She saw business leaders as heroic figures whose enterprises exemplified all that was best about humanity, and would have sided with another tradition in the USA of wanting companies to be treated as individuals before the law.[41] Insofar as the USA's lack of political leadership on issues such as climate change is hampering the pursuit of global solutions, the way these traditions are influencing policy is important to understand, hampering for instance legislation on emissions trading, and questioning the mandate of the government's Environmental Protection Agency to regulate GHG emissions. (See also Chapter 10.)

Second, recognizing the firm as a legal entity is important because when people argue that companies have to behave in ways detrimental to sustainability, these behaviours often have a legal foundation. It is the law that permits companies to make a profit (unlike charities), and moreover imposes legal duties on directors to ensure they do so. Maine USA is not a renowned hub of private enterprise, but its company law is typical in requiring that 'the directors and officers of a corporation shall exercise their powers and discharge their duties with a view to the interests of the corporation and of the shareholders'. This provision—and the many like it in jurisdictions around the world—makes clear that those who run companies have a legal duty to shareholders, and that duty is to make money.[42] There may not be an inherent contradiction between profit and sustainability, but many people have noted that a short-term perspective on profit is at odds with sustainability challenges that play out over a longer time horizon.[43] In India, where the Companies Act dates back to 1956, contradictions between sustainability and the fiduciary duties of directors are addressed through a vast body of case law. In the UK, the much more recent Companies Act 2006 contains provisions that recognize the duties of companies as wealth creators and as responsible members of society. Thus, for instance, directors have a duty to promote the success of the company, and this has been interpreted as meaning a *long-term* increase in value, something that could be affected by demographic change, biodiversity loss, and other sustainability challenges.[44]

Liability

Indian law is currently being revised, and it will be intriguing to see how recent debates about the social and environmental responsibilities of business inform any new companies act in this fast-growing economy. For some, the outcome is a foregone conclusion because they believe that it is increasingly agreed around the world that the legal purpose of the firm is to maximize long-term shareholder value.[45] Others argue that this is a normative position based on what companies do in practice, not what they are legally compelled to do, and claiming that a particular action cannot be taken despite any sustainability benefits is a cop out rather than a legal obligation.[46]

The narrow, normative interpretation of the law is to an extent being challenged from a governance perspective. A narrow definition of corporate governance is that it 'deals with the ways in which suppliers of finance to corporations assure themselves of getting a return on their investment'.[47] However, a succession of governance reforms has gone at least some way to broadening the scope of corporate governance beyond shareholder returns (e.g. encouraging board diversity; incorporating ethics into governance). Along with this, attention has been paid to corporate accountability. Accountants have been identified as playing a potentially crucial role as scorekeepers when it comes to understanding corporate performance in a sustainability context. Management accountants could help companies understand the true costs of their products and processes on the environment, perhaps resulting in missed opportunities to make them more efficient.[48] This is an element of the emerging field of true cost or full cost accounting where what have hitherto been considered external costs (e.g. pollution, toxic spills) become internalized as a result of legislation, taxes, and fines, and start to find their way into company reports.

However, this shift in management and financial accounting is still in its early days despite many years of academic study, and the upsurge in social and environmental reporting. It might be self-evident that companies have complex relationships with society that arise from 'doing business', but mainstream accounting—the principle means by which companies give an account of themselves—uses very narrow performance measures, and a qualified accountant is one who understands liquidity, profitability, and solvency ratios, not the gamut of interconnected events that companies are variously responsible for or affected by.[49]

Another legal aspect affecting business' relationship to sustainability is ownership. Most companies in the formal economy have limited liability which separates the assets of the company from those of its principles and agents, allowing owners to invest in and enjoy the profits of a company while limiting their liability for its debts beyond the nominal value of their shares. Limited liability has been an essential element in the rise of business, even though the pioneer of liberal economics, Adam Smith, feared it would lead owners and managers to pursue separate paths of self-interest.[50] This fear has persisted, and the tension between the principle (owner) and her agent (manager) has manifested itself in innumerable cases of malfeasance from Enron in the USA to Dubai's Damas International to the UK's Polly Peck. For some, limited liability is part of the 'genius of capitalism' in that it encourages risk taking by investors;[51] for others, it separates the interests of the company from those of wider society.[52]

Although limited liability has been criticized for fostering some patterns of corporate behaviour that are at odds with being a responsible citizen, sustainability theory has not seriously posited its overhaul or overthrow. There is interest, however, in different types of ownership and how they affect sustainability. For instance, the attention paid to the consequences of short-term investment horizons for sustainability amongst publicly traded companies has led some to argue that ownership structure is a determinant of company responses to social and environmental issues.[53] Thus, an employee partnership such as John Lewis could have different opportunities and constraints than a listed company such as Unilever even though both have high-profile sustainability programmes. Equally, John Lewis might behave differently to a private-equity owned company such as Georgia Pacific because the latter was acquired with particular expectations about returns on investment over a particular period. A related area of enquiry is how companies with a reputation for corporate responsibility or sustainability behave when they are acquired by other companies (e.g. The Body Shop after the L'Oreal buy-out, innocent's acquisition by Coca-Cola). Research to date does not yet show convincing empirical correlations between ownership and sustainability performance, but it does enough to remind us that ownership needs to be considered as a factor affecting companies' responses to sustainability challenges.

Social factors

Talk of companies' legal obligations to investors reveals one constraint on progress in a sustainability context. However, another barrier could be the primacy attached to the roles of principles and agents, and how this excludes others that have a legitimate interest in what a company does. Since the 1980s, there has been renewed interest in the idea that companies pay attention not only to the interests of investors, but also to other stakeholders defined as those whom the firm has an impact upon and those who have an influence over the firm. Stakeholder theory takes various forms: Freeman, for example, adopts an instrumental approach whereby the significance of stakeholders lies in their power to jeopardize the firm's success; Goodpaster, in contrast, says the interests of stakeholders should be considered as a moral duty irrespective of any material consequences for the firm.[54]

Such distinctions have led to the separate development of stakeholder management (cf. Freeman) and stakeholder engagement (cf. Goodpaster), although from a business practice perspective the former predominates. However, both recognize that investors are only one constituency that companies need to consider. Stakeholders such as NGOs, consumers, and community groups have played a big part in persuading companies to consider sustainability issues, and in particular determining what issues are given priority. Retailer Marks & Spencer, for example, initially focused on organic foods and responsibly managed timber because this was what focus groups identified as consumer priorities. The role stakeholders play in shaping company behaviour is discussed in Chapter 10, but when thinking about why companies take a particular course of action, it is important to remember the potential barrier stakeholders can pose. Consumer demand, for example, can drive a company to produce goods such as bottled water that from a sustainability perspective are undesirable (Chapter 11); pressure group campaigns can push companies to focus on a particular issue without allowing a rational examination of whether there might be more important issues to address. The prevalence of conservation efforts targeted at aesthetically appealing mammals such as orangutans, rather than ones aimed at conserving biodiversity across an ecosystem is a good example of this.

Political factors

Companies are reluctant to deny consumers goods and services that are legal and profitable. They argue that it is the responsibility of governments to prohibit damaging products. However, since the 1980s, OECD country governments have been reluctant to interfere with demand in the belief that this hampers economic growth and overall societal well-being. Instead, through supply-side policies, governments have strived to reduce taxes and stimulate demand. This is a very different type of economic policy to the Keynesian ones that preceded it, and which aimed to use demand-side interventions such as taxation, government investment, and policies stimulating particular sectors to drive prosperity. President Reagan and the British prime minister, Margaret Thatcher, exemplified the shift to supply-side economics, and ushered in an era when politicians saw their role as enabling free market competition rather than promoting particular industries in the national interest.

This was not true worldwide, and it has been argued that economies such as China's and Vietnam's have prospered because they ignored the advice of supply-side economists.[55] Moreover, whether one is thinking about promoting clean energy, taxing carbon emissions, adopting emissions reduction targets, or establishing green banks, a return to demand-side policies is evident in government policy. This was apparent in some of the green stimulus packages of the late 2000s, and will be at the heart of the German government's renewable energy programme in the 2010s. However, we should not underestimate the shift this requires in political orthodoxy, and in countries such as Australia, the UK, and Japan economic recovery has been regarded as separate from—and a priority over—sustainability. In truth, the situation is more complex than this (Chapter 10), but governments are much more at ease treating sustainability as a supply-side issue where technological innovation and mostly private sector investment brings economic growth. Frustrated by this laissez faire attitude, some major companies around the world have lobbied for greater government leadership through initiatives such as the 'Corporate Leaders Group on Climate Change' (Chapter 2). There is also a growing sense, not least amongst NGOs, that more regulatory intervention is essential if sustainability challenges are to be met, and yet the political appetite for demand-side policies is largely absent.

Economic factors

The fiduciary duty to maximize shareholder value, the paramountcy awarded to investors above all other business stakeholders, and the political emphasis on supply-side economic policies all serve as barriers to private enterprise tackling sustainability challenges. They are also interrelated in that the law, politics, and business' overall relationship with society all reflect and reinforce the fundamental principle that business is the primary creator of wealth and economic prosperity in the modern world. In day-to-day parlance, the proxy for wealth, well-being, and prosperity is economic growth, typically measured in terms of GDP. The emphasis on GDP as a measure of wealth is itself problematic in a sustainability context because it is a measure of economic activity, not value. Thus, an event such as BP's Deepwater Horizon leak in the Gulf of Mexico, could ironically increase GDP by causing government spending on the clean-up, creating jobs for clean-up workers, and increasing the revenues of companies tackling the oil spill. This is another example of how conventional thinking is incongruent with sustainability. However, even without this incongruity, economic growth can easily be seen as at odds with addressing sustainability issues.

The laws, government policies, and societal norms that support growth are based on the assumption that economic growth is needed to ensure lasting prosperity. The dilemma according to some is that economic growth is not compatible with ecological sustainability. It is not that growth is essential to capitalism: a capitalist economy can function even if there is stagnation. But it is common to associate growth with 'good capitalism' where entrepreneurs and large corporations generate profits through innovation and efficiency.[56] The necessity for growth to achieve human well-being is taken for granted in Stern's analysis of economics and climate change, but as Helm (2008, p. 211) notes:

> The easy compatibility between economic growth and climate change which lies at the heart of the Stern Report is an illusion. The truth is that there is as yet no credible, socially just, ecologically sustainable scenario of continually growing economies for a world of nine billion people.

It is easy to understand why so much importance is attached to growth. Without it, financial capital loses its value, jobs are lost, consumer spending falls, and the positive feedback systems associated with growth falter, leading to recession and instability. Yet, from a sustainability perspective, less growth means less pressure on natural resources and the opportunity to reach an equilibrium between production and the throughput of resources. This balance is at the heart of Daly's 'steady-state economics' which posits that sustainable prosperity can only be achieved if there is a stable population with sustainable levels of consumption that do not surpass the carrying capacity of particular ecosystems or the Earth in general.[57]

One way of achieving this equilibrium that has gained traction in government policy is decoupling economic growth from emissions growth (Key concept 3.1). Market mechanisms such as cap and trade, and carbon taxes all have this intention (Case study 3). In OECD countries, the amount of energy and materials used for every unit of GDP has declined, and this has encouraged governments in particular to believe that not only is economic growth compatible with tackling climate change and other sustainability challenges, but is an essential condition for it because it creates the wealth needed to invest in mitigation and adaptation.

However, the OECD's drop in energy and material intensity is an example of 'relative decoupling', and as the earlier examples of retail and aviation show this does not mean there has been a fall in total emissions. Overall, emissions for OECD countries are 40 per cent higher today than they were in 1990, and since 2000 they have grown by three per cent a year. Material consumption in these countries has either increased or been offshored: for example, the UK experienced a six per cent emissions reduction in 1990–2004, but this masks an 11 per cent increase once emissions from the manufacture of imports are included.[58] What is required to address the worsening sustainability situation described in 'How well is business doing?' is absolute decoupling, i.e. absolute reductions in global carbon emissions that enable stabilization targets to be met without stifling economic growth.

Environmental economics

For environmental economists such as Daly and Jackson, absolute decoupling is an impossible challenge. They argue that decoupling must be measured as follows:

$$I = P + A + T$$

Where I refers to the impact of human activity from P (population size), A (society's affluence, normally measured as GDP), and T (the carbon intensity of technology). Relative decoupling has brought a decline in T but has not affected the growth of P or A, and has therefore meant an overall rise in I. In absolute decoupling, for I to decline the reductions in T, P, and/or A must be sufficient to offset any increases. However, as the section 'Political factors' shows, politicians raised on supply-side theories of prosperity are reluctant to hamper growth in A, and moreover do not want to address population growth for ethical reasons. We are therefore almost exclusively dependent on T (technological innovations that reduce carbon intensity) to address climate change. According to Jackson (2009), in order to meet the emissions reduction targets necessary to stabilize GHG emissions at 450 ppm by 2050 (Chapter 1), carbon intensity must improve by seven per cent a year. This is 10 per cent greater than has been achieved to date, and implies that by 2050 the carbon content per unit of economic output needs to be less than 40g CO_2: this is a reduction of 21-fold on the current global average.

Again, we know more about the economics of climate change than other aspects of sustainability, but not everyone agrees with the ecological economists. For instance, the Economics of Ecosystems and Biodiversity initiative (TEEB) is based on the principle that ecosystems and species will only be appreciated if their economic value can be demonstrated. In theory, this allows them to be included into a calculation of affluence (A), although probably not current measures such as GDP (See Chapter 1, Snapshot 1.2). More likely though is that it could enable biodiversity etc. to be factored into management accounting systems (e.g. as an element in calculating net present value), something that is relevant for relative decoupling, but not for absolute decoupling. Indeed, the experience of assigning market value to biodiversity is mixed, leading for instance to damaging levels of big game hunting, and record high prices for bluefin tuna as rarity encourages, rather than discourages, increased exploitation.[59]

For Jackson, anything that does not result in absolute reductions in the throughput of natural resources begs the question whether we are ultimately prepared to take on sustainability challenges such as emissions, biodiversity loss, and deforestation, or are we shying away from the challenge by protecting conventional economic wisdom? John Stuart Mill, an early thinker on liberal economics, once said 'the increase of wealth is not boundless: that at the end of what [economists] term the progressive state lies the stationary state, that all progress in wealth is but a postponement of this, and that each step in advance is an approach to it' (Mill 1848, Book IV, Chapter VI). Innovation and efficiency have stopped us reaching that stationary state, but sustainability presents three basic questions for economists that need to be answered if infinite growth is not a possibility:

- Can the affluence created by economic growth fund the degree of technological innovation required to reduce the throughput of natural resources?
- Can market instruments that put a price on ecosystems and biodiversity prevent their over-exploitation, and promote more sustainable models of production and consumption?
- Can economies be structured in such a way that they optimally balance affluence, population size, and technological development to reduce human impact?

If economic theory cannot answer these questions, then the plausibility of infinite growth is brought into doubt, and conventional economics which is built on that premise could be seen as a barrier to tackling sustainability in its own right. This is troubling for business which defines success according to the tenets of neo-liberal economic theory, and implies that if orthodox economic theory is itself a barrier to tackling sustainability challenges, the uncertainties business encounters will be exacerbated.

 ## Discussion points

Business is not a free agent when it comes to sustainability: its possibilities for action are constrained by an array of other factors.

- Which of the SLEPT factors in the section 'Barriers to progress' poses the most serious barrier to business' tackling sustainability issues?
- Why do governments prefer supply-side to demand-side policies?
- Do you agree with Jackson and Daly that economic growth is incompatible with sustainability?

 ## Summary

Business is a very important element in addressing the world's sustainability challenges, but the nature of the challenges means that conventional business thinking is not guaranteed to work: indeed, in some instances, it may increase business risk. Private enterprise is variously praised as a solution to society's difficulties in achieving sustainability, and blamed as the begetter of our problems. But regardless of whether business is considered a saviour or a sinner, the bulk of what companies are doing under a sustainability umbrella is connected to innovation and efficiency. This is in line with established ideas about corporate strategy, but despite many examples of individual companies incorporating sustainability into their strategic thinking, it is not obvious if these will help achieve the kinds of transformation sustainability appears to demand.

At a time when the gap between targets and performance in areas of sustainability such as carbon emissions is growing rapidly, it is understandable that business should look to other elements of society for assistance. However, if one looks at the law, consumer behaviour, politics, or economics, it is easy to conclude that business is being encouraged to continue practices that exacerbate rather than mitigate the wider problem.

We can conclude from this that business should be doing more, but that could simply result in it doing more ineffective or even harmful things. We might also conclude on a desperate note that business should do as little as possible because the cause is lost, but that would put in jeopardy its licence to operate, and could increase the pressure to seize assets and limit its activities. Business might feel it is in a fire at the cinema and its future is at risk, but rather than speed up the rush to the exits, or sitting pessimistically in its seat, it needs to recognize why it behaves as it does, and what would need to be different in order for it do more.

 ## Further reading

Chang, H. 2010, *23 things they don't tell you about capitalism*, Allen Lane, London.
Not a book about business or about sustainability, but it challenges all sorts of conventional wisdom about why some countries prosper and the way capitalism works in the real world.

Jackson, T. 2009, *Prosperity without growth: Economics for a finite planet*, Earthscan, London.
A well-constructed argument against the need for economic growth from an ecological economics perspective.

PwC 2011, Low Carbon Economy Index, PricewaterhouseCoopers LLC, London.
A biannual assessment of how well global society is doing in reducing GHG emissions.

Sandberg, P., Khan, N., & Leong, L. 2010, *Vision 2050. The new agenda for business*, World Business Council for Sustainable Development, Geneva.
Scenarios for achieving a sustainable world economy by 2050 based on consultations with several multinational companies.

Senge, P.M. 2008, *The necessary revolution: How individuals and organizations are working together to create a sustainable world*, Nicholas Brealey, London.
Business strategist take on the implications of sustainability for the way companies are run in the future.

 ## Case study 3   European Emissions Trading Scheme—a market approach to sustainability

In 2012, the trading price of carbon permits on the European Emissions Trading Scheme (ETS) fell to little more than €5 a tonne. This was a long way off the market's peak of €35 in 2008, and a significant drop from the €15 at which permits had been trading for much of 2009–2011. Nonetheless, the EU remains committed to the scheme, announcing in January 2012 that it would push ahead with plans to get foreign airlines to pay for carbon emissions from flights landing in Europe. The airlines would thereby join other high polluting industries such as steel, energy, and cement in having to buy permits to offset carbon emissions.

The ETS was the brainchild of Michael Grubb who was pessimistic that international negotiations would ever lead to countries agreeing to cut their emissions equally. He turned instead to the acid rain regulations being developed in the USA under which the government would give polluters allowances for their emissions. Polluters could trade these allowances amongst themselves so that companies that reduced their emissions could sell unused allowances to ones that were struggling to do so. Over time, allowances would be gradually retired, and as they became rarer, their price would rise forcing companies to choose between investing in emissions-reduction techniques, or paying an ever higher price to pollute.

Grubb saw that a similar regulated carbon market would help the negotiation of global emissions reductions. Countries would agree to allowances that they could buy and sell amongst themselves. As Grubb recognized early on, there would be problems in deciding how to allocate emissions permits to countries, and which countries should be allowed to participate. His ideas were integrated into the Kyoto Protocol (Chapter 10), but these problems have continued to haunt climate change negotiations.

The EU was the first region to recognize the advantages of emissions trading. After initial hostility to what was seen as an American-led free-market approach, it embraced a market-approach to emissions reduction in preference to carbon taxes and other policy alternatives. The ETS was launched in 2005, and since then about half of the carbon emissions of a region that accounts for 17 per cent of energy-related emissions have been subject to a carbon price. The ETS has become the flagship in the EU's claim to be playing a leadership role in combating climate change, not least as the champion of market-based solutions to managing the global commons.

It has, however, encountered numerous difficulties, many of them predicted from the outset. 2005–2007 was always intended to be a learning period, wrestling with the problem of permit allocation. A simple auctioning of permits as advocated by some economists was never practicable because it would put European-based companies at a disadvantage compared to overseas competitors who would not have to buy permits. This would be economically disastrous and would do nothing to reduce overall global emissions. Without auctions, however, it was difficult to know how many permits to allocate, and as it turned out the estimates of emissions made in 2005 were wildly inaccurate, and many companies found they had more than enough allowances to cover their emissions. Consequently, trading almost stopped.

Auctioning was increased, however, in Phase 2 (2008–2012) and national allocations were revised downwards to create a genuine demand for permits. For much of this period, the carbon price has been stable, and although not as high as some people hoped for, trading has been sufficient to support market exchange and a sophisticated derivatives market. Although the final figures are not yet known, indications are that the ETS has led to significant reductions in company emissions. Beyond 2012, it is planned that the European Commission itself will allocate allowances, meaning that individual governments will have less room to favour particular industries. The scope of the scheme is also being extended, notably to include the aviation industry. In addition, two-thirds of permits will be auctioned.

According to some policy analysts, the ETS has been a success because it offers the prospect of a cycle of economic growth promoting decarbonization. Yet E.On CEO, Johannes Teyssen, has said, 'The ETS is bust, it's dead. I don't know a single person in the world that would invest a dime based on ETS signals'. Companies such as E.On and Shell that have invested in clean technologies are calling for the European Commission to prop up the carbon price; but heavy industries such as steel say that meddling with prices makes a mockery of a market-based system. The idea that ETS fosters decarbonized growth has been strongly challenged on the one hand by industries claiming that carbon trading costs jobs and could see industries moving abroad, and on the other hand by those worried that the Commission's current focus on increasing energy efficiency will further reduce the value of permits.

Other countries and groupings such as the Canadian and US provinces and states involved in the Western Climate Initiative, New Zealand, China, and India continue to watch developments in the ETS as they look to build their own trading schemes, and there is hope that a critical mass of national and regional schemes will eventually lead to a global system as Grubb originally envisioned. But short-term political imperatives have trumped the ETS's long-term goals from the outset, and they will continue to be a major influence on this and other schemes moving ahead.

Sources: Chaffin 2012; Ellerman, Buchner, & Carraro 2011; Newell & Paterson 2010.

Questions

1. Emissions trading (also known as cap and trade) has been widely touted as a market-based solution to emissions reduction.

   a. What are the main advantages of cap and trade over international negotiations, carbon taxes, and other approaches?

   b. Why is the cement industry generally opposed to it, and the energy industry generally in favour?

   c. Why is the European Union eager to champion its ETS?

(*continued*)

2. The EU ETS has been the flagship of Europe's fight against global warming.

   a. What have been the main achievements of the ETS?

   b. Why has it not been the success some hoped for?

   c. Is Teyssen right to say it is bust?

3. Cap and trade has engendered a lot of political controversy worldwide.

   a. Why are Russian and Chinese airlines angry about the European system being extended to their industry?

   b. Compare the EU ETS's development with trading schemes in the USA and Australia. Why have national governments in those countries opposed such schemes?

   c. Is it likely that a cap-and-trade type approach will be extended to other sustainability challenges such as biodiversity and ecosystems management?

Endnotes

1. (Neale 2008)
2. (McKibben & McKibben 2007; Tickell 2008)
3. (James 2007)
4. (Singer 1972)
5. (Frank 1999, 2000; Schor 2010)
6. (Sandberg, Khan, & Leong 2010)
7. (Daly 1996)
8. (Gray 2003)
9. (Peattie & Belz 2009)
10. (Jackson 2009)
11. (Krosinsky & Robins 2008)
12. (Lydenberg 2005)
13. (Porter & Kramer 2011)
14. (Elkington & Hartigan 2008)
15. (Blowfield & Dolan 2010a, 2010b)
16. (Sandberg, Khan, & Leong 2010)
17. (Friedman 1962)
18. (Newell & Paterson 2010)
19. http://www.basf-admixtures.com/en/sustainability/EEA/Pages/default.aspx, accessed 23 June 2011.
20. (Newell & Paterson 2010)
21. (Newell & Paterson 2010)
22. (Pinkse & Kolk 2009)
23. (Senge, Smith, & Kruschwitz 2008)
24. (James 1918)
25. (Frank 1999, 2000; Jackson 2009)
26. http://www.guardian.co.uk/sustainable-business/britain-biggest-retailer-green-growth, accessed 25 June 2011.
27. http://www.tesco.com/climatechange/carbonFootprint.asp, accessed 25 June 2011.

28. http://www.iata.org/SiteCollectionDocuments/Documents/Global_Approach_Reducing_
    Emissions_251109web.pdf, accessed 25 June 2011.

29. (SSEE 2009)

30. (SSEE 2009)

31. (Senge 2008)

32. (Jones 2010)

33. (Jones 2010)

34. (PwC 2011)

35. (Stern 2008)

36. (Jackson 2009)

37. (Krupp 2008)

38. SLEPT and its close relative PESTLE (political, economic, social, technological, legal, and environmental)
    are common diagnostic tools for informing strategy, and is a feature of Porter's five forces analysis
    (Porter 1980).

39. (Matten & Crane 2007; Greenfield 2006)

40. (Rand 1966)

41. (Kelly 2001; Mitchell 2001)

42. (Hinkley 2002)

43. (Krosinsky & Robins 2008; Lydenberg 2005)

44. (Fisher 2009)

45. (Hansmann & Kraakman 2000)

46. (Lee 2005)

47. (Shleifer & Vishny 1996)

48. (Weybrecht 2009)

49. (Gray, Kouhy, & Lavers 1996)

50. (Carney 1998)

51. (Friedman 1962; Novak 1982)

52. (Ellsworth 2002)

53. (Barnea & Rubin 2010; Oh, Chang, & Martynov)

54. (Evan & Freeman 1988; Goodpaster 1991)

55. (Chang 2010)

56. (Baumol, Litan, & Schramm 2007)

57. (Daly 1996)

58. (Jackson 2009)

59. For similar examples, see the research described at http://www.wildcru.org/research/.

Section 2

Managing sustainability

Leadership, entrepreneurship, and change

Key terms

Individual leadership	Entrepreneurship
Transformation	Values
Leadership organizations	Sensemaking
Social enterprise	Intrapreneurship

Online resources

- Signposts to information on sustainability leadership.
- Resources on sustainable entrepreneurship.
- Suggestions for case studies on leadership.

  http://www.oxfordtextbooks.co.uk/orc/blowfield/

Chapter in brief

This chapter examines leadership, something that is often cited as the essential ingredient to tackle sustainability effectively. It looks at individual leadership, highlighting the levels of leadership, the significance of values, and the role of entrepreneurship. It examines what actions leaders take, their skills and competencies, and why they make the decisions they do. It explores the idea of collective or communitarian leadership. It also discusses the current state of leadership, and ends by examining the possibilities and constraints on business as a sustainability leader.

Introduction to leadership

Leadership is a very appealing word. When faced with sustainability's complex challenges, it is not surprising that great weight is attached to a term that is both optimistic and yet unspecific. Leadership in a sustainability context is often presented as something unique, distinct from previous forms of leadership. Sustainability leaders could be ones who have 'internalized the spiralling threat [of sustainability issues] and are striving to make a difference. . . . The gift of sustainability leaders is their commitment to consciously embrace choices that serve common interests'.[1] In other words, it is claimed sustainability leadership is about discovering and then embedding values associated with sustainability into a company. Alternatively, leaders could be identifiable by their success in getting their companies to meet certain external criteria: for instance, the United Nations Global Compact defines 'corporate sustainability leadership' in terms of integrating UN principles into company strategies and operations.[2] In this case, leadership is about taking predefined criteria and finding ways of integrating them into the company.

As we will see in this chapter, there is controversy about whether a values-orientation or a technical-instrumental one is the proper focus of sustainability leadership. However, what both imply is that there is something special about sustainability leadership that distinguishes it from other kinds of leadership and innovation. Senge has called the shaping of a sustainable, flourishing world as the greatest learning challenge ever faced by humanity,[3] but does the nature of the challenge mean that it needs to be distinguished from conventional notions of corporate leadership? For example, the values-oriented approach to leadership fits comfortably into the well-established traditions of trait-based and behavioural theories of leadership that hold successful leaders use their inherent or acquired capabilities to gain an organization's commitment to particular values. Similarly, if the focus is more on the leader's role in taking a company through the technical process of change, this fits in the traditions of transactional and context leadership.[4]

By recognizing these traditions, it can be argued that 'sustainability leadership should not be seen as a different school of leadership, but rather a particular blend of individual leadership characteristics applied within a definitive context' (CPSL 2011, p. 20). However, this raises two further questions. First, how much weight should be given to an individual's characteristics and actions, and how much to the context they have to operate within? It may be that what is crucial are the specific actions individuals inside and outside of a company take that lead to change;[5] but it could be that events and circumstance determine what leadership approaches are appropriate.[6] Second, to what extent is leadership an institutional or group quality rather than one associated with individuals? Given all the emphasis in modern management theory on teamwork, collaboration, and participation, it might be misleading to view sustainability leadership—to paraphrase Thomas Carlyle—as merely the stories of great men. These questions underpin the following sections where we will look at individuals, organizations, and context.

Individual leadership

There are numerous testaments to the power of individuals as agents of change in the sustainability context. Leaders such as social entrepreneurs stand out because of their 'self-assurance, their emotion, their insane ambition': 'Their endeavors are transformative, not

Key concept 4.1 Leadership

According to Peter Drucker, the only useful definition of a leader is someone who has followers. Sustainability leadership is about the skills, styles, competencies, and actions individuals and organizations take to build this followership. It is not necessarily about leadership from the top: innovation from across the company can be an important element in transforming companies. There is also no single approach, and quite different leadership approaches are used to motivate, inspire, and win commitment from those whose lives will be affected by any change.

palliative, with the power to catalyze and shape the future' (Elkington & Hartigan 2008, p. 6). There is much talk of sustainability champions inside and outside of companies, and individuals such as Interface's Ray Anderson—a pioneer of executing The Natural Sep (Chapter 3)—are singled out as sustainability heroes. This is not unique to business: the environmental movement has built its own pantheon of heroes such as Chico Mendes, the Brazilian environmentalist and union leader, and Wangari Maathai, the Nobel Peace Prize-winning environmental campaigner from Kenya. It is also not unique to sustainability, and magazines such as *Fortune* have a long history of cover stories such as the CEO of the Decade, Business Person of the Year, and the Top People in Business.

There are good reasons for telling stories about change by focusing on an individual. While some might agree with Brecht's character who says 'Pity the land that is in need of heroes', there are many who find it more convincing, compelling, or comprehensible to attribute change to individual leaders. For instance, IBM's turnaround in the 1990s is widely attributed to CEO Lou Gerstner, just as John Mackey as founder of Wholefoods is credited with establishing a retail company with a unique philosophy.[7] People such as Mackey or Apple's Steve Jobs are so closely associated with the identity of their firms that much attention is paid to their individual leadership qualities and philosophies. As we seek to understand and learn from companies' experiences, we look with hindsight at what happened to draw out lessons for the future, and as innumerable business school case studies demonstrate, this is most easily done by concentrating on individuals.

Two problems emerge from this, however. First, understanding past events from the perspective of the present is fraught with danger as, for instance, the experiences of some individuals are brought to the foreground while those of others are forgotten or overlooked. Equally, there is a tendency to start with the outcome and explain why that happened, rather than examining how the situation looked at the time, the range of options, and the full variety of actions taken (many of which failed or were missteps).[8] An example of this is the aforementioned IBM turnaround story: depending on what sources one uses, this has been presented as case of heroic leadership by the CEO, and as one of the struggle by mid-level 'intrapreneurs' (i.e. entrepreneurs within the company) to enact their ideas and overcome the inertia of senior management.[9] Second, as the IBM example demonstrates, there is a high risk that what emerges as the leadership story is the one that flatters the current leadership rather than sheds genuine insight into what has occurred as became evident in 2001 when Enron entered bankruptcy a year after its management team won *Fortune* magazine's Quality of Management award. This has been recognized by IBM itself, one of whose strategists warns 'senior managers are often only told the stories they want to hear, [and] are insulated from negativity or they simply succumb to the very human tendency to hear what we want to hear'.[10] As we will see, the debate about sustainability leadership is not immune from these problems.

Leadership aims

Sustainability leadership is often singled out for attention because the situation is depicted as unique. This can be because the sustainability challenge is exceptional, demanding that companies be reengineered to be fit for purpose in a resource-constrained economy (Chapter 3). More often, however, the leaders' role is depicted less as envisioning a new type of company, and more as a guide responsible for leading the change from one state to another, more appropriate one. The sustainability leader's role, therefore, is to steer the company through a transformation process. Typically, in large companies at least, it is not the leader's vision of sustainability that matters, but his 'organizational intelligence': the knack of connecting with what matters most to others in the company so as to unleash their 'latent collective imagination and energy'.[11] A common theme is that it is insufficient to exchange one set of management practices for another: sustainability leadership is often depicted as needing practices that are rooted in a sense of purpose and values.[12]

This is not as original as some sustainability authors might claim. The different sustainability leadership models described in this chapter fit within conventional leadership categories (Figure 4.1). Likewise, any business student familiar with the change theories associated with Lewin, Kotter, or Bennis will recognize elements of their diverse thinking in sustainability leadership.[13] We should not be surprised by this: goals may vary from company to company, but the strategic challenges are shared.[14] Indeed, if they were not shared, then it would be impossible to discuss leadership as a science or discipline. However, in identifying the unique elements of sustainability leadership, we need to know if these strategic challenges differ because of sustainability. A comparison of conventional strategic challenges and the sustainability management challenges discussed in Chapter 3 reveals that with the exception of growth, there is little difference (Figure 4.2). Given the predicament of growth in a sustainability context (Chapter 3), this might be considered a major

Great man theory	Leaders are innately exceptional people, destined to lead
Trait theory	Leaders are those with the myriad traits/qualities associated with leadership
Behaviourist theory	Focuses on the actions of leaders rather than their qualities. This gives rise to different styles of leadership
Situational leadership	Leadership suited to a particular situation. For instance, an autocratic style might be appropriate in some cases; a more participative style in others
Contingency theory	A refinement of situational leadership intended to identify the situational variables that predict what form appropriate/effective leadership will take
Transactional theory	Emphasizes the leader—follower relationship, and the mutual benefits associated from their 'contract.'
Transformational theory	Focusing on the change process, and the role of leaders in envisioning and implementing the transformation process

Figure 4.1 Conventional theories of individual leadership.

distinction, however this is not something addressed in sustainability leadership theory. Treating the outcomes of sustainability leadership in this way leaves it open to criticism of arrogance (i.e. the outcomes are self-evident truths) or ignorance (i.e. the outcomes are unclear). It can be argued that one of leadership's aims is to bring clarity to an uncertain situation (see 'Sensemaking'), but uncertainty is not unique to sustainability, and nonetheless many mainstream management thinkers have been overt and transparent about the outcomes by which leadership should be measured. Drucker, for example, in *Concept of the Corporation*, says that the goal of business leadership is to secure 'genuine capital formation' that is of necessity built on profit. Indeed, despite writing in the 1940s, he is clearer on sustainability-related goals than some current thinkers, highlighting that successful companies should never substitute the exploitation of natural capital for genuine capital formation: 'Capital formation [must] be based on the one resource which, instead of being destroyed by being used, reproduces itself, namely profit' (Drucker 1946, p. 234). Where Drucker has more in common with sustainability leadership theory is the importance he attaches to values: in his case, it is the values of free enterprise, and the importance of companies to the US model of capitalism; in the case of sustainability leadership, it is the values that emerge from the concept of sustainability.

Figure 4.2 Typical elements of strategic challenge for leaders.
Sources: adapted from Collins & Porras 1994; Rouse 2006; Senge 1999.

Values-based leadership

We have already mentioned a distinction in discussions of sustainability leadership between a technical-instrumental orientation and a values-based one. The former concentrates on the application of conventional behaviour and strategy theories to sustainability challenges (see 'Leadership actions'); the latter builds on a belief that there is something intrinsically problematic about free enterprise in its current forms, and that the role of the leader is to move the company from what is variously described as an outdated, unsustainable, or morally wrong position to one where the company can thrive, be it in a very different business environment. As Senge posits, 'Climate change is a particular sort of gift, a time clock telling us how fast the Industrial Age is ending' (Senge 2008, p. 27).

Much of the values-oriented leadership thinking elicits a very subjective response, typically reflecting one's existing values. Declarations such as 'We must live and work, caring for ourselves and others. We must love openly all human beings and the earth'[15] will appeal to some and be objectionable to others. Such views often reflect religious beliefs, but political, philosophical, and psychological theories also underpin values-based thinking. For example, Gauthier's theory of leadership draws on the psychology of generative change the aims of which include creating more life-affirming, holistic ways of working;[16] Allen draws on Confucian and Western philosophical traditions to explain what she calls 'archetypal change journeys'.[17]

The idea of a journey is common in individual leadership, again drawing on psychological theory. Sustainability is not unique in this sense in that conventional organizational change from Lewin to Mintzberg has been rooted in psychology. Reflecting Kübler-Ross's idea of the stages of grieving,[18] authors such as Fisher, and Lewis and Parker have developed transition curves where individuals go through different phases of change (Box 4.1). Scharmer's 'Theory U' has been promoted as a model of individual change appropriate to sustainability.[19] This breaks the process of change into three stages (downloading, reacting, embodying) during which the individual again moves from the rejection of old ways to an acceptance of something new to the embedding of those new ideas.[20]

Such theories emphasize not only the individual's journey, but the part played by collaboration and teamwork in undertaking such journeys for the benefit of the firm. It is the leader's role to guide this process to the point where they are embedded in performance, practice, and infrastructures. Various qualities are associated with successful leadership of this kind. Eliatamby, for example, lists personal virtues such as humility, self-denial, and respect; Senge talks about qualities and capacities, notably the ability to think in terms of systems rather than narrow impacts, collaboration, and the ability to bring things leaders desire into reality.[21] In both cases, the responsibility of the leader is to drive systems change. Their role, therefore, is to clarify the organization's values, frame relevant questions, and help create a vision for the future. This in turn will often involve dealing with uncertainty about how to undertake the journey, courage given the likely scepticism amongst peers, and having the insight to build the company's adaptive capacity.[22] 'In cultivating these change leaders and agents [it is] imperative that they are helped to connect their actions to a deep sense of purpose and meaning for a world in which living systems, happiness and well-being are central to human endeavour' (Birney, Salazar, & Morgan 2008, p. 26).

Box 4.1   Typical elements of transition curves

- Immobilization or anxiety: shock. Overwhelmed mismatch: expectations vs reality.
- Denial of change: temporary retreat. False competence.
- Incompetence: awareness and frustration.
- Happiness: excitement at prospect of change.
- Acceptance of reality: letting go of the past.
- Disillusionment: rejection of the new future.
- Testing: new ways to deal with new reality.
- Search for meaning: internalization and seeking to understand.
- Integration: incorporation of meanings within behaviours.

Sources: Parker & Lewis 1981; http://www.businessballs.com/personalchangeprocess.htm, accessed 1 August 2011

 Discussion points

Sustainability is seen by some as an opportunity to embed values into commercial enterprises.

- What are the underlying principles and values in your organization's mission or vision statement?
- Are these congruent with your own values?
- Have you experienced conflict between your values and the organization's?

Sensemaking

The notion that part of the leader's function is to provide a purpose and mission to the change process echoes the idea of leadership as a process of sensemaking. Developed by the organizational theorist Karl Weick, sensemaking is particularly relevant to emergencies, disasters, and other situations characterized by chaos or when the current state of the world is at odds with how we expect it to be. This is clearly the situation with sustainability challenges that contest the tenets of 'business as usual'.

Weick argued that there were three stages of reaction to such situations: (a) superficial simplicity during which individuals seek ready-made (but typically erroneous) explanations for what is happening; (b) confused complexity during which a potentially paralysing array of explanations for the situation emerge; and (c) profound simplicity when seasoned explanations for the event gain acceptance, and enable people within the organization to progress once more.[23] The leader's role in such circumstances is to help people with their struggle to make sense of complexity by manipulating their experiences so as to give meaning to what they have experienced. Through sensemaking, the leader guides them to the stage where profound simplicities become accepted as a reality, not because they tell an objective truth necessarily, but because they provide an explanation strong enough to generate a new commitment to take particular courses of action. The leader, therefore, is someone who wins others' commitment, and implicit in many ideas about sustainability leadership is Weick's belief that strong commitments are essential to enact change, or conversely that weak commitments seriously limit what a company can achieve.

Snapshot 4.1   Sensemaking at the top—Paul Polman, Unilever

Since joining Unilever from Nestlé in 2008, CEO Paul Polman has garnered a reputation as champion of the consumer goods company's sustainability agenda. His predecessors, Patrick Cescau and Niall Fitzgerald, had both taken significant steps in identifying sustainability with Unilever's brands, but it was under Polman that the Sustainable Living Plan was launched with the aim of doubling the company's size while reducing its environmental footprint.

By tackling the issue of absolute decoupling (Chapter 3) in this way, Polman challenged his company, its industry peers, and governments to think seriously about what a sustainable business means. He has set out three big goals for 2020: sustainable sourcing for all of Unilever's agricultural raw materials; halving the environmental impact of its products; and reaching a billion poor people to improve their health and well-being. He is open in saying that the company's brands should have a social mission, and is outspoken in acknowledging the constraints financial analysts put on long-term company thinking. 'Unilever recognizes that growth at any cost is not viable. We have to develop new ways of doing business which will increase the positive social benefits arising from our activities while at the same time reducing our environmental impacts'.

Sources: CPSL 2011; http://www.sustainable-living.unilever.com/news-resources/news/sustainable-sourcing/paul-polman-on-sustainability/, accessed 1 August 2011.

Questions

Paul Polman's role as CEO could be described as sensemaker in the sustainability context.

1. What uncertainties and anxieties within the company is he addressing?

2. Is sensemaking about a social mission more important for some Unilever brands than others?

3. How important are Polman's own values in the sensemaking process?

Leadership actions

An important feature of sensemaking is that it is not a static model. Change theory such as Lewin's Unfreeze, Change, Refreeze model has tended to divide the change process into discrete chunks, each needing particular leadership skills. This persists today in well-known tools such as the think–plan–do–check approach to continual improvement. Weick, however, sees change as a dynamic process requiring simultaneous thinking while doing. This might seem to be common sense, but segmenting actions is common in sustainability leadership literature. AA1000, an accounting standard to promote responsibility and sustainability, provides a very structured approach to enable to leaders to engage with stakeholders, based on a blend of the Six Sigma and related think–plan–do–check approaches to continual improvement that are also evident in ISO (International Organization for Standardization) environmental and corporate responsibility series. Other sustainability leadership authors such as Epstein and Doppelt have built models that reflect Kotter's eight-step model of organizational change.[24]

There is often a strong tone of optimism in these theories: the leader may be referred to as someone who can empower others to make change, releasing the latent creativity of the work-force in the process. Reflecting features of the broader field of transformational leadership, values such as freedom, engagement, and democracy are commonly cited as positive, and failure to address sustainability challenges is attributed to factors such as 'entrained patterns of thought', outdated routines, and fixed constructions of reality.[25] When leaders do not succeed, the blame tends to be interpreted as a failing on the part of the led. The change recipient is portrayed as someone irrational or dysfunctional, and the emphasis is placed on what can be done to or for the resistant parties. However, this itself could be a self-serving interpretation by leaders trying to make sense of resistance. Less noticed is resistance as a conscious, deliberate act, a reaction for instance to the actions of the leaders who may be felt to have eroded trust or broken agreements, or part of the process of generating commitment to new ideas.[26]

This is a weakness in some empowerment-oriented perspectives on sustainability leadership. As we will see with intrapreneurship later, the spotlight is shone on the potential contribution of the change recipient, but this assumes a particular relationship between employer and employee. In an era of employment mobility, job insecurity, and worsening terms and conditions in OECD countries, the incentive to assist a company that may have no concern about the employee's long-term interests can be hard to discern. As with other types of transformational leadership, sustainability leadership's appeal to commitment and empowerment can be interpreted by an insecure workforce as a confidence trick. As Boltanski and Chiapello observe (2005), it is a feature of contemporary capitalism—exemplified by modern management theory—that individual achievement, personal reward, and entrepreneurship are reified as values, whereas the values of the social sustainability discourse lean towards joint endeavour, communal benefit, and collaboration. Communitarian leadership is a vigorous area of practice and scholarship with a historical tradition dating back to early industrial commentators such as Morris and Blake, and emphasizing collaboration and civic identity over individualism.[27]

The disconnect between the values of the modern workplace and of a sustainable civic society is ignored in sustainability leadership literature, even though the implied social contract with other stakeholders is a recurring theme. Ironically, this flies in the face of some seminal management thinking. Drucker, for example, states that failure to meet workers' expectations about fairness disengages them from an interest in company success, and what he calls the 'worker's citizenship' (i.e. her role in the company and wider society) is of central importance to industrial society (Drucker 1946). As he stresses, this relationship is especially important in a transitional situation. Deming, the pioneer of total quality management, echoes this in his view on managers during transformation:

> The job of management is inseparable from the welfare of the company. Mobility, here a while and gone, from the management of one company to the management of another, is something that . . . industry can no longer afford. Management must declare a policy for the future, to stay in business and to provide jobs for their people, and more jobs.
>
> (Deming 2000, p. xi)

Deming concurs with some sustainability theorists that an emphasis on short-term profits and the lack of constancy of purpose prevent transformation. However, in what he calls the 'deadly diseases' that damage transformation, he dismisses elements that have been lauded in sustainability leadership such as constant evaluation of performance and the measurement of visible figures. The New Economics Foundation, in setting out its views of a sustainable planet, argues that what gets counted counts, but according to Deming this can lead to the exclusion of unknown and unknowable elements that equally need to be managed.[28]

NEF's position echoes a wider tension in sustainability leadership thinking which on the one hand emphasizes empowerment and similar transformational qualities, but at the same time alludes to quantification, incentivization, and performance measurement associated with the quite different 'transactional' school of leadership. For many years, as companies grew through mergers and acquisitions, or increased their bottom lines through efficiency, transactional leadership was highly desirable where incentivization and punishment were key management tools. At times, sustainability leadership theory implies the tools of transactional leadership legitimize sustainability goals, but overall its emphasis is on transformational leadership where fostering collaboration, networking, and 'followers' (i.e. workers) commitment to the vision and mission of the organization are the leader's goals.[29] Moreover, different leadership qualities are required for different elements of transformation. In his theory of the 'tipping point', Gladwell (2000) identifies three types of transformation: contagion (a new idea is quickly taken up), connection (a few well-connected people adopt an idea and disseminate it), and rapid (after a slow start, a tipping point is reached and adoption of a new idea is sudden and rapid). The tipping point has been applied to sustainability, and three types of leader have been suggested as essential to change: connectors (the well-connected individuals who feed new ideas into the mainstream), knowledge holders (those with specialist knowledge about sustainability), and marketers (those who can sell knowledge of sustainability to others).[30] In each case, leaders require specific competencies to carry out their role, but for the most part the emphasis in sustainability leadership is on a general set of qualities and values rather than specific skill sets.

A survey of senior managers involved in sustainability highlighted the mix of transactional and transformational leadership approaches they consider desirable. They identified seven characteristics they thought important for individual leadership approaches (Box 4.2). They also noted that leadership does not consist of one-off, isolated actions, and that the embedding of sustainability into how the business is run required more of a transactional approach, rewarding performance and delivering tangible results. The same cohort felt that leadership is not about the leader being in command of everything, and an important element of leadership is creating opportunities for innovation across the company (see 'Intrapreneurs'). Similarly, leadership should not be restricted to within the company, but involves using one's influence in the wider business community, and initiating new ideas that challenge the status quo.[31]

It would be misguided to assess what is appropriate leadership based on theory alone, but it can be difficult to assess how much of what is being proposed is evidence-based and how

---

Box 4.2   Desirable characteristics for individual sustainability leadership

1. A systemic, interdisciplinary understanding of the situation.
2. Emotional intelligence and a caring attitude.
3. A values orientation that is used to shape the corporate culture.
4. A strong vision for making a difference.
5. An inclusive style that engenders trust.
6. A willingness to innovate and be radical.
7. A long-term perspective on impacts.

Source: CPSL 2011.

much relies on an a priori notion of good sense. Some sustainability leadership theories do not refer to empirical experience, and some that do use snapshots (sometimes called case studies) that seem to support the theory, but these are not systematic enough to claim that they are its basis. Various surveys concur that sustainability is an important issue for business, and moreover that many corporate leaders view it as a competitive advantage.[32] However, this kind of data needs to be treated cautiously because of the inevitable respondent biases in surveys that have sustainability or corporate responsibility as their primary concern. An IBM study of complexity more generally, involving face-to-face interviews with over 1500 CEOs, found that sustainability ranked seventh in importance as a leadership concern (IBM 2010). Another reason to question leadership commitment is the gap between beliefs and actions. An Accenture study of 766 business leaders found that 93 per cent believed sustainability is important or very important to the future success of their companies, and 96 per cent said that environmental, social, and governance issues should be fully embedded into the strategy and operations of a company. Taken at face value, the fact that 81 per cent of CEOs believe this integration is already happening should be a cause for good cheer. However, given the significance of the sustainability challenges for business noted elsewhere (Chapters 1 and 2), these figures could be interpreted as a sign that leaders are underestimating what needs to be done.

Discussion points

The Cambridge Programme for Sustainability Leadership (CPSL) is a well-established organization which educates business leaders on sustainability. Its model of leadership was developed through consultation with alumni from its courses over a 20-year period (Figure 4.3).

- What do you think are the most important external factors that affect what leaders do?
- What traits would you expect to see in a good sustainability leader?
- Why is people empowerment important as a leadership action?

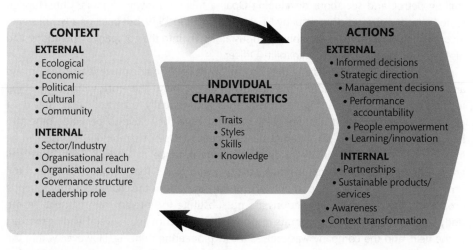

Figure 4.3 CPSL Model of leadership.

Entrepreneurs and intrapreneurs

So far, we have discussed leadership mostly as a quality and action associated with senior managers, typically within large companies. This is only part of the sustainability leadership landscape: for every Ray Anderson (Interface) who led his company in a sustainability direction from the very top, there are examples of change being initiated at other levels of the company. Per Carstedt who introduced biofuel cars to Sweden found that it wasn't senior managers or auto engineers who bought into his idea, but people in the car manufacturers' marketing departments (Snapshot 3.1). Likewise, this kind of 'intrapreneur' played a crucial role in embedding sustainability into the retailer Marks & Spencer (Appendix 1, Extended case study A)

Furthermore, sustainability leadership is not limited to large companies. Insofar as sustainability represents a breakthrough opportunity for new products and new types of business, much of the leadership can be expected to happen in SMEs. Sustainability is now an important element of the wider field of social entrepreneurship, which in addition to product and service innovation also promises alternative kinds of business model of the kind that sustainability sometimes appears to demand (Chapter 3).

Intrapreneurs

An intrapreneur is an employee who is given the freedom to work independently within a company with the objective of introducing innovation to revitalize and diversify its business.[33] The term was first used by management consultant George Pinchot in the 1970s, and it has become popular in sustainability because the knowledge, values, and commitment necessary to make sustainability part of the management process have not been the monopoly of corporate leaders. Hamel has written extensively on cases where management innovation has happened in unlikely places within the corporation,[34] and there are similar examples of intrapreneurs influencing their companies' sustainability agendas. BP Australia's Gerry Hueston, for example, discovered that young children were being brain-damaged from sniffing petrol, and set about developing Opal, a fuel with lower vapours. Chris Tuppen joined telecommunications company BT as an engineer in 1979, but became a key player in incorporating corporate responsibility and sustainability into the company's operations, and his final position was Chief Sustainability Officer.

A feature of intrapreneurs is that they do not have a ready-made power base: a command and control approach to leadership is not an option for them. Therefore, while many of the features of individual leadership described earlier apply equally to intrapreneurs, they must also be able to truck and bargain, using what leverage they have to persuade others to become allies. In some cases, external alliances with NGOs or shareholder activists can be important to stirring up activity inside the firm. For instance, at Marks & Spencer a small group of sustainability champions built relations with NGOs that had been hostile to the firm, eventually creating a support network for the innovations the champions subsequently proposed. However, external relations are no substitute for internal commitment. At the Body Shop in the 1990s, the corporate responsibility team contained several leading thinkers in the field, and the company was praised for its pioneering thinking. However, within the company the team was often viewed as outsiders, and struggled to win the credibility that would allow it to lead.[35] Nowadays, it is widely accepted that successful intrapreneurship depends as much on a knowledge of how the company works as it does on knowledge about sustainability. Indeed, anecdotal evidence suggests that companies that have established a reputation for their sustainability practices are ones that have retained a corpus of sustainability intrapreneurs such as Rahul Raj, Walmart's Senior Manager of Sustainability, Jan Kees Vis, Unilever's Global Director Sustainable Sourcing Development, and Sarah Severn, Director of Stakeholder Mobilization for Nike. What these very different individuals share, in addition to their views on sustainability, is that they did not come to their respective companies as sustainability champions, and they had many years of experience inside the company enabling them to understand how their businesses function.

We can get a sense of the current work of intrapreneurs from surveys of employees with a sustainability function.[36] At present, most of their time is spent on promoting understanding about sustainability and why it is valuable to the company, rather than on particular actions to address sustainability issues. Intrapreneurs expect this situation to change in future, but for the time being they are more likely to think about market advantage, mindsets, and not least fund raising than water availability or low carbon production.[37] Much of their time, therefore, is spent building a consensus within the company through the kind of actions listed in Box 4.3. In large companies in particular, overcoming internal resistance and winning employee support are far more important than new management systems or sustainability reporting. Consequently, the skills an intrapreneur needs to influence her company tend to be soft rather than hard skills. Communication skills, industry knowledge, and consensus facilitation are currently more important than hard skills such as strategic planning, systems thinking, or project management. Risk assessment and scientific expertise, both of which are interlinked with the business-sustainability challenge (Chapter 2), seem to be ranked low in the skills needed for success at present.

We need to exercise caution when taking lessons from this kind of data. The sustainability intrapreneurs are describing the current situation, and are aware that their skills base will change once sustainability is more integrated into company strategy. Furthermore, the competencies listed are those recognized by sustainability experts, and may not reflect the views of others in the company. However, accepting these limitations, they nonetheless reflect the opinions and experience of people most engaged in day-to-day sustainability management, and therefore provide as good a picture as any of current leadership issues.

Box 4.3   Key current activities for company sustainability specialists

- Getting top management buy-in.
- Developing the business case.
- Educating customers/clients about the company's activities.
- Getting funding for sustainability initiatives.
- Overcoming internal resistance to change.

Sources: ISSP 2010; Sustainability & GlobeScan 2010.

Snapshot 4.2   Act now, apologize later—Adam Werbach

Adam Werbach had been an environmental activist since his school days. He ran the Sierra Student Coalition, and by 1996 was president of the Sierra Club. He also had a place on Greenpeace's international board. But in 2004 he alienated many environmentalists when he announced the 'death of environmentalism'. Having witnessed the aftermath of Hurricane Katrina in New Orleans, USA, he concluded that major companies rather than governments or NGOs held the capacity to deal with the biggest problems.

Werbach's Act Now consultancy began to work with Walmart. He saw the long-term nemesis of the environmental movement as an ideal conduit for reaching the average American, and designed a programme to encourage every employee to make a change that would benefit themselves and wider society. Act Now was acquired by advertising firm Saatchi and Saatchi, and under the label Saatchi and Saatchi S has worked with companies such as McDonald's, Johnson and Johnson, and General Mills to foster intrapreneurship amongst workers.

Sources: CPSL 2011; Werbach 1997, 2009.

Questions

Werbach's career path highlights one of the ways sustainability leadership has been accepted by companies.

1. Why did environmental NGOs reject Werbach's shift in direction?

2. Is Werbach an example of intrapreneurship?

3. Is there a role for intrapreneurs in NGOs and government agencies?

Sustainability entrepreneurs

Sustainability leadership is not the preserve of large companies. On the contrary, such firms face the obstacles of inertia and incumbency that may help explain the gap between what is required to tackle sustainability issues and what is currently being achieved (Chapter 3). By contrast, SMEs offer the promise of disruptive innovation and flexibility that sustainability challenges seem to demand. This is not to pretend that sustainability is always greeted as an opportunity by SMEs. As with corporate responsibility, many entrepreneurs see it as an unnecessary cost, something that might be affordable to large firms but not to them.

These different attitudes remind us that SMEs are not homogeneous: the owner of rickshaws in Jogjakarta, Indonesia, is likely to have little in common with a software engineering start-up in Iceland even if the number of workers is about the same. Indeed, SMEs often appear to be defined as much by what they are not (i.e. they are not multinational enterprises) as what they share in common. One reason SMEs are not homogeneous is that they represent different types of entrepreneurship. The entrepreneurs that generate excitement in a sustainability context are a specific type, called variously 'opportunity entrepreneurs' and 'gazelles'.[38] They are often the serial entrepreneurs who derive enormous satisfaction from establishing new businesses, and whom it is hoped will be attracted by the opportunities found in tackling major societal challenges. The opportunities connected with sustainability such as demographic change and global warming (Chapter 2) are already being seized on by such people. It has been argued that they should get preferential treatment in the allocation of resources (e.g. government funding). Even if their products do not have a sustainability orientation, their growth orientation provides an incentive to be aware of their social and environmental footprint, increases the importance of a robust and more complex approach to stakeholder management, and opens the door to new sources of capital (e.g. venture philanthropy).[39] Richard Reed, Adam Balon, and Jon Wright, founders of the innocent smoothie company are examples of this type of 'gazelle'.

Therefore, when entrepreneurs are mentioned in a sustainability context, the term refers to gazelles, but these represent a small section of the entrepreneurial universe. There has been little analysis of sustainability and 'lifestyle' entrepreneurs, those who have chosen to work for themselves or have been left little choice given the changing nature of employment in wealthier economies. They have little desire or indeed potential to grow, and they may regard running a SME not as an exciting springboard to business success, but more as a trade-off between factors such as independence, income, employment, and other lifestyle-related decisions.[40] In developing countries in particular, where entrepreneurship is increasingly espoused as a way out of poverty, there are also 'necessity entrepreneurs', i.e. small operations (often in the informal economy) where own-account enterprise is the option of last resort, and where the opportunities and incomes are typically worse than in formal employment. Examples include the female small market traders in Nairobi, food hawkers in Manila, and the laid-off Detroit car worker who is trying to run his own machine shop. Unlike lifestyle entrepreneurs, necessity entrepreneurs may see their business as a temporary occupation until something better comes along, and there will be little capital to invest in anything that does not show an immediate return.

Sustainability as a strategy for lifestyle entrepreneurs is discussed elsewhere (Chapter 5). Some claim that SMEs are by their very nature more responsible than other types of company by reason of their close relationship to communities, long-term family ownership of the enterprise, paternalism towards workers, and lesser compulsion to maximize shareholder value.[41] The key in these cases is to engage company heads in the issues. Grayson and Dodd (2007) highlight five factors that can affect SME receptiveness toward these ideas:

- Using acceptable, understandable terminology: a term such as sustainability could have a very different impact than one such as sustainable enterprise or good citizen.

- Targeting: given the sheer number of SMEs and the fact that some are likely to be more receptive to ideas of sustainability than others, prioritizing which companies are involved in awareness raising and capacity building initiatives is crucial.

- The messenger: support for improving SME sustainability management may have to come from government, but this does not mean that the public sector is best placed to deliver the message. There is evidence that anything that makes sustainability issues seem part of a political agenda generates indifference or even hostility, and that organizations known and respected by SMEs such as chambers of commerce and trade associations are better conduits.

- An evolutionary journey: sustainability is not a state to achieve but a definitional construct, and managerial process is essential to understand direction and progress.

- Think of SMEs as people: following the theory that SMEs are different in character as well as size from larger companies, some argue that they exhibit more 'human' traits. For example, while larger firms value orderliness, formal systems, planning/strategy, and accountability, SMEs might be as comfortable with informality, intuitiveness, and trust.

 ## Discussion points

People have very different motivations for becoming entrepreneurs.

- Why might 'gazelles' be more interested in sustainability than other people?
- Why did necessity entrepreneurs increase in number in North America and Europe in 2008–2009?
- Are all small enterprises producing 'green' products social entrepreneurs?

 ### Key concept 4.2   Social enterprise

Social enterprise is a collective term for a range of organizations that trade for a social purpose. They adopt one of a variety of different legal formats but have in common the principles of pursuing business-led solutions to achieve social aims, and the reinvestment of surplus for community benefit. Their objectives focus on socially desired, nonfinancial goals, and their outcomes are the nonfinancial measures of the implied demand for and supply of services.

Source: Haugh 2006, p. 183.

Social enterprise

The link between sustainability leadership and social entrepreneurship was made early on. Anita Roddick at the Body Shop, and Ben Cohen, co-founder of Ben & Jerry's are recognized as early social entrepreneurs with a strong environmental commitment. An international phenomenon, social entrepreneurship is spreading around the world, applying much of the innovation and management theory associated with entrepreneurship in general to addressing social and environmental challenges. By some measures, start-up rates and employment growth in social enterprises is outstripping that in conventional commercial enterprises, and they are having an impact on significant numbers of people: for example, Grameen Bank has 2.4 million microcredit customers in Bangladesh and Afghanistan, while the Bangladesh Rural Advancement Committee is the country's second largest employer after the government.[42] For some, social enterprise is not limited to SMEs, therefore GE's ecomagination initiative or the retail company Wholefoods both deserve the label social entrepreneurship as much as Fairtrade's web of small producers in developing countries.[43]

Some of the claims made about social entrepreneurship's impact clearly rest on employing as inclusive a definition as possible, For example, classifying all not-for-profit organizations as social enterprises allows proponents to claim the sector is worth over a trillion dollars; and subsuming the long-standing credit union sector within social enterprise enables the claim that 25 per cent of the US population is affected by social enterprise.[44] However, such self-serving use of data does not help us to understand the role of social entrepreneurs as sustainability leaders. From the outset, 'social entrepreneurship' has been used to embrace a wide range of entrepreneurial activity. A collection of 14 academic articles on social enterprise used ten different definitions of the term, including basic disagreements about whether it applied to individual entrepreneurs or to organizations; whether trade and financial objectives were an essential element, or if it were as likely to be found in public and non-profit sectors as the private sector; and whether the defining characteristics are the goals and outcomes (e.g. tackling social problems) or the process (e.g. employing ideas of innovation to create new social value).[45] In a field where practitioners and theorists can often appear intoxicated by the excitement of their endeavours, it is not surprising that many define social enterprise in terms of its ambition and intent. The entrepreneurs are called 'disruptive change agents' and 'sectoral iconoclasts', and their enterprises are described as 'social justice in motion' and world changers.[46]

> The real measure of social entrepreneurship should be 'direct action that generates a paradigm shift in the way a societal need is met'. What such people do, in effect, is to identify and attack an 'unsatisfactory equilibrium'. Their endeavors are transformative, not palliative, with the power to catalyze and shape the future.
>
> (Elkington & Hartigan 2008, p. 6)

In what remains an important introduction to the field, Dees (1998) sets out a continuum of social entrepreneurship organizations defined by the way they are funded. On one side are organizations with a social or environmental mission that are run by and largely funded by volunteers; at the other end are socially-oriented ventures conducted within commercial private sector organizations. In between, lie an array of not-for-profit and for-profit enterprises that variously are funded through grants, capital investments, and revenues. Although this spectrum includes large as well as small companies, private and public sector organizations, what is important here is sustainability innovation in the private sector. Haugh's (2006) definition is broad enough yet not too inclusive to act as a working definition of social enterprise in this chapter. (See Key concept 4.2.) It needs to be expanded to explicitly include environmental benefits, but it does emphasize the importance of business-led solutions in pursuit of social and environmental outcomes. While some would contest this as too narrow, it fits the purposes of this chapter, and also chimes with an important strand of business-focused (though not necessarily for-profit) social enterprise. Haugh's definition also helps highlight that even if social enterprises are run at a profit, this is not their primary purpose.

It is common to emphasize the upside of social entrepreneurs as leaders; their innovation, courage, creativity, and stubbornness, for example. But as with any entrepreneurs, qualities can be a double-edged sword. The strengths of such single-minded visionaries (e.g. their self-assurance, their emotion, their 'insane ambition'; Elkington & Hartigan 2008) can create institutional weaknesses (e.g. unwillingness to delegate or build organizational capacity, reluctance to recognize criticism or fault, inability to think strategically or objectively), and these in turn can prove a barrier to achieving goals such as genuine empowerment, democratization, and indeed the scaling up of the enterprise. However, a greater barrier in terms of the impact entrepreneurial leadership might have is the nature of entrepreneurship itself. Even if a significant number of social enterprises prosper and have a distinctively strong impact in dysfunctional markets, there may be limits on the change they can bring about. Muhammad Yunus, founder of the Grameen Group of social enterprises, says that the 'future of the world lies in the hands of market-based social entrepreneurs. The more we can move in the direction of business, the better off we are—in the sense that we are free'.[47] But this assumes that entrepreneurship is an abundant quality that simply needs to be harnessed. However, most entrepreneurs are 'necessity entrepreneurs' of the kind discussed in 'Sustainability entrepreneurs' rather than the 'gazelles' that advocates of social entrepreneurship idealize. As one social entrepreneur puts it, 'One does not decide to be an entrepreneur. One is an entrepreneur [from birth]'.[48] If this is true, then there may never be enough social entrepreneurs to make a significant impact on the social and environmental challenges of the twenty-first century. But if what Yunus refers to are the hordes of necessity entrepreneurs who would rather not be entrepreneurs at all, then it seems unlikely the innovation hoped for from social enterprises will ever be realized.

 ## Summary

Leadership is frequently emphasized as an essential quality in getting companies to transform to the requirements of a resource-constrained economy. Sustainability leadership has been touted by some as a distinct field requiring unique leadership traits, particularly when it comes to soft skills. Amongst these traits, special importance is attached to values, and the sustainability leader is often portrayed as someone who can build a consensus and commitment around values that support social and environmental outcomes as an objective.

These traits are relevant to executives, but they are important throughout the company. Change does not always come from the top, and various companies show the importance of intrapreneurship, i.e. innovation within a firm to revitalize and diversify its business. There has also been a lot of attention paid to sustainability entrepreneurs, normally as an aspect of social entrepreneurship where SMEs pursue business-led solutions to achieve social and environmental aims.

Sustainability leadership has generated considerable excitement, but it is questionable how far it is unique. Examination of traits-based leadership in action shows that it is significantly influenced and restricted by context, and that while there is an emotional bias towards transformational leadership styles (e.g. inspirational motivation and intellectual stimulation), in practice transactional leadership is equally important (i.e. motivation through rewards, praise, and promises). The reality, therefore, appears to be that sustainability leadership is an example of contingency and situational leadership theory where particular variables related to the internal and external business environment determine which particular style of leadership is best suited to the situation. No single leadership style is best in all situations, and different styles of leadership are better or worse suited to specific types of decision-making.

Although leaders in a sustainability context confront specific challenges, it is not possible to say that sustainability leadership itself is unique. Indeed, ideas of sustainability leadership sit comfortably within existing leadership theory. This is not to say that there are not interesting examples of leadership aimed at achieving discernible sustainability-related outcomes: there are numerous such examples at individual and group levels, within large and small companies. However, it is possible that by stressing its originality, proponents of sustainability leadership are not making good use of the wealth of knowledge about business leadership in general, or using this to make informed decisions about what leadership actions are feasible, effective, and necessary.

Further reading

CPSL 2011, *A journey of a thousand miles: The state of sustainability leadership in 2011*, **Cambridge Programme for Sustainability Leadership, Cambridge.**
Lessons about sustainability leadership drawing on 20 years' experience of teaching senior private sector managers about the significance of sustainability to their companies.

Drucker, P.F. 1946, *Concept of the corporation*, **The John Day Company, New York, NY.**
A seminal and eloquent explanation of the importance of corporations and corporate leadership in free market economies. Not only does it spell out the role of company leaders, it even touches on why they should sustain human and natural capital.

Elkington, J. & Hartigan, P. 2008, *The power of unreasonable people: How social entrepreneurs create markets that change the world*, **Harvard Business School Press, London.**
Two advocates of social entrepreneurship explain the leadership role of entrepreneurs.

Senge, P.M. 2008, *The necessary revolution: How individuals and organizations are working together to create a sustainable world*, **Nicholas Brealey, London.**
An influential mainstream leadership thinker adapts his ideas about the learning organization to the issue of business and climate change.

Weick, K.E. & Sutcliffe, K.M. 2001, *Managing the unexpected*, **Jossey-Bass, San Francisco, CA.**
An introduction to sensemaking and its importance to companies in periods of risk and uncertainty.

 ## Case study 4   Finance leads the way—green venture capital

Green technology is not a risky investment. 'I'm so dead certain that we're solving the next huge problem for the planet. I'm not very good at hitting the bull's-eye. I need a big target. And this is the biggest target I've ever seen in my life.' This is the opinion of Randy Komisar, a partner at Silicon Valley venture capital firm Kleiner Perkins Caulfield & Byers. Greentech is one of KPCB's three big investment plays, and its pure cleantech fund raised US$500 million, putting the firm in the top five of green technology fund managers.

Leadership by venture capital (VC) firms such as KPCB is seen by some as essential to creating a low carbon economy. Governments might fund scientific research and set the regulatory framework, multinational companies might invest huge amounts in R&D, but it is venture capitalists who get new technologies ready for the marketplace. This was true in the case of Amazon, Google, and Sun Microsystems, all of which KPCB bought into early on. Now, KPCB hopes it will be true of Transphorm Inc, developing energy saving technologies, Mascoma, developing affordable cellulosic ethanol production, and APTWater, developing water reuse technologies.

A small group of KPCB partners became convinced of the potential for greentech in the early 2000s, and were impressed by the array of technologies that had already been developed. But they were also perplexed by how few of these had been commercialized. They concluded that the low price of oil had blocked these innovations' journey to market, but an analysis of 'the grand challenges' facing global society showed that impediments would be removed in the near future. Building on co-founder Tom Perkins's philosophy of 'When you have a great opportunity, push all the chips to the center of the table', the company announced a US$100 million greentech fund in 2006.

Launching a greentech fund was a leadership statement in its own right, but it also made KPCB a hub where sustainability entrepreneurs would bring their ideas. An early investment, predating any special fund, was K.R. Sridhar's idea for the Bloom Box, an energy server using solid oxide fuel cell

(continued)

technology to generate enough off-grid energy for a house or office block. Bloomenergy, the maker of these servers, is now taking its products to market, suggesting it has found its way through what entrepreneurs call 'the valley of death', i.e. the often long period between invention and commercial deployment. An appetite to keep investing in enterprises throughout this journey will be a test of KPCB's leadership. The partners are used to investing significant sums to get start-ups ready for public offerings—it took US$25 million of venture capital to get Google ready for its IPO. However, Google went from start to IPO in five years; not only has Bloomenergy needed US$250 million to get into business, it has taken ten years and as yet no public offering.

Given that VC firm profits are a factor of the amount of money invested over what period of time, lengthy journeys through the valley of death may dull the attraction of greentech opportunities. A greentech bet may well pay off in the long term, but investing too early in ideas that the market is not yet ready for is a sure-fire recipe for VC failure. Recognizing this possibility, KPCB's greentech partners have agitated for more favourable energy policies, confirming the opinion of some that sustainability leaders should take on a public role. But this does not go down well with everyone. Financial analyst Paul Kedrosky observes, 'Clean tech brings out a really emotional response in people in [Silicon Valley]. They react strongly to the idea that this has to succeed because it's really important, because it's too big to fail. But that has nothing to do with whether or not you can make money on it'.

In the VC community, therefore, leadership in a sustainability context is not so much about technology or finance—both of which KPCB partners would say are already in place—as it is about creating the right environment for technology diffusion. It is nearly 60 years since the discovery of silicon solar cells hit newspaper front pages as a world-changing technology. VC firms, used to the relatively fast returns from their investments in the internet revolution, will need to learn the quality of patience when it comes to greentech. The most innovative products are costly to produce, not least because they require new industrial processes. These costs will come down once there is a large enough market to justify mass production, but at present the prices are often too high even for early adopters. The enterprises most likely to succeed may be ones able to stake out a niche early on, irrespective of any larger market potential. As journalist Jon Gertner phrases it, KPCB is gambling on financial outcomes that aren't certain in a future that isn't yet real. However, perhaps this is a different type of gamble than it first appears. KPCB funds are often by invitation only, and attract very wealthy individuals such as Google founders Sergey Brin and Larry Page. While they are probably not looking to lose money, their investment aims and horizons are not the same as most people's: perhaps the opportunity to have a stake in KPCB's investees fits well with their vision. VC, after all, has always been about risk, foresight, and courage.

Sources: Gertner 2008; http://www.kpcb.com; http://www.bloomenergy.com; http://www.venturesource.com

Questions

1. KPCB is one of the Silicon Valley venture capital firms that came to prominence during the internet boom.
    a. What are the similarities and dissimilarities between investing in greentech and internet startups?
    b. Is KPCB right to take what Kedrosky calls an emotional view of green technology's importance?
    c. Is greentech a sensible choice for KPCB's investors?

2. VC firms are sometimes described as leaders in a sustainability context.
    a. Are KPCB's partners showing leadership by promoting greentech as an investment priority?
    b. What does it mean to say that KPCB is a hub for sustainability entrepreneurs?
    c. What other VC firms have made a serious commitment to greentech? Are their strategies different to KPCB's?

3. In 2011, greentech venture capital in the USA remained strong despite the state of the wider economy. Solar, electric vehicles, and energy efficiency technologies won the most funding, but 79 per cent of this went to later stage start-ups.

    a. What does continued VC investment in cleantech say about the VC industry?

    b. What does the current focus of investment say about VC's claim to be a leader?

    c. What is the value-added proposition that VC firms offer greentech start-ups?

 Endnotes

1. Sustainability Leadership Institute, http:// www.sustainabilityleadershipinstitute.org/different.php, accessed 30 July 2011.

2. (UN Global Compact undated)

3. (Senge 2008)

4. See Hammer and Champy (1993) and Bennis (2007) respectively.

5. (Birkinshaw, Hamel, & Mol 2008)

6. (Bennis 2007)

7. (Austin, Nolan, & Harvard Business School 2000; Hamel 2007)

8. (Alvesson & Sveningsson 2007)

9. Compare, for instance, Gerstner (2002) with Hamel (2000).

10. (Snowden 2001, p. 1)

11. (Senge 2008, p. 99)

12. (E.g. Bennis 1989; Birney, Salazar, & Morgan 2008; Gearty & Galea 2004; Kotter 1996; Lewin 1963)

13. (Bennis 1989; Kotter 1996; Lewin 1963)

14. (Rouse 2006)

15. (Eliatamby 2010, p. 14)

16. (Gauthier et al. 2008)

17. (Allen 2002)

18. (Kubler-Ross & Kessler 2005)

19. (Birney, Salazar, & Morgan 2008)

20. (Scharmer 2009)

21. (Eliatamby 2010; Senge 1999, 2008)

22. (CPSL 2011)

23. (Daft & Weick 1984; Weick & Sutcliffe 2001)

24. (Doppelt 2010; Epstein 2008)

25. (Gearty 2008, p. 84)

26. (Ford, Ford, & D'Amelio 2008)

27. (E.g. Redekop & Benjamin 2010)

28. Compare http://www.neweconomics.org/programmes/valuing-what-matters, accessed 1 August 2011, with Deming (2000, pp. 97–8).

29. (Bass & Avolio 1994)

30. (Birney, Salazar, & Morgan 2008)

31. (CPSL 2011)

32. (E.g. BSR & GlobeScan 2010; Haanaes et al. 2011)

33. *Oxford English Dictionary.*

34. (Hamel 2000, 2007)
35. (Wheeler 1997)
36. (E.g. BSR & GlobeScan 2010; ISSP 2010; Sustainability & GlobeScan 2010)
37. (ISSP 2010)
38. (Grayson & Dodd 2007; Patricof & Sunderland 2006)
39. (Grayson & Dodd 2007)
40. (Jenkins 2009)
41. (Grayson & Dodd 2007; Morsing & Perrini 2009; Murillo & Lozano 2006)
42. (See Nicholls 2008, p. 3)
43. (Elkington & Hartigan 2008)
44. (Salamon 2003; Smallbone et al. 2001, cited in Nicholls 2008, p. 3)
45. See the contributions in Mair and Noboa (2006).
46. (Bornstein 2004; Mawson 2008; Nicholls 2008)
47. (Elkington & Hartigan 2008, p. 17)
48. (Elkington & Hartigan 2008, p. 22)

Strategy and execution

Key terms

Sustainability strategy
Competitive strategy
Stakeholder engagement

Innovation
Risk management
Marketing

Online resources

- Case study of Cadbury's ethical and sustainability strategy.
- Links to third-party sustainability cases.
- Guidelines for executing sustainability as part of corporate strategy.
- Links to resources on executing sustainability programmes.

  http://www.oxfordtextbooks.co.uk/orc/blowfield/

Chapter in brief

This chapter explores the relationship between sustainability and company strategy. It looks at evidence that companies have treated sustainability as a strategic issue, and examines the different ways it has been interpreted from a strategic perspective. It analyses how sustainability has been integrated into corporate strategy in specific companies, and identifies common features from these experiences. It takes an in-depth look at marketing as a particular example of how sustainability can influence strategy. It concludes with lessons about executing sustainability strategy.

Strategy and sustainability

Strategy can be a difficult concept to pin down. It has strayed a long way from when business first borrowed the term from the military where it referred to the art of a commander-in-chief in projecting and directing the movements and operations of a campaign. Since the term was adopted by business, its meaning has been broadened and in some senses diluted.

While it still refers to the grand idea of determining and acting upon the corporate purpose, it can also refer to quite narrow business functions, so that a company can have a marketing or an ICT strategy, and even a health and safety or public relations strategy.

Mintzberg (1994), following Andrews, attempted to reclaim strategy as the grand idea by identifying five forms of strategy:

- Strategy as a consciously and purposively developed plan for how to get from one place to another. This is the original meaning of strategy in a business context.
- Strategy as a ploy to gain typically short-term advantage over competitors.
- Strategy as a pattern in a stream of decisions and actions over time. For example, targeting a particular group of consumers will give rise to an array of actions intended to meet their wants.
- Strategy as a position: the offering by companies of particular products to specific markets.
- Strategy as a perspective. More than a position, strategy reflects ingrained ways of perceiving the world, and is to the company what personality is to the individual.

Like a battle plan, corporate strategies can be decided in advance, but they rarely last in their pure form once they are launched. Real strategy is not the plan, but what emerges over time as intentions collide with reality, and is the upshot of accommodating shifts in the internal and external environment of the firm.

Different notions of strategy gain and shed popularity over time. There has been a loss of faith in strategy as a plan in recent years with the demise of iconic business figures such as Jack Welch at GE or Rupert Murdoch, and shareholders' wariness of the overly powerful CEO. In the 1980s when green marketing first came to prominence, sustainability was often linked to strategy as a ploy with companies developing so-called green products to outwit their competitors. However, today obvious ploys are treated with suspicion, not least because the products and marketing lost credibility amongst consumers. Companies that have established and leveraged social or environmental credentials over time are more likely to be ones with strategies discernible from a pattern of actions. For example, Aveda has built its hair and skin care business by targeting fashion-conscious but also ecologically aware consumers, tailoring its product development, marketing, price structure, and value chain management around this clearly defined audience.

For larger companies, strategy is more likely to be about position, with diverse innovation, customer, market segmentation, and geographical strategies. Strategy as position is determined by an array of factors such as the products on offer, the nature of the customer, production capability, technology, size and growth, and return and profit.[1] Some sustainability thinkers have treated sustainability strategy and position as synonymous, arguing, for instance, that strategic environmental management is the positioning of business to take advantage of environmental challenges, turning them from threats into opportunities.[2]

Treating sustainability as part of position is still common but perhaps less so than it used to be. For example, in the late 1990s, supermarkets such as Migros and Sainsbury's were lauded for giving shelf space to fairtrade and ethically traded products, but a few years later they were being asked why more of their product lines did not carry this assurance, and now the multiple retail sector in many countries from the UK to South Africa to Holland has adopted ethical criteria. In each case, early adopters of sustainability-related production or marketing have found that it is impossible to be a little bit pregnant, and instead of being celebrated for having a few specialized sustainability items, they are pressured into making sustainability as fundamental as quality control.

Cadbury is an interesting example of how this can evolve. In the late 1990s, it was largely resistant to pressure to more actively manage its social or environmental impacts, but in 1999 it became embroiled in accusations that forced labour and child labour were being used to produce cacao in Côte d'Ivoire and Ghana. The force of the media and public back-lash caught the company unawares, but also showed how powerful a particular market segment could be. Not only did Cadbury tackle the child labour and slavery issue, it started to take an interest in ethical brands, and in 2005 bought the organic chocolate brand, Green & Black's. Cadbury's offered Green & Black's all manner of advantages in terms of marketing, production, and scale, just as Unilever had done when it took over Ben & Jerry's, and Coca-Cola would do for innocent, the smoothie maker. But Cadbury was also a risk to its acquisition in that if its own mass market chocolate offerings were unsustainably or unethically produced, this could have a knock-on effect for Green & Black's. Therefore, Cadbury stepped up its plan to develop a sustainable supply chain for all of its products, and in 2008 launched the Cadbury Cocoa Partnership to invest in sustainable cocoa pro-duction in producer communities. In 2009, it also announced that its top selling line, Dairy Milk, would only use Fairtrade-certified cacao beans, and the Fairtrade label is now found on a range of Cadbury products. In other words, no sooner had the company realized the value of sustainability-related brands in its growth strategy, than it recognized it could not maintain its position in a niche consumer market without strengthening the sustainability reputation of the rest of the company.

Strategy as perspective is a type of strategy that appeals most to pioneering sustainability advocates. Influential thinkers to the business and sustainability field such as Porritt (2005) and Elkington (2001) both emphasized early on that sustainability needs to be embedded into the firm as part of its vision and direction. Lush, for example, the cosmetics manufac-turer and retailer, was established with a very specific set of ethical, sustainability, and com-mercial beliefs that inform all of its business decisions. Likewise Seventh Generation, the green household products brand, has as its mission statement, 'To inspire a revolution that nurtures the health of the next seven generations'. Such companies are relatively rare, but as we shall see later in this chapter, there are examples of mainstream companies that appear to be rethinking their strategies from a sustainability perspective.

 Key concept 5.1   Strategy

Business consciously borrowed the term strategy from the world of military leadership where it originally referred to generalship and the art of commanding armies. Early on, strategy was essentially about defining and executing corporate goals. Nowadays, strategy can refer to: (a) a plan of how get from here to there; (b) a pattern of actions identifiable over time (e.g. targeting high net worth individuals); (c) a position, offering particular products to specific markets; and (d) a perspective, i.e. the company's vision and direction, and the decisions and actions that result (Mintzberg 1994).

Interpretations of sustainability strategy

Embedding sustainability into corporate strategy is widely touted as an advantageous and essential element of contemporary business success. This chapter highlights many companies that have done this, but the connection between sustainability and strategy is still an awkward one, not least because there are quite separate interpretations of what sustainability strategy means. In many instances, it remains the case that for all of the talk about integrating sustainability into business operations, it is often an add-on to existing policies and practices such as legal compliance, the commitments of individual executives, eco-efficiency targets, voluntary guidelines, and chance formulations that appear in business performance profiles.[3] However, even if we discount sustainability as an ad hoc element of other strategies, we can still discern three distinct interpretations of what a sustainability strategy means.

Interpretation 1: sustainability of the company

First, there are strategies that deal primarily with the sustainability of the company. It is common to think of the modern company as confronted by an array of external threats associated with globalization, international justice, and sustainability (Chapter 2). Thus, Trafigura could not hide its export of toxic waste to Côte d'Ivoire from international public scrutiny because of social networks, international activism, and access to courts in different jurisdictions.[4] Likewise, Nike found itself before the US Supreme Court because of its labour practices in Asia due to scrutiny by a worldwide web of human rights campaigners.[5]

This emphasis on the sustainability of the company can present firms with a long list of disparate issues (Figure 5.1). For instance, the company is required to uphold the principles of fairness in business relations, employment rights, and ensuring a financial return to investors, each of which can be justified in its own terms. Companies are then expected to meld these together within a coherent strategy, but more typically they will have a series of, at best, loosely connected policies that may seem worthy on their own, yet when brought together result in a mix of unrelated or even contradictory goals. Gap Inc., for example, found its competitive advantage depended on contractual relations with suppliers that made it difficult for them to meet Gap's own human rights criteria, particularly in relation to pay and overtime.[6] Epstein argues that each of these principles is important in its own terms, and that they all be integrated into every-day management decisions, and quantified and monetized (Epstein 2008).

1. Ethics
2. Governance
3. Transparency
4. Business relationships
5. Financial return
6. Community involvement and economic development
7. Value of products
8. Employment practices
9. Environmental protection.

Figure 5.1 Nine principles of sustainability.

Sources: Eccles 2010; Epstein 2008.

Moreover, there may be good reasons for having a strategy to tackle these issues if doing so moves the company from being crisis prone to crisis prepared, and reduces business costs by allowing it to avoid legal costs and reputational damage. However, despite any spin-off benefits for workers, communities, and the environment, the fact remains that the main focus of such a strategy is the sustainability of the company.

Interpretation 2: integrating sustainability into corporate strategy

The second interpretation of sustainability strategy is one in which sustainability refers to a coherent external environment that affects and needs to be accommodated within overall corporate strategy. In contrast with sustainability of the company, it does not present companies with an ad hoc list of issues to address; it identifies an interconnected set of social and environmental factors that as a whole have implications for the company's strategy. For example, PepsiCo's corporate strategy was focused on increasing market share, and it recognized that public health issues such as obesity could be an obstacle to that. In response, it did not change its strategy, but instead incorporated health concerns into its strategy and acquired Tropicana fruit drinks and Quaker Oats. Similarly, GE's corporate strategy emphasized increasing profitability, and it saw that climate change was both a threat and an opportunity to realizing its goal. Focusing on the opportunity side, it decided to invest in clean technology, and in particular wind power, gas turbines, hybrid locomotive engines, efficient jet engines, and nuclear power.

In these situations, companies are looking for what Savitz (2006) calls the 'sustainability sweetspot'—the point at which business objectives overlap with sustainability benefits. The balance between business and sustainability outcomes is represented in Figure 5.2. Ideally,

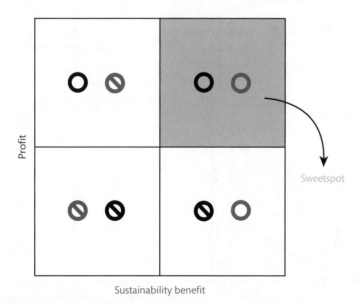

Figure 5.2 Identifying the sustainability sweetspot.

Sources: adapted from Elkington 1997; Savitz & Weber 2006; Willard 2002.

company strategy would focus on actions in Quadrant 4, but more likely most options will fall into Q2 or Q3, and the challenge for managers is to increase the size of the sweetspot in these quadrants to find the optimal business and sustainability benefits. In evaluating company sustainability performance, stakeholders are consciously or subconsciously making a judgement about optimalization of the sweetspot. It is acceptable for PepsiCo, for instance, to pursue a strategy of cost reduction by conserving natural resources, but the board will want to know the net savings, and external stakeholders will want to know the sustainability benefits of company programmes on water, packaging, and energy use.

Some strategy thinkers have taken this a step further and argued that the strategies associated with particular types of enterprise architecture are better equipped for addressing sustainability as a strategic issue. Piepenbrock (2010) argues that until recent times the business environment favoured modular architectures in which a firm, its investors, its suppliers, the labour pool, and its customers were functionally independent actors. The firm's strategy reflected its singular objective function of shareholder maximization, and it built competition-based relationships that supported this, i.e. ones that drove down labour, capital, and product costs. In terms of Schumpeter's concept of creative destruction where all industries pass along an evolutionary pathway from irruption to decay (Figure 5.3), these modular architectures come into ascendancy as an industry approaches the peak of its life cycle. Prior to that, product innovation and differentiation is the main determinant of success as new technologies supplant their predecessors at a rapid rate. The personal computer is a good example of this with companies such as Acorn, Hercules, and Texas Instruments prospering early on by virtue of the significant technological leaps they spearheaded, but then losing

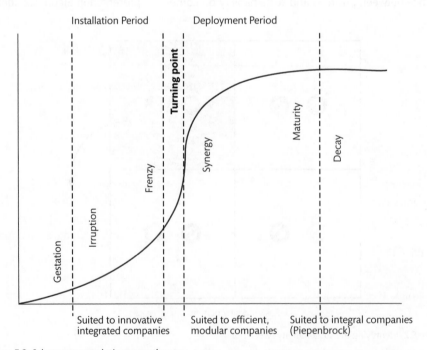

Figure 5.3 Schumpeter evolutionary pathway.

out to companies focused on cost leadership such as Dell and Acer once improvements became incremental rather than radical.

In sustainability terms, we might expect to find companies and technologies to be at an early stage, perhaps beyond gestation but still relatively immature in terms of installation (Figure 5.3). However, as we will see in 'Interpretation 3: sustainability as the determinant of change', this is a different, relatively marginal interpretation of sustainability strategy. If we focus on sustainability as an influence on corporate strategy, then as Piepenbrock points out, what we are looking at is not innovative companies going from gestation to irruption to frenzy, but rather companies in well-established industries looking to prosper even though the industry is mature and in decline. He argues that incumbent companies dependent on modular architectures and with a shareholder maximization focus are not suited to this situation; instead, they are susceptible to challengers that have a very different strategy built on an integral architecture (Piepenbrock 2010). These companies are process innovators and they thrive in saturated markets by taking on the modular incumbents. They are characterized by a plural objective function of stakeholder optimization which means creating interdependent, lasting relations amongst investors, suppliers, customers, and labour. In contrast with the profit maximizing incumbents, they do not seek to commoditize labour, or adopt promiscuous sourcing practices amongst suppliers, and because they are seen as newcomers, they need patient capital rather than access to impersonal capital markets. For example, newcomer Airbus has been able to take on the industry incumbent Boeing because its strategy is based on a very different set of relations and objectives; Nucor has bucked decades of industry decline and demonstrated that steel production can be profitable in the USA (Snapshot 5.1).

Integral architectures are not unique to sustainability, and it is possible that implemented successfully they will extend the life of companies and industries that from a sustainability perspective are harmful. However, there is significant overlap between the features of integral architectures and the qualities associated with sustainability strategies. There is also dissonance between those qualities and the features of modular architectures such as simplified relations based on competition, efficiency focus, and a short, rapid, volatile business cycle. In integral architectures, there is competition but this is informed by trust and a recognition that long-term relations are beneficial; strategic goals are plural and more complex; collaboration and effectiveness are associated with business success rather than competition and efficiency; and companies see the benefit of taking a long-term perspective.

Each of these features has echoes in sustainability strategy theory where there is repeated mention that sustainability depends on companies taking a long-term viewpoint, sustainability goals can only be funded by patient capital, and the company needs to think about stakeholders, not simply shareholders.[7] I will return to these features in more detail later on, but the point to stress at this stage is that if integral strategies are more effective it is another example of how sustainability not only influences but complements corporate strategy.

Interpretation 3: sustainability as the determinant of change

Referring back to Mintzberg's types of strategy, there are many who would like to see companies treat sustainability as perspective, i.e. central to the vision and direction of the organization. McDonough and Braungart, for example, argue that while it is commendable

Snapshot 5.1   Sustainability issues as corporate strategy—Nucor

Nucor is one of the top 300 companies in the USA. It has sales of over US$11 billion, and employs more than 20,000 workers. It is an unlikely standard-bearer for sustainability with its origins in the nuclear industry, its anti-union stance, and the fact that it is a steel producer—a highly energy-intensive industry that has largely moved to countries where its environmental practices are less subject to scrutiny.

However, in contrast with the fiery blast furnaces of popular imagination, Nucor's business is built on mini-mills that use electric arc furnaces that recycle scrap steel. It is the largest steel producer in the USA, and has over 50 facilities managed through a highly decentralized system. It owns one of North America's largest scrap metal brokers, and manufactures a wide range of steel products from girders to wire. Nucor attributes its success to three main factors: its innovative use of arc furnaces, its decentralized management (less than 0.5 per cent of its workforce is at corporate headquarters), and its egalitarian employment practices. Its mills' appetite for scrapped cars (ten million a year) makes it one of the world's biggest recycling operations, but it is also renowned for lifetime employment policies, egalitarian benefits, and performance-related incentives. The company has delivered a 371 per cent return to investors in the last five years, and has never laid anyone off because of the business cycle. Despite having the best paid workers, it claims to have the lowest labour costs in what remains of the USA steel industry.

Sources: http://www.nucor.com, http://money.cnn.com, accessed 12 August 2008; *Metal Bulletin Daily*)

Questions

Nucor has positioned itself as a company with a strategy to prosper in a resource-constrained economy.

1. What distinguishes Nucor as a challenger from incumbents in the steel industry?

2. Is Nucor an example of an integral or modular business architecture?

3. Is its strategy an example of sustainability-related ploy, plan, position, or perception?

that many companies seek to minimize their environmental impacts, this is ultimately a case of doing things in a less bad way: genuine sustainability strategy, by contrast, requires companies to maximize their contribution to maintaining and expanding the stock of natural capital, and making this central to product design, production, financing, and marketing (McDonough & Braungart 2002). Their interest is in what they call 'cradle to cradle' whereby a company takes into account the sustainability impacts of a product throughout its lifetime all the way through to when it is disposed of. 3M has conducted life-cycle assessments of all of its products to identify where they have a negative or positive impact on the environment. However, the cradle-to-cradle maximization model goes beyond this, and challenges companies to ask why they are producing a particular product or service in the first place, and what positive contributions it makes to a sustainable world.

Elements of the maximization model are apparent in Belz and Peattie's (2009) work on sustainability marketing. Just as sustainability raises questions about established production processes and products, so too it challenges consumption behaviours and how these are influenced by marketing. Marketing has long been more complex than simply selling more stuff, but a sustainability-based approach to marketing is one that takes into account the carrying capacity of the planet. Its ultimate purpose is building and maintaining sustainable relations with customers, society, and the natural environment. Echoing cradle to cradle, sustainability marketing does not consider the cost to customers to be limited to the sticker price, but extends it to the social and environmental costs of obtaining, using, and disposing of a product. Marketing as an example of strategy is discussed in the section 'Sustainability's impact on strategy: the example of marketing'.

Comparison of interpretations

There are good reasons for seeing sustainability as something that could change the rules of business and hence become a determinant of strategy (Chapter 3). Not everyone accepts the severity of current or anticipated events, however, and many feel that technological, regulatory, and economic interventions can be made that will allow a more sustainability-aware but otherwise unchanged model of business to prosper. If that is the case, then the second interpretation whereby sustainability is incorporated into corporate strategy seems appropriate, and it is not surprising that this is where we see most activity by companies at the present time.

However, if we regard aspects of sustainability as fundamental shifts in the environment in which business operates, then failing to build business strategy around the new realities of that environment is as hazardous as ignoring gravity when engineering a new building, or designing a better mousetrap when we are hunting big game. This is not a situation strategy theory is used to dealing with because until now the environment in which business operates has largely been taken for granted. It is one in which company growth has been treated as a virtue not a problem, consumer choice has been the main determinant of a product or service's utility, and natural and social capital have been best managed by a mixture of market and regulatory systems. As discussed in other chapters, none of these premises can be taken for granted in the light of our sustainability challenges. Yet the growing gap between what is required and what has been achieved in areas such as emissions reduction (Chapter 3) suggests that current strategies do not recognize or accept this possibility.

There are examples of social entrepreneurs that have built businesses around a sustainability perspective: d.light, for instance, describes itself as a consumer products company serving people without access to reliable electricity, and produces the solar-powered light that was selected as an icon of the future in the BBC series *A History of the World in a Hundred Objects*; Spier is a Stellenbosch (South Africa) vineyard and tourist lodge founded on sustainability principles; and CRELUZ is a cooperative established to provide electricity from localized hydropower in rural Brazil. Some believe that if issues of scale and finance are resolved, companies such as these will dominate what is described as a paradigm shift in business.[8] Returning to Schumpeter's evolutionary pathway, it is claimed that these enterprises are at the forefront of the creative destruction that may destroy some industries and will certainly see incumbent companies replaced by sustainability-driven challengers (Figure 5.4).

There are also those who believe that incumbent companies are in the process of transforming towards a sustainability perspective. We will discuss this in relation to Unilever in Case study 5, but other examples include Nike's introduction of its Considered Design principles on sustainability to all top volume products, and BYD's commitment to hybrid and

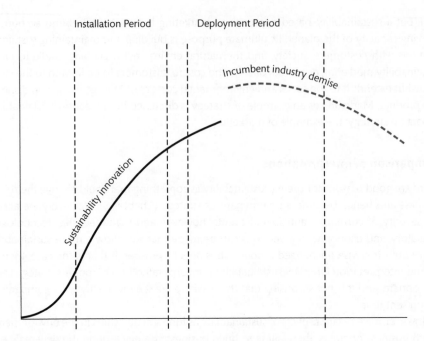

Figure 5.4 Sustainability perspective companies and creative destruction.

electric powered vehicles. In these and similar cases, the companies concerned will always be subject to questions about how far this represents a unique strategic approach rather than recognizing the potential of sustainability in terms of positioning, innovation, differentiation, and customer relations. The history of corporate change shows how difficult it is for incumbent companies to transform, and it may be that those attempting to rebuild themselves around sustainability will fail. Nonetheless, their role remains important, in terms of both influencing other stakeholders in order to retain their position for as long as possible, and assisting the companies that may ultimately replace them.

 Discussion points

Sustainability is often portrayed as crucial to corporate strategy.

- What are the business-sustainability sweetspots for Nucor (Snapshot 5.1) and Toyota (Snapshot 5.2)?
- Which companies do you think have done well at integrating sustainability into corporate strategy?
- Which companies have made sustainability their strategic determinant?

Features of sustainability strategy

In the late 1990s, Unilever, a multinational company owning many famous consumer product brands in foods, beverages, cleaning agents, and personal care, was a struggling giant. It had pursued a strategy of growth through mergers and acquisitions that had left it with an enviable portfolio including Birds Eye, Wall's, Hellmann's, and Lipton, and a strong worldwide presence, not least in emerging markets. But markets were not inclined to reward this strategy, and the share price underperformed industry rivals such as Procter & Gamble and Nestlé who were able to beat Unilever to the top spot in categories such as shampoo, washing powder, instant coffee, and frozen food. CEO Niall Fitzgerald recognized social and environmental issues as something relevant to Unilever, and during his tenure the company produced its first social and environmental reports, became a co-founder of the sustainable fisheries initiative, the Marine Stewardship Council, and also of what was to become the Ethical Tea Partnership. The company, which is a major buyer of palm oil used in its food and personal care products, was also amongst the first to recognize the environmental and reputational dangers associated with the rapid expansion of oil palm production in Malaysia and Indonesia.

These initiatives were typically examples of intrapreneurship (Chapter 4) with individuals such as Chris Pomfret, Mandy Cormack, and Jan Kees Vis championing aspects of sustainability they were concerned about from very different functions within the company. Their work was not connected by a coherent strategy, and there were a lack of formal channels to enable them to work efficiently together. We will see how such people contribute to the creation and execution of strategy in the section 'Executing strategy', but the success of their early efforts were restricted not only by their isolation and lack of a sustainability mission, but by the disconnect between corporate strategy and the evolving understanding of sustainability issues.

Nonetheless, Unilever was developing a reputation in corporate responsibility circles, not least for its award-winning social and environmental reports. Although Fitzgerald's 'path to growth' strategy became less and less trusted by investors, and the continual restructuring that strategy required led some initiatives to stall, it was also apparent that there were important overlaps between corporate strategy and sustainability. For example, the company believed that developing and emerging markets offered its biggest opportunity for growth, and it had the advantage of 35 per cent of its revenues already coming from those markets. Its Indian subsidiary, Hindustan Lever, believed that success in such markets would require distinct approaches to product development, marketing, and retailing, and in 2000 began pilot projects that would eventually form the basis for Project Shakti. Shakti saw Hindustan Lever work with local NGOs to create a network of female entrepreneurs providing rural consumers with products that met their ideas of convenience and affordability. Over ten years, it aimed to reach 500,000 villages through 100,000 micro-entrepreneurs, in what became a high profile case of bottom of the pyramid enterprise.[9] Today, although Unilever has altered its investment in Shakti, this and other experiences have provided the lessons that have led the company to obtain a market leadership position in many developing economies by selling products costing less than five per cent of the daily wage. In Nigeria, for example, products with a unit price of less than US$0.10 account for over 30 per cent of sales.[10]

Project Shakti can also be seen as complementing another element of the 'path to growth' strategy, winning with customers, which required the company to build stronger bonds with consumers, distributors, and retailers. Its network of entrepreneurs not only sold Unilever's products; they provided continual marketing intelligence that was fed into product development and other business operations. Moreover, Shakti was only one of a number of sustainability-relevant initiatives that Unilever could draw on in executing its corporate strategy (see Box 5.1).

> **Box 5.1** How Unilever's corporate strategy was complemented by its sustainability focus
>
> **Strategy priority 1:** developing and emerging markets represent the biggest opportunities for company growth, and the company's existing presence in those markets represents a competitive advantage.
>
> *Sustainability opportunities:* extensive 'fortune at the bottom of the pyramid' opportunities to make products available to the poor.
>
> **Strategy priority 2:** the personal care category (soaps, deodorants, hair care) has above average growth rates in a fragmented market where consumers exhibit a strong personal relationship with their favourite brands.
>
> *Sustainability opportunities:* by focusing on green issues of concern to the affluent LOHAS category (lifestyles of health and sustainability), Unilever can strengthen and extend consumer loyalty. For example, the Dove brand was produced, packaged, and marketed with attention to the needs and attitudes of LOHAS consumers.
>
> **Strategy priority 3:** vitality innovation (i.e. products offering health and energy benefits) was an area where Unilever could leverage its existing market position with brands such as Slim-Fast, Snapple, and Lipton.
>
> *Sustainability opportunities:* LOHAS consumers again represent a market responsive to healthy and sustainability related brands; presence in frozen foods provides the company with an opportunity to influence sustainable agriculture and fisheries.
>
> **Strategy priority 4:** creating stronger bonds with consumers, distributors, and retailers in order to increase the effectiveness of product development, marketing, and distribution.
>
> *Sustainability opportunities:* consumer, government, customer, and civil society interest in sustainability issues provides companies with significant sustainability programmes to establish its credibility and reputation amongst influential stakeholders.
>
> *Sources:* Clay 2005; Neath 2008; Savitz 2006; C. Pomfret pers. comm.

The Unilever strategy is brought up to date in this chapter's case study, but the earlier story, which covers the final years of Fitzgerald's tenure and his replacement by Patrick Cescau in 2004, highlights features common in many companies' experience of sustainability. It is not an unalloyed success story: 'path to growth' was ultimately judged a failure, and when Cescau took over, the company issued its first ever first profits warning. But in 2007, he reiterated the importance of sustainability to the company:

> The agenda of sustainability and corporate responsibility is not only central to business strategy but will increasingly become a critical driver of business growth . . . I believe that how well and how quickly businesses respond to this agenda will determine which companies succeed and which will fail in the next few decades.[11]

Strategy steps—defence, offence, and integration

Unilever's accommodation of sustainability within its corporate strategy during the 1990s exhibits key features common to a number of companies. The initial concern was regulatory compliance, ensuring that the company's products and plants met legal requirements on pollution, product safety, workplace health and safety, and honest advertising. Indeed, Unilever could claim from the outset to have gone beyond compliance: not only did it operate its manufacturing facilities according to worldwide standards that in many cases exceeded what was required locally, Unilever's employment practices were highlighted as examples of what profitable multinationals could achieve at a time when famous brands such as Reebok and Nike were being criticized for low wages, excessive overtime, child labour, and hazardous working conditions.[12]

Like many companies, it then came to view sustainability as a risk strategy, protecting the company's reputation and supply chain integrity against bad publicity and unsustainable raw material practices in areas such as fisheries, agriculture, and water management. This was true of Gap Inc. which was one of 26 retail companies found guilty of labour exploitation in what is commonly known as the Saipan Settlement. Unwilling to see its reputation damaged again, it embarked on a series of initiatives to improve labour practices in its supply chain. Shell found its reputation similarly damaged following the Brent Spar incident in the 1990s when its plans to decommission an offshore oil storage facility were condemned as environmentally disastrous by campaign groups. The company's subsequent commitment to innovative scenario planning can be traced back to the various short- and longer-term responses developed as a result of this event.[13]

Some companies treat sustainability solely in terms of risk, and invest in defensive strategies that protect the company. They will often bolster their legitimacy by using standards such as the Global Reporting Initiative's sustainability reporting guidelines, or submitting sustainability reports for competitions such as the CERES-ACCA Sustainability Reporting Awards. Labelling schemes such as Rainforest Alliance's certification programme offer another way that companies can defend themselves. Other companies, however, may see opportunity in sustainability. Unilever was not defending itself when it initiated Project Shakti, or when it became a founding partner in WSUP (Water & Sanitation for the Urban Poor), a partnership tackling inadequate access to water and sanitation in developing country cities. Similarly, the development of PUR by P&G (Chapter 2) was not a defensive action, but an offensive one attempting to harness the competencies of the company in order to address a sustainability issue. As Kramer and Kania (2006) point out, a defensive approach can protect the brand, but it will not enhance its reputation; an offensive approach, by contrast, can enhance the brand, but will not protect it. Unilever discovered the truth of this when despite being well respected amongst sustainability advocates for its work in advancing sustainable fisheries, sustainable agriculture, and water management, it nonetheless found its reputation damaged by a Greenpeace campaign that included people dressed as orangutans squatting outside of the company's headquarters to highlight the damage oil palm production was causing to tropical forests.[14]

As companies begin to understand the relevance of defensive and offensive approaches to sustainability, they begin to develop a basis for integrating sustainability issues into corporate strategy as highlighted in the aforementioned second interpretation of sustainability as strategy (see 'Competitive strategy'). Arguably, companies that are defensive are focused on the sustainability of the company (Interpretation 1), but this can generate an awareness of the social and natural environment they operate within (Interpretation 2). Integration means that sustainability considerations are factored into all of the forces affecting a strategy: products and services, customer, type of market, production, technology, sales and marketing, distribution, natural resources, size and growth, and return on investment and profit.[15] The goal, it is argued, is that sustainability is so integrated it becomes hard to distinguish from the company's day-to-day business.[16] This means understanding sustainability issues in the company's own products and operations, but equally throughout its value chain. The Guardian Media Group, for example, relates its commitment to 'creating a fair society that lives within the means of our planet' not just to its own products, services, advertising, and governance, but to its relations with its audiences and customers, its procurement, its workforce, and local and business communities. As companies have found to their reputational cost since the early 1990s, responsibility does not stop at the factory gate, and now there is a strong expectation that companies will understand and utilize the leverage they have in their value chains to raise the performance standards of all stakeholders they come into contact with.

BHP Billiton, the multinational mining company, provides an example of how companies think about integration, and also of how the form it takes will vary from industry to industry. It recognizes that long-term economic growth must be socially and environmentally sustainable, and its corporate strategy comprises two interdependent dimensions. On the one side, there are the business dimensions such as the quality and long life of its assets, its inventory of growth projects, the diversity of its portfolio, business excellence, and customer focus. On the other side, there are the sustainability dimensions: a policy of zero harm from mining, social responsibility, economic contributions to society, governance, and risk management. One of its competitors, Anglo, has adopted a similar approach, and is highly regarded because of its comprehensive and consistent sustainability reporting.

Anglo has also developed SEAT, its socio-economic assessment toolbox that allows it assess how its operations affect society. Other companies seeking to integrate sustainability into corporate strategy have also developed specific tools to assist them. Nike adapted Kaplan and Norton's strategic management tool, the balanced scorecard, to include sustainability, and this has matured into the Nike Considered Index used to evaluate new products for their total life-cycle impact. Herman Miller and Starbucks have also adapted the scorecard to help integrate sustainability.

3M is a technology-driven company best known for its market-leading home and office products such as Post-It and Scotch Tape. Its interest in sustainability arose out of a corporate emphasis on reducing costs and risk. In 1975, it launched 3P (Pollution Prevention Pays), a programme to reward workers who find ways to reduce pollution at source and that have a financial benefit. At that time, 3M's main problem was the use of solvents in fuel cells and adhesives, and cleaning up solvent-related emissions was costing the company hundreds of millions of dollars. As a result of 3P, it moved to water-based solvents in adhesives, and removed toxic solvents from other products. By one estimate, 3P gave birth to over 5,600 projects, avoided a billion kilograms of pollutants, and brought savings of US$1 billion during just the first year of each project.[17]

Competitive strategy

A feature of sustainability integration is that it is often associated with companies that consider sustainability as a competitive advantage. A company may have what it considers a sustainability strategy, but this could be strategy in its most basic sense, on a par with saying the company has a recruitment strategy, a work–life balance strategy, or a strategy for developing its canteen. These are very specific subsets that may ultimately feed into overall corporate strategy, but are best seen as policies, projects, or initiatives. Sustainability issues only begin to have meaning for a company in strategic terms when they are integrated into high-level strategy. This will normally mean moving beyond defensive or offensive tactics, and treating sustainability as a factor in competitive strategy. For example, as was evident to a degree in Unilever's corporate strategy of the early 2000s (see 'Features of sustainability strategy'), sustainability should be related to the three 'value disciplines' of mainstream strategy theory:[18]

- Operational excellence: the production and delivery of goods and services in ways that lead the industry in terms of price, convenience, reliability, etc.
- Customer intimacy: the tailoring of goods and services to particular customers so as to establish a trust dividend based on long-term customer loyalty and profitability.
- Product leadership: developing and rapidly commercializing a continual stream of innovative goods and services to retain consumer attention.

Porter's theory of competitive strategy posits that companies win competitive advantage in one of three ways: cost leadership, differentiation, and concentration on particular market segments (Porter 1980). It is possible that a defensive approach on sustainability issues could contribute to cost leadership (e.g. reducing production costs through eco-efficiency, avoiding costly litigation), but if it is the case that sustainability is best addressed by integral companies, and such companies lose out on cost leadership to modular ones (see 'Interpretation 2: Integrating sustainability into corporate strategy'), then sustainability is best integrated into companies focused either on differentiation (innovation and unique product offerings) or concentration (dominating niche markets). Apple, for example, is a world-leading example of success through differentiation, and increasingly this is built not only on innovation, understanding consumers, and timely product offerings, but also a recognition of sustainability issues as intrinsic to its brand. Affresol is a company aiming to carve a niche in the social housing market by offering affordable housing out of recycled plastic that meet the highest level of sustainable housing standards.

Stakeholders and long-term relationships

A further area of common ground between the different interpretations of sustainability strategy is the importance of companies being as inclusive as possible. In contrast with conventional management wisdom in the latter half of the twentieth century, which emphasized the singular objective function of serving shareholder interests, people interested in the business–sustainability relationship seem in universal agreement that companies need to build a diverse stakeholder base of those they affect and those who have an influence on the firm (Chapter 8).

Understanding one's stakeholders helps managers answer two important questions in a sustainability context: 'What am I responsible for?' and 'To whom am I responsible?'. A legalistic answer to these questions is inadequate given the shortcomings of the law, and the limitations of regulatory regimes discussed in other chapters. Corporate responsibility theory

Key concept 5.2   Stakeholders

IBM's CEO, Sam Palmisano, calls the shift in business from shareholder companies to stakeholder companies as a defining element of the modern corporation. In the 1980s, stakeholder entered management's vocabulary to identify the array of organizations that companies needed to manage if they were to maximize shareholder returns. In the 1990s, stakeholders came to be seen not as something to be managed, but as groups with legitimate claims on business and needs that should be met. 'Stakeholder engagement' became a popular element of corporate responsibility and sustainability practice, and management looked beyond the traditional categories of consumers, customers, workers, and investors, to consider the voices affecting local and international discussion of issues from human rights to conservation to climate change and more. Today, the importance of stakeholders continues to grow as companies collaborate with NGOs and international agencies to achieve sustainability outcomes, and seek input from all sectors about how to address their sustainability challenges.

offers a great deal of advice on how to conduct a consistent, robust, and credible discourse with stakeholders. The AA1000 Series, for example, sets out rules for reaching consensus on sustainability through stakeholder participation, comprising four main elements that are underpinned by the principle of stakeholder engagement: (a) company commitment to social and ethical accounting, auditing, and reporting, with stakeholders playing a key role; (b) defining and accounting for the company's actions through stakeholder consultation that identifies issues relating to social and ethical performance, the scope of the social audit, relevant indicators, and the collection and analyses of information; (c) preparation of a corporate responsibility report to be audited by an external group, and subjected to external feedback; and (d) embedding social accountability systems into mainstream management practice.[19]

Building long-term relations is another common theme in sustainability management theory, and stakeholder engagement offers ways of achieving this. It also complements the relationship-based approach to innovation and marketing that some consider an important element of the business–sustainability relationship (Chapter 5). There are numerous resources available suggesting ways of executing stakeholder engagement, something that is also touched on in Chapter 8. However, it should also be noted that even if implemented in line with best practice guidance, problems can arise. Freeman, a pioneer of stakeholder management, abandoned some of his ideas when he saw how companies were picking and choosing who to accept as stakeholders, largely on the basis that they served instrumental ends.[20] Yet this leaves unanswered the problem of identifying the crucial stakeholders from a sustainability perspective, rather than a corporate one. This is evident in stakeholder engagement today, in which consultation and dialogue is carried out with the aim of gathering important input and ideas, anticipating and managing conflicts, improving decision-making, building consensus among diverse views, and strengthening the company's relationships and reputation. There can be a strong business case for stakeholder engagement, including reduced costs, opening new markets, and protecting the company against activism. But this leaves companies open to criticism that they are picking and choosing who to call a stakeholder, and hence whom to listen to, and some managers feel that they are under pressure to respond to some stakeholders rather than others, based on who corporate headquarters regards as important rather than who the company affects.[21] A company may claim, and indeed believe, that its approach to sustainability is built on stakeholder engagement, but if the stakeholder model is to become part of a new way of managing the business–society relationship, companies will need to give up some of their power and influence in order to become accountable to, rather than simply in discussion with, the wider stakeholder community.[22]

Sustainability's impact on strategy: the example of marketing

Marketing is a powerful example of how sustainability can affect strategy. In its early days, the goal of marketing was to sell more things to people. This is the antithesis of what is required to meet sustainability challenges, and a resource-constrained economy is one in which the resource intensity of products will drastically decline, and consumption—at least in its present form—will be problematic (Chapters 2 and 11). Marketing emerged as a business philosophy and management discipline after the Second World War. Market segmentation, brand image, and the mix of marketing approaches became central elements of marketing strategy in the 1950s. In the 1960s, the Four Ps concept was introduced and became perhaps the single most influential marketing idea into the twenty-first century. The Four Ps of product, price, place, and promotion set out the parameters that marketing managers can control, and these became the basis for decisions about the marketing mix. They provide a framework for deciding the tactics of a marketing plan. More than this, they put marketing at the centre of the company's operations.

Traditionally, marketing had been part of a relay team that received a baton that had already been through corporate planning, product research and development, and costing, and was now handed over to the marketing team to run with on the final leg to success. The Four Ps made a persuasive argument that aspects such as brand image, warranties, packaging, and functionality were part of marketing, and needed to be central to product development. Likewise, in addition to the traditional marketing territory of promotion, marketing should inform pricing, and where and how the product should be placed. When Per Carstedt decided that working with automotive engineers was not helping him to get biofuel cars into the Swedish market, and that marketing departments held the key (see Chapter 3, Snapshot 3.1), he was acknowledging the shift in power that had been happening in many industries since the 1960s. Unilever's commitment to developing standards for sustainable fisheries was driven by people in its marketing team who could see that major changes in the availability or price of fish would damage the Birds Eye brand that had been built around an image of health, affordability, and quality.

Marketing continued to evolve, often in response to external conditions and the challenges they posed for business prosperity. For example, during the socially turbulent 1970s, marketing teams put greater focus on targeting and positioning, and introduced ideas such as social marketing that applied marketing skills to addressing social and environmental challenges.[23] (Social marketing was widely used, for instance, in combating the spread of HIV/AIDS.)

Economic globalization and the technologies that enabled it presented new possibilities for marketing in the 1980s. On the one hand, global marketing campaigns by multinationals took

Snapshot 5.2   Societal marketing—Toyota Prius

The Toyota Prius is a cool car. It is driven by movie stars. It is stylish. It is technologically innovative. It looks distinctive but not out of place in the high street or on the open road. The Prius is also held in high esteem by consumers, procurement professionals, and sustainability champions. A Prius in the driveway or a fleet of Prius in the car pool make an environmental statement, but the hybrid of internal combustion and electric battery technology that is the backbone of its powertrain is efficient and reliable. In the city, a Prius can achieve 50 miles per gallon; it emits 104 grams of CO_2 per kilometre; and seats five people.

When the Prius hit the North American market in 2000, it was an instant success, and almost since its launch demand has exceeded supply. However, consumer response was not a shock to Toyota. Two years before the car appeared in showrooms, the company began educating the public. It established a dedicated Prius website, and sent out e-brochures. The pre-launch tag line in advertisements was, 'A car that sometimes runs on gas power and sometimes on electric power, from a company that always runs on brain power'. But while the pre-launch ads emphasized technological innovation, the post-launch ones targeted consumers' emotions. Toyota made good use of green events such as Earth Day, but knew it also had to appeal to other market segments. Hence, the emphasis on innovation when targeting technology-driven early adopters, and on fuel economy and low maintenance costs for the value conscious.

The Prius has been a success in its own right, reaching a million units worldwide in 2008. But it has also enhanced Toyota's image as a leader in environmentally friendly technologies, deflecting attention from its strong presence in the gas-guzzling four-wheeled drive segment. It has also given the company invaluable real-world experience not only in developing and launching green technology, but also in incorporating sustainability issues into marketing strategy.

Sources: Belz & Peattie 2009; Esty & Winson 2009; Makower 2009.

Questions

The Toyota Prius is an example of successful societal marketing.

1. What are the immediate consumer desires and long-term societal needs the Prius meets?
2. How has the Prius experience benefitted Toyota more broadly?
3. From a marketing perspective, why was the Prius more successful than the Honda Insight hybrid launched in the USA seven months earlier?

off, but at the same time direct marketing, local marketing, and customer relationship marketing became more feasible. Thus, towards the end of the century, we saw both the rise in global brands, and the rise in ever more sophisticated, targeted marketing through emotional and experiential marketing, something that has continued to evolve with tribal, viral, guerrilla and turbo marketing. These last ideas are often presented as examples of revolutionary, post-modern marketing—a rejection of the Four Ps—but on closer examination they are more accurately seen as new tools in a Four P-based strategy.[24] Indeed, the co-option of the language and image of revolution by marketing professionals is a feature of contemporary consumerism.[25] Although there have been shifts in the goals of marketing—for instance, from selling products to satisfying and retaining customers, from one-to-many transactions to a more one-to-one relationship—the ultimate purpose has been the sale of goods and services.

However, we should not disregard the significance of the changes that have occurred. Belz and Peattie (2009) argue that the move away from transactions with customers to building and maintaining relationships has implications in the sustainability context. As noted in relation to leadership (Chapter 4), stakeholders ('Features of sustainability strategy' section), and partnerships (Chapter 8), cooperation, collaboration, and trust are highly valued, and approaches such as relationship and total relationship marketing, co-marketing, loyalty marketing, solution marketing, and symbiotic marketing all leverage and foster these kinds of interaction.

A criticism of marketing in the sustainability context is that it encourages the consumer behaviour that erodes natural capital. However, there are examples of marketing that address the disjoint between conventional marketing and ecological realities. Societal marketing, for example, markets products that give immediate consumer satisfaction but also serve long-term societal interests. The Toyota Prius is a well-known example of this (Snapshot 5.2). Social marketing applies the marketing professional's toolkit to social change, and is now widely used in health care; ecological marketing draws attention to the negative effects of human activity on the environment, and promotes solutions.

In the 1980s, environmentally aware consumers applied the knowledge they had acquired from a plethora of green guide books in their shopping decisions about products such as batteries, beverages, food, cars, and cleaning products. Marketing professionals seized this as a win–win opportunity, and an array of green products and brands emerged such as Ecover, Philips's compact fluorescent lights, and Odwalla. Some of these were built on new business propositions. New York's Greystone Bakery's tagline is 'We don't hire people to bake brownies. We bake brownies to hire people': much of its workforce is made up of former drug addicts and prisoners.[26] Not all were successful. Nau, Inc. attempted a new, sustainably-based model for outdoor clothing design and retail: its mission statement was 'To combine the generosity of the human spirit and the power of technology with business innovation to increase shareholder equity, protect the environment, enhance social justice, and provide humanitarian relief worldwide'. It sought to harness new technologies such as additive manufacturing, introduce distribution and retail innovations, integrate philanthropy, and foster customer-directed marketing, melding these elements into a new business model. In the face of an economic downturn, Nau folded after a year, although its experience has informed mainstream brands such as Nike and Patagonia.[27]

The experiences of social, societal, and green marketing have informed the field of what Belz and Peattie (2009) call sustainable marketing. Sustainable marketing is a macro-marketing concept that sees the object of marketing as changing the behaviours of consumers, producers, and across the value chain. In contrast with green marketing, where the focus has been on individual problems (e.g. detergents contaminating water sources), sustainable marketing recognizes the interconnected economic, social, and environmental dimensions of sustainability, and considers how actions affect all three dimensions of this 'triple bottom-line'.

Belz and Peattie (2009) and Kotler, Kartajaya, and Setiawan (2010) take this a step further in what they respectively refer to as 'sustainability marketing' and 'Marketing 3.0'. The objective of sustainability marketing is to build and maintain sustainable relations with customers, and the social and natural environments. Rather than see the company as at the centre of a set of relationships with consumers and other stakeholders, it places the company within a web of many-to-many relationships that at different times will benefit the company but also contribute to sustainability objectives. Just as nobody is simply a consumer, the company is not simply a provider of goods and services: it is a social institution that has multiple roles. Its marketing strategy cannot be short term and sales oriented because selling things is just one of the company's roles: a sustainability marketing strategy will be long term and relationship oriented (Box 5.2).

Procter & Gamble's 'connect and develop' approach is an alternative to conventional research and development. It is a model of open innovation that leverages the company's worldwide network of entrepreneurs, suppliers, and consumers to provide fresh and innovative product ideas.[28] This is an example of collaborative marketing. As well as the pipeline of new products it has generated, it has created new kinds of relationship that offer mutual benefit to participating stakeholders. Companies engaged in sustainability marketing have to collaborate: 'They cannot do it alone. In the interlinked economy, they must collaborate with one another, with shareholders, with their channel partners, with their employees, and with their consumers' (Kotler, Kartajaya, & Setiawan 2010, p. 11).

Collaboration of this kind is made possible but equally made necessary by the technological and social features of economic globalization. Globalization is at once the source of new opportunity and the cause of social anxiety (Chapter 1). Holt claims that certain brands are able to ease our anxieties about globalization: these 'cultural brands' become icons, and beyond providing people with a sense of identity, they offer myths that help us deal with society's contradictions. They are at once channels for expressing desire, and means of relieving anxiety.[29] The Body Shop, for example, became an icon because it addressed anxieties about inequality and injustice: its success as a cultural brand was not due to any ploy to align its brands with social or environmental causes, but its readiness to serve as a catalyst for those interested in such issues.

Less ambitious perhaps than The Body Shop, there are nonetheless companies for whom sustainability marketing marks a shift from an emphasis on products to solutions to customer needs. Building on knowledge from life-cycle assessment, some companies have taken responsibility for the impact of their products from cradle to grave. Interface is a famous example of this (Chapter 4), but another is Sun Microsystems which has been a pioneer of energy-efficient servers, and of the cradle-to-grave management of its hardware. The success of these examples highlights the importance of long-term customer relations, but they are quite conventional in other respects. However, there are signs that companies are developing a new solutions orientation that is less about minimizing the impact of their current offerings, and more about tailoring their offerings around sustainability. For example, the Connected Urban Development partnership involving Cisco has been a pioneer in working with a variety of organizations to develop low carbon communications infrastructures. Cisco had potential products it wanted to sell into this underdeveloped market, but more significantly recognized that its real contribution was the competencies and convening power it brought to the problem, and its real benefit would be information and insight from engaging with other stakeholders that could be fed into later innovation and marketing strategy.

Box 5.2   Areas for attention in a sustainability marketing strategy

- **Socio-economic issues**: how does the company contribute to, and how can it help resolve them.
- **Consumer behaviour**: using the tools of marketing to encourage sustainable consumption and production.
- **Marketing values and objectives**: what is the perspective of the company (its vision and direction) in the wider societal context.
- **Marketing strategies**: harnessing conventional marketing competencies to optimize the sustainability impact of innovation, segmentation, targeting, positioning, and timing.
- **Marketing mix**: altering the seller's viewpoint typical of the Four Ps, and taking the buyer's viewpoint about what is feasible, affordable, convenient, and societally beneficial.
- **Marketing transformations**: engaging with stakeholders to enable societal transformation.

Sources: summarized from Belz & Peattie 2009; Kotler 2010.

Discussion points

Marketing has been highlighted as a key element in sustainability strategy.

- Why are some people cynical about considering sustainability from a marketing perspective?
- What are the key differences between sustainability marketing and previous types of marketing strategy?
- Have any companies adopted sustainability marketing or Marketing 3.0 as a strategy?

Executing strategy

Many resources exist advising on how best to implement sustainability as part of corporate strategy. Some of these are listed at the Online Resource Centre (http://www.oxfordtextbooks. co.uk/orc/blowfield/), which also contains more detailed examples of how to execute strategy. Makower makes the point that whatever else sustainability offers, it must have value within the company: if it does not fit with the story the company would like to tell about itself now and tomorrow, and if it cannot be shown to work in terms of real-world accomplishments, then social and environmental commitments will come to nothing (Makower 2009). He argues that effective sustainability strategies are built on the following criteria:

- Credibility: why anyone should believe the company.
- Relevance: how the company leverages sustainability to create value.
- Effective messaging: how the company translates complex data on sustainability into compelling messages.
- Differentiation: the company's unique goals and achievements.[30]

These criteria are echoed in other sustainability guidance,[31] but they can be criticized for putting too much emphasis on appearance and appealing to external audiences. Kotler,

Kartajaya, and Setiawan (2010) say that very different strategies are required to communicate sustainability mission and values to consumers, employees, channel partners, and shareholders. However, communication effectiveness ultimately depends on substance, and this requires the company to consider its sustainability vision. There are a number of commonly advocated background checks that companies can conduct to help with this: What are the economic, political, legal, and public sentiment factors on the horizon that could affect the company? What risks do different aspects of sustainability represent for the company? How will sustainability affect the company's industry? The answers to these questions are discussed in Chapters 3, 1, and 2 respectively.

In addition to this, it is important for the company to understand its position. Porter's Five Forces framework is a widely-used tool in analysing the competitive forces affecting a company or industry. Weybrecht (2009) applies this tool as a way of developing a sustainability dimension to corporate strategy, posing the following questions:

- **How hard is it for new companies to enter the industry?** Low entry barriers are normally considered a negative because they increase the possibility of competition, although in a sustainability context the entrance of large companies may increase the overall market size as proved to be the case with energy drinks and green cleaning products.

- **What is the threat of substitute products or services?** Will your existing offerings be challenged by ones that are less environmentally harmful, more energy efficient, healthier, or otherwise more appealing from a sustainability perspective? Equally, how easy is it for others to imitate your own sustainability-based offerings?

- **What is the level of competition in the industry?** In highly competitive industries, sustainability could aid companies either by helping to drive down costs (e.g. eco-efficiency), or by creating opportunities for innovation (e.g. clean energy). As noted earlier, it could also be that in competitive, saturated industries, the relationships and business architectures associated with sustainability offer the greatest competitive advantage.

- **What is the bargaining power of customers?** A lot of attention in sustainability debates is given to consumers, but business to business relations are also very important. Walmart as a buyer has been able to exert considerable influence on the waste and efficiency practices of suppliers such as Cargill, and Unilever as a buyer of palm oil has been able to encourage more responsible social and environmental practices amongst plantation owners and oil palm processors.

- **What is the power of suppliers?** In situations where the balance of power in the value chain favours suppliers over buyers, this can limit the opportunities of the company. For instance, suppliers of famous brands in computers and apparel have become huge companies in their own right, and consequently less susceptible to their buyers' demands. As a consumer you may incorporate sustainability factors into a decision whether to buy a Raleigh, Schwinn, Trek, or Kona bicycle, but each could have been manufactured by a single company, Kinesis Industry of Taiwan.

Five Forces applies a tool managers are familiar with to sustainability, and offers a means of identifying and refining the company's sustainability purpose and the business need. It provides a rational basis for strategizing, and can inform the alignment of sustainability thinking with company policies and guidelines in areas such as governance, ethics, and business principles.

There is no universal structure that guarantees successful execution, but leadership from the top to give legitimacy is widely cited as essential, even if the ideas and initiatives can come from across the organization (Chapter 4). The imprimatur of the CEO and others in the C-suite is seen as vital because sustainability challenges accepted norms and practices. For instance, we have seen the importance attached to a long-term perspective, and this flies in the face of the short-termism that dominates contemporary business practice. Unilever CEO Paul Polman's decision to abandon quarterly financial statements was seen by some as complementary to his company's commitment to sustainability. Successful approaches to sustainability are also commonly linked to partnership, not least with customers, suppliers, and even competitors, and this kind of change in business thinking requires endorsement at the highest level.

As noted earlier, sustainability is a cross-cutting issue: it needs to be built into supply chain management, brands, and everyday working, as well as being evident in particular sustainability initiatives. The meaning of and rationale for addressing sustainability need to be communicated and discussed internally as well as with external stakeholders. We have already seen examples of how creativity within companies and channel partners can generate important sustainability initiatives, and this kind of involvement moves sustainability from being the preserve of the committed few to part of the knowledge base of the company as a whole. Although accepted as a goal rather than a current reality, company sustainability practitioners as well as management theorists are judging progress less and less by individual programmes, and more by how far sustainability becomes the way the company does business.

➕ Summary

Strategy in its grandest sense means determining and acting upon the corporate purpose. Over time, its meaning has been extended and diluted so that companies have multiple strategies. A sustainability strategy can be one of these; directing the company on tackling sustainability issues. Hopefully, but not necessarily, the sustainability strategy will complement other strategies within the company, especially any overarching corporate strategy. It will identify the risks and opportunities that sustainability issues represent, and provide the basis for developing defensive or offensive ways of addressing them.

However, a purer concept of strategy is something that embraces the entire organization, and moreover stretches beyond the company to influence how it relates to all of its stakeholders. Strategy theory teaches five forms of corporate strategy, and each affects how companies view sustainability. The company may treat a sustainability issue as an instant opportunity, a ploy that will give it a short-term advantage over competitors. Or it may regard sustainability as central to the company's personality, informing its perspective on business and the wider world.

For the most part, contemporary strategic thinking on sustainability is either about understanding how a sometimes rambling list of social and environmental issues could affect the sustainability of the company, or attempting to integrate sustainability issues into long-term planning and mainstream business functions. However, there are signs of a fundamentally different approach to the strategy-sustainability relationship. Building on the idea that sustainability challenges will fundamentally alter the nature of business success, it is being argued that sustainability defines corporate strategy, requiring that companies shift their focus away from maximizing benefits to shareholders or even a broader group of stakeholders, and thinking instead in terms of optimizing the company's societal contribution.

 ## Further reading

Belz, F. & Peattie, K. 2009, *Sustainability marketing: A global perspective*, John Wiley & Sons, Hoboken, NJ.
Perspectives on marketing in a resource-constrained economy, and an introduction to sustainability marketing.

Esty, D. 2011, *The green to gold business playbook: How to implement sustainability practices for bottom-line results in every business function*, John Wiley & Sons, Hoboken, NJ.
A recent addition to the library of books on executing sustainability strategy.

Evan, W.M. & Freeman, R.E. 1988, 'A stakeholder theory of the modern corporation: Kantian capitalism', *Ethical Theory and Business*, 3, 97–106.
An introduction to and discussion of stakeholder management.

Husted, B. & Allen 2011, *Corporate social strategy: Stakeholder engagement and competitive advantage*, Cambridge University Press, Cambridge.
A recent addition to the library of books on executing sustainability strategy.

Neath, G. & Sharma, V. 2008, 'The Shakti revolution', *Development Outreach*, 10(2).
A brief introduction to Unilever's Project Shakti and its fit with corporate strategy.

Savitz, A.W. 2006, *The triple bottom line: How today's best-run companies are achieving economic, social, and environmental success-and how you can too*, Jossey-Bass, San Francisco, CA.
Arguments for treating sustainability as a strategic issue.

 ## Case study 5   Unilever—Sustainable Living Plan

Unilever announced its Sustainable Living Plan in November 2010. It sets out the company's sustainability commitments and targets until 2020, and according to CEO, Paul Polman, is more than a sustainability plan, more than a business strategy: it represents a new business model:

> Growth at any cost is not viable. We have to develop new ways of doing business which increase the positive social benefits arising from Unilever's activities while reducing our environmental impacts. We want to be sustainable in every sense of the word.

The Plan promises three headline outcomes:

- Helping over a billion people to improve their health and well-being.
- Decoupling company growth from its environmental impact.
- Enhancing the livelihoods of people in the company's supply chain.

Moreover, this will be achieved while doubling the company's sales. Achieving these goals involves addressing social, economic, and environmental challenges relating to all of Unilever's product lines and brands, from shampoo to tea, from Marmite to Vaseline. The Plan also applies to the company's entire value chain: from the cultivation and sourcing of raw materials to consumer use and waste disposal. As the company frequently points out, with somebody somewhere in 280 markets using Unilever products every day, this represents a massive undertaking.

The Plan did not appear out of nowhere. Throughout the 2000s, Unilever produced well-respected sustainability reports that told a consistent story about the company's footprint in areas such as energy and water use. It was an early partner in sustainability initiatives such as the Roundtable on Sustainable Palm Oil and the Marine Stewardship Council, and has sold eco-labelled tea since 2007. The company had also commissioned two groundbreaking studies by NGOs and academics on its relationship to local economies in Indonesia and South Africa, and in 2007, then group CEO, Patrick Cescau, had said that not only was sustainability central to business strategy, but also a critical driver of growth.

At the time, Cescau's speech had been celebrated by some people for putting Unilever to the fore of the multinationals engaged in sustainability as strategy. However, some questioned whether it amounted to anything more than a recognition that Unilever's prosperity depended in large part on making consumers wealthier and having access to raw materials. Furthermore, the company's long spell of sluggish growth and under-performance compared to its peers meant the CEO's words could be interpreted as another flawed attempt to rebrand the company.

When Polman left Nestlé to become CEO in 2010, nobody was sure if he would continue Unilever's commitment to a sustainability strategy. Yet the Sustainable Living Plan marks the clearest statement of the company's ambitions to go beyond what was largely a compliance approach to sustainable sourcing, to thinking of itself as part of a complex ecosystem in which all of its actions affected ecosystem prosperity. Hence, the Plan includes stretch targets such as halving the environmental footprint of its products, sourcing all of its agricultural raw materials sustainably, and linking over 500,000 smallholder farmers and small-scale distributors to its supply chain.

One could argue that it is simple business sense to target a billion new consumers with products such as soap, toothpaste, and safe drinking water, because beneficial though these may be, Unilever has a strong brand presence in these areas. However, Unilever argues that its strategy is not just to sell more products, but to help people to change their behaviour so that healthy habits such as brushing teeth twice a day become part of everyday living. For example, Lifebuoy soap is a strong brand in many developing and emerging economies where diarrhoeal disease and respiratory infections are two of the biggest killers of children under five. Handwashing with soap would be good for Lifebuoy, but could also potentially reduce diarrhoeal disease by 25 per cent, and increase school attendance by up to 40 per cent.

Actions beyond the factory walls are crucial to achieving the Plan's goals. The company will only be able to halve its GHG emissions, for instance, if it can have an impact on consumers whose behaviour accounts for 68 per cent of emissions relating to the company. Manufacturing and transport are relatively straightforward areas of intervention compared to changing people's behaviour when it comes to showering, hair-washing, and doing laundry. To succeed, Unilever will have to provide consumers with more products that use less water, and readily admits that it doesn't yet know how it will achieve its target.

Reading the Plan's smallprint, it is apparent that Unilever's environmental footprint will be no smaller in 2020 than it is today, but the company itself will be twice the size meaning that it is committed to zero environmental growth. At present, the emphasis is on how to achieve this by changing sourcing, production, marketing, and consumer behaviour, but it will be interesting to see how it affects other strategic decisions. For instance, will the company offload brands that jeopardize the Plan (e.g. because of their water footprint), or withdraw from markets that put targets in danger (e.g. countries with a high reliance on coal and oil)? Will the Plan be a factor in decisions about acquisitions, either because a target company is financially attractive but unattractive in sustainability terms, or vice versa? As these kinds of decisions get made, what will be the reaction of shareholders and analysts?

Sources: http://www.sustainable-living.unilever.com/the-plan/; http://www.guardian.co.uk/sustainable-business/unilever-sustainable-living-plan; http://www.businesswire.com/news/home/20110503007585/en/Unilever-Sustainable-Living-Plan-Advances-Recyclebank-Partnership, all accessed 30 September 2011.

(continued)

Questions

1. The Sustainable Living Plan is the latest step in Unilever's strategic thinking on sustainability.

    a. How is it different from the earlier steps described in this chapter?

    b. Is it an example of a defensive, offensive, or competitive strategy?

    c. Do you think it shows that sustainability is being genuinely incorporated into the company's strategy?

2. The Plan will have an impact on many aspects of Unilever's decision-making over the coming years.

    a. What parts of the business pose the greatest challenge for delivering the Plan's outcomes?

    b. Will the Plan affect the company's strategic direction?

    c. Why might shareholders be worried about the Plan? Are their fears justified?

3. The Sustainable Living Plan is readily available online.

    a. Under sustainable sourcing, what agricultural commodities is Unilever committed to source sustainably?

    b. How will sustainable sourcing in this way contribute to the company's enhancing livelihoods target?

    c. Can its sourcing strategy help the company reduce its GHG emissions?

Endnotes

1. (Robert 1995)
2. (Schaltegger 2003)
3. (Schaltegger 2003)
4. http://www.bbc.co.uk/news/world-africa-10735255; http://www.guardian.co.uk/world/2009/sep/16/trafigura-african-pollution-disaster; http://www.ft.com/cms/s/0/32634a10-a210-11de-81a6-00144feabdc0.html, accessed 20 April 2012.
5. (Blowfield 2011)
6. (Vogel 2005)
7. (E.g. Laszlo 2003; Lydenberg 2005; Makower 2009)
8. (E.g. Gilding 2011); see also seminar 4 of the Incongruence seminar series, http://www.smithschool.ox.ac.uk/good-growth-and-other-paths-to-congruence/, accessed 11 August 2011.
9. (Neath & Sharma 2008)
10. (Savitz 2006)
11. http://www.wbcsd.org/plugins/DocSearch/details.asp?type=DocDet&ObjectId=MjQ3ODI, accessed 11 August 2011.
12. (Ballinger & Olsson 1997)
13. (Mirvis 2000; Savitz 2006)
14. http://www.guardian.co.uk/environment/2008/apr/21/wildlife, accessed 11 August 2011.
15. (Robert 1995)
16. (Weybrecht 2009, p. 280)
17. (Savitz 2006)
18. (Treacy 1995)

19. (Leipziger 2003)
20. (Evan & Freeman 1988)
21. (CCC 2005)
22. (Rasche & Esser 2006)
23. (Kotler 2008)
24. (Peattie & Belz 2009)
25. (Thrift 2002)
26. (Makower 2009)
27. (Makower 2009)
28. (Kotler, Kartajaya, & Setiawan 2010, p. 11)
29. (Holt 2004)
30. (Makower 2009, p. 181)
31. (E.g. Epstein 2008; Esty 2011; Husted 2011)

Innovation, planning, and design

 Key terms

Technology   Cradle to cradle
Innovation   Cap and trade
Cleantech   Clean Development Mechanism
Geoengineering   Extended producer responsibility

 Online resources

- Additional examples of company innovation for sustainability.
- Links to resources for companies.
- More discussion topics.

  http://www.oxfordtextbooks.co.uk/orc/blowfield/

Chapter in brief

This chapter provides an overview of the different types of innovation that business is making use of to address sustainability challenges. This means more than just technological innovation, and includes economic innovations that use market mechanisms to limit carbon emissions and boost investment in clean technology. The chapter covers emissions trading, project financing, and other economic innovations. It then looks at the different types of technological innovation, distinguishing between those focused on efficiency, and ones that substitute unsustainable processes with sustainable ones. It examines the distinction between these and innovations that use technology to enhance the sustainability of products and our living environment. It concludes with a discussion of high impact technologies such as geoengineering that could protect us from changes in ecosystems without requiring major changes in our lifestyles.

Innovation for sustainability

Sustainability is often presented as a challenge demanding a two-pronged solution. One prong is economics—both encouraging and discouraging behaviours through economic incentives and sanctions, and the use of financial markets to put an accurate value on different dimensions of sustainability according to their impacts on economic activity. The second prong is technology—discovering and deploying technological innovations that enhance sustainability and resilience. Therefore, it is not surprising that there has been a lot of effort put into both economic and technological innovation. This includes, for example, the development and introduction of cap-and-trade systems that make carbon tradable just as other commodities such as coffee and copper are (see Chapter 3, Case study 3). It also includes the development of clean energy technologies such as photovoltaics and wind, as well as rethinking urban development and sustainable design.

All of these areas of innovation and more besides are covered in this chapter. However, before that it is useful to remind ourselves what this innovation is for. Other chapters depict the size of the sustainability challenge: for instance, Chapter 1 sets out the pressures that social and economic systems are under from demographic, ecosystem, and climate change; Chapter 2 describes how life could be different in an economy where these changes are played out. The picture that emerges from those chapters is the backdrop to the innovation for sustainability discussed here. Put briefly, sustainability challenges require innovation that addresses the following:

- Reducing CO_2 emissions to a level that avoids catastrophic climate change (Chapter 1).
- Enabling humans to prosper without exceeding the Earth's carrying capacity (Chapter 3).
- Increasing the quality of life for all of humanity (Chapter 2).

Key concept 6.1 summarizes these challenges more bluntly in terms of emissions, ecological footprints, and measures of human development. Rising populations along with resource depletion and degradation mean that human aspirations will have to be fulfilled from less and less resources. Someone living in 1900 had the equivalent of 7.91 hectares at their disposal to provide the food, water, materials, housing, and other components of their well-being. Now that figure—our ecological footprint—is about two global hectares per person, and by 2050 it is estimated to be 1.44 global hectares per person. In other words, the innovation challenge is how to do more with much, much less. Moreover, because of the danger of GHGs, innovators will need to figure out how to reduce our ecological footprint whilst slashing our emissions. One of the reasons Malthus's famous prediction that the Earth would be unable to sustain growing populations proved false (Chapter 2) was that we shifted from being something akin to a sun-powered economy (one where solar radiation was transformed into energy) to being a carbon-powered one (one where energy came from fossil fuels). For any innovator today, the challenge is how to increase the prosperity of an unprecedentedly large and growing population as we shift back to being a sun-powered economy again. Furthermore, mention of 'prosperity' in the last sentence is deliberate: although there may be many arguments for curtailing population growth, or for ignoring poverty as a sustainability challenge (Chapter 2), innovations in those areas are unlikely to pass the litmus tests of public opinion or political will. Hence, against the backdrop of smaller ecological footprints and lower emissions, increasing human prosperity is an aspect of sustainability innovation. This does not necessarily mean that everyone should have a luxury car, but it does mean there should be progress in the basic areas fundamental for human well-being, as measured for instance in the UN Human Development Index.

What innovation is needed?

The word 'innovation' is most commonly associated with technology, and this is certainly the case in the context of sustainability. As discussed in Chapter 2, the search for low carbon mobility is inspiring innovation in hybrid electric vehicles, batteries, and hydrogen cells, as well as increased efficiency from internal combustion engines. In this chapter, we will also explore new technologies in areas such as renewable energy, fossil fuels, construction, urban planning, transport, agriculture, and manufacturing.

However, it would be a mistake to treat innovation as synonymous with technology. As we will see shortly, there have been significant economic and financial innovations that clearly address sustainability challenges. Not discussed in this chapter, but dealt with in detail in Chapter 11, is behavioural innovation. There are many who think that humans will respond rationally to sustainability challenges given the right economic framework and/or the appropriate technologies. Yet, whether we are talking about the rise in carbon emissions since 2000 (Chapter 3) or the reluctance of investors to factor sustainability into their analysis (Chapter 7), an emphasis on economics and technology has not delivered the changes many sustainability champions once hoped for. The barrier here is not the lack of innovative ideas, but a human reluctance to change behaviour in order to adopt those ideas, and thereby establish patterns of sustainable consumption and production (Chapter 11).

Economic innovation

Emissions trading

The atmosphere is part of the global commons. Nobody owns it, and we all rely on it regardless of where we live or how wealthy or poor we are. Modern economic and political thinking is very suspicious of anything held in common, arguing that people have no

---

 Key concept 6.1   Sustainability innovation

Sustainability innovation refers to technological and economic innovation enabling humanity to meet the major sustainability challenges. As with any innovation, it encompasses the idea, its development, its financing, its deployment, and its promotion to customers. However, to be a genuine response to sustainability challenges, sustainability innovations must also contribute to critical issues. For example, they must address one or more of the following:

- Reducing CO_2 emissions by 80 per cent by 2050.
- Enabling humanity to prosper from an ecological footprint equivalent to 1.44 global hectares per person by 2050.
- Achieving a continual rise in human well-being as measured in the UN Human Development Index.

incentive to look after something if they do not own it (Chapter 2). This seemed to be true of GHG emissions where a highly industrialized country emitting ample CO_2 did not suffer any more or less from climate change than a country with a small carbon footprint. It might be possible to reach some kind of international agreement to regulate emissions as happened with the 1970 Nuclear Non-proliferation Treaty or the 1989 Montreal Protocol which cut chlorofluorocarbons (CFCs) associated with ozone depletion. However, the process of reaching such agreement was always likely to be tortuous given the link between emissions and economic growth (Chapter 3).

A different approach to environmental regulation tried in the 1980s was the Canada–USA Air Quality Agreement which gave polluters emissions allowances that they could use to offset their own emissions, or that they could sell to other polluters if their emissions were lower than expected. In other words, the allowances were a potential source of revenue that could be realized as a result of investments in emissions reduction.

Michael Grubb, an economist at Chatham House, recognized the potential of allowances to form the basis of a global carbon market (see Chapter 3, Case study 3). Countries would be given emissions allowances that they could then trade. The total number of allowances would be tightly regulated, and like in a game of musical chairs, the total would be reduced so that over time there would be less and less opportunity to emit GHGs. Countries that chose to use up all of their emissions (e.g. because high-polluting plant was central to their economies) would eventually find themselves with an allowance deficit, and would have to buy allowances from other countries in the carbon market. Over time, as the number of allowances decreased, it was hoped that the price of allowances—known as carbon credits—would rise to the point where it made more economic sense to cut emissions than buy credits. Equally, for countries with low emissions (or for ones that successfully cut their emissions), the global carbon market idea promised revenues as polluters sought to offset their emissions with credits. This had particular appeal to developing economies that would have ample surplus emissions that they could monetize by selling to richer, more polluting economies.

These are the underlying principles of what is variously known as emissions trading or cap and trade. It is a market-based instrument that allows countries to seek out the cheapest and most cost-effective ways of reducing their emissions. From the outset, emissions trading received strong support in the USA, but less so from Europe where governments thought it would lead to countries trading their way out of reducing their domestic emissions. It is ironic, therefore, that the EU only agreed to emissions trading being part of the Kyoto climate change protocol (Chapters 2 and 10) in order to keep the USA on board, yet it became the champion of trading when the USA pulled out of the Kyoto process in 2001. Nonetheless, the emissions trading scheme (ETS) established under Kyoto was a pioneering innovation. The Protocol sets emissions targets for the 2008–2012 period for every signatory country, and each country is allocated a tradable allowance (i.e. credit) for every tonne of CO_2e. Countries with lower emissions than their tradable allowance can then sell their surplus to countries with higher emissions. High-emitting countries can either buy these surplus credits or earn credits from investments in the Clean Development Mechanism (CDM) and Joint Implementation (see later sections).

Subsequent ETSs have elaborated on the Kyoto model. In 1998, the EU decided to develop its own ETS as a way of meeting its Kyoto emissions reduction target. Launched in 2005, the

EU ETS has commoditized a large part of the carbon emissions from a region that accounts for 20 per cent of global GDP and 17 per cent of energy-related CO_2 emissions.[1] It requires companies in a slowly expanding range of high-emission industries to have emissions allowances—one allowance for each tonne of emissions. A coal-fired power plant in Poland, for example, must have allowances equivalent to its annual emissions before it can operate. If it does not have enough allowances it can trade to obtain more, knowing that because the number of allowances is deliberately reduced over time, the price of credits will rise, making it a strategic decision whether to pay for credits or pay for less polluting facilities.

The first phase of the EU ETS was called 'learning by doing', in the full knowledge that nobody to that point knew exactly how this kind of market would operate. Despite the opposition of economists, credits were distributed through allocated rather than auctions. As Case study 3 reveals, in some instances, notably amongst electricity companies, companies ended up with a windfall of free credits that they could trade without having to tighten up on their emissions, and overall imprecise calculation of emissions led to a flood of credits that meant companies had no need to trade. Not surprisingly, the trade in emissions credits practically stopped.

In some people's minds—not least amongst opponents of ETS—the experience of the EU ETS Phase 1 marked the end of global carbon markets as a scalable innovation. However, Phase 1 was always meant to be about experimentation, and in Phase 2 (ending in 2012) the European Commission has been a tougher negotiator with member states, there has been more auctioning of allowances, and there is evidence that companies affected by the system have reduced their overall emissions.[2] ETSs similar to Europe are now running in Switzerland, Japan, New Zealand, and New South Wales (Australia), and are being proposed for South Korea, several states in the USA, and Canada. Nonetheless, the USA's failure to adopt a federal-level ETS has been seen by some as a sign that ETS innovation has gone as far as it can. Given the USA's position as the largest total emitter of CO_2, its attitude to ETS was always going to be crucial, and early on in his administration, President Obama was firmly committed to it. However, political resistance to any form of ETS and its image as a barrier to the USA's prosperity and economic growth means that it is highly unlikely to be adopted in the foreseeable future.

This sense of gloom about the future of ETS as a whole has been exacerbated by the poor performance of emissions credit as an investment with prices persistently hovering at about £10 per tonne where they have languished since the 2008 financial collapse. Nonetheless, it is probably too early to write-off ETS as an innovation. Existing schemes continue to function, and the EU ETS will enter its third phase in 2013 irrespective of any post-Kyoto agreement. Although for ETS to have the impact initially hoped for, they will need adoption worldwide, the EU's scheme has not damaged Europe's economy and is not strongly opposed by the industries it has targeted. Furthermore, for all the controversy such schemes generate, the need for this kind of potentially far-reaching innovation is as great as it has ever been.

Clean Development Mechanism

Emissions trading complements another economics-related innovation that grew out of the thinking of Norwegian climate change expert, Ted Hanisch, in the early 1990s. The problem that he sought to address was that wealthy nations had grown rich without having to pay much attention to their carbon emissions, while emerging economies that historically had low emissions could end up having to share the burden of creating a worldwide resource-constrained economy. Hanisch's insight was that rather than a strictly regulated framework of rules and conditions, countries should be allowed to develop flexible responses that, while demonstrably contributing to the goal of emissions reduction, recognized the different conditions of particular countries. Thus, for example, a wealthy, high-emissions country could partner with a poorer, low-emissions one to reduce both of their emissions, or rich nations could invest in poor ones to offset their higher emissions. This kind of bespoke, flexible approach appealed to the USA which made it a key feature in negotiating the Kyoto Protocol. Although the USA withdrew from the Protocol, the principle of flexibility lives on in the Joint Implementation and the more famous CDM elements of the eventual agreement.

Joint Implementation applies to countries that seek to meet their emissions reduction commitments through joint projects. Because it can be cheaper to reduce emissions in another country other than one's own, high-polluting countries were willing to invest in projects overseas, projects that could lead to investment in clean energy infrastructure in emerging nations. In terms of climate change, emissions savings are equally beneficial no matter where they are made. In terms of economic development, it encouraged wealthier nations to invest in renewable energy, energy efficiency, forestry, and clean technologies in places that were otherwise not a priority.

Joint Implementation still exists as an element of the Kyoto Protocol, but for political reasons it has not been as successful as its sibling, the CDM. The CDM is similar in that it enables countries to invest overseas to offset their own emissions. However, it differs in two important ways. First, under Joint Implementation there was confusion about what would happen if emissions reduction by one partner was offset by emissions increases by the other (e.g. due to economic growth). Under the CDM, the net emissions are not considered, and hence any emissions growth in a developing economy cannot derail the reductions in a developed one. This is important to developing countries that have been very reluctant to agree to emissions reduction targets, and to industrialized ones that do not want to see their industries put at a competitive disadvantage by countries without reduction commitments. Second, the CDM applies only to projects in developing economies (Annex 1 countries) where the cost of project implementation is lower, and hence it is much easier to make a cost-benefit case.

The financial workings of CDM are described in Chapter 7, but in innovation terms it generates emissions credits for countries that invest in emissions reduction projects overseas. To return to the earlier example of a coal-fired power station in Poland, instead of trying to reduce emissions from that plant, the company could invest in a solar energy facility in Zambia, and the credits generated by that project would then count towards Poland's emissions commitments under the Kyoto Protocol.

Other economic innovations

The earlier examples are both connected to climate change, and watching the effort involved in putting these market-based innovations into practice has influenced the responses from people tackling other sustainability challenges. They show that commoditizing transboundary natural resources and the creation of markets is far from easy, and moreover is divisive even amongst free marketeers. But they also demonstrate that tradable credits as part of offtake contracts can be made to work. The Economics of Ecosystems and Biodiversity (TEEB) initiative has promoted economic instruments as a way of protecting ecosystems (Chapter 1), including, for instance, the Hunter River Salinity Trading Scheme in North South Wales, Australia.[3] Started in the mid-1990s, it tackles the problem of salt discharges by industry making the river unsuitable for farm irrigation. The total amount of dischargeable salt is capped at sustainable levels, and allowances in the form of credits are distributed amongst dischargers at different sections of the river. The amount of allowable discharge by any one party is controlled by the number of credits they have, and the total salinity is controlled by the total number of credits available. If a company in one section has a temporary need to discharge more than it holds credits for, it can buy extra credits on the market from companies that have a surplus.

At the micro-level, economic instruments are being used to build up community resilience, provide water and sanitation, and promote sustainable resource utilization, not least amongst poor communities. The influence of microfinance, itself an economic innovation, is often felt in these types of scheme, and they are discussed in more detail in Chapter 7.

 Discussion points

Cap and trade has created a regulated market for carbon credits.

- What are the advantages of a cap-and-trade system compared to government regulation?
- How does cap and trade benefit emerging and underdeveloped economies?
- Why are some countries resistant to cap and trade?

Technological innovation

Sustainability is the catalyst for a wide array of innovations; far too many to cover comprehensively in this book. In order to better understand the types of innovation that are taking place, technologies can be divided into different broad categories. The purposes of technologies within a category are discussed below, and examples are given to show what is being achieved and what is likely to happen in the coming years. For anyone wanting to learn about technologies in a given category, a list of useful books is attached to each category. The categories are as follows:

- **Efficiency**: technologies using existing resources more efficiently (e.g. home insulation, anaerobic digestion of waste).
- **Substitution**: technologies to allow alternative resources to be used as substitutes for depleted or harmful ones (e.g. hydrogen fuel cells, nuclear fission).
- **Effectiveness**: technologies that add value in sustainability terms (e.g. portable solar-powered lighting, green roofs).
- **Mitigation**: technologies that negate any sustainability risk (e.g. geoengineering, nuclear fusion).

In some cases, technologies are discussed in more detail elsewhere in this book. Clean energy technologies, for example, are covered in Chapter 2, and transport, low carbon retail and aviation are covered in Chapter 3. There are also examples of technologies to do with more sustainable consumption and production that are dealt with in more detail in Chapter 11 than they are here. The fact that examples crop up throughout the book shows the pervasiveness and importance of technological innovation in thinking about sustainability challenges. It also shows that thinking about technology in isolation from the wider social, political, economic, and cultural context often leads to poor decision-making. In 2009, for example, the Australian government announced a multi-billion dollar home insulation programme as part of its economic stimulus package and also to boost federal government action on climate change. In 2010, the programme had to be abandoned because despite the low cost to homeowners and the promise of lower electricity bills, the technology had met with increasing consumer resistance. Young installation workers were killed installing the insulation, roofs caught fire, and unqualified installers eager to reap the financial bonanza nailed the foil insulation to electricity cables resulting in several deaths.[4] Instead of a flagship programme that would use proven technology to create jobs and reduce energy emissions, the government found itself dealing with contractor fraud, homeowner compensation claims, unemployed installers, and a severely damaged reputation that would affect any future efforts to tackle sustainability issues. It was also a valuable lesson that successful innovation is as much about application as invention.

 Snapshot 6.1   Buildings standards—LEED

Leadership in Energy and Environmental Design (LEED) is a building certification system to promote environmentally responsible, profitable, and healthy places to live and work. It is similar to systems such as the BRE (Building Research Establishment) Environmental Assessment Method in the UK, and Haute Qualité Environnementale in France.

LEED came out of the US Green Building Council, and was launched in 2000 as a voluntary standard that provides guidelines, certification, and education for green buildings. Green buildings are ones that are intended to create greater economic and social benefits over their lifetime than conventional ones, can reduce or eliminate adverse human health effects, and make a contribution to improved air and water quality. They can achieve this through, for example, low-disturbance land-use techniques, improved lighting design and water fixtures, materials selection, energy efficient appliances and heating/cooling systems, on-site water treatment, and recycling. Other innovations include natural ventilation and cooling, green roofs that provide wildlife habitat and reduce storm water runoff, and artificial wetlands that help preserve water quality while reducing water treatment costs.

By 2010, 6,000 buildings had been LEED certified, and over 155,000 building professionals had LEED accreditation. Government buildings in particular were increasingly required to be LEED certified. However, LEED is not simply a certification system. In addition to creating a green building standard, it seeks to promote integrated, whole-building design practices, to recognize environmental leadership in the building industry, stimulate competition, and build public awareness. Projects pay to be certified, and there are three levels of certification, silver, gold, and platinum.

There is plenty of debate about whether LEED-compliant projects are more expensive than conventional ones or not. Any higher construction costs need to be offset against claims that maintenance costs are lower. Prominent architect Frank Gehry has dismissed LEED standards as 'bogus', and a distraction from genuine environmental improvements. Certainly, LEED has been criticized for over-emphasizing energy efficiency at the expense of creating healthier, non-toxic working environments. It has also been criticized for diluting calls for stringent regulation, and at present green buildings represent only ten per cent of new construction.

(continued)

However, LEED has created interest in green buildings and made them not only desirable but achievable. The standards are subject to continual improvement, and are being adopted internationally. Although not as large or profound as some might have hoped for, LEED and similar systems elsewhere have helped stimulate a new market for environmental innovation while avoiding the resistance that often meets other areas of sustainability.

Sources: Belz & Peattie 2009; Bokalders 2009; Eichholtz, Kok, & Quigley 2009; Esty & Winston 2009, Makower 2009; http://www.usgbc.org/DisplayPage.aspx?CMSPageID=1988, accessed 15 October 2011.

Questions

LEED was established to change behaviour and foster innovation in the building industry.

1. Why is change important from a sustainability perspective in the building industry?
2. How does LEED encourage technological innovation?
3. Is a voluntary approach the best way to improve standards in this industry?

Efficiency technologies

The major impact that business can have in meeting sustainability challenges is to use resources more efficiently. Eco-efficiency has long been a focus of management because it equates with lower costs and reduced liabilities. Long-time Timberland CEO, Jeff Swartz, calls it 'the CFO [chief financial officer] case' because the financial logic is readily apparent. The evolution of the humble light bulb depicts the eco-efficiency journey quite well. Incandescent bulbs have been around for over a century, and were a major factor in improving productivity because of how they brought superior artificial light into the workplace. However, by the mid-1950s, fluorescent bulbs were starting to out-sell incandescent ones in factories and offices because they convert electrical power into light more efficiently. In the 1970s, rising oil electricity prices prompted some firms to consider the possibility of smaller fluorescent units as a replacement for the traditional light bulb. This required two further innovations: first, finding an alternative to the electronic ballasts that cause the flicker associated with normal fluorescent lighting; second, developing high-efficiency vapours to allow more power to be used in a smaller space. Throughout the 2000s, the long-term efficiency benefits of compact fluorescent lights have spurred a variety of initiatives to speed up their adoption. European governments, for example, have sought to defray the higher upfront costs of buying CFLs by subsidizing their price or making them free to early adopters. There have been all manner of awareness campaigns involving government agencies, environmental groups, and power and electronics companies. Philips, for example, aligned its brand with eco-efficient lighting, and now not only manufactures bulbs but offers a wide range of efficient lighting products and services. However, the CFL itself is now being challenged by LED lighting that is more energy efficient, longer lasting, and is easier to dispose of without harming the environment. In 2009, Google gave all of its workers two LED bulbs to celebrate Earth Day just as Home Depot had handed out free CFLs at its stores on Earth Day two years earlier.[5]

Innovations in efficiency are happening in a number of areas. Energy-related innovations are the most prominent because climate change is often treated as an energy challenge. Thus, as discussed in other chapters, we have seen the rise of hybrid-electric vehicles that seek to combine the relative strengths of current petrol and electric engine technology to create more efficient cars and trucks. Governments in particular have invested in improved energy efficiencies in homes and other buildings, subsidizing for example, loft and wall insulation. Governments also play a huge part in designing more efficient infrastructure so that, for example, the public has convenient alternatives to cars and their associated emissions when they are in towns.

Bicycles may not seem an obvious area for major innovation. However, Chinese manufacturers have benefited from a rapid growth in the domestic and overseas markets for electric bikes, producing 22 million units in 2010 and achieving sales of US$11 billion, similar to the British car industry.[6] Technologically, the industry has taken advantage of improvements in batteries, but its success is also due to more affluent consumers in Asia's congested cities, government legislation that means 'e-bikes' can compete with motorbikes, environmental concerns in Europe, and an ageing but healthy population in many parts of the world for whom electrically powered bikes are more appealing than pedal-powered ones.

However, bicycle innovation is not simply a story of motorization. In the Netherlands, for instance, extensive investment was made in bike paths in the 1980s, but with little increase in bike usage. The many Dutch citizens who were already regular cyclists appreciated the well-lit, well-maintained network of paths, but non-cyclists were unconvinced. In 1990, a national bike plan was introduced as part of overall transport policy, and with the specific aim of creating better alternatives to car use. Innovations included creating safe, high-quality infrastructure, and separating places where cyclists and fast vehicles met. Bike use was actively promoted through subsidies, improved cycling experience, and companies and government agencies drawing up cycling plans for their employees. Subsequently, fatalities amongst cyclists fell significantly even as car and bike use rose, and nearly 30 per cent of trips involved cycling.

Away from energy and buildings, there are other efficiency innovations in areas such as water. The Coca-Cola Company, for instance, has emphasized water stewardship as part of its wider Live Positively sustainability strategy. By 2012 it says it will have improved its water efficiency by 20 per cent compared to 2004 levels as part of a pathway intended to make it a zero water company by 2020, i.e. it will replenish to nature and communities an amount of water equivalent to what is used in its finished beverages.[7] To achieve this, the company is focused on three areas: reduction, recycling, and replenishing. On current production figures, Coca-Cola will need to make efficiency inroads into the 309 billion litres of water it uses annually. It claims that it will replenish 130 billion litres, meaning that it will need to reduce or recycle 179 billion litres. Much of what has been achieved to date, particularly under the 'replenish' heading, has been to understand more about the company's relationship to water supplies and hence its impact, and this is a reminder of the information that is required to evaluate any innovation's effectiveness. Now, Coca-Cola's data are being processed to inform its investments. Coca-Cola Enterprises, The Coca-Cola Company's bottling partner in Europe, has installed recycle-and-reclaim loops in a dozen of its water treatment facilities so that processed water can be reused in cooling, heating, and cleaning. As part of its reduction commitment, it is reassessing the water usage in manufacturing, packaging, and ingredients. At present, a 500-ml plastic bottle of Coca-Cola has a water footprint of 35 litres.[8] Not only is it committed to reducing the footprint per unit, if overall output expands it will either need to reduce or recycle more, or be left with an ever larger commitment to replenish whatever water it uses.

The Coca-Cola Company is also innovating in areas other than water. Coca-Cola Enterprises had the largest hybrid electric truck fleet in North America when it sold off its operations there in 2010, and the same technology is being deployed in parts of Europe. The Coca-Cola Company is collaborating with fuel cell manufacturer, Bloom Energy, to power some of its plants with electricity from natural gas. Its commitment to replace all traditional vending machines with HFC-free systems that use intelligent energy management by 2015 is estimated to be the equivalent in carbon emission reductions of taking over eleven million cars off the road.

The types of initiative being undertaken at Coca-Cola operations reflect innovations happening in water, waste, and manufacturing more generally. Improved water capture, storage, recycling, and the separation of potable from 'grey' water mains are something found in new factories, offices, and retail facilities. In some instances, products are being designed so that once they are no longer used they can be retrieved, disassembled, and reused in future reduction. Sun Microsystems (now part of Oracle) developed servers and storage products that could be returned by the user, and significant parts of which were then reused in building new models. This is part of another area of innovation known as 'extended producer responsibility' by which waste from one product is used as a resource for future ones. Considered Design is Nike's approach to incorporating sustainability into product design that includes the facility to have shoes recycled into new ones at the end of their useful lives. 'Extended producer responsibility' stems from earlier thinking about cradle-to-grave, and subsequently cradle-to-cradle design. Cradle to grave considers the impact of a product from development and manufacture to distribution and use, and tries to reduce negative impacts where possible. Cradle to cradle extends this further by treating a product as something with potentially perpetual impacts that go beyond the moment it is no longer of use to the buyer. Under cradle to cradle, the manufacturer as the creator of the product has responsibility for the impacts of the product beyond its useful life into its disposal and reuse. We will explore this further in the 'Effectiveness technologies' section.

Sources of more detailed information

Technology area: energy efficiency

Boyle, G. (Ed) 2007, *Renewable electricity and the grid: The challenge of variability*, Earthscan, London.

Club of Rome & Natural Edge Project 2009, *Factor five: Transforming the global economy through 80% improvements in resource productivity: A report to the Club of Rome*, Earthscan, London.

Harvey, L.D.D. 2010, *Energy and the new reality*, Earthscan, London.

Patterson, W.C. 2007, *Keeping the lights on: Towards sustainable electricity*, Earthscan, London.

Technology area: buildings

Bokalders, V. 2009, *The whole building handbook: How to design healthy, efficient, and sustainable buildings*, Earthscan, London.

Harris, C. & Centre for Alternative Technology (Great Britain) 2005, *The whole house book: Ecological building design & materials*, 2nd edn, Centre for Alternative Technology, Machynlleth.

Smith, P.F. 2010, *Building for a changing climate: The challenge for construction, planning and energy*, Earthscan, London.

 Discussion points

Efficiency innovation is about doing more with less.

● To what extent is efficiency a behavioural challenge rather than a technological one?
● How does 'extended producer responsibility' differ from conventional eco-efficiency?
● Do you agree that eco-efficiency is always about making the 'CFO case'?

Substitution technologies

The significance of substituting energy derived from fossil fuels with ones from alternative, cleaner sources is a recurring theme in talking about business and sustainability. Alternative energy including hydro, wind, biomass, solar, and nuclear are dealt with as part of the major sustainability challenges in Chapter 2. At present clean energy power generating capacity accounts for about 13 per cent of total energy supply.[9] The major part of this comes from hydro and biomass, in particular biofuels. These are not especially new technologies, and they are controversial for a number of reasons, not least their impacts on poor and marginalized people. Wood has been used since time immemorial as a source of heat, and more recently in the early twentieth century Rudolf Diesel and Henry Ford both designed their engines to run on biofuels (peanut oil and hemp respectively). However, the potential of biomass as a renewable energy source has clearly attracted much attention because of interest in sustainability as well as issues to do with energy security and oil prices. The potential of biofuels for aviation is actively being explored, and future generations of biofuels will not compete so much with human food cultivation although they cost of processing is very high.

The appropriate alternative energy technology depends significantly on one's location. Although there is talk of using the deserts of North Africa as an energy farm for Europe and elsewhere,[10] the sources of alternative energy cannot be transported to where they are needed in the same way oil, coal, or even natural gas can. Consequently, biomass is a good source of renewable energy in land-rich Brazil, but wind farms are more suited to Britain (the windiest country in Europe), and solar power more likely to succeed in Egypt. Solar and wind are the major clean energy technologies in terms of investment at present, and the techno-logical challenges with each are quite different. Wind energy is already competitive with natural gas, but to develop further there will need to be major investment in distribution and storage as well as generation, and the deficiencies of wind power in terms of providing a stable base load have not been solved. Solar photovoltaic cells face some of these same problems, but there is also a serious cost issue. It is the most costly of the current renewable energies because the proven photovoltaic materials are expensive, and their alternatives have a short lifespan.

The future promise of these kinds of technology has generated a lot of entrepreneurial and to a lesser degree investor enthusiasm. China is celebrated as the 'superpower' of alternative energy because of its growing strength in solar and wind development and manufacturing; Germany has committed itself to taking the lead on alternative energy innovation after outlawing nuclear power facilities. However, Germany, Spain, and Australia have all experienced difficulty in establishing a balanced policy environment for expanding renewables, and it is unclear how much the growth in solar panels in China is because of high state subsidies, and how long those can continue. The USA also has aspirations to be a technology leader in this area, and in 2009 as part of its economic recovery package the government guaranteed a loan of US$523 million to one solar manufacturer, Solyndra. In 2011, Solyndra filed for bankruptcy and in the process caused a vociferous public debate about the viability of alternative energy, the role of government in choosing technologies, corporate fraud, and subsidies to the oil and gas industries.

Solyndra's failure, although not unique, garnered extra attention because President Obama had visited its factory and highlighted it as an emblem of the Green New Deal. However, although this meant that there was a lot of political capital to be had from the bankruptcy, more importantly it was a reminder that governments and the financial markets are a long way from knowing how to bring such new technologies to market in an environment that still favours incumbent, fossil fuel-based power. This situation can attract attention away from the other alternative energy technologies that are being developed.

Oil or tar sands are not a clean technology by any means, but the increased availability of crude oil from separating bitumen from clay or sand has had an effect on arguments about how close we are to reaching peak oil, and how long it will be before renewable energy is price competitive with oil. Oil sands are expensive and energy intensive to exploit, involving the heavy use of natural gas to produce the oil. Ironically, the potential of accessing new sources of natural gas by a process called fracking (hydraulic fracturing) means that oil sands could become cheaper to exploit. Fracking, in the USA in particular, is being promoted as a contribution to clean energy as well as energy security. Rock is fractured by pressurized fluids, and this releases natural gas. Natural gas produces about half of the GHG emissions of coal, but fracking itself has been associated with aquifer contamination and land subsidence. Moreover, natural gas causes methane emissions, and these are potentially far more harmful than CO_2.

A similar problem arises with methane hydrates, a plentiful source of natural gas trapped on the sea floor as a result of decaying marine life. It is difficult to extract, and there is a high risk of uncontrolled methane gas release. However, its abundance makes it a very appealing untapped reservoir of natural gas, even if its commercial exploitation is a long way off.

Another abundant resource mentioned in the search for alternative energy is hydrogen. Hydrogen fuel cell vehicles are discussed in the transport context in Chapter 3, but the potential for hydrogen goes beyond this.[11] However, we need to be clear that when we consider hydrogen we are not talking about energy per se, but about a way of storing and distributing energy. Before a hydrogen fuel cell can be used, energy has to be converted to hydrogen, something that is costly and technologically challenging. Moreover, its benefits in sustainability terms ultimately depend on the original source of energy, and without a ready supply of clean energy, hydrogen could increase the demand for oil and coal. Nonetheless, hydrogen is appealing to politicians and to the general public because if the hurdles are surmounted, it does not require fundamental changes to economies or lifestyles.

Sources of more detailed information

Technology area: alternative energy general

Boyle, G. 1996, *Renewable energy: Power for a sustainable future*, Oxford University Press, Oxford.

Harvey, L.D.D. 2010, *Energy and the new reality*, Earthscan, London.

Miller, D. 2009, *Selling solar: The diffusion of renewable energy in emerging markets*, Earthscan, London.

Skea, J., Ekins, P., & Winskel, M. (Eds) 2011, *Energy 2050: Making the transition to a secure low carbon energy system*, Earthscan, London.

Technology area: photovoltaics

Kurokawa, K. (Ed) 2003, *Energy from the desert*, Earthscan, London.

Wenham, S.R. (Ed) 2007, *Applied photovoltaics*, 2nd edn, Earthscan, London.

Technology area: biomass

Morris, N. 2009, *Biomass power*, Franklin Watts, London.

Wissenschaftlicher Beirat der Bundesregierung Globale Umweltveränderungen (Germany) 2010, *Future bioenergy and sustainable land use*, Earthscan, London.

Technology area: wind energy

Burton, T., Jenkins, N., Sharpe, D., & Bossanyi, E. (Eds) 2011, *Wind energy handbook*, 2nd edn, Wiley, Oxford.

Wagner, H. 2009, *Introduction to wind energy systems: Basics, technology and operation*, Springer, Berlin.

Effectiveness technologies

The term eco-effectiveness was coined by McDonough and Braungart in their influential book *Cradle to Cradle* (2002). It is used to distinguish certain types of innovation from the technologies of eco-efficiency described earlier. They summarize eco-efficiency as being 'less bad' than business as usual, but argue that approaches such as reduce, reuse, and recycle may enhance our ability to do more with less, but ultimately still eat away at natural capital. Recycling, for example, is typically 'downcycling', i.e. the downgrading of a resource so that at each reincarnation it can be used as a lower-quality input. They cite the example of recycling aluminium cans which involves mixing manganese and magnesium, resulting in a weaker metal than the original can. Every time a product is downcycled in this way, additives may be needed to give it a new lease of life (e.g. the bleaching of recycled paper to extend its usefulness), and these additives may have negative impacts of their own. They conclude:

> Eco-efficiency is an outwardly admirable, even noble, concept, but it is not a strategy for success over the long-term, because it does not touch deep enough. It works within the same system that caused the problem in the first place, merely slowing it down with moral proscriptions and punitive measures. It presents little more than the illusion of change.
>
> (McDonough & Braungart 2002, p. 62)

Head (2008) makes a similar distinction in a different, less critical way. He distinguishes between innovations that assist a soft transition from an unconstrained to a resource-constrained economy (what he calls the 'ecological age'), and innovations that help create a long-term sustainable lifestyle. Eco-efficiency and indeed some of the other innovations we have discussed so far may have an important part to play in the process of transition. Eco-effectiveness aims to enable long-term sustainable lifestyles. The function of innovation in this context is not to create economic growth per se, but to ensure that either economic activity contributes to the stock of natural capital, or any ecosystem loss is offset by economic benefits that can then be invested in mitigating harm from that loss.

Closed loops are essential to eco-effectiveness. We touched on Nike's Considered Design concept earlier, in the context of 'extended producer responsibility' (see 'Efficiency technologies'). In its present form, Considered Design is a good example of eco-efficiency because of its emphasis on less toxics, less waste, and more environmentally friendly materials. The shoe recycling component of the model introduces a further step in producer responsibility, but the longer-term goal is to close the loop so that products are designed not simply to do less bad (in McDonough and Braungart's language), but constitute a net good.

Interface, the modular flooring company, is probably the most well-known example of a company that has embraced eco-effectiveness. Its aim, in an industry that uses toxic chemicals to manufacture its products and which generates large amounts of waste, has been to achieve a zero environmental footprint by 2020. Its vision reads as follows:

> To be the first company that, by its deeds, shows the entire industrial world what sustainability is in all its dimensions: People, process, product, place and profits – by 2020 – and in doing so we will become restorative through the power of influence.[12]

Its mission statement continues:

> We will honor the places where we do business by endeavoring to become the first name in industrial ecology, a corporation that cherishes nature and restores the environment. Interface will lead by example and validate by results, including profits, *leaving the world a better place than when we began*, and we will be restorative through the power of our influence in the world. (Emphasis added.)

Ecological principle	Example of application in technology
Use waste as a resource	Wheat and straw used in fire-retardant walls
Diversify and cooperate	Mix-use urban planning
Gather and use energy efficiently	Smart metres
Optimize rather than maximize	Real term journey information
Sparing use of materials	Eco-efficiency
Clean up (do not pollute)	Anaerobic digestion
Avoid drawing down resource capital	Green roofs
Use local resources	Better water capture
Foster information flows	Investment in high-speed broadband

Figure 6.1 Ecological principles as a guide to sustainability innovation.

Sources: Benyus 1997; Hawken 1995; Head 2008.

The idea that companies and commerce can leave the world a better place than it was before is central to effectiveness innovation. Interface's business model—and in particular its commitment to using renewable energy, fitting form to function, recycling everything, and creating no waste—is based on Paul Hawken's work on the 'ecology of commerce', seeing business from an ecological perspective (Hawken 1995). The ecology metaphor is common amongst effectiveness innovators, and Hawken describes its elements in his 'Natural Step' framework (Chapter 8). Design and planning company, Arup, refers to Benyus's *Biomimicry Principles* (1997) when describing the transformation of urban areas, manufacturing, and food production (Figure 6.1), and various authors talk about natural capitalism and the creation of value in social and environmental as well as economic asset classes (Chapter 3). The attraction here, as exemplified by McDonough and Braungart's example of the ant colony, is that nature creates balanced ecosystems, whereas contemporary human societies are not in balance, and it should be innovation's aim to address this.

Living roofs such as those at Barclay's London headquarters, California's Academy of Sciences, and the Confederation of Indian Industries' building in Hyderabad are early examples of how cities might eventually become carbon neutral or even negative. City farms stacked up like current car parks, buildings and roads designed to optimize natural cooling and warming, and waste to energy systems are all being integrated in urban planning. The Connected Urban Development initiative saw Cisco partner with companies such as HSBC, Arup, and CH2M HILL on discovering ways ICT could contribute to creating low carbon cities. Masdar, the 'zero-carbon, zero-waste, energy exporting' city being constructed in Abu Dhabi, along with Dongtan in China, are high profile examples of what future urban centres could look like.[13] However, older cities such as Malmö and Copenhagen are examples of what can be achieved even if one does not start with a blank sheet of paper.

What Malmö has tried to address, and what Masdar is sometimes criticized for, is the separation of environmental development from human development. Although Malmö has its share of prestige, elite sustainability icons such as the 'Turning Torso', it has also retrofitted housing and redesigned facilities in the poorer sections of what was an industrial town in serious decline. By contrast, Masdar has been criticized for being a 'gated community', its inhabitants selected by the government, and its innovations restricted to the wealthy and well connected. In many ways this is an unfair criticism because Masdar is not a normal city; it is an experiment in sustainability innovation. However, it highlights a tension between the enthusiasm generated by some innovations, and fears that they might exacerbate wealth divides.

The scale of Masdar's ambitions have been scaled back considerably since the 2008 financial crisis,[14] begging the question that if effectiveness innovation is too costly for one of the richest states in the world, how can it be implemented in the fast-growing urban areas of developing economies. For cities that lack basic amenities at present, the choice is between installing new or old technologies. For example, when bringing sanitation to growing cities in sub-Saharan Africa or South Asia, systems could be designed from the outset to accommodate separating toilets where solid waste is taken away in vacuum tubes for anaerobic digestion, and liquid waste goes for treatment, reuse, and nutrient extraction. These technologies are not necessarily new: for instance, Disney World in Florida, USA has used vacuum garbage disposal since the 1970s. Moreover, current resource use is so inefficient that there is ample low-hanging fruit that requires innovative thinking rather than new technologies. For example, urban developments where people can easily get to work, school, shops, and leisure by foot, bike, or public transport result in less pollution and are less costly to maintain compared to spread out urban centres.[15]

Sources of more detailed information

Technology area: buildings and the built environment

Hankins, M. 2010, *Stand-alone solar electric systems: The Earthscan expert handbook for planning, design, and installation*, Earthscan, London.

Kats, G. 2010, *Greening our built world: Costs, benefits, and strategies*, Island Press, Washington, DC.

Schiller, P.L., Bruun, E.C., & Kenworthy, J.R. 2010, *An introduction to sustainable transportation: Policy, planning and implementation*, Earthscan, London.

Technology area: engineering and design

Chick, A. 2011, *Design for sustainable change: How design and designers can drive the sustainability agenda: required reading range course reader*, Ava Publishing, Lausanne.

Fletcher, K. 2008, *Sustainable fashion and textiles: Design journeys*, Earthscan, London.

Stasinopoulos, P. (Ed) 2009, *Whole system design: An integrated approach to sustainable engineering*, Earthscan, London.

Technology area: urban development

Calthorpe, P. 2010, *Urbanism in the age of climate change*, Island Press, Washington, DC.

Farr, D. (Ed) 2008, *Sustainable urbanism: Urban design with nature*, John Wiley & Sons, Hoboken, NJ.

Lehmann, S. 2010, *The principles of green urbanism: Transforming the city for sustainability*, Earthscan, London.

Snapshot 6.2   Eco-effectiveness—Herman Miller

Herman Miller's environmental goal is 'to become a sustainable business—manufacturing products without reducing the capacity of the environment to provide for future generations'. This manufacturer of office furniture was an early adopter of the principles of cradle-to-cradle product design and responsibility. Its founder, D.J. De Pree was a strong believer that companies should have a moral purpose, and as a publicly listed company since the 1970s, it has grown to become one of the top suppliers of office furniture in the USA.

Herman Miller was an early mover in environmentally informed innovation. In the 1980s, it established an Environmental Quality Action Team that sought out solutions for achieving the company's environmental goals. In the 1990s, it adopted a zero waste to landfill policy, and in the early 2000s launched its Perfect Vision initiative that as well as zero landfill included zero hazardous waste generation, zero water and air emissions from manufacturing, buildings built to LEED standards (Snapshot 6.1), and 100 per cent renewable energy commitments.

Meeting its own high goals has not always been easy. The Mirra chair was its first offering designed under cradle-to-cradle, eco-effectiveness principles, and it soon became apparent that it required not only engineers, but also supply chain managers, manufacturers, and design consult-ants to work differently. All had to be trained in a new design protocol devised for the new product. By insisting that the chair be reusable or easily recyclable, for example, elements such as the chair's spine (a mix of difficult to separate plastic and metal) had to be reengineered. PVC is a cheap and durable material for padding, but also results in toxic emissions during manufacture and disposal.

The same eco-effectiveness ethos that Herman Miller applies to its products is applied to its facilities. Its Michigan factory was designed so that workers felt as if they were working outdoors. It has a tree-lined interior, roof skylights wherever people are working, and views of the outside from the manufacturing floor. The factory site is built to encourage wildlife, and waste water and storm water are channelled into a series of wetlands. The same principles were subsequently used in the company's Netherlands' factory.

Despite admitting that its environmental commitments can increase immediate costs, the company is not only acclaimed as one of the USA's best employers, but also shows strong financial performance. Although it is seen as a purveyor of premium products, it has ridden out the recessions of the early and mid-2000s. Furthermore, it has not only adhered to but flaunted its environmental commitments, something that runs in the face of perceived wisdom about public companies being constrained in how far they can be sustainability champions.

Sources: Belz & Peattie 2009; Esty & Winson 2009; Makower 2009; McDonough & Braungart 2002; Rossi et al. 2006; http://hermanmiller.com.

Questions

Herman Miller is a profitable international company that has taken on a role as a champion of eco-effectiveness.

1. What are the company's major achievements?

2. What are the benefits its position as a sustainability champion bring to the company?

3. Should companies take on the role of sustainability champions?

Mitigation technologies

There is a final category of technologies that could make the threats posed by climate change and resource depletion irrelevant. As Heinberg notes:

> [If] we had enough energy available we could make up for shortages in fresh water by desalinizing ocean water in vast quantities. The oceans may be running out of stocks of wild fish, but with enough available cheap energy we could simply farm as many fish as we needed. Eventually, using biotechnology and nanotechnology, we should be able to synthesize any substances we desired. Even if wild nature disappears altogether . . . [we] could create artificial environments of any kind we choose – so long as we had enough energy.
>
> (Heinberg 2004, p. 133)

This abundance of low-cost renewable energy is what is promised by nuclear fusion, a technology that if successful would make zero-carbon energy available without long-life nuclear waste using readily available fuels such as deuterium. Nuclear fusion technology is proven to a degree but we are a long way from being able to harness it to produce energy in any significant amounts. However, as with several of the mitigation technology ideas, its ultimate promise gives it a degree of attraction despite how long it will take to develop and deploy it.

Geoengineering has attracted considerable attention as a way of moderating climate change by deliberate, large-scale intervention in the Earth's climate system. Geoengineering technologies can be divided into two types:

- CO_2 removal technologies (CDR) that address the root cause of climate change by removing GHGs from the atmosphere.
- Solar radiation management (SRM) techniques that attempt to offset the effects of heightened greenhouse gas concentrations by shielding the Earth from increased solar radiation.[16]

CDR techniques include enhanced weathering processes to remove CO_2 from the atmosphere, and enhancing the oceans' uptake of CO_2 through artificial fertilization of nutrients, and increased upwelling processes to improve the nutrient content of surface waters. Not all CDR techniques, however, are especially innovative. Biomass fuels can be considered part of CDR, and they could also have a role to play in carbon sequestration. Land-use management offers a low-technology way of removing carbon by protecting or enhancing carbon sinks such as forests.

SRM techniques directly modify the Earth's radiation balance and include some of the most radical innovations associated with climate change. Ideas include desert reflectors to increase the albedo (reflecting power) of deserts to produce large negative radiative forcings; increasing cloud albedo by creating whitening clouds over the ocean; stratospheric aerosols that release particles into the stratosphere to scatter sunlight back to space; and shields in space to reduce the amount of solar energy reaching the Earth.

The difficulty with CDR and SRM technologies at present is that none has been shown to be effective at an affordable cost and with acceptable side effects. In theory, CDR techniques are more attractive because they permanently return the climate system to something like its natural state. However, they can be costly, and their impact is slow, measured in decades. SRM techniques, although involving radically new technologies, are probably less expensive, and could have an effect within a few years. They can be thought of as a performance booster that could be introduced for a limited period if efficiency and substitution technologies are not delivering emissions reductions at the necessary rate. However, not only are they a long way from realization, they create an artificial balance between increased GHG concentrations (e.g. from conventional manufacturing emissions) and reduced solar radiation, and this would need to be managed and maintained potentially for centuries. Depending on one's viewpoint, this represents an exhilarating challenge or a terrible threat to the idea of the Earth as a self-regulating system of the kind described in the works of James Lovelock.[17] It also poses unprecedented challenges for global governance because interventions at a national or company level that have international consequences are well beyond the competence of current governance mechanisms. A British Royal Society report on geoengineering concluded that, 'Solar Radiation Management methods should not be applied unless there is a need to rapidly limit or reduce global average temperatures' (Royal Society 2009, p. xi).

 ## Discussion points

Geoengineering is amongst the areas of innovation where a breakthrough could cause us to rethink how we tackle threats to ecosystems.

- What are the main differences between mitigation technologies and effectiveness ones?
- Why is geoengineering a governance challenge as much as a technological one?
- What dangers or threats do geoengineering and some aspects of eco-effectiveness pose to developing economies?

 ## Summary

Economic and technological innovation are often considered the most important elements of finding solutions to our sustainability challenges. The creation of a regulated market in carbon emissions may not have been an overnight success and continues to be highly controversial, but it is a major innovation that has had some impact on emissions. It also needs to be acknowledged that the much maligned Kyoto Protocol has played a part in creating the means for channelling funding to low carbon development projects in poorer countries.

Technological innovations fall into four different categories. The most common are efficiency technologies associated with companies trying to reduce their environmental footprint without fundamentally altering the way they do business. Particularly in the area of energy, there is a lot of innovation in alternative technologies that can be deployed as a substitute for ones that depend on finite and polluting resources. Solar and wind power have become increasingly important in some countries, but hydro and biomass are still the main sources of renewable energy, and in the longer term the most successful technologies are likely to be the ones best suited to particular locations.

The distinction between innovations that are an improvement on the current situation, and those that help business maintain or improve ecosystems is one that has cropped up frequently since the early 2000s. Eco-effectiveness has been adopted as a principle by a small but nonetheless successful group of companies, all of which are able to compete in mainstream industries. These companies typically see themselves not only as innovators, but also promulgators of sustainability innovation, demonstrating what can be achieved without sacrificing competitiveness. Nonetheless, effectiveness technologies still tend to be seen as a cost to business, and not a business opportunity in their own right. The situation is different with mitigation technologies such as those associated with geoengineering. Not only do these have the potential to alter the sustainability situation, they hold out the promise of a technological revolution However, they are a long way from being commercially or politically viable, and could in the end be too late or too hazardous to make a significant contribution.

Further reading

Fletcher, K. 2008, *Sustainable fashion and textiles: Design journeys*, Earthscan, London.
Insights into the ways sustainability innovation is being introduced to the garments and textile industry: the learning is applicable to a host of industries interested in substitution and eco-effectiveness technologies.

Miller, D. 2009, *Selling solar: The diffusion of renewable energy in emerging markets*, Earthscan, London.
Observations on the successes and failures of solar innovation provide the basis for an explanation of how solar technology can be deployed in emerging economies.

McDonough, W. & Braungart, M. 2002, *Cradle to cradle: Remaking the way we make things*, North Point Press, New York, NY.
Groundbreaking early book on cradle-to-cradle design and manufacturing, and an introduction to the principles of eco-effectiveness.

Royal Society 2009, *Geoengineering the climate: Science, governance and uncertainty*, The Royal Society, London.
Concise overview of the types of geoengineering being developed, their prospects, their strengths and limitations, and what it would take to bring them into being.

Skea, J., Ekins, P., & Winskel, M. (Eds) 2011, *Energy 2050: Making the transition to a secure low carbon energy system*, Earthscan, London.
An exploration of how a major economy can meet its emissions reduction targets by substituting high carbon energy for clean energy.

 Case study 6   SELCO-India—bringing energy to the rural poor

Like many of the largest emerging economies, India is fuelling its economic growth with high carbon energy plus nuclear power. The country has substantial coal reserves, and in international fora it is at pains to assert its right to exploit these just as OECD countries have done in the past. Yet, according to SELCO founder, Harish Hande, coal and nuclear—the backbone of India's electricity grid—are an irrelevance to vast sections of the population. Forty-four per cent of Indians lack mains electricity, and for many more the supply is erratic.

Hande established SELCO in 1995. It is based in Bangalore and employs nearly 200 people at its HQ and 21 branch offices across South India. SELCO's purpose is to provide sustainable energy services to photovoltaic (PV) solar home systems to low-income households and businesses. It has served over 150,000 customers, and in the process developed a unique business model that makes solar energy available at an affordable price to underserved markets.

SELCO's success hinges on two types of innovation that are welded together in the company's business model. The first type is technological innovation. SELCO designs and sells photovoltaic energy systems for the home. These are primarily to provide lighting that is cleaner, more reliable, and more affordable than the kerosene lamps found in most rural homes. A typical unit is sufficient to power four 7-W compact fluorescent lights, although consumers also use electricity for radios and fans. SELCO's engineers install the systems which typically comprise a 35-W PV module on the house's roof, and a lead-acid battery to store the power inside. Both the cells and batteries have been specifically designed to meet the needs of their users so that, for example, the batteries can cope with daily discharge in a way that would destabilize conventional car batteries.

Technological innovation is not limited to PV and batteries. SELCO helps customers modify their homes to get the most use out of their installations. For example, a lamp installed in a corner can serve several rooms if parts of the dividing walls are removed; or bulbs can be moved from one room to another if sufficient wiring and sockets are installed. Whether it be the hardware, the installation, or the subsequent service contract that forms part of the package, SELCO sources as locally as possible. Its PV modules are made in India, although the success of the Indian solar energy industry has resulted in one supplier ceasing manufacture of the smaller units SELCO needs. SELCO has developed a network of local installers in what has become a new trade in the areas where the company operates.

Installations typically cost about Rs 18,000: a significant outlay for customers whose daily income could be Rs 400 (under £5) a day. However, energy is a significant outlay for poorer people, and while SELCO's target market could not afford Rs 18,000 in one payment, paying in instalments of about Rs 400 a month over five years is an attractive proposition. Moreover, in many cases the extra productivity that a steady supply of light throughout the day brings is more than sufficient to pay for the installation and maintenance. For street traders, PV modules might be too expensive, but a battery and a fluorescent lamp are within their means, so SELCO has encouraged a network of PV battery-charging businesses. To pay the initial deposit and to organize monthly payments, potential customers can go to local development banks that India's state-owned banks were compelled to set up in the 1980s. Government has also supported SELCO's expansion with 33 per cent subsidies of installations, but this agreement has now ended.

SELCO itself says its model is sustainable. It has a long-term financing partnership with E+Co, a non-profit that provides debt and equity investments in clean energy businesses in developing countries. More recently it has received support from the Lemelson Foundation (USA) and Good Energies (Switzerland). Amongst its proudest claims is that its success has demonstrated that clean energy need not be expensive, and that a low carbon economy does not have to deprive poor people of electricity. The next step in innovation will be making better use of the power people have access to. For example, many women would like to power sewing machines, but the PV modules do not generate enough watts. However, on further investigation, the problem is that the sewing machines on the market are over-powered for what rural women need them to do, and if a less powerful machine were available it could run off the current modules and still meet the women's aspirations.

Sources: conversation with Harish Hande, Oxford, 29 October 2011; http://www.selco-india.com/; http://www.ft.com/cms/s/0/cb0b871a-0f98-11de-a8ae-0000779fd2ac.html#axzz1cMJCaiDZ, accessed 20 October 2011.

Questions

1. SELCO-India is an example of innovation by a social enterprise.

    a. What are the essential elements in the company's success so far?

    b. Is the SELCO model replicable in other countries?

    c. Is the SELCO model only applicable in rural areas?

(continued)

2. The company has won various awards for creating a viable business model that addresses social and environmental issues.

   a. What are the main sustainability impacts the company delivers?

   b. Could a mainstream energy company adopt a similar approach?

   c. What will the company need to do differently in order to increase its impact?

3. SELCO-India is an example of technological and financial innovation.

   a. Under what conditions is PV technology more affordable than coal-based energy?

   b. How could you develop a similarly innovative approach to a different sustainability challenge such as clean water?

   c. Are there other examples of clean energy being provided to poor communities? How are they similar and how are they different to SELCO?

 Endnotes

1. (Newell & Paterson 2010)

2. (Convery 2009; Ellerman, Buchner, & Carraro 2011)

3. http://www.environment.nsw.gov.au/resources/licensing/hrsts/hrsts.pdf, accessed 12 October 2011.

4. http://news.bbc.co.uk/1/hi/8507538.stm; www.abc.net.au/news/2010-02-19/garrett-scraps-insulation-scheme/336610, accessed 12 October 2011.

5. http://googleblog.blogspot.com/2009/04/happy-earth-day-earthlings.html, accessed 13 October 2011.

6. http://www.economist.com/node/16117106?story_id=16117106, accessed 13 October 2011.

7. (Coca-Cola Company 2010)

8. (Coca-Cola Company 2010, p. 29)

9. (IEA 2010a)

10. (Anonymous 2003)

11. (Rifkin 2002; Romm 2004)

12. http://www.interfaceglobal.com/Company/Mission-Vision.aspx, accessed 14 October 2011.

13. http://news.bbc.co.uk/1/hi/world/middle_east/8586046.stm, accessed 14 October 2011.

14. http://www.businessweek.com/news/2011-09-15/world-s-first-solar-building-exporting-energy-shelved-by-masdar.html, accessed 14 October 2011.

15. (Head 2008)

16. (Royal Society 2009)

17. (Lovelock 2000, 2006, 2010)

Financing sustainability

Key terms

Sustainable investing	Engagement
Green capital	Asset classes
Green investment	Venture capital
Investing strategies	Screening

Online resources

- Additional case study on sustainable investing in China.
- Additional case study on impact investing.
- Links to major initiatives.
- More discussion topics.

  http://www.oxfordtextbooks.co.uk/orc/blowfield/

Chapter in brief

This chapter explores the role of finance and investment in the sustainability context. It discusses the importance of the financial markets in successfully addressing sustainability challenges, and how global capital has contributed to the challenges we face today. It describes the array of current initiatives through which investing and banking communities engage in sustainability, and the emergence of sustainability-oriented financial instruments. Particular attention is paid to the sustainable investing movement that has emerged out of the long-established field of socially responsible investment. It examines the impact of sustainability on funds, analysis, investment strategies, and other elements of financial markets, and concludes with a discussion of whether we are progressing towards the kind of changes in investment behaviour that some aspects of sustainability seem to require.

Importance of the financial markets

Financial markets provide the oxygen of the capitalist system. Their role in raising capital, sharing risk, and enabling liquidity has made them the pre-eminent institution of free market capitalism: one that is both admired and feared. There are many who regard investors and bankers as the enemies of a sustainable world in the same way as some consider capitalism and sustainability to be at loggerheads (Chapter 3). However, with more than US$50 trillion of the world's wealth accounted for by the market capitalization of the top eighteen stock exchanges, and equally eye-watering amounts invested in other tradable asset classes from corporate bonds to property to hedge funds and commodities, it is manifestly obvious that markets are an inevitable part of any equation seeking to solve sustainability challenges.

There are good a priori and empirical reasons for claiming that sustainability is a huge opportunity for investment and wealth creation. Authors such as Esty and Winston (2009) and Laszlo (2003) explore the business opportunities arising from sustainability, and Krosinsky and Robins (2008) and Sullivan and MacKenzie (2006) demonstrate the performance advantages of factoring sustainability into investment decisions. Equally, some of the earliest attention from the finance community came from reinsurance companies wanting to learn more about the material risks associated with sustainability, and since then many people have examined how sustainability can threaten financial performance and wealth creation.[1] Relating to this, there has been specific research into the strengths and weaknesses of the tools and beliefs that inform investment decisions. Academics and practitioners such as Gray and Beddington (Gray 2003; Gray & Beddington 2001) have challenged the inadequacy of conventional accounting practices in assessing the value of the firm, and companies such as Innovest and Trucost have developed alternative analytical tools intended to give a more accurate picture of companies' performance than conventional ones that encourage firms to treat social and environmental issues as externalities.

There are examples of investors of different stripes responding to this kind of information, and we will explore these later on (see 'Different asset classes'). Sustainable investing as a development of socially responsible investment is growing (see 'Current initiatives'), but although there may be advocacy reasons for organizations such as the US Social Investment Forum to claim social and environmental investments account for over 20 per cent of the investment marketplace,[2] the reality is that sustainability challenges are not a major factor in the vast majority of public or private equity transactions, and the situation is no better in the case of cash, fixed income, real estate, or commodity assets (see 'Sustainable investing'). There may have been a significant increase in sustainability reporting and the integration of sustainability information into financial reports,[3] but the fact remains that stock exchanges such as London, Sao Paolo, Moscow, and Toronto still have 20–30 per cent of their market capitalization tied to fossil fuels.[4] Moreover, dimensions of sustainability other than climate change such as water, land degradation, and biodiversity are barely recognized as potential issues with material consequences.

Sustainability's hunger for capital

This mismatch between the apparent size of the sustainability opportunity and risk to investors and the behaviour of financial markets is a source of continual perplexity for those who regard sustainability as an important business issue. HSBC's Nick Robins talks of a

Key concept 7.1   Investment

Investment is the allocation of capital with the aim of gaining a profitable return. Profit can take the form of interest, income, or appreciation in the value of the asset in which capital has been invested. The asset can be in any number of forms including property, shares, bonds, savings accounts, and natural resources. Investments are often made through intermediaries such as pension funds, insurance firms, brokers, and banks. Much investment is facilitated by financial markets where investors and buyers meet to trade assets. Financial markets is a broad term that includes capital markets (shares and bonds), commodity markets, and insurance markets amongst others.

'dialogue of the deaf' between companies and their investors; a chasm in understanding resulting in investor behaviour that stops business addressing sustainability challenges.[5] A former KPMG senior partner, now investment analyst, claims that 'the majority of large institutional investors have . . . been sleepwalking through the early part of the twenty-first century', blind as he sees it to the 'extraordinary economic and sociopolitical transformation' that is the 'sustainability revolution'.[6]

There are those who see this mismatch as a minor irritant at most, and one that will be alleviated once the sheer size of the financial opportunity associated with sustainability becomes apparent. Jaeger et al (2011) estimate that over 20 per cent of investment in the European Union by 2020 will go into addressing climate change: not only is this necessary to reduce emissions, they argue, it represents the best opportunity for economic growth. According to the World Business Council for Sustainable Development (WBCSD), US$40 trillion will need to be invested in urban infrastructure worldwide by 2030, and the International Energy Agency estimates that US$13 trillion is needed for energy transmission and distribution networks.[7] Similarly huge numbers are bandied around in relation to energy, water, and mobility (Chapter 2), and estimates rarely include other high-investment challenges such as biodiversity and land degradation. Addressing drinking water and sanitation in developing economies is estimated to cost US$113 billion by 2020.[8]

The investment required to address sustainability challenges is not simply new or different; in some instances it will be more costly. Hydro and wind power are an important part of the anticipated shift to renewable energy, but could require US$5.7 trillion of investment, making them significantly more capital intensive than fossil fuels.[9] Overall, the market size for renewable energy is estimated to be US$325 billion by 2020. It is easy to feel queasy as the jumble of numbers—all different, all marked 'urgent', and all very large—flies past, but the implication is clear: much of this investment will have to come from financial markets. A significant amount will come from government, but not enough. In developing economies, overseas development assistance has been surpassed by foreign direct investment as the main source of foreign capital, marking a shift away from government-to-government lending and grants, to private capital investment. Emerging economies such as China and Brazil have bought large amounts of OECD country debt, limiting what they can spend on sustainability. OECD countries themselves are too burdened with debt and uncertainties about their economies to launch the kind of sustainability-focused public sector investment binge envisaged by some prior to the 2008 financial crisis.[10] In countries such as the USA, Australia, and the UK there is in any case an ideological aversion to the public sector choosing what to invest in—something that was not the case during crises such as the Great Depression or the Second World War—and more generally a reluctance amongst politicians to increase tax revenues to extend the pool of public money. Furthermore, governments prefer to invest in particular aspects of sustainability, for example, favouring investments in efficiency rather than technology when it comes to climate change, or education rather than infrastructure in the context of poverty alleviation (Chapter 2). For all of these reasons, the financial markets are not only the oxygen of capitalism; they are the oxygen of meeting sustainability challenges.

Different types of capital

There is a marked tendency amongst people whose main interest is sustainability and consider the role of business as an afterthought to treat capital as something homogeneous. In reality, however, the estimate of US$10 trillion for infrastructure investment between 2008 and 2015, for instance, is needed by companies of different sizes and evolutionary stages located in different jurisdictions and operating within different sectors. Company size and type, geography, and sector all influence the cost and availability of capital, but typically sustainability investment is viewed from a demand-side rather than supply perspective. Moreover, investment gaps often appear when supply is examined. In the case of infrastructure, the majority of the US$10 trillion required remains unfunded even though we are half way through what WBCSD regards as a critical period: if the funding is not found by 2015, the need will not go away, but the cost of action will increase.[11] The life insurance and pension industries propose playing a role in bridging the investment gap, but in 2012 the solution still seems to depend on innovative models of public–private financing partnerships that have not even been tested yet. The British government's Climate Change Committee has said that capital markets will need reconfiguring if climate change-related investment needs are to be met.

Often, the financing sustainability debate is contradictory. On the one hand, sustainability is presented as a great opportunity for entrepreneurs and start-up companies, and is considered comparable to personal computing or the Internet in terms of creating a demand for innovation. Yet, on the other hand, it is described as an opportunity for institutional investors which manage 50 per cent of the global capital pool and have little if any interest in early stage businesses. It has been estimated that only 0.001 per cent of the global capital pool is allocated to early stage funds even though start-ups account for 60–80 per cent of all innovation.[12] The fervour of many involved in lobbying the financial sector to take sustainability seriously means that many figures need to be treated cautiously, but in the absence of analysis of important issues they are often useful to highlight weaknesses in our current understanding. Having the wrong type of capital can be just as problematic as having no capital at all, and investment gaps are likely to occur when the types of investment on offer are inappropriate given the type of companies seeking finance.

In light of this, the role of institutional investors is especially important. The world's largest pension funds have combined assets under management of about US$30 trillion, and along with insurance companies, major endowments and foundations, and sovereign wealth funds they own a significant share of the world economy with interests in every asset class, industry sector, and national market. The size and breadth of their assets has led them to be called 'universal owners' because they have an economic interest not only in the prosperity of individual firms, but the productivity of the economy as a whole.[13] The largest individual funds such as ABP in the Netherlands, CalPERS (USA), the sovereign wealth funds of China or UAE, or Norway's Government Pension Fund have a common interest in global economic, social and environmental prosperity, and also the financial power to significantly influence corporate behaviour. The P8 Group recognizes this and brings together major pension funds such as CalPERS, New York State, AP7 (Sweden), ACSI (Australia), and the National Pension Service (South Korea) to advance investment strategies to address climate change. However, as we will explore further later on (see 'Sustainable investing'), universal owners have been slow to use their economic power and investment strategies to address sustainability challenges. Ironically given the 'masters of the universe' image financial markets have amongst some sustainability campaigners, universal investors can seem timid and conservative, something that was very apparent when trustees of the UN's staff pension fund refused to sign the UN's own Principles for Responsible Investment in 2006.[14] As one particularly hostile critic puts it:

> There is simply too much inertia 'hard-wired' into the current system. A toxic cocktail of overly timorous, deferential pension fund trustees and fiduciaries, egregiously bad, uninformed advice from spuriously self-confident investment consultants, and equally smug and myopic money managers, hopelessly archaic interpretations of what fiduciary responsibility really constitutes, and serious agency problems have created an enormously uphill battle for those who seek to mitigate [this] modern-day Tragedy of the Commons.
>
> (Kiernan 2009, p. 8)

We will explore later if these comments are in any way justified, but such anger—and from an industry insider—is evidence in itself of the importance attached to financial markets in tackling sustainability challenges.

 Snapshot 7.1   Pension funds—Hermes

Hermes is the pension fund manager for the UK's biggest pension fund, BT. It was established when BT was privatized and its pensions were no longer underwritten by the government. During its 30-year existence, it has grown to manage £22.6 billion of assets, and expanded beyond the UK to Australia and the USA. Hermes is unique in the pension fund world in that it has a headline commitment to responsible asset management, and delivering sustainable risk adjusted alpha across all of the asset classes it invests in.

Sustainability is a centrepiece of Hermes's investment and engagement activities. It is well known for exercising shareholder voting rights, and engaging with companies on social, ethical, environmental, and governance issues. Through Hermes Equity Ownership Services, it advises clients on how to vote at companies' general meetings. It also acts on their behalf in direct engagements, and advises them on sustainability issues affecting investment returns. An important point of leverage has been the focus funds under Hermes Focus Asset Management. These funds invest in companies deemed undervalued because environmental, social, and governance (ESG) issues are impeding their growth. It then uses its leverage to get executives and directors to improve in these areas. To date, the logic that poor ESG performance equates with poor overall performance appears sound: the funds, which are invested in five regions around the world, have outperformed their benchmarks, and exceed US$5 billion.

Through its investment strategies and activism, Hermes has become a leading example of a responsibility-driven pension fund manager. It exemplifies the long-term outlook and active engagement that many see as essential to align financial markets with sustainability. Although its ESG focus has not been widely imitated, Hermes's persistence in putting shareholder activism at the heart of its

(continued)

strategy is gaining traction, recognized not only in numerous awards but also in policy thinking as governments try to figure out how best to regulate financial markets.

Sources: Belz & Peattie 2009; Davis, Lukomnik, & Pitt-Watson 2006; Esty & Winson 2009; Green 2009; Kiernan 2009; Makower 2009.

Questions

The role of pension fund managers such as Hermes in financing sustainability is often talked of as crucial.

1. Why are pension funds considered to be so important?
2. Why have more pension funds not followed Hermes or BT's example?
3. What are the key features of Hermes's work for its client that address sustainability?

Legitimization

Irrespective of their role in providing the sustainability-oriented company access to global capital, the financial markets have a key sociological, psychological, cultural role: not only with investors, but also with politicians, the media, corporate managers, and sections of the public, they grant or deny legitimacy to what companies do. They do this overtly by rating the finance-worthiness of companies and industries, and as we will see (see 'Global Reporting Initiative and UN Principles for Responsible Investment') a frequent criticism of sell-side analysts and others in the financial value chain is that they do not properly incorporate sustainability factors into their company valuations. They do it covertly as well, for instance by the questions they ask or do not ask at conference calls between analysts and corporate executives: if sustainability is not raised at such events, then the pressure on a CEO to put it at the top of his to-do list is reduced. However, financial markets also grant or deny legitimacy in what can appear to be subconscious, unintended ways. Financial markets have enormous power over the language that is used, the models employed to understand business, and the aspects of corporate behaviour that are considered important. Terms such as return on investment, efficiency, and liquidity have all found their way into sustainability thinking, and initiatives such as TEEB (see Chapter 3) are blatant attempts to make aspects of sustainability comprehensible to people steeped in the norms and language of finance.

Different asset classes

The main emphasis on this chapter is financial investments, and reflecting current interests of theorists and practitioners it pays particular attention to public equities. However investing in sustainability is broader than this, and each asset class presents opportunities and risks for investors in a sustainability context (Figure 7.1) Real estate, for example, is probably the largest asset class in the world, not simply because of the size of the mortgage market, but also because of the array of financial instruments that relate to the owning, rehabilitation, and construction of building stock.

1. Cash and cash equivalents—low-risk, low-return, liquid investments. Examples: bank accounts, Treasury bills, corporate commercial paper, certificates of deposit.

2. Fixed-income—low-risk, fixed-return investment. Examples: government bonds, corporate bonds, asset-backed securities.

3. Public equities—publicly traded shares on regulated stock exchanges.

4. Private equity—capital raised from retail and institutional investors to invest directly into private companies or to purchase publicly listed companies.

5. Real estate—investments tied to owning, rehabilitating, and creating new building stock. Examples: debt financing, investment properties, real estate investment trusts.

6. Infrastructure—relatively new asset class concentrating on private funding of the renewal of existing infrastructure, and the demand for new infrastructure especially in emerging markets. Examples: airports, privatized rail, toll roads, power plants.

7. Commodities—capital invested directly into the ownership of commodities and natural capital. Examples: agricultural commodities, energy, land, agricultural futures.

8. Hedge funds—private investment vehicles investing in publicly listed shares and bonds. Characterized by aggressive trading strategies, often across different asset classes.

Figure 7.1 Different asset classes.

Arguably, those seeking to address sustainability challenges through investment channels could have more impact by increasing their focus on asset classes such as real estate, infrastructure, and commodities, even if this were at the expense of attention to public equities and fixed income. For example, in commodity investing, capital is directed towards a diverse range of commodities including agriculture, metals, minerals, water, and energy. A vibrant commodities market improves the liquidity of the commodity which in turn helps producers achieve greater price stability. Investors that choose to eliminate or underweight commodities with a negative sustainability impact, or emphasize those that have a positive one encourage improved performance. The most famous example of this is the advent of emissions trading schemes that treat carbon as a commodity traded through regulated markets (see Chapter 3, Case study 3). It is unlikely that similar specific markets for other sustainability-related commodities such as water, methane, or fisheries will be created in the foreseeable future, but it is still possible to factor sustainability into investment decisions in established markets. For instance, investors can buy natural gas instead of coal; aluminium instead of other metals.

Similarly, real-estate investment offers ample opportunity for global capital to be deployed for sustainability-positive outcomes. Buildings are the major user of overall energy; up to 45 per cent of carbon emissions stem from buildings.[15] Property specialists in pension fund managers such as TIAA-CREF and CalPERS have set reasonably aggressive targets to reduce energy by property owners and managers, and there is considerable potential for investors to promote efficient building management by working with managers to increase energy efficiency across their portfolios. Organizations such as the Responsible Property Investing Center and the UNEP Finance Initiative define and stimulate thinking about responsible property investment and management practices, although the credibility of some of their members is open to doubt: for example, RPIC announced that the Universities Superannuation Scheme (USS) had adopted its policies at about the same time USS was slashing benefits to its members.[16]

Infrastructure has only appeared relatively recently as a separate asset class, largely in response to the increased role of the private sector in infrastructure projects such as car parks, toll roads, airports, power plants, water utilities, and public transport systems. Previously, such investments were the domain of public sector investment, but this has altered to a degree, not least with the advent of public-private finance initiatives. Because of this shift, the risks and responsibilities associated with such projects have also been taken on by the private sector. There is likely to be significant investment opportunity in creating the new power grids necessary for low carbon economies (Chapter 2), but there is also the risk of redundant assets if high carbon technologies are replaced with low carbon ones. Equally, anyone investing in high-speed rail, new airports, and the privatization of water will find themselves at the heart of sustainability debates.

It is also worth mentioning cash and cash equivalents as an asset class. When banks are discussed in the context of sustainability, it is often their investment activities that are referred to. Nowadays, the existence of investment and retail banking within a single company (and with shared liabilities) is increasingly being questioned, but if we consider just the retail operations their role in the cash/cash equivalent asset class is still considerable. Retail banks are often the originators of mortgages and loans for home improvements, both of which relate to energy efficiency. Triodos has built a successful European business around ethical savings and investment products, the UK's Ecology Building Society has been lending to promote sustainable construction since the 1980s, and in Germany GLS specializes in loans to sustainable businesses and social enterprises.

Current initiatives

There are a number of flagship initiatives that indicate financial institutions' awareness of sustainability. Individual companies such as the Co-operative Bank in the UK have built successful businesses on the back of ethical principles and products, and some of the largest investment houses such as JP Morgan Chase are involved in carbon credit trading. In 2007, JP Morgan also launched its Environmental Index (JENI-Carbon Beta) to assess corporate bonds from a carbon footprint perspective, and since the mid-2000s 'green bonds' have been issued in Europe and North America to fund sustainability-related projects. However, rather than individual organizations' initiatives, the focus of this section is initiatives that address core elements of financing sustainability, and represent a clear, often multi-organizational attempt to alter practices in the financial markets. For example, the Equator Principles bring together 70 financial institutions, and provide them with a framework to assess social and environmental risks in project financing. Launched in 2003, they were primarily intended to reduce risks associated with the financing of large-scale projects in countries where corruption was rife or governance was otherwise weak. This has involved not simply developing a code of practice, but a system of voluntary governance involving reporting, grievance, and disclosure components.

Indexes

Indexes employing common criteria to grade companies have long been a feature of mainstream investment, and were recognized early on by those engaged in financing sustainability as necessary for reliable performance measurement. Three of the major socially responsible investment (SRI) indices are KLD's Domini 400, the Dow Jones Sustainability Group Indexes, and the FTSE4Good Index, which is produced jointly by the Financial Times and the London Stock Exchange. Each of the indices uses a different weighting system for financial and non-financial performance.

The Domini 400 Social Index (DSI) was launched in 1990 to set a benchmark for SRI fund managers, similar to the S&P 500, but subject to social and environmental screens. Today, approximately 250 DSI companies are S&P 500 companies, a hundred are non-S&P 500, and 50 others are chosen for their 'exemplary' records of environmental, social, and corporate governance practices. A decade later, the Dow Jones Sustainability Indexes (DJSI) became the first indices to track sustainability-driven companies on a global basis. They were launched together by the Dow Jones Indexes, STOXX Limited (a European index provider) and SAM Group (a pioneer in SRI). There are over US$8 billion assets in DJSI-based investment vehicles. The DJSI uses a rules-based methodology and focuses on best-in-class companies. Assessment criteria include corporate governance, risk and crisis management, codes of conduct, labour practices, human capital development, sustainability and project finance (for banks), climate strategy (including eco-efficiency and protection of biodiversity), and emerging markets strategy.

The FTSE4Good Index was launched in July 2001 and is derived from the FTSE Global Equity Index Series as an initiative of FTSE, in association with EIRIS and the United Nations Children's Fund (UNICEF). Today, there are two series: a benchmark index and a tradable index. The initial screening process looks at the starting universe—FTSE All-Share Index, FTSE Developed Europe Index, FTSE US Index, FTSE Developed Index—and screens against tobacco producers, companies providing parts, services, or manufacturing for whole nuclear weapon systems, weapons manufacturers, and owners or operators of nuclear power stations that mine or produce uranium. Positive screens are applied on the subsets of companies, corresponding with each of the original indices, to include companies that are working towards environmental sustainability, have positive relations with stakeholders, and uphold and support universal human rights. The inclusion criteria originate from globally recognized codes of conduct such as the UN Global Compact and the Universal Declaration of Human Rights. Since 2004, FTSE4Good has launched a series of regional indexes including ones for Japan, Australia, the USA, South Africa, and emerging economies. New climate change criteria were introduced in 2007, and it also operates an index of European environmental leaders.

Global Reporting Initiative and UN Principles for Responsible Investment

The Global Reporting Initiative (GRI) is now in its third major iteration. Launched in 2000, its main aim has been to provide a disclosure framework that companies can use to report on their sustainability performance. Its framework sets out principles and performance indicators that allow companies to measure and report on ESG performance. Approximately 1,800 companies worldwide used GRI guidelines as part of their reporting in 2010, and about 450 of these were externally verified. Financial services has been the most active sector in terms of reporting, and

1. To incorporate ESG (environmental, social, and corporate governance) issues into investment analysis and decision-making processes.

2. To be active owners and incorporate ESG issues into our ownership policies and practices.

3. To seek appropriate disclosure on ESG issues by the entities in which we invest.

4. To promote acceptance and implementation of the Principles within the investment industry.

5. To work together to enhance our effectiveness in implementing the Principles.

6. To report on our activities and progress towards implementing the Principles.

Figure 7.2 UN Principles for Responsible Investment.

Sources: http://www.unpri.org http://www.uss.co.uk; http://www.unepfi.org.

along with energy and mining has sector specific guidelines. This is a small fraction of the total companies producing reports, but by some measures sustainability reporting has become synonymous with corporate reporting, and the GRI is involved in high-profile initiatives such as the International Integrated Reporting Committee aiming to demonstrate linkages between an organization's strategy, governance, and financial performance and the social, environmental, and economic context within which it operates.

Another international initiative, but one specifically focused on finance is the UN PRI. Signatories to the principles make six commitments (Figure 7.2), but they also represent a network, coordinated by the UNEP Finance Initiative and the UN Global Compact, working together to put the principles into practice. There are currently more than 900 signatories to the Principles including many of the largest pension funds, and different types of investment manager such as BlackRock, Nomura Asset Management, and AXA Private Equity.

As part of its mission to improve the practice of responsible investment, the PRI has launched or acquired a number of capacity building initiatives. The Enhanced Analytics Initiative, for example, was launched in 2004 by major buy-side clients including pension funds to incentivize analysts to produce better research on the less tangible performance indicators associated with sustainability. It was incorporated into the PRI in 2008, and now exists under the PRI Enhanced Research Portal.[17]

Carbon Disclosure Project

Arguably, at least as influential on the financial community as the aforementioned initiatives has been the Carbon Disclosure Project (CDP). Established as an independent NGO in 2003, it asks companies to measure and disclose their GHG emissions, water management, and climate change strategies as the basis for establishing reduction targets and improving performance. These data are primarily for institutional investors, and CDP claims they are used by over 500 investors with over US$71 trillion under management. They are also used by companies such as Dell and Walmart as well as governments and civil society organizations.

The CDP is simple but seemingly effective. It asks companies about their emissions (and more recently their use of water), and makes this information available to the buy side and others in ways that enable users to leverage their influence to get companies to improve performance. In 2010, 3000 companies reported, including 82 per cent of the Global 500 and 70 per cent of the S&P 500.[18]

⬛ **Discussion points**

In the light of what we have discussed, consider the following.

● What is the significance of the discussed initiatives in influencing the investment community?

● Please describe and comment on the Global Reporting Initiative. What are its merits and limitations?

● In terms of financing sustainability, is it a mistake to concentrate on public equities and private equity rather than other asset classes?

Sustainable investing

Since the mid-1960s, retail funds have been available to allow private investors to invest according to ethical principles. Over time, these have grown into the field called socially responsible investment (SRI), although in this sense 'social' can also include environmental and governance issues. Various political events such as the Vietnam War and apartheid in South Africa boosted this movement as investors sought to divest themselves of shares for ethical or non-financial reasons. Today, concern about the different aspects of sustainability are providing another of these boosts, and one can discern a shift from concerns about tainted money (i.e. capital allocated to unethical or socially and environmentally harmful businesses) to finding ways of deploying capital to address major societal challenges. Some people now use SRI as an abbreviation for 'sustainable and responsible investment', but some talk about a separate field known as 'sustainable investing'.

Sustainable investing recognizes the social, environmental, and governance goals of SRI generally, but stresses the need for patterns of finance and investment focused on long-term value creation, sustaining natural as well as financial assets, and a needs-based orientation to financial innovation that serves the poor. Underlying sustainable investing are two claims: one, that fully incorporating long-term social and environmental trends will deliver superior risk-adjusted returns; two, that global sustainability of the kind discussed in Chapters 1 and 2 requires the mobilization and recasting of the world capital markets. For some it is entirely distinct from SRI because while ethically motivated investors' decisions are affected by the societal consequences of business, sustainable investment is built on the premise that sustainably managed enterprises are better able to add value over the long term.[19] The former is highly subjective (i.e. what values are given priority), and taken to its logical conclusion could be an argument for business as usual if one believed (as many do) that 'the business of business is business' is a strong moral position in itself. Values-derived SRI may be profoundly attractive to some for ethical reasons, but it is not underpinned by an encompassing financial discipline. Moreover, it is often defensive: the avoidance of certain companies and industries as if to demonstrate that—in defiance of modern portfolio theory—it is possible to build efficient investment portfolios despite excluding parts of the investment universe.

In contrast, it is argued, sustainable investing positively seeks to invest in companies with practices and policies aligned to sustainability goals, not because of ideological reasons, but because the best investments are companies that adhere to long-term drivers of performance, i.e. companies that exhibit superior sustainability. This is a powerful argument (although its persuasiveness hinges in part on an investor's beliefs), and one that gains force from (a) the uncertainty about conventional financial analysis and innovation that is the fallout from the 2008–2009 financial crisis, and (b) the apparent flood of investment opportunities emerging from addressing climate change (e.g. alternative energy, energy reduction, low carbon construction, geoengineering). However, as we return to later, there is a need for caution; both because of the interpretation and reliability of the historical data produced to support the thesis that sustainable investing outperforms conventional investment, and because the analytical and predictive tools needed to deal with sustainability are only in their infancy. Without a stronger basis for accounting for the past, and for predicting the future, extrapolating too much from a narrow range of companies and industries associated with tackling climate change could be as mistaken as the over-investment SRI fund managers made in IT and health stocks in the late 1990s when their funds eventually slumped and underperformed the market.

Types of sustainable investing strategy

There are several different strategies used to help investors leverage their power so that companies tackle sustainability issues (Figure 7.3), and this section reviews the main ones used today. Screening has a long and venerable history in SRI, and has become part of sustainable investing. Religious groups have long limited their investment universe by avoiding industries and activities that offend their moral principles. It is a pre-investment stage question that asks if a company is engaging in business practices that support or go against the investor's social, ethical, or environmental principles. Individual and institutional investors take different approaches to answering this question, and to determining which companies are therefore 'responsible'.

Negative screening

'Negative' screening eliminates from an investment portfolio companies that are engaging in what are perceived to be negative business or environmental practices. In conventional SRI the most commonly applied social screens were tobacco, alcohol, and gambling, but in sustainable investing negative screens could include nuclear power, coal, and oil and gas. It includes 'norms-based' screening, a variation on negative screening which involves monitoring corporate compliance with internationally accepted norms, such as the Millennium Development Goals, the International Labour Organization core conventions, or the UN Global Compact. Like other negative screening it is used to eliminate specific risks to the portfolio, and to communicate with the general public and corporate members on the ethics of the organization. Because the screen itself makes an ethical statement, it might also be used to guard the reputation of the investor.

The risk associated with negative screening is the possibility of biasing the geographic or sector allocation of the investment portfolio. As noted earlier, screened SRI funds appeared to outperform conventional ones in the late 1990s but this was because they were overexposed to IT and health stocks which subsequently dropped in value at the turn of the decade. Equally, anti-ethically screened funds such as the Vice Fund (VICEX) have outperformed the S&P 500 for significant periods, but are now struggling to return to their 2005 value following

Style	Overview
Negative screening—ethical	Avoiding companies/industries on moral grounds
Negative screening—environmental or social	Avoiding companies/industries because of their social or environmental practices
Norms-based screening	Avoiding companies because of non-compliance with international standards
Positive screening	Active inclusion of companies because of social and environmental factors
Extra-financial best in class	Active inclusion of companies that lead their sectors in social/environmental performance
Financially-weighted best in class	Active inclusion of companies that outperform their sector peers on financially material social/environmental criteria
Community investing	Allocating capital directly to enterprises and projects based on their societal contributions
Sustainability themes	Selecting companies on the basis of sustainability factors (e.g. renewable energy)
Blended value investing	Active allocation based on a blend of financial and social/environmental return on investment
Engagement	Dialogue between investors and company management to improve management of environmental, social, and governance issues
Shareholder activism	Using shareholder rights to pressure companies to change environmental, social and governance practices
Integrated analysis	Active inclusion of environmental and social factors within conventional fund management

Figure 7.3 Different styles associated with sustainable investing.

Sources: Adapted from (Krosinsky 2008, Lydenberg 2005, Sparkes 2002) the latest major financial crisis. I discuss performance later in this chapter, but one needs to be cautious about leaping to conclusions on screened fund performance.

Positive screening

Unlike negative screening, a particular industry is not excluded from positively screened portfolios. Rather, 'positive' screening is the selection of investments that perform best against corporate governance, social, environmental, or ethical criteria, and which support sustainability. Positive screening is associated with a 'triple bottom-line' investment approach, ensuring that a company performs well according to financial, social, and environmental criteria. 'Best-in-class' screening is one such strategy, which selects the best performing companies within a given sector of investments, while 'pioneer' screening chooses the best-performing company against one specific criterion.

Examples of positive screens might include: improvement of health and safety conditions; integration of environmental criteria into the purchasing process; prevention of corruption; elimination of child labour; promotion of social and economic development. Such screens have the advantage of encouraging companies to improve extra-financial performance irrespective of their industry, but they can be problematic. There is the challenge of how to measure performance in a robust, replicable manner, and professional organizations such as the Certified Financial Analysts Institute are only starting to find ways to incorporate this into their certification and career development programmes. More fundamentally, there is the question of whether such screens result in significantly different investment portfolios. Benson, Brailsford, and Humphrey (2006) found that SRI mutual funds were virtually no different to mainstream ones, reinforcing Hawken's (2004) conclusion that SRI fund managers were no less likely than conventional ones to put financial returns ahead of trying to combat social injustice or environmental degradation.

In practice, funds may offer a mix of positive and negative screens. BankInvest Global Emerging Markets SRI, an emerging market equity fund, was one of the pioneers. Its negative screen excludes companies that have continuing violations of human rights, the environment, and labour rights, and those that derive more than 10 per cent of turnover from war material, alcoholic beverages, gambling, tobacco, or three per cent from pornography. The positive screen rewards the best and fast movers, and companies that have a high score in supporting human rights, labour standards, the environment, and corporate governance. The first investor in this fund was Mistra, the foundation for strategic environmental research, that is based in Sweden and which manages its assets in a socially responsible way. Some 80 per cent of its capital of SEK3.6 billion is invested on the basis of environmental and ethical criteria.

⊙ **Discussion points**

Values-based investing strategies require consideration of ethical, moral, ESG issues.

- What is the difference between SRI and sustainable investing?
- What are some initiatives that try to ensure that companies are disclosing their social or environmental business practices, so that investors can make an accurate assessment?
- What do investors expect from values-based investments and how might their expectations differ from those of traditional investments?

Engagement

Screening and the use of sustainability indexes (see 'Indexes') are strategies used at the pre-investment stage. Another set of strategies arise at the post-investment stage. Engagement is the process by means of which investors become involved with the business to influence its activities, behaviours, and operations. This section discusses some of these engagement strategies, including shareholder activism, proxy voting, policy statements, and engaging at different levels.

Engagement occurs in response to the company's approach to sustainability. Other issues that might be cause for concern include the company's overall performance, internal controls, compliance, or general business practices, and responsible investors may raise these matters. Innovest go as far as to claim that a company's approach to sustainability is a key indicator of good management, and have developed a matrix for assessing this.[20]

Shareholder activism

Shareholder activism includes activities that are undertaken in the belief that investors and shareholders can work together with management to change course and to improve financial performance over time. These activities can be conducted privately or publicly. Private methods might include letters to other shareholders, or to company management, to raise concerns. Institutional investors might raise issues during their routine meetings with company managers, or communicate their concerns to other investors to build pressure on the company; they might even join forces with other like-minded investors to take subsequent public actions. Public mechanisms for shareholder advocacy include raising questions during annual general meetings, or calling an extraordinary general meeting to propose shareholder resolutions. Investors might also issue press statements, or arrange briefings to make their reservations known to the wider international community of investors.

It is difficult to quantify the degree and effectiveness of shareholder activism because some of it is public and some of it behind the scenes. There are examples such as the nuns who threatened a shareholder resolution at a GE AGM about pollution of the Hudson River where activists have affected corporate behaviour. There are also famous individual and institutional activists such as CalPERS, Robert Monks, and John Bogle who have fought for more shareholder power, not least in the arena of governance. Hermes has made a name for itself in sustainability-related activism (Snapshot 7.1). But overall, given the primacy accorded to shareholders by law, company owners have not had the huge influence on extra-financial issues that one might have expected. Even companies with a strong stance on particular social or environmental issues may lack a clear sustainability policy for their pension funds, although the emergence of groups such as the P8 (see 'Different types of capital') suggest that this might be changing.

Proxy voting

To understand the relative paucity of shareholder activism, one only needs to look at proxy voting. At a company's annual general meeting, shareholders are given the opportunity to vote on a number of issues on the agenda. Following major corporate scandals such as

Enron, AIG, and RBS, more shareholders are beginning to understand the importance and relevance of their voting and active participation. Usually, proxy voting applies to issues of corporate governance and, by voting against the mandatory approval of annual accounts and reports, investors register their protest against company practices. Leading sustainability issues that are likely to be the focus of attention include climate change, environmental reporting, and corporate political contributions.

 Discussion points

Please review the preceding section on 'Engagement'.

● As a private investor, what are some of the ways in which you might make others aware of your concerns about a company's sustainability practices?

● As a fund manager, how might you communicate to the company your concerns about its business practices?

● What are some of the ways in which you think international investors might better coordinate on their engagement efforts, either as institutions or as members of organizations such as the UN Global Compact?

Sustainability capital initiatives

In addition to the initiatives aimed at encouraging the inclusion of sustainability factors into investment decisions (see 'Current initiatives') and the strategies associated with sustainable investing (see 'Sustainable investing'), there are initiatives seeking to make capital available for sustainability-related investments specifically. The four discussed next are environmental venture capital, alternative finance vehicles, the clean development mechanism, and green investment banks.

Environmental venture capital

We have already noted that sustainability creates a demand for different types of capital, from large-scale investments in infrastructure to small, early-stage investments in new technologies (see 'Importance of the financial markets'). At the early-stage end, transformation to a low carbon economy has created a significant demand for capital in areas such as alternative energy, geoengineering, and green buildings. Part of this demand is served by 'environmental venture capital', or 'cleantech' which looks at investment opportunities in entrepreneurial environmental projects and companies that will reap financial, social, and environmental rewards for the investors. Opportunities for these investments include sustainable energy technologies, such as renewable energy, transportation, and distributed generation of power. The size of some of these initiatives means that much of the capital will have to be raised from conventional financial markets and from government-backed bonds. Certainly, some of the immediate investment needs such as nuclear power and an energy distribution system matched to the specifics of alternative energy are not suited to venture capital. Nonetheless, in 2009 venture investors put $5.6 billion into cleantech start-ups based in North America, Europe, China and India, and although this was down about 33 per cent on 2008 this was due to global economic decline rather than loss of faith in the technology. Furthermore, green technology is an important part of the recent economic stimulus packages in some countries. For example, South Korea, the European Union, and China have allocated 81 per cent, 59 per cent, and 31 per cent of their respective stimulus packages to green investment (US$31 billion, US$23 billion, and US$221 billion).[21]

There are a multitude of renewable projects presently active in the USA and in Europe. Germany has been a leader in developing wind power, with some German states sourcing more than more than 1,800 megawatts of their power from wind. To date, solar and wind power have attracted the most investment dollars, while other experimental technologies are being tested, such as biomass—producing electrical power from agricultural crops—and photovoltaics—producing electricity from sunlight (Chapter 6).

Cleantech investors expect both high environmental and financial returns. Fluctuations in oil prices, global concerns about water supplies, and an attention to fossil-fuel dependency have inspired both technological innovation and entrepreneurs looking to build enterprises to address the environmental challenges. Cleantech investors are supporting this new wave of innovation. There is, however, also evidence of caution, because investment dollars deployed in cleantech have fluctuated and decreased at times, owing to the high risk involved with the development of new technology.

Alternative investment vehicles

This is a catch-all heading for an array of relatively recent, innovative approaches to financing that increasingly have a sustainability element. Community Development Investing began as finance to generate resources and opportunities for economically disadvantaged people in urban and rural communities who are under-served by traditional financial institutions. Community-level sustainability initiatives such as Low Carbon West Oxford and Zerowaste (New Zealand) have created a demand for similar investment for a wider range of projects. Community Development Investment funds deploy equity and equity-like investments into small businesses in geographic areas that are traditionally overlooked by venture capital and private equity funds. Other development investment funds pool together investors, such as banks, corporations, insurers, foundations, and public pension funds, to provide support that can enable the provision of affordable housing, education, community centres, and small businesses.

Microcredit is another vehicle that has been linked to the poverty aspect of sustainability (Chapter 2). The fundamental idea is to make money available to the poor, based on terms and conditions that are appropriate and reasonable. The concept emerged out of initiatives in the 1970s by organizations, such as Accion International and the Grameen Bank, which wanted to provide economic opportunity to poor people looking to start small businesses. Traditional banks were not interested in making small loans to what were considered 'the unbankable' (i.e. people without collateral), so a system of community banking was set up, under which small informal groups (called 'solidarity groups' within the Grameen Bank) were formed. Their collateral was the social networks these savers and borrowers formed so that loans were effectively guaranteed by a combination of peer pressure and social cohesion. Women's groups in particular proved successful, and loan repayment far exceeded the normal percentage in traditional banking.

Originally the brainchild of NGOs, microcredit is now offered by mainstream banks such as Deutsche Bank and Standard Chartered. However, it is not an unalloyed success. A little money can support the development of a one-person business or the beginnings of a small shop, for example, but scaling up the business to the next level is not always easy when further financial support is needed. If one looks at a country such as Bangladesh where microcredit is the main form of banking, the signs that it has lifted people out of poverty (e.g. growth in incomes or GDP) are not obvious. This may be due to the entrenched nature of poverty, and microcredit could be as much a strategy for survival as a means of growth. Moreover, in the drive to scale up microcredit, there is evidence from around the world that the solidarity group based model has been increasingly bypassed in favour of direct loans to borrowers. Interest rates are also often very high compared to other formal moneylending. This may make the lending organizations more viable, but it raises questions about the social impact and how microcredit is ultimately different from traditional banks other than in the size of their loans.[22]

Clean Development Mechanism, REDD, and offtake contracts

Offtake contracts have become a feature of climate change finance. Under these, emitters of GHGs enter into contracts with those demonstrably reducing or abating pollution. The CDM is one of the earliest examples of this having been set up under the Kyoto Protocol (Chapter 6). Its aim is to incentivize advanced economy investment in low carbon technologies and activities in developing economies (known as Annex 1 countries in the language of the protocol). When an investment is made in technologies or activities that demonstrably reduce or sequester emissions, the investor receives credits (Certified Emissions Reductions) that can be used to meet advanced economies' emissions targets. CDM projects are open to public and private investors.

There are various requirements that need to be met for a project to be considered CDM-valid, and there have been criticisms that the system works against the needs of the poorest countries. Nonetheless, it is estimated that by 2012 1.5 billion CO_2e will have been removed due to CDM projects, and could generate up to US$24 billion in direct revenues.[23]

Until now, CDM projects have needed to be new projects, and credits cannot be issued for existing activities, even if they have climate change benefits. This has been particularly controversial in relation to standing forests that are essential to absorb CO_2, but not recognized under the CDM. Annex 1 countries such as Brazil and Indonesia, both with large standing forests, have protested about this, asking might it not better financially for a forest community to tear down its forests and put up a hydro-power facility because the latter would be eligible for CDM investment. However, despite the absence of a formally regulated market, voluntary carbon credits for the conservation and reforestation of forests have been created. Merrill Lynch, for example, announced in 2008 that it had reached an agreement with the government of Aceh, a province of Indonesia, which would see US$9 million invested over a four-year period to help protect the 750,000-hectare Ulu Masen forest (Case study 7).

Ulu Masen is an example of Reducing Carbon Emissions from Deforestation and Forest Degradation (REDD) schemes. For the past decade investors have been able to enter into offtake contracts whereby they put money into the regeneration of forests and avoided deforestation in return for credits. However, these 'voluntary' credits have not had the same status as those from CDM projects. That situation may well change as a result of the ongoing renegotiation of climate change protocols. Once Kyoto expires, it is hoped that REDD projects will generate credits that can be more easily traded on formal markets as part of what is being called REDD+.

Green investment banks

The idea of special banks investing only in greening the economy has been talked about for several years. Typically, their inspiration has been the state-owned specialized finance institutions that have a long tradition around the world as an effective way of stimulating investment in specific public policies, or responding to emergencies. In France, Caisse de Dépôts et Consignations (CDC), which dates back to the Napoleonic era, has used its position in mobilizing long-term savings for social housing to provide low-interest energy efficiency loans for the social housing sector. It works closely with the OSEO Group, a government-backed entity that provides long-term financing through government-backed bond issues and other means. OSEO itself was modelled on the German KfW, a government-owned financial institution with its origins in the Marshall Plan after the Second World War, and which now is heavily involved in climate change investments.[24]

In 2010, the British government announced the creation of the first new green investment bank, promising £3 billion of state-funding by 2015. However, it will not be able to borrow from capital markets until 2015, and that is conditional upon the strength of the UK's economic recovery. If successful, it will remove some of the risk in investing in low carbon economy projects, offer innovative finance mechanisms, and bridge capital gaps. The bank's current focus is only on climate change, but in order to be a significant contributor to the transformation to a low carbon economy it will need to generate a major part of the £750 billion the government believes is necessary to invest by 2030.[25]

Performance

There is a long-standing and ongoing argument about whether incorporating sustainability criteria into investment decisions is harmful or not to investors. A number of arguments have been made as to why environmental, social, or even governance issues should not be factored into investment decisions (Figure 7.4). One of the most persistent of these is investments that take into consideration sustainability factors perform less well than others. One way to compare company performance with and without sustainability factored into it is to look at the various indices available. An analysis of 29 SRI indices (not investment funds), found that they did not exhibit a different risk-adjusted return to that of conventional benchmarks.[26] In other words, there was no significant difference in SRI and conventional index performance. Separating sustainable investing from SRI, Krosinsky (2008) concludes that sustainability-oriented funds outperform values-based investments. The latter underperform or at best are comparable to mainstream indices depending on what time horizon one uses; the former outperform the mainstream irrespective of the time period being compared. Moreover, sustainable investing funds have not only outperformed values-based ones, but also even the best of the mainstream indices (18.7 per cent versus 17 per cent for 2002–2007).

The most recent analysis, covering the 2008 Western stock market crash, shows that sustainable investing funds lost slightly less of their value in 2008, produced net positive returns over the 2003–2008 period (compared to a net loss on the mainstream indices), and outperformed mainstream indices in the first half of 2009 (Figure 7.5).

Other studies have found there is no firm correlation between extra-financial factors and investment performance,[27] and a review of 16 academic and broker studies concluded that there was a positive correlation between fund performance and attention to extra-financial issues in 38 per cent of cases, and a neutral correlation in 44 per cent.[28]

Despite such evidence, there is continuing criticism of including sustainability in investment analysis. Advocates of sustainability investment have been guilty of over-emphasizing the positive, preferring to highlight the funds with five-year returns of 50 or 60 per cent, and turning a blind eye to shorter-term returns that might only be three per cent or lower.[29] For example, a

1. Sustainability factors are irrelevant or damaging to risk-adjusted financial returns.
2. Attention to sustainability factors could run contrary to fiduciary duty.
3. Research does not support the argument that sustainability and good performance are interconnected.
4. Sustainability analysis is less rigorous than conventional investment analysis.

Figure 7.4 Arguments against integrating sustainability considerations into investment decisions.

Sources: Kiernan 2009; Krosinsky 2008; Robins 2008.

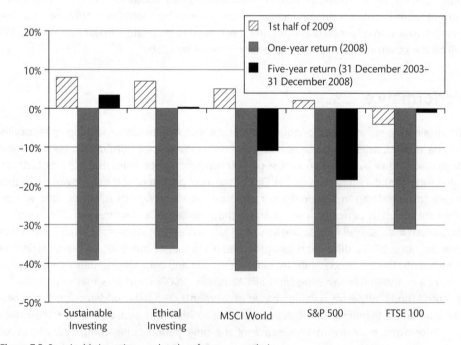

Figure 7.5 Sustainable investing–updated performance analysis.

Source: Krosinsky & Robins, original unpublished research, 2011.

comparison in late 2007 of the Winslow Green Growth Fund (WGGF), a Morningstar five-star rated fund with an aggressive growth policy focused on small growth companies that have a positive or neutral environmental impact, with Berkshire Hathaway (BRK-A), investment sage Warren Buffett's holding company, would have found that the latter grew by 100 per cent in the preceding five years, but the sustainable investing fund grew by 200 per cent. However, from 2008 onwards, BRK-A consistently outperformed WGGF: as of April 2010 it had delivered roughly 90 per cent growth on 2003, compared to WGGF's approximately 60 per cent.

Another commonly voiced argument against including sustainability in investment analysis is that the tools are insufficiently robust. Much of what we know about sustainability is about what has happened and why, and therefore falls within the explicative concerns of accounting. Analysis, in contrast, is predictive, so that, for instance, financial analysis—no matter how imperfectly—allows one to forecast future flows in order to obtain the net present value. In the case of sustainable investing, for example, an analyst would want to integrate ESG factors into financial valuation tools, but while as we have seen throughout this book there are plenty of ideas about how such factors are material to companies, their incorporation into areas such as risk analysis is not yet commonplace.[30] Equally, companies are not always aware of what investors are interested in when it comes to sustainability, and the sustainability reports that are often cited by companies as a sign of their commitment may be irrelevant for investment decision-making.[31]

Kiernan (2009), however, lays the blame firmly at the feet of the finance community. He argues that those involved in investment decisions are deluding themselves that the tools they currently use are sophisticated and robust, and are demanding a standard of excellence from sustainability—in terms of performance and analysis—that is far beyond anything required in conventional accounting-driven investment analysis. Moreover, the latter is still held up as best practice despite evidence that it is increasingly unable to capture the actual risk profile or value potential of companies.[32] Yet by omitting sustainability factors, this type of analysis could be ignoring factors fundamental to the risk and value of a firm. Until this is recognized, it puts at jeopardy the 'efficient markets hypothesis' (EMH) that underpins investor behaviour. EMH assumes that information is available to all market participants, and if it is material it is accurately and promptly incorporated into market prices. However, if factors such as sustainability are material but are not being incorporated because of the practices and mindsets of financial experts, then the very idea that markets are accurately valuing companies is questionable.

 Snapshot 7.2 Investing for Good—impact investing

Investing for Good (IFG) was founded in 2005 by Geoff Burnand and Caroline Mason to meet a growing need for investment advice and market information in the impact investing space. Inspired by a new breed of entrepreneurial organizations that directly tackled the world's most pressing problems, IFG realized that financial advisors, financial intermediaries and asset managers lacked the capacity to advise appropriately on social investing deals. In response, IFG was founded to focus on the emerging asset class of impact investments, a niche market where investments were made in companies that delivered positive social and environmental impact as their core goal. IFG supports investment advisors and mainstream asset managers that offered foundations and high-net-worth individuals access to this newly emerging market.

(continued)

Social investing is a broad term that refers to investments that consider social and environmental issues. It includes investments made with the intention of having a positive impact, investments that exclude 'harmful' activities, and even investments that are driven by investors' values and do not necessarily correspond to having a positive social or environmental impact. Social investing covers a range of possible investment combinations depending on the extent of financial return desired, risk appetite and social/environmental mission: these include philanthropy, impact investing, and socially responsible investing. Impact investing refers only to the social investing that actively seeks to have a positive impact. It represents investments for financial return in companies or projects that have social and/or environmental benefit as their core goal. Investments that promote energy efficiency provide credit to rural farmers or test drugs that would mainly benefit the poor exemplify impact investing: investments seeking both social and financial return.

Impact investing, as distinct from either market-rate investing or philanthropy, can leverage economic performance while also creating social and/or environmental value within a single, unified approach to investing. It is, by definition, a market-based approach to addressing many of the challenges facing the global community and seeks to engage capital in creating sustainable, long-term solutions to those same challenges. Such strategies are defined as 'blended value' since they view the value being created as neither solely economic nor solely social/environmental, but a blend of both. This approach recognizes that economic value can create various forms of social and environmental impact and cannot be viewed as a separate component of the value proposition found within any given investment. Therefore, it seeks not a multiple bottom-line (*pace* triple bottom-line), but rather a single bottom-line with multiple value components.

Questions

1. What are the unique features of impact investing?

2. What services does IFG offer investors?

3. What is distinctive about blended value strategies?

Challenges

Taking into consideration the low starting point, the knowledge and practice associated with financing sustainability has come a long way in a relatively short space of time. Sustainability has become a central and vibrant part of values-based investing with the influential industry organization UK Social Investment Forum now defining its mission as advancing *sustainable development* through financial services. Sustainable investing builds upon, but is trying to go beyond, the SRI niche by making the case that sustainability is not a value that is an optional part of an investor's portfolio, but is a determinant of the prosperous firm for the foreseeable future. It is aided by the existence of high-profile initiatives such as UN PRI, the Carbon Disclosure Project, and the International Integrated Reporting Committee, none of which are more than ten years old. Major investment banks, accountants, retail banks, and financial managers such as Goldman Sachs, PwC, HSBC, and State Street all have operations focused on sustainability. Although many proponents of greater integration of sustainability into finance are frustrated at the speed of progress, the advancements listed above are relatively impressive compared to the ones made over a similar period in fields such as sustainability marketing (Chapter 5) and alternative accounting.

Nonetheless, the arguments that sustainability protagonists find so compelling still fall on deaf ears amongst much of the financial community. One commonly cited reason for this is that sustainability factors are material in the medium to long term whereas much investment activity is short term. Sustainable investing advocates are keen to emphasize the importance of time horizons in evaluating fund performance and investment strategies. In part, this is because the high turnover of stocks in mainstream funds is blamed for investors' disinterest in extra-financial dimensions of business performance, and the disconnect between corporations and their owners. But there is also evidence that funds with a low turnover (i.e. their portfolios change every three to five years) exhibit stronger performance.[33]

Irrespective of any time horizon, however, successful investing depends on an accurate valuation of the investee, and there is evidence that in a sustainability context investors are measuring the wrong things. Campanale and Leggett (2011), for example, have calculated that the fossil fuel reserves held by the top 100 listed coal companies and top 100 listed oil and gas companies represent potential GHG emissions of 745 GtCO$_2$. If all of these reserves were used, the resultant emissions would take the world 180 GtCO$_2$ over its remaining carbon budget (Chapters 1 and 2). 'This means that using just the listed proportion of reserves in the next 40 years is enough to take us beyond 2°C of global warming' (Campanale and Leggett (2011, p. 2). Moreover, further oil, gas, and coal resources are held by states as well as non-listed companies. It is possible that once all of these other sources are factored in, listed companies will only be able to use 20 per cent of their reserves. If that were the case, then investors would be exposed to the risk that a major part of the value of these companies could never be realized because if they were it could result in catastrophic climate change.

However, for as long as investors base their decisions on inaccurate information, and this goes unpunished because of the short-term nature of contemporary markets, then progress on financing sustainability will be incremental and run the risk of becoming a niche interest. One way of resolving this would be the introduction of new regulatory regimes, but if the history of the evolution of corporate governance is used as a historical comparison, such change would be slow and filled with compromise.[34] Furthermore, although there has been considerable activity around the rethinking of financial markets in the latter part of the 2000s, sustainability's concerns with short-termism, and the inadequacies of the efficient market hypothesis and accounting-driven analysis have not been a feature of any reforms. On the contrary, the financial crisis that prompted changes in regulation has bolstered belief in market portfolio theory, and the need to avoid overexposure in any asset class or investment vehicle. For as long as sustainability is considered an extra-financial consideration rather than something integral to company valuation, the screening for sustainability factors will always be seen as opposed to the creation of a balanced portfolio.

We have already noted another challenge, the need for the right types of capital for different sustainability investments (see 'Different types of capital'). Much of the thinking about financing sustainability has focused on public equities and private equity which for the most part is synonymous with incumbent industries and large companies. Green venture capital has been held out as a way of helping early-stage companies, but the venture capital markets in the USA and Europe have shrunk in recent years. Add to this the large sums of cash held by major companies that are holding back on investment due to global economic uncertainty, the increasingly large reserves banks are obliged to hold, and the sovereign wealth funds investing in advanced economy national debt, then the likelihood of significant investment gaps increases further. In addition, in the wealthiest economies there are ageing populations dependent on their pensions and social security for an enjoyable old age. This is a wealthy demographic segment but not one that has an appetite for risk. The pension funds may need higher returns on investment to meet their commitments to longer-living members, but they are by nature risk averse, and forays in pursuit of alpha to try to fill deficits have only drawn criticism.[35] It is easy to make the case that pension funds by their sheer size have a vital role to play in financing sustainability, but it remains to be seen whether their own investors (i.e. pension fund contributors) will allow them to do this.

There are, of course, rapidly growing savings pools in emerging economies that could be harnessed to finance sustainability. However, this brings out another contradiction. Economists around the world are calling for emerging economies to save less and spend more in order to revitalize the global economy and stimulate growth. As discussed elsewhere (Chapter 3), economic growth and sustainability are uneasy bedfellows, but at the present time the largest economies are begging for growth irrespective of what this might do to emissions, resource depletion, and biodiversity. Furthermore, the growth they seek is the same kind as dominated in the past in which any adverse impact on society and the environment was treated as an externality. For those who saw the 2008 financial crisis as an opportunity to shift to a sustainability focus, the irony is that the failure of the financial system they consider unsustainable has been given a new lease of life by its own excesses.

 ## Summary

Finance is the oxygen of capitalism, and sustainability does not alter this fact. Addressing the sustainability challenges outlined in other chapters requires huge amounts of capital, but from the financial markets' perspective they are just some of the opportunities available to investors. A relatively thriving segment of sustainability funds has emerged backed by sustainability indexes and analysis. This has a lot in common with SRI, and many of the strategies developed as part of SRI are employed for sustainability ends. However, many of those who have pushed for more attention to be paid to sustainability in investing make a more fundamental claim: sustainability is not just a values-based decision, but concerns factors that are determinants of companies' long-term prosperity and success.

Although sustainability is relevant across all asset classes, advocates of sustainable investing have concentrated mostly on public equities and to a degree private equity and venture capital. They have argued, and made a strong evidence-based case for sustainability factors to be fundamental to the valuation of the firm. In a relatively short period of time, a number of international initiatives have been established to enable sustainability to be integrated into investment decision-making, and major institutions such as pension funds are collaborating on how to bring about change.

Nonetheless, there is considerable resistance to change, and arguments are commonly made that treating sustainability as central to investment decisions is harmful, a breach of fiduciary duty, contradictory to portfolio theory, or is already factored into valuations. In part as a result of this, but also because of troubles in the global economy, there are few signs that the huge amounts of capital needed to make a successful transformation to a prosperous resource-constrained economy will be available in the short or even medium term. This raises questions not only about the financing of sustainability initiatives, but also the valuation of firms with the greatest exposure to sustainability risk.

Further reading

Davis, S.M., Lukomnik, J., & Pitt-Watson, D. 2006, *The new capitalists: How citizen investors are reshaping the corporate agenda*, Harvard Business School Press, Boston, MA.

Arguments from investment professionals about the increasingly strong role of normal savers with pensions and life insurance in influencing the behaviour of corporations.

Hudson, J. 2006, *The social responsibility of the investment profession*, Research Foundation of CFA Institute, Charlottesville, VA.

An introduction to social responsibility from a financial analyst's perspective.

Krosinsky, C. & Robins, N. 2008, *Sustainable investing: The art of long-term performance*, Earthscan, London.

Prominent professionals from the sustainable investment world examine the case for sustainable investing, and how it differs from SRI.

Louche, C. & Lydenberg, S.D. 2011, *Dilemmas in responsible investment*, Greenleaf Publishing, Sheffield.

An introduction for investment professionals on how to invest to achieve positive social and environmental impacts.

Sullivan, R. 2011, *Valuing corporate responsibility: How do investors really use corporate responsibility information?*, Greenleaf Publishing, Sheffield.

An explanation of investment professionals' reasoning to people managing corporate responsibility issues; and an explanation of corporate responsibility professionals' reasoning to people making investment decisions.

 Case study 7   Merrill Lynch—carbon farming in the rainforests

Rain forests play a key role in maintaining the world's environmental balance, their trees and plants soaking up CO_2 through photosynthesis. Nine million hectares of rainforest are lost each year when they are cleared by fire for alternate use. These fires account for about 20 per cent of the world's CO_2 emissions—more than the total from all vehicles, airplanes and ships. Such fires make Indonesia—the world's 22nd largest economy—the third-largest emitter of CO_2 after the USA and China.

Curbing forest destruction is gaining more attention as a strategy to combat climate change. The Kyoto Protocol, the global treaty intended to cap GHG emissions, allows companies to earn the right to pollute by funding emission-reducing projects in developing nations. Credits to pollute are traded around the world, and major buyers include heavy-emitting companies in Europe and Japan, which are subject to Kyoto-related emission caps. Currently, the treaty allows companies to generate credits by planting new trees, but does not reward them for preserving existing trees. However, in the debate about Kyoto's successor, there is increasing talk of changing the rules to permit tradable emission credits derived from forest-preservation, or what is called 'avoided deforestation'.

In February 2008, Merrill Lynch announced it had reached an agreement with the government of Aceh, a province of Indonesia, that would see US$9 million invested over a four-year period to help protect the 750,000-hectare Ulu Masen forest. But this was no philanthropic gesture on the part of the Bank of America-owned Wall Street investment bank. On the contrary, the agreement marked Merrill's first entrance into the market for carbon credits derived from 'avoided deforestation'. If the people of Aceh reduced logging of the forest to a verifiably sustainable level, then Merrill would buy US$2 million worth of credits a year (with an option to buy US$1 million more). The money would be made available for community development projects so that people are no longer dependent on illegal logging and converting forests into farmland. In return, investors would receive credits based on how much CO_2 would have been emitted if the forests had been burned.

(continued)

Ulu Masen is an example of a REDD project, a still somewhat contentious element of the emissions trading system. If successful, the environmental NGO Flora and Fauna International that set up the project reckons it will reduce deforestation in Ulu Masen by 85 per cent through a combination of forest guards, community conservation, and social development projects. As well as the revenue from the voluntary carbon market, income will be generated through the development and marketing of specially labelled 'Aceh Green' forest products such as sustainable palm oil, coffee, and cacao.

From the investor's perspective, each credit represents a ton of carbon dioxide that is prevented from entering the atmosphere. Merrill Lynch has agreed to buy credits at the fixed price of four dollars each, and is betting that the price in the voluntary market—which has ranged US$2–20—will increase. For Merrill Lynch, success depends equally on growth in demand for credits from REDD projects, and the credibility/quality of the credits it has to offer.

Regarding market demand, Abyd Karmali, global head of Carbon Emissions at Merrill Lynch, says he expects to see strong demand from customers because the Ulu Masen credits deliver a number of benefits in addition to carbon emission reductions. 'Merrill Lynch's thesis on the carbon market is that the days of vanilla credits [that simply deliver emission reductions] are nearing an end', he says. 'Companies will be looking for credits that deliver more benefits, and the Aceh project is a prime example of this approach – there are five endangered species in this region that will benefit from biodiversity protection while the income will also aid development in an area badly affected by the 2004 tsunami.'

It is too early to talk about outcomes from such a recent initiative. Success is by no means guaranteed, and there are a variety of factors that will ultimately influence the project. Much depends on whether REDD-related credits are recognized under whatever agreement succeeds the Kyoto Protocol. While much attention will be paid to how much or little Merrill Lynch and others make from deals such as Ulu Masen, such projects could generate enormous sums for tropical forest conservation according to Johannes Ebeling, a senior consultant with emissions-credit developer EcoSecurities Group. He estimates that reducing the loss of forests by as little as ten per cent could generate as much as $13.5 billion a year for conservation. However, that is unlikely to happen until investors have some sort of a reliable framework to start investing, and while support for avoided deforestation is growing, the future is still uncertain.

Sources: Efstathiou 2008; Gunther 2008; Murray 2008; Wright 2007.

Questions

1. Ulu Masen was one of the first examples of a financial institution getting involved in a REDD scheme.

   a. What arguments do you think Abyd Karmali made to Merrill Lynch decision-makers to convince them of this investment opportunity?

   b. Is the role of NGOs in Ulu Masen a positive or negative feature?

   c. What other examples can you find of major companies investing in forest credits? How are these similar or different to Ulu Masen?

2. REDD projects have been controversial.

   a. Why are REDD-related credits marked down compared to those associated with CDM projects?

   b. Why has avoided deforestation historically not been viewed as having the same usefulness as reforestation and other CDM projects?

   c. What are the key features of REDD Plus which has a good chance of becoming part of any post-Kyoto climate change agreement?

3. Emissions credits are emerging as a new asset class.

   a. How large are the current markets for regulated and voluntary credits?

   b. What are the biggest threats to these markets?

   c. What kinds of service are companies working in this area offering to their clients?

Endnotes

1. (E.g. Kiernan 2006; Lydenberg 2005)

2. http://ussif.org/resources/sriguide/srifacts.cfm, accessed 16 September 2011.

3. http://www.unpri.org/publications/2011_report_on_progress_low_res.pdf, accessed 16 September 2011.

4. (Campanale & Leggett 2011)

5. (Sullivan 2011)

6. (Kiernan 2009, p. 3)

7. (Sandberg, Khan, & Leong 2010)

8. (Sandberg, Khan, & Leong 2010)

9. (IEA 2010b)

10. (Prins & Rayner 2007)

11. (Sandberg, Khan, & Leong 2010)

12. (Podmore 2009)

13. (Hawley & Williams 2000)

14. (Kiernan 2009). The trustees relented on the day the Principles were launched, but the World Bank's pension fund has still refused to endorse them—see http://www.unpri.org/signatories/, accessed 16 September 2011.

15. (Wood undated)

16. See http://www.responsibleproperty.net/ and http://www.unepfi.org/work_streams/property/. For information on the reduction of USS member benefits, see http://www.timeshighereducation.co.uk/story.asp?storycode=412540, accessed 22 September 2011.

17. http://www.unpri.org/research/. For more information on the lessons from the Enhanced Analytics Initiative, see http://www.unpri.org/research/Four%20years%20of%20the%20Enhanced%20Analytics%20Initaitive.pdf.

18. http://www.cdproject.net/en-US/Programmes/Pages/CDP-Investors.aspx, accessed 22 September 2011.

19. (Krosinsky & Robins 2008)

20. (Kiernan 2009)

21. Nick Robins presentation at London Business School, March 2010.

22. (Bateman 2010)

23. (World Bank 2010)

24. (Lecacheur 2010)

25. (Holmes & Mabey 2010)

26. (Schröder 2007)

27. (John 2006)

28. (Jewson Associates Research report on ethical investment for Oxford University 2008)

29. (Monitor 2009)

30. (Krosinsky & Robins 2008)

31. (Sullivan 2011)

32. (Litan & Wallison 2003)

33. (See, e.g. Kreander et al. 2005)

34. (See Blowfield & Murray 2008, chapter 7)

35. (Desai 2012)

8

Cooperation, collaboration, and partnership

 Key terms

Stakeholder management	Multi-stakeholder
Stakeholder engagement	Power
Partnerships	Supply chain collaboration
Co-governance	Pluralist purpose of the firm

 Online resources

- Additional business–NGO partnership case study.
- Supply chain partnership case study.
- Guidance on implementing partnerships.
- Links to resources on partnership.

  http://www.oxfordtextbooks.co.uk/orc/blowfield/

Chapter in brief

This chapter addresses partnerships and other forms of collaboration that have come to prominence because of the business–sustainability relationship. It begins by examining why partnerships have garnered attention, and then identifies the main types of collaboration that business engages in. Partnerships involve various arrays of stakeholders, and company perspectives are affected by whether they want to manage or engage with stakeholders. Stakeholder theory provides insights into the power relations that are a strong influence on how partnerships operate and what they can achieve. This is explored further with examples of inter-firm collaborations, supply chain partnerships, and multi-stakeholder partnerships in different regions of the world.

Key concept 8.1   Sustainability partnership

Partnerships can usefully be defined according to the sectors involved, their purpose, whether they are open-ended or for a fixed period, and the extent to which they are a way of managing stakeholders or a kind of ecosystem where business and other members of society come together. Broadly, partnerships can be divided between those that set rules, those that provide services, and those that generate resources. They rarely have contractual relations at their core. The United Nations describes partnerships of the kind that are relevant in the sustainability context as voluntary and collaborative relationships between various parties in which all participants agree to work together to achieve a common purpose or undertake a specific task, and to share risks, responsibilities, competencies, and benefits.

The rising significance of partnership

Business has long run on networks, the labyrinth of personal relationships and long- or short-term alliances that are the often hidden web that weaves its way through the day-to-day functioning of business. At various historical moments, collaborations of this kind have met with a political and public backlash when they become the backbone of collusion, oligopoly, and other practices that run against the principles of free market capitalism. As Adam Smith pointed out, 'People of the same trade seldom meet together, even for merriment and diversion, but the conversation ends in a conspiracy against the public, or in some contrivance to raise prices' (Smith 1776).

Despite this, alliances and collaborations of one form or another have thrived, especially in recent years, often with the full support of governments. Competitive clusters of complementary businesses in a given geographical area are often seen as essential to competitive advantage,[1] and public–private sector partnerships have gained traction in some countries as a way in which to deliver public services, from schooling to incarceration. Civil society groups that might historically have been expected to be wary of business alliances, have come to favour what are called multi-stakeholder partnerships, i.e. alliances between actors from the private, public, and civil society sectors. As we will see, there are many types of partnership, but the United Nations, which has taken a great deal of interest in alliances with business, offers a broad working definition, describing partnerships as 'voluntary and collaborative relationships between various parties . . . in which all participants agree to work together to achieve a common purpose or undertake a specific task, and to share risks, responsibilities, competencies and benefits' (cited in Mouan 2010, p. 368).

The aims of partnerships range from the broad and grand, to the narrow and specific. For example, the 2002 World Summit on Sustainable Development, which is attributed with stimulating various partnerships between government and civil society, placed business at the centre of international efforts to reduce poverty. In contrast, a partnership might be formed between airport authorities, local government, local community groups, and environmental NGOs, with the specific purpose of negotiating a runway extension. Equally, as we shall discuss further, partnerships involve different levels of participation and involvement, ranging from a company promising to report on social and environmental performance to stakeholders, or to fund a specific project, to civil society, business, and government groups collaborating together to achieve certain ends. It is not that one type of partnership is necessarily better than another—the question is what is fit for purpose—but it must be recognized that there are different types, each with implications for goals, design, and implementation.

The principle of partnership has been widely lauded both within and outside the business community. It has been called the 'collaboration paradigm of the twenty-first century' that allows actors to exceed their individual capabilities, the 'development approach of our time', and 'the last remedy to the stresses [of] intense globalization'.[2] A large number of companies have spoken out in favour of partnerships. Hershey acknowledges that 'corporations cannot address the challenges of ensuring a truly sustainable supply chain without working in partnership with [our] particular industry and, increasingly, without the help of outside non-governmental organizations' (Long 2008, p. 317). Accenture sees business–NGO partnerships as essential to improving the performance of civil society organizations.[3] The International Commission on Mining and Metals (ICMM) says that a partnership approach is essential in establishing and strengthening sustainable development approaches in mining areas.[4] As Warner and Sullivan describe it:

> Tri-sector partnerships are, in essence, a new form of strategic alliance . . . [A] voluntary collaboration to promote sustainable development based on the most efficient allocation of complementary resources across business, civil society and government.
>
> (Warner & Sullivan 2004, p. 17)

Partnership as ideology?

Around the world, there are examples of partnership, particularly of the multi-stakeholder variety, and these are being discussed and replicated not just as a methodology, but an ideology—what Bendell (2010) terms the ideology of 'partnerism'. In the 1990s, partnerships such as the Ethical Trading Initiative were considered radical; now partnering of some kind has not only entered into mainstream corporate thinking, it is an indicator of a company's commitment to good governance, social responsibility, and sustainability; and it has become an indicator of good performance in these fields in its own right.

There are some widely accepted reasons as to why this has come about. Stakeholders in their broadest sense are putting pressure on companies to act on ESG issues. Some companies will react to stakeholders as a threat, and seek to manage them accordingly. Other companies, however, might see them as groups to engage with in order to help them navigate the uncertainties that confront modern business.[5] This reflects a fundamental philosophical difference in stakeholder management theory that we will explore later on (see 'Stakeholders'). However, the role of stakeholders, including how they have been empowered by the social interconnectedness and opportunities for transparency that are features of contemporary globalization, is an important factor in the evolution of partnerships. Other factors discussed in Chapter 1 also shed light on the emergence of partnerism. There is a sense that governments are less able than before to regulate business, and certain partnerships have arisen to fill this governance vacuum (Chapters 10 and 11). The perceived diminishing power of governments is often linked to the drop in government overseas development assistance as a percentage of capital flows into developing economies, and partnerships have to a degree been a response to this shift.[6] There are also various instrumental benefits companies associate with partnership such as employee satisfaction and morale, effective risk management, and above all, brand image, which in one survey was rated as three times more important than other benefits.[7]

A challenge to convention?

Given the enthusiasm for, and proliferation of partnerships and other variations on collaboration in the broad ESG arena, it is easy to forget that partnering of the kind relevant to sustainability is recent and a significant change from conventional business models. For example, mainstream management theory still promotes a corporation perspective model of the firm in which the primary goal is to create value for shareholders. An exemplar of this is Porter's 'five forces' framework which seeks to limit the number of competitors by putting one's company in a dominant position, and optimizing outcomes for shareholders (and typically executives) over those for suppliers, customers, employees, and regulators.[8] Stakeholder engagement is not precluded by such a model, but its purpose is always to benefit the company (i.e. its shareholders and executives) rather than society as a whole.

The ideological value awarded to partnerships is that they offer an alternative to the corporation perspective model, but in examining and evaluating partnerships in practice, we should always remember the power of well-established conventions, and therefore be wary of the distinction between collaborations that mark a radical shift away from the status quo, and ones that are the refurbishment of existing structures. In particular, we should be aware of the differences in sustainability outcome that result from these distinctions. If partnerships that reinforce the aims of the corporation perspective model deliver real benefits from a sustainability perspective, then it would be mistaken to criticize them. There are those involved in sustainability who are hostile to business because of its competitive nature (Chapter 3); they may well favour partnerships where there is a genuine sharing of power, and the pursuit of common interest rather than self-interest. However, that is not what is at issue here: the success of partnerships in a sustainability context is to be measured by how well they deliver outcomes that demonstrably improve the sustainability situation, not how well they conform to particular actors' preconceived ideologies. As we will see throughout this chapter, this is no easy task. The reality is that much of the coverage of partnerships in a sustainability context exists in order to promote the ideology of partnering, and there is a dearth of reliable empirical evidence to show the benefits of partnership beyond the many individual case studies that tell interesting stories, but do not comprise a comparable, analysable data set.[9]

 Discussion points

Partnerships have become one of the ways companies manage sustainability issues.

- Why do companies think partnerships are well-suited to sustainability challenges?
- What specific advantages do multi-stakeholder partnerships offer?
- Why is the 'five forces' framework at odds with the intentions of partnership approaches?

	Business to business	Multi-stakeholder
Rule-setting partnership	EUREPGAP/GLOBALGAP International Council on Mining and Metals	RSPO FSC MSC
Service/implementation partnership	Sustainable Agriculture Initiative Platform	Better Cotton Initiative Cadbury Cocoa Partnership
Resourcing partnership	Connected Urban Development	Accenture Development Partnership

Figure 8.1 Examples and types of partnership.

Types of partnership

There are various ways of categorizing partnerships (Figure 8.1). We have already mentioned *multi-stakeholder partnerships* that in contrast with *business to business partnerships* bring together actors from different sectors of society to achieve an agreed set of goals. The Forest Stewardship Council is an example of business partnering with social development and environmental NGOs to further the goal of responsible forest management. It stands out from other partnerships created in the 1990s in that it includes organizations from developing as well as developed economies. It is a voluntary partnership in that there are no legally enforceable elements bringing the organizations together, in contrast to most conventional business-to-business or business-to-other party relationships. It also does not include government or its agencies, although in common with some other pioneering international collaborations, it has received direct or indirect government funding.

Rule-setting, implementation, and resource partnerships

The FSC operates a certification standard that is applied to well-managed forests, and compliance is recognized by the FSC logo applied to certified products using the output of those forests (e.g. paper, wooden furniture, sawn timber). As such, it is an example of a *rule-setting partnership*, along with the Marine Stewardship Council, and the IFOAM organic agriculture standard. Not all such partnerships are multi-stakeholder in nature: for example, EUREPGAP is a partnership of retailers and producers that develops certifiable criteria for good agricultural practice.

The environmental NGO, the World Wildlife Fund (WWF), played an important part in creating FSC and the Marine Stewardship Council, and that experience was carried over into the creation of the Roundtable on Sustainable Palm Oil (RSPO). The RSPO is a collaboration of companies throughout the palm oil value chain and NGOs, and oversees a standard for the cultivation of socially and environmentally acceptable oil palm at the plantation and smallholder levels. However, as well as a rule-setting function, the RSPO is involved in creating a market for sustainable palm oil, and in improving cultivation standards. As such, it can also be seen as an *implementation or service partnership* that not only fulfils a governance function, but also a pastoral one in regards to oil palm growers (Case study 8). There are a large number of service partnerships, and often they are found in developing countries where they offer distinct models for increasing local producers' capability to meet sustainable production best practice.[10] The Cadbury Cocoa Partnership brings NGO and government partners together to improve the livelihoods of cacao farmers and their communities, and the Sustainable Agriculture Initiative Platform is a food industry-wide initiative to promote sustainable agriculture practices.

Roundtables such as RSPO have become a popular partnership model: there are roundtables on sustainable sugar cane, soy, and biofuels, and such is the momentum behind this approach, a traditional industry body like the International Cocoa Organization is now imitating it in its industry–government collaboration, the Roundtable for a Sustainable Cocoa Economy. They are examples of 'co-regulation' in which civil society and business representatives jointly regulate business policies and practices.[11]

Another attraction of roundtables is that they offer the potential to provide resources that might otherwise be unavailable. The RSPO generates revenue from the sale of certified palm oil and this is available to build up the capacity of growers, but resources need not just be financial: rule-setting partnerships such as the Fair Labor Association have given companies access to the grassroots level knowledge of NGOs about working conditions, and a service partnership such as the Better Cotton Initiative has made available the competencies of agriculturalists, manufacturers, and designers for the common goal of more environmentally acceptable cotton cultivation. *Resourcing partnerships* are considered by some a separate type of partnership, especially when their primary aim is to provide particular groups with additional competencies. For example, Accenture Development Partnerships which makes the skills of management consultants available to NGOs, is a resourcing partnership. This category also includes partnerships to conduct systematic dialogues, i.e. forums that allow business and other stakeholders to come together to discuss particular aspects of sustainability, including sharing best practice.[12] The UN Global Compact and the UN Principles for Responsible Investment (Chapter 7) can be seen as resourcing partnerships because although they set out criteria for best practice, these do not constitute rules comparable to the FSC or MSC's certifiable standards, and their contribution is probably best measured in terms of improved dialogue rather than improved governance.

There are various sub-types of partnership that fall under the above three broad headings (Figure 8.2). Employee volunteering, for example, is a common form of resourcing partnership, as is company sponsorship, and short-term business-NGO consultations. Philanthropy is often dismissed as a lesser form of partnership, in part because it does not imply a substantive change in company behaviour. However, from a company's perspective, philanthropy can be a prized form of partnership because of its demonstrable impact on employee morale, and its measurable effects on reputation and brand value. Finnish forest products company, Stora Enso, for example, engages in rule-setting partnerships and systematic dialogues about sustainability, but its support of children's charities is still a key part of its partnership approach.[13]

Company perspectives

Company perspectives are another way of categorizing partnerships. It is common for multi-stakeholder partnerships in particular to be described in terms of their social and environmental outcomes, but improved social and environmental performance is only one

1.   **Knowledge sharing**

Long-term voluntary agreements between stakeholders to share information about the company's activities (e.g. feasibility studies, proposals, and evaluations).

2.   **Dialogue**

Medium-term voluntary agreement that key stakeholders will consult with each other on specified activities, such as preparing regional plans, developing environmental standards, and deciding on reporting requirements.

3.   **Informed consent**

Voluntary agreement by each party not to take action without the prior consent of others.

4.   **Contractual**

Medium-term agreement between certain stakeholders to provide specified services to others in the partnership.

5.   **Shared work plans**

Medium-term voluntary agreement between stakeholders to carry out separate, defined tasks in pursuit of common goals.

6.   **Shared responsibility**

Long-term agreement between stakeholders to share responsibility for implementing tasks and to be responsible to each other for their delivery.

Figure 8.2 Partners' obligations to each other.
Sources: Seitanidi 2010; Steger 2009; Warner 2004.

motivation. The contribution partnerships can make to reputation and brand value is highly important, not least when those within companies are making an internal case for tackling sustainability challenges (Chapter 4). Various studies have shown that this is what resonates with company managers,[14] and as Johnstone, Wilkinson, and Ackers argue (2010), there can be a gulf in expectation between what those inside companies and those outside consider to be a partnership's value. Nevertheless, there are other motivations that are recognized within companies, such as improved performance from integrating social and environmental issues into management practice (integration benefits), and the creation of new business models (innovation benefits).

Snapshot 8.1   How sustainable is Kate Winslett?—Albert, TV's carbon calculator

In 2010, the BBC developed a carbon calculator named Albert to measure the footprint of its TV shows. The footprint of shows varies considerably depending on where they are made, their budgets, and production intensity. Quiz shows, several of which can be made on the same day, are less carbon intensive than news broadcasts, for instance, and ironically a nature documentary on the Arctic might leave a larger footprint than a car show. Big stars can make high carbon demands such as limousines and luxury trailers, but lighting, heating, and transport mean all TV shows have a significant footprint.

Albert was designed by Richard Smith of the BBC's Sustainability Team, and developed by Share-point City, an IT consultancy specializing in applying Sharepoint collaboration software. However, the BBC recognized that unilaterally introducing a carbon calculator would have little impact on the industry as a whole, and could put the BBC at a disadvantage. Fox's *24* was already committed to becoming the first carbon neutral TV show, and a year before political chat show host Bill Maher had struggled to answer if he would cancel his show to reduce his carbon footprint. Yet, in a highly competitive industry, it was unlikely that any of the BBC's competitors would want to adopt the BBC's measurement tool.

The BBC therefore went looking for a partner with sufficient respect to get the industry to adopt Albert, and make it their own. The British Academy of Film and Television Arts (BAFTA) does a lot of cross-industry work in addition to running its prestigious awards programme. By handing Albert over to BAFTA, an inter-company partnership could be created, ensuring that programme producers and commissioners were working to the same standard. BAFTA announced it would be managing Albert at the Edinburgh TV Festival in 2010, and since then it has been adopted by Channel 4, IMG, ITV, Kudos, Shine, Sky, Talkback Thames, and Twofour. The partnership also comprises other companies responsible for design and branding, carbon assessment, web-hosting, and footprint checking, and including Microsoft which has granted BAFTA a licence to use SharePoint. BBC has now made calculating carbon footprints compulsory for all of its in-house produced shows, and its raunchy puppet-based sitcom, *Mongrels*, is trying to catch up with *24*'s Jack Bauer to become the first carbon neutral TV show.

Sources: http://www.bafta.org/the-academy/sustainability/; http://www.bbc.co.uk/pressoffice/pressreleases/stories/2011/05_may/19/albert.shtml; http://www.nytimes.com/2009/03/02/arts/television/02twen.html, all accessed 30 October 2011.

Questions

Albert is an inter-firm partnership in a highly competitive industry.

1. Is it an example of rule-setting, implementation, or resourcing?
2. Why did the BBC not want to own Albert once they had developed it?
3. Why was BAFTA chosen to host Albert?

A further company motivation can be that partnerships offer an alternative to formal regulation by government, and in the process create rules of the game that are favourable to business' interests (Chapter 10). This is, however, only part of the story. It is not that anyone can choose between civil regulation and state regulation: civil regulation refers to the process by means of which business and others in society are compelled to take action, not because of the law, but because civil society demands it (Chapter 10). Partnerships can therefore be seen as a way in which to comply with the types of civil regulation imposed by social media, campaigns, and advocacy groups. This compliance is optional only in so far as an organization can decide whether or not to comply: non-compliance with civil regulation entails risks no less than does failure to abide by the law.

Characteristics of partnership

Partnerships can operate at different levels of society (e.g. local, regional, national, and international), and can evolve over time to meet changing needs and expectations. For example, a mining company may convene a partnership comprising local communities, international development and environmental NGOs, and national government agencies when it begins exploration, but as the project progresses through construction, operation, and, eventually, closure, the partnership may well change to include local NGOs and government representatives. It may even spawn different partnerships to address particular aspects of the mine's presence.

It is clear from the examples so far that most partnerships are voluntary, even though there may be contractual and other legally enforceable elements within them. However, this does not necessarily mean that the partnership is non-binding, or that failure to implement the partnership properly goes without sanction. The array of expectations, especially in multi-stakeholder partnerships, means that there is an inherent tension amongst members about whose aims are being met, and many of these stakeholders will be able to punish failure in one way or another. For example, in the Ethical Trading Initiative (ETI), a multi-stakeholder partnership aimed at improving the monitoring of labour standards in supply chains, companies that fall short of raising standards in their supply chains are open to various levels of criticism from their peers in industry forums, from other companies, NGOs and trade unions in the ETI working groups, and from the public when the ETI reports its progress in its annual report.

Rule-setting partnerships are a relatively small, if high profile, group, and the voluntary nature of partnerships is not considered problematic in relation to resource or service partnerships. Moreover, there is a degree of competition between partnerships, especially at the international level. For example, the ETI has often been seen as in competition with the international labour standard, SA 8000, and the Fair Labor Association; more recently, the Better Cotton Initiative has fought for recognition with the Textile Exchange. This situation, although a cause for frustration amongst companies because it causes duplication and confusion, means that partnerships are to a degree subject to market discipline. Furthermore, despite initial predictions that competing partnerships would result in a race to the bottom in terms of social and environmental outcomes, the most credible partnerships have often proven to be the ones with the most rigorous requirements.

Stakeholders

Partnerships are variously depicted as competitive and collaborative, as noted earlier. Some believe that collaborative partnerships wherein the company is but one element of a joint enterprise delivering sustainability outcomes represents a desirable, and radically different new model of business compared, for instance, to the corporate perspective model of the firm (see 'Stakeholder management'). In reality, partnerships sit somewhere on a spectrum with collaborative enterprise at one end and managed self-interest at the other. Svendesen and Laberge (2005) argue that most partnerships are formed because companies have to engage with stakeholders in order to comply with regulations, to solve operational problems, or to respond to public pressure for greater accountability. They claim that companies tend to approach these partnerships as if they were closed systems and seek to control stakeholder relationships in order to meet organizational goals. This situation reflects Freeman's seminal work on stakeholder management which placed the company at the hub of numerous bilateral relationships, the purposes of which are, typically, to reduce risks, to enhance reputation, to improve the bottom-line or to develop new business opportunities. In contrast, there are a number of partnerships that are best thought of as stakeholder networks.[15] These may be convened by a company to tackle challenges that it cannot address on its own, but, once the network is formed, the partnership has a life of its own that cannot be controlled by a single organization and is inherently dynamic, unpredictable, and evolving. In conventional partnerships, company managers manage stakeholders, and behave as gatekeepers and benefactors; in networks, the theory is they create the space in which the network can grow— and must then relinquish control.

Stakeholder management

When Freeman originally wrote of business engaging with stakeholders, he was largely talking about bilateral partnerships between a company and another organization. Dating back to the 1930s, business leaders have typically used the term 'stakeholders' as a way of distinguishing between the main groups towards which companies have different kinds of duty: in particular, shareholders, customers, consumers, and employees. (See also Chapter 5.) Freeman treats stakeholders as something more extensive, complex, and nuanced than this. Furthermore, he regards effective stakeholder management as essential to the survival and prosperity of the enterprise. In what he calls 'radical externalism', Freeman proposes that managers pay attention to stakeholders as a matter of course by adopting integrative strategic management processes.

In the light of subsequent scepticism about stakeholder management, it is important to put Freeman's ideas in context. It might seem surprising now, but business at the time Freeman wrote was seen as weak and 'on the ropes':[16] stagflation was undermining major capitalist economies; US business, in particular, was under threat from Japanese competitors; there were unprecedented levels of mergers and acquisitions; and companies were increasingly targets of consumer and environmentalist advocacy. The business world that Freeman sought to help was something weak and troubled, and he adopts a very instrumental approach to stakeholder theory under which companies choose who their stakeholders are, based on their potential to jeopardize the firm's survival.

It can be difficult to identify who stakeholders are. At the broadest level, they are individuals, groups, or entities (including, some would argue, the natural environment) that claim rights or interests in a company and in its past, present, and future activities. Freeman initially drew a distinction between 'primary' and 'secondary' stakeholders. Primary stakeholders are those without whose participation a company cannot survive (e.g. investors, employees, suppliers, customers, and the governments and communities that provide infrastructure and markets). Secondary stakeholders are those that influence the company or are affected by it, but who are not essential to its survival, although they may be able to help or harm the company (e.g. the media, terrorists). The manager's duty, therefore, is to create sufficient wealth, value, or satisfaction for primary stakeholders to ensure that they remain part of the stakeholder system. He may pay attention to secondary stakeholders as well, but there may often be circumstances under which the interests of primary stakeholders are pursued at the expense of those that are secondary (e.g. taking a money-losing product sold to poor communities off the market).

The distinction between primary and secondary has proved controversial, and was eventually abandoned by Freeman himself.[17] It ignores any moral claim a stakeholder might have to be recognized by a company, and has left companies open to criticism that they do not respond to those with the greatest need or strongest entitlement. Moreover, stakeholder management can be considered incomplete if it does not weigh the significance of the identified options for the different stakeholder groups, and makes a normative judgement that integrates this information into a decision.[18]

Stakeholder engagement

At the end of *Strategic Management: a stakeholder approach*, Freeman raises a question that has subsequently been a recurring visitor in partnership thinking:

> Can the notion that managers bear a fiduciary relationship to stockholders . . . be replaced by a concept of management whereby they must act in the interests of the stakeholders of the organization?
>
> (Freeman 1984, cited in Walsh 2004, p. 249)

In contrast to sets of discrete, typically bilateral, relationships upon which the company chooses to embark with stakeholder groups, more recent stakeholder theory treats the firm as an organism that is embedded in a complex web of relationships, and requires the company to see these other organisms not as objects of managerial action, but as subjects with their own objectives and purposes. The stakeholder management model therefore involves the company being aware of, and responsive to, the demands of its constituents, including employees, customers, investors, suppliers, and local communities. An important consequence of this is that shareholders are no longer regarded as the most important constituents and shareholder value is not the sole criterion for assessing the company's performance.

This pluralist notion of the company's responsibilities clearly runs counter to the liberal economic model of the firm. Fundamental to that model is the belief that business contributes to the public good by pursuing its narrow economic goals and, hence, that managers should concentrate on maximizing the market value of their companies. The pluralist model, by contrast, holds that, in real life, the distinction between economic and social ends is seldom as clear as liberal economists pretend, because economic decisions have social consequences and vice versa, and the very idea of separate social and economic worlds is seen by some as mistaken.[19] Unlike Freeman's model of stakeholder management, the pluralist model of stakeholder engagement concerns the interactive, mutually engaged, and responsive relationships that 'establish the very context of doing business, and create the groundwork for transparency and accountability' (Andriof 2002, p. 29).

Stakeholder engagement is meant to be mutually beneficial, and requires that all concerned assume rights and responsibilities in relation to each other. It is not enough that companies pursue stakeholder partnerships purely for instrumental ends, but it is equally unacceptable that the company's stakeholders fail to consider the rights and interests of the company, and act accordingly.[20] There is no shortage of advice on how to build and recognize engagement.[21] Friedman and Miles (2006) have adapted Arnstein's *Ladder of Citizen Participation* to provide a way of evaluating the quality of engagement (Figure 8.3). Advocates of stakeholder engagement as an essential element of the business–sustainability relationship typically aspire to the highest rungs of the ladder where stakeholders have a degree of discernible authority over company decision-making. Two surveys of the quality of engagement both conclude that this is rarely the case in practice, and if it does occur it is because there are legal requirements about stakeholder representation on the Board (e.g. as in Spain and Germany).[22] There are plenty of cases of stakeholders having an input into the company's planning and decision-making, and these are widely publicized both by companies, and by third parties. P&G, for example, says that it has raised millions of dollars for NGO partners in Latin America, worked with NGOs to deliver 10,000 sanitary kits in tsunami-affected areas of Japan, and prevented 115 million days of disease through its safe drinking water programme (see Chapter 2, Snapshot 2.2). The University of Oxford, for instance, announced that the P&G–UNICEF partnership was 'conquering a deadly disease'[23] by sponsoring vaccines through nappy purchases. However, the majority of cases of stakeholder engagement fall under the category of informing, placation, or mitigation.[24] This should not be taken as a criticism: many stakeholders on the ground do not expect co-determination of decisions, and may value information sharing and consultation.[25] Nonetheless, the claims made for partnership and stakeholder engagement in the sustainability context are much grander than this, and mark a fundamental shift in the way business is managed. It may be that this is just hyperbole; but if it is not, then the consequences of the current situation and how it has arisen need to be recognized and understood.

Power in partnerships

The most common types of partnership either fall under the category of stakeholder management, or exist at the lower rungs of the hierarchy of stakeholder engagement (Figure 8.3). This is a disappointment to some champions of business as a positive force in tackling sustainability challenges because for them the potential is to harness the power of stakeholders to jointly discover and agree on innovations relevant to major sustainability issues. Pioneers of stakeholder engagement in the sustainability context such as Porritt (2005) and Elkington (2001) envisioned creative collaborations that would come up with answers that no single group could reach on their own. Furthermore, the power within the partnerships would create a countervailing force to the short-termism of shareholders and executives that is often blamed for unsustainable behaviour (Chapter 7).

In order to explain why such ambitions are still unfulfilled, we need to understand something about the nature of power in partnerships. Since the emergence of partnerships as a management approach in the late 1990s, the power dimension has largely been ignored, at least amongst practitioners. Nonetheless, we can see some of its consequences. For example, the gender dimension to sustainability—how sustainability affects and is affected by

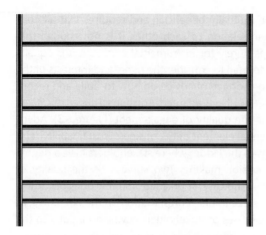

	Citizen control: stakeholders control decision-making
	Delegation: stakeholders have some formal authority (e.g. board level)
	Partnership: stakeholder input into planning and decision-making
	Informing, consultation, placation: one and two-way flow of information between company and stakeholders. Information may not always be acted upon
	Manipulation and therapy: the management of stakeholders for instrumental ends

Figure 8.3 Ladder of stakeholder engagement.

Sources: data from Friedman 2006; Manetti 2011.

women as a social group—is almost entirely missing from business-related initiatives.[26] Likewise, although considerable emphasis is put on the role of intrapreneurs and champions of sustainability within a company (Chapter 4), valuing the workforce as a co-creator of the enterprise is very rare, and workers are typically treated as suppliers, the costs of which must be limited wherever possible.[27] Case studies in Africa and Asia suggest that companies, even when committed to having a positive social or environmental impact, can influence what is perceived as a benefit, and cause stakeholder dependency rather than empowerment.[28]

In business management, power is most commonly associated with negotiation and books such as *Getting to Yes* (Fisher 1981) are hugely popular. However, this is only one type of power. Lukes (1974), for example, identifies three dimensions of power that are evident in the partnership context. First, there is a one-dimensional model of power in which decisions are made by clearly identifiable actors, and identifying power is a straightforward process of looking at those decisions. Thus, for instance, at a Board meeting there is a tied vote on a particular issue, and the Chair exerts her power through a casting vote. Second, there is two-dimensional power in which power is 'covert', i.e. it cannot be measured simply by looking at decisions; it needs to take into account such features as what was on the meeting agenda and what was excluded, any informal influence that lay behind the Chair casting a vote in the way she did, and the significance of any coercion, inducement, persuasion, and other behaviour by particular actors in deciding the eventual outcome.

Most of the discussion of power in a stakeholder context focuses on one or other of these two types of power. However, Lukes adds another type of power: three-dimensional power. This includes the overt and covert expressions of power described previously, but also comprises the less discernible factors that affect outcomes such as existing norms, values, and ideologies. This is what Lukes calls 'the mobilization of bias', something that affects what issues are dealt with and which ones are suppressed. Power is not simply about who wins in a conflict: 'the most effective and insidious use of power is to prevent . . . conflict from arising in the first place' (Lukes 1974, p. 23).

An example of this described by Mannell (2010) is a business–NGO partnership through which management consultants collaborated with NGOs on international development projects. There were several expected benefits from this collaboration: the consultants would be exposed to the challenges of poverty and sustainability inside developing economies; NGO staff could tap into management expertise that would otherwise be inaccessible; and management capabilities could be harnessed for the benefit of the poor and marginalized. However, in practice the partnership came to be seen as addressing the deficiencies of NGOs; deficiencies that were defined from a business perspective such as inefficiency, transparency, and accountability. Furthermore, measures of business success, notably profitability, came to be reified as development success, and it is easy to imagine that over time ideas that did not conform to these perspectives and goals were not only rejected, but were not even acceptable topics of discussion. In other words, the bias towards a business mindset was being mobilized, driving out alternative ways of thinking about development.

 ## Discussion points

Stakeholder theory has had a considerable influence on management since the 1980s.

- What are the main objections to stakeholder theories of the firm?
- Why is stakeholder engagement regarded as important for companies tackling sustainability challenges?
- What are the barriers that prevent partnerships reaching the higher rungs of Arnstein's ladder?

Inter-firm collaborations

Earlier this year, the world's twenty largest economies (G20) came together and agreed an unprecedented, coordinated response to the global economic downturn . . . World leaders now need to demonstrate the same level of coordination and resolve to address climate change. Economic development will not be sustained in the long term unless the climate is stabilized. It is critical that we exit this recession in a way that lays the foundation for low-carbon growth and avoids locking us into a high-carbon future.

(Prince of Wales Corporate Leaders Group on Climate Change 2009)

At first glance, one could be mistaken for thinking this statement was issued by a partnership of NGOs. In fact it came from a partnership of mainstream companies from around the world, and was issued in the run up to the Copenhagen Summit on Climate Change (Chapter 10). The Prince of Wales's Corporate Leaders Group on Climate Change, which issued the statement, is one example of inter-firm partnerships. Referring back to the earlier categorization of partnerships, it is a collaboration intended to generate a systematic dialogue, and is similar in this respect to the UN Global Compact and the UN Principles for Responsible Investment (Chapter 7). Its aim is to communicate the consensus opinion of the alliance members on climate change to governments, something that originally came about because governments believed business would be hostile to actions to combat global warming. Signatories to the communiqué quoted included Warner Brothers, Rolls-Royce, L'Oréal, and Bayer; the core members include AXA, Cemex, T-Mobile, and Shell.

The other examples of inter-firm partnerships in this section give a taste of the array of different forms and goals such collaborations take.

Equator Principles

The Equator Principles is an example of a rule-setting partnership. The Principles stipulate how financial institutions should consider environmental and social issues in their project finance operations. The signatories are primarily European and North American banks, and the standard clearly reflects reputational concerns about their portfolios of lending to developing countries. These arise from the potentially high risk of adverse social and environmental impacts that are attached to the infrastructure, energy, extractive, and other projects financed in this way (e.g. relocation, ecological damage, impact on communities). The Principles commit banks to formulating environmental and social policies and processes against which individual projects can be assessed for compliance. Their provisions are based on the social and environmental policies and procedures of the International Finance Corporation, which, among other things, require banks to screen proposed projects according to their potential social and environmental impacts. The outcome of the screening process, in turn, triggers a range of follow-up activities, and the most dangerous projects are subjected to more rigorous assessment, public consultation, and information disclosure requirements.

While signatory banks agree to adopt these policies and procedures, implementation is left up to the individual bank and, in contrast with FSC or SA8000 (see 'Rule-setting, implementation, and resource partnerships'), there is no requirement that companies independently verify how they are implementing the standard. Indeed, the Principles explicitly state that they are a benchmark for use in the development of each member company's policies. There is, however, an implicit assumption that, by involving large project finance banks, the Principles will create an environment within which good social and environmental policies are the norm, and will encourage industry-wide improvements. Recent signatories such as Banco Sabadell (Spain) make clear statements about when they will employ the principles, but there is no readily available information on industry-wide impacts. At present, success is still being measured in terms of the number and size of the signatory companies, with about 73 banks currently signed up to the Principles.[29]

New Zealand's fishing industry

A very different partnership, but one relevant to many SMEs, is the informal one that evolved around the fishing industry in Nelson/Marlborough, New Zealand.[30] Like many fishing industries, Nelson/Marlborough's has suffered from depletion due to over-powerful capture technologies, pollution, and habitat loss. Quota management systems adopted in New Zealand in the 1980s, have not stemmed this decline, and in the search for alternatives, the potential of partnerships as a means of fostering innovation and generating practical solutions, and the experience of competitive clusters of companies in close geographical proximity were explored.

Although companies within the partnership are in competition, they also stand to benefit from collaboration. For example, resources and capabilities can be shared; there is a wider selection of skilled employees to choose from; and there is the potential to develop a more complex, innovative industry because of the critical mass of expertise.

Long before partnership became a topic, the basis for a competitive cluster already existed in Nelson/Marlborough: there are large and small fishing fleets, harbours, chandlers, marine engineering, distribution, processing, marine lawyers, and marine research and education institutes. In contrast with many other examples of partnership where the creation of the partnership and its subsequent management are the central focus, in Nelson/Marlborough partnerships emerged from the pre-existing competitive cluster. However, the goals of sustainable fisheries set out in the government's Fisheries 2030 strategy (Ministry of Fisheries 2009) made it clear that the conventional business competitiveness orientation of the established cluster would not by itself be enough to prevent decline. Instead, partnerships began to emerge from within the cluster to complement the strategy. For example, in place of more intensive fishing, emphasis was put on value-adding innovations in processing and waste reduction, something that involved collaboration by the different sectors of the industry value chain plus the local research institutes. Likewise, partnerships evolved to improve the processes linking capture fisheries and aquaculture (e.g. mussel farming), and there have been several attempts at improving the supply chain. In each case, the strength of the cluster, the framework of government policy, and the involvement of non-commercial institutions enabled the partnerships to look beyond immediate profit motives towards sustainable futures. Furthermore, at a time of industry decline, fisheries in Nelson/Marlborough has seen an increase in the number of people employed, and signs of renewed investment in R&D.

Business sponsored partnerships

A relatively recent form of inter-firm partnership is the organization created to help business tackle specific sustainability issues. The Sustainable Agriculture Initiative Platform was an early example of this, established in 2002 by Nestlé, Unilever, and Danone to share knowledge on sustainable agricultural practices. In 2001, the Organic Exchange was created to develop a market for organic cotton in response to demand from the textiles industry. Nike was one of the companies that helped conceive and launch the Exchange (now called Textile Exchange) because it saw that only a value-chain wide approach could facilitate growth in the organic cotton industry. Now, organic cotton farmers can find buyers for their products in international markets through the Exchange whose other services include acting as 'matchmaker' between buyers and sellers of organic fibres, providing advice on sustainable fibre production processes, and developing standards and assessment tools.[31]

However, perhaps worried by Organic Exchange's focus on creating a market for organic cotton more than the benefits that it could bring for farmers in developing economies, international donor agencies established the Better Cotton Initiative (BCI) in 2005. The BCI has broadly similar aims to the Organic Exchange, although it is more explicit about the promotion of sustainable cultivation practices, and showing the economic benefits to farmers (e.g. a 69 per cent increase in net profits for farmers on the pilot projects).[32] Companies such as Levi Strauss & Co, IKEA, H&M, and Marks & Spencer support BCI, compared to Nike, Patagonia, adidas, and Nordstrom which support Organic Exchange. It is by no means the first case of seemingly competing partnerships: in the early 2000s, Verité, SA1000 and the Fair Labor Association seemed to offer similar partnerships on labor standards; the Sustainable Food Laboratory and the Sustainable Agriculture Initiative Platform have overlapping missions and membership; and there is a history of competition between international and national standards (e.g. Forest Stewardship Council and Indonesian Ecolabelling Institute; Ethical Trading Initiative and Kenya's Horticultural Ethical Business Initiative). There is often a suspicion that competing partnerships are linked to attempts to soften standards, but it can also be because certain companies are reluctant to collaborate with their peers.

Supply chain collaborations

An important type of inter-firm partnership is the one along supply chains. With the growth of outsourcing and offshoring as a feature of economic globalization, the governance function of supply chains is almost as prominent as its production one. Company reputations are at risk as much from what companies allow to happen in their supply chains as any acts they perform themselves. Furthermore, companies cannot credibly claim to be adopting sustainable practices if they do not know, or deny, responsibility for what is happening amongst their suppliers.

The early examples of such partnerships were to do with rule-setting, and in particular labelling initiatives such as the stewardship councils mentioned earlier (see 'Types of partnership'). As well as producers, manufacturers, and retailers, these partnerships required a standard-setting body and audit organizations to make them work. More recently, partnerships of market-based members have emerged such as EUREPGAP (now GLOBALGAP), which aims to harmonize standards for good agricultural practice.

Such initiatives share the assumption that inter-firm supply chain cooperation, influenced by Western consumer and civil society pressure, are effective in improving social and environmental conditions.[33] Retailers in particular have instigated such partnerships (e.g. Wal-mart, Tesco, WH Smith), but other organizations such as banks (e.g. Lloyds TSB) and health services (UK National Health Service) are involved in sustainable procurement partnerships. Power relations have always been part of such supply chains, and historical suspicion and distrust influences today's supply chain partnerships. Suppliers can be told to join partnerships, e.g. by powerful retailers, but this does not mean they will participate in any meaningful sense. Furthermore, in some industries, the growth in mega-suppliers in Asia means that power has shifted back to the manufacturer. Therefore, supply chain partnerships can rarely rely solely on coercion alone. Sharfman, Shaft, and Anex (2009) identify seven conditions that support cooperation around sustainability in supply chains:

- There is a high level of uncertainty about environmental issues.
- There is a high level of uncertainty about how to respond to these issues.
- Companies are unclear about the effects of their actions.
- Cooperation demonstrably benefits the bottom-line.
- Companies face strong regulation.
- Companies share a commitment to be proactive in tackling sustainability issues.
- There is a high degree of trust/respect within the supply chain.

Their study of 14 companies' supply chains shows that in addition to financial and compliance benefits, uncertainty, shared values, and trust all affect supply chain partnerships. These types of condition are not unique to sustainability, and broadly reflect an earlier wave of supply chain collaboration during the quality management revolution of the 1980s.[34]

The most famous supply chain partnership examples are of international supply chains, typically those linking poorer producing countries with wealthy consumer markets. With the growth of emerging economies as consumers in their own right, this situation has shifted somewhat. In South Africa, for instance, the multiple retailer, Woolworth SA, has been marketing what it calls the 'Good Food Journey' for a decade since it introduced organic fruit and vegetables in 1999. In 2007, it launched its 'Good Business Journey' based on the principle that the company has responsibilities to communities and the environment. Suppliers are an important part of this journey, and many of the areas of high risk identified by Woolworth management relate to suppliers (e.g. reducing energy consumption, reduced packaging and increased recycling, local sourcing of clothing, addressing water scarcity).[35] Initially, as with many multiple retailers around the world, the company focused on getting suppliers to comply with a code of business principles. However, this type of approach by itself can often exacerbate the tensions that already exist between buyer and supplier, especially if the latter already feels it is being squeezed in other areas of its contract. Moreover, Woolworth SA is not a retailer in the sense that retailers such as Ahold, Carrefour, and Tesco are. These latter companies sell a mix of own-brand and name-brand items, but companies such as Woolworth and Marks & Spencer are best described as fast moving consumer goods companies that happen to own their own retail outlets. The bulk of the products on Woolworth's shelves are own-brand items designed to its own specifications. This creates a direct relationship with the supply chain that gives the company potentially more influence, but also an opportunity to work more collaboratively.

A compliance-only approach left the company falling short of its social and environmental goals, and so it introduced Eco-Efficiency Awards.[36] Water is one of the company's largest challenges because over 90 per cent of the country's catchment areas are already over-allocated, and agricultural produce—a major part of Woolworth's business—uses over half of the country's water for irrigation alone. Therefore, again, the company adopted a mix of compliance and collaboration, on the one hand requiring all non-organic farmers to adhere to the GLOBALGAP standard (mentioned earlier in this section), and at the same time working with WWF in South Africa to work on water neutrality, a 20-year commitment which commits the company to releasing enough water into South Africa's water system to offset the water used in its operations each year.[37]

Multi-stakeholder partnerships

The example of Woolworth SA extending its supply chain collaboration to include partnering with the NGO, WWF, to achieve water neutrality, is an example of the multi-stakeholder partnerships that have become increasingly popular in the business-sustainability arena (see 'Supply chain collaborations'). Multi-stakeholder partnerships take many forms, but what singles them out is that they are voluntary collaborations that involve business and organizations from the public and/or civil society sectors. The underlying principle is that, in

Snapshot 8.2   Multi-stakeholder governance—Extractive Industries Transparency Initiative

Extractive Industries Transparency Initiative (EITI) is an example of a strategic multi-stakeholder partnership with an explicit governance function. It was launched by the British government at the 2002 Johannesburg Summit, and although it is primarily an inter-firm partnership, it has always enjoyed strong political support from OECD governments. Furthermore, its successful implementation depends on active civil society organizations, not least at the national level.

EITI is based on the idea that greater transparency and accountability in countries that depend on revenues from oil, gas, and mining will help those countries avoid the 'resource curse' which in the past has been blamed for the mismanagement of finances and corruption in resource rich but economically poor countries. Relief from the resource curse, it is argued, will enable the revenues from extractive industries to become an engine for sustainable development. EITI tackles this in three ways. It provides a universal standard for companies to promote revenue transparency by getting companies to publish what they pay.

At the international level, EITI is based on a set of 12 principles that were developed under the stewardship of the British government through discussions involving multi-national extractive companies, NGOs, institutional investors, and international institutions such as the World Bank Group. At this level, companies agree to disclose what they pay to governments in resource-rich countries. At the national level, the EITI is a government-led initiative, and governments agree to publish the revenues they receive from extractive industries. But it is also recognized that for this information to be used effectively, there has to be a formal role for other stakeholders from the private sector and civil society. In this way, not only is the information on payments and revenues disclosed in a transparent, accessible, and comprehensible manner, but it can be acted upon, for instance by exploring if the revenues are being used for development programmes.

The initiative has earned itself a mix of praise and criticism, often for the same reasons. For example, its narrow focus on financial transparency means it does nothing about many other sustainability issues in the extractive industry value chain, and depending on one's point of view this is a strength or a weakness. It has also been accused of omitting stakeholders that have historically helped local people tackle the resource curse (e.g. trade unions), and of shifting power to community-level government officials regardless of whether they have local people's trust or not.

A recurring criticism is that EITI is a Western-led initiative that not only has failed to gain the support of the increasingly important extractive industries from emerging economies, but may promote values that are not aligned with those economies' culture, philosophy, and business interests. For example, China's national oil companies have not supported EITI even though they have pursued a programme of rapid international expansion since 2002. This expansion is paid for through the 'Angola' mode of investment in which development aid, debt relief, low interest loans, and infrastructure development are given to the host country in return for access to its resources. This type of barter relationship is not suited to the EITI system which assumes a much more Western capitalist model of exchange.

Sources: Bracking 2009; EITI 2005; Mouan 2010.

Questions

EITI is a widely acknowledged example of an international multi-stakeholder partnership.

1. What category of partnership does it represent?

2. Is its narrow focus a strength or a weakness?

3. Are extractive companies from emerging economies right not to join EITI?

line with our earlier broad typology of partnership (see 'Types of partnership'), organizations such as companies, government agencies, and trade unions or NGOs each bring unique competencies when it comes to governing, implementing, and resourcing sustainability-related activities. For example, a European company might lack the capacity or credibility to understand the environmental impacts of its suppliers in the Philippines, and therefore seeks to collaborate with organizations already working with workers and surrounding communities. In the 1990s, this was a controversial idea, but now the principle of increased effectiveness by harnessing the relative strengths of the different sectors is widely accepted.

Business–NGO partnerships in particular have become very common at local, national, and international levels, wherever there is a functioning civil society. Kourula and Halme (2008) identify eight types of business–NGO engagement (Figure 8.4). Thus, in this chapter, the aforementioned Woolworth SA–WWF collaboration on water neutrality (see 'Supply chain collaborations') is an example of a common project, the UN Principles of Responsible Investment are a type of systematic dialogue, and the Marine Stewardship Council is an eco-labelling programme (see 'Rule-setting, implementation, and resource partnerships').

From a company's perspective, multi-stakeholder partnerships promise three broad types of benefit:

- Reputation protection and enhancement.
- Improved social and environmental performance.
- Fostering innovation and the penetration of new markets.

Reputation is the most widely acknowledged benefit, and genuine innovation is probably the least evident. One aspect of multi-stakeholder partnerships missing from the categorizations, though, is their role in governance, and how particularly at the international level they serve to fill a governance vacuum at a time of greater globalized trade. Eco-labelling is one example of this, but multi-stakeholder governance is not limited to certification of the kind associated with the RSPO or the FSC. The example of the EITI is explored in Snapshot 8.2, and the UN Global Compact and the Global Reporting Initiative are examples of global public

- Sponsorship: company financial support of a NGO.
- Single issue consultation: company consults NGO on specific issue.
- Research cooperation: company and NGO provide resources for research topic.
- Employee training and volunteerism: company workers work on NGO projects or are trained by NGO workers.
- Certification and labelling: NGO certification of company production processes.
- Systematic dialogue: structured forums for company–NGO interaction around sustainability issues.
- Common projects: company and NGO collaborate on implementing a particular project.
- Strategic partnerships: company and NGO act under a partnership agreement to achieve long-term common goals.

Figure 8.4 Types of business–NGO engagement.

Sources: created from Edwards 1995; Kourula 2008; Warner 2004.

policy networks within which business plays an overt role in sustainability governance.[38] We examine this phenomenon further in Chapter 11.

The Munich Climate Insurance Initiative (MCII) is a somewhat different example, seeking to improve the performance of the insurance industry, and foster innovative insurance solutions in the context of climate change-related events. While many of the best-known partnerships involve NGOs, MCII concentrates more on linking business with research organizations, and it is hosted at the United Nations University's Institute of Environment and Human Society. It is also one of several examples of partnerships being hosted by partnership management organizations (what are sometimes called 'referent organizations').[39] Other examples include the Renewable Energy and Energy Efficiency Partnership which hosts a business–NGO partnership to promote renewable energy, and the BioCarbon Fund which is a resourcing partnership using government and private sector funding to purchase greenhouse gas.

 ## Discussion points

Multi-stakeholder partnerships are a particular approach to stakeholder engagement.

- What examples can you find for each type of business–NGO partnership?
- Why are these partnerships treated with less suspicion than they were a decade ago?
- What are the particular advantages of multi-stakeholder approaches compared to inter-firm partnerships?

 ## Summary

Partnerships in their many guises have become an important part of the language of sustainability management. In the space of little more than a decade, voluntary collaborations between companies and between companies and their stakeholders have gone from being something radical and alternative to something acceptable if not essential. Partnerships can serve governance, implementation, or resourcing functions, and can range from one-off projects to shared long-term commitments.

For all of the support partnerships enjoy, there is little comprehensive data on how effective they are at meeting their objectives. One can point to the progress made by specific collaborations, particularly rule-setting ones that have created markets for certified sustainability products. However, overall the effectiveness of partnerships compared to other possible approaches to implement and resource sustainability initiatives is unknown, and many companies view success in terms of their reputations rather than the more ambitious goals of enhanced social and environmental performance, or sustainability innovation.

This is not to deny that there are examples of partnerships that have been innovative, progressive, and impactful, but it would be surprising if the majority of them lived up to the high aspirations some people have of them. There are good reasons why many partnerships are best described as examples of stakeholder management rather than stakeholder engagement, and the shift to power sharing and collaboration some consider crucial for sustainability runs counter to established theories of competitive enterprise. In sustainability theory, the prospect of this situation changing is often debated, but for the time being most companies are wary about any further shift from shareholder responsibility to stakeholder accountability.

Further reading

Friedman, A.L. & Miles, S. 2006, *Stakeholders: Theory and practice*, Oxford University Press, New York, NY.

Comprehensive review of how stakeholder theory is evolving.

Husted, B. & Allen 2011, *Corporate social strategy: Stakeholder engagement and competitive advantage*, Cambridge University Press, Cambridge.

An exploration of the business reasons to adopt a stakeholder approach to strategic thinking.

Seitanidi, M.M. 2010, *The politics of partnerships: A critical examination of nonprofit-business partnerships*, Springer, Dordrecht.

A discussion of the nature of stakeholder partnerships based on in-depth studies of two major business–NGO collaborations.

Steger, U. 2009, *Sustainability partnerships: the manager's handbook*, Palgrave Macmillan, Basingstoke.

Guidance on how to implement partnerships.

Zakhem, A.J., Palmer, D.E. & Stoll, M.L. 2007, *Stakeholder theory: Essential readings in ethical leadership and management*, Prometheus Books, Amherst, NY.

A collection of articles on stakeholder management theory.

 Case study 8   Roundtable on Sustainable Palm Oil—international multi-stakeholder partnerships across the value chain

The RSPO was formed in 2002; one of several partnerships fostered by the environmental NGO, WWF. Building on its experience with the Forest Stewardship Council and then the Marine Stewardship Council, WWF mobilized an array of industry actors. Palm oil is a major global commodity used in foodstuffs, soaps, cosmetics, and now biofuels. It is produced from the fruit of oil palms that grow in tropical regions on plantations and smallholdings. Production has escalated rapidly since the 1980s, most notably in Malaysia and Indonesia. This expansion has often resulted in the deforestation of tropical forests. This has negative consequences for biodiversity, and conservationists were amongst the loudest early protesters against oil palm; but when it also involves deforestation of forests in areas of peat, it results in the release of large amounts of what was previously sequestered CO_2.

RSPO was launched as a joint initiative of NGOs, palm oil processors and traders, financiers, retailers, food manufacturers, and industry bodies such as the Malaysian Palm Oil Association. After two years of negotiation, it was formally established as a not-for-profit association in Switzerland, although its secretariat is located in Kuala Lumpur. It was intended to be a demand-side coalition creating a demand for sustainable palm oil much as FSC had created a market for certified timber. Unilever and Migros had already set standards for sustainable palm oil, but it was felt that retailers and manufacturers working together would be able to put more pressure on producers to conform to the new standards. Moreover, by involving NGOs, it was felt that the demand-side could build consumer awareness and support, and reduce what sometimes felt like ill-informed campaigns by advocacy groups.

Not all NGOs accepted this offer, and ones such as Greenpeace have continued to mount anti-palm oil campaigns since RSPO's launch. There was also disagreement between companies and the participating NGOs, notably on how much the supply side should be involved, and whether the primary focus should be on oil palm as a cause of deforestation. Unilever, for example, which was the most influential of the initial companies, did not think the causal link between oil palm and deforestation was as strong as NGOs claimed, and moreover did not believe that simply using buyer strength was sufficient to bring about substantial changes in producer practices. Disagreement about this latter point was keeping producers away from the initiative, but after the first roundtable meeting in 2003 it was agreed that producers, NGOs, and buyers would all have equal representation.

Achieving an acceptable balance between different sectors, and different parts of the value chain was a major step in RSPO's evolution, and while there continued to be disagreements, there was also a sense of common ownership. In 2005, RSPO members adopted the 'principles and criteria for sustainable palm oil production', comprising eight principles and 39 criteria on economic, environmental, and social aspects of palm oil production. Thus, RSPO had evolved from being a partnership for systematic dialogue to one that included rule-setting as a central focus. However, in doing so, it developed standards that its multiple stakeholders could agree on, and the elaborate governance structures and procedures emphasized consensus rather than coercion; common positions rather than differences.

This approach, which was also time-consuming, was frustrating for some outside of the process who wanted rapid change, and interpreted the symptoms of consensus-building as evidence of failure. Greenpeace published a report, *Cooking the Climate*, and sent people in orangutan costumes up the outside of Unilever's HQ. Nonetheless, certification began in 2008 with 106,000 hectares of productive area, and that figure is now over 1.2 million hectares (March 2012). Over 5.1 million metric tonnes of certified palm oil has been sold on the international market, accounting for approaching ten per cent of global production. Despite this significant rise, and the support of some of the largest palm oil producers such as Sime Darby and Wilmar, there are major energy and food markets where non-certified oil can be sold (e.g. China and India), and the European market represents no more than 20 per cent of world demand. Because growing units are certified, not companies, plantation owners can benefit from the certified and non-certified markets, and continue deforestation. At present, certified palm oil attracts a premium, but this is likely to drop as supply increases, and because RSPO was pioneered largely by technical experts, the marketing side of sustainable palm oil has only recently started to get any serious attention.

Nonetheless, RSPO has demonstrated the adaptability of its partnership model over time. Early on, its challenge was to bring together powerful organizations to create an immediate legitimacy, but this led to problems in engaging with some parts of the value chain, not least the smaller producers who saw RSPO as a threat, a cost, or an irrelevance. RSPO changed from a demand-based to a supply-demand orientation, and also accepted a role for NGOs. It achieved consensus around a sustainable production standard, but members found that the standard itself, rather than protecting their image, became a target for civil society criticism. Producer unease has been partly offset by the growth in the market for certified oil, but the challenge now is to get yet more of the cultivated area certified even if global demand is uncertain.

Sources: Nikoloyuk 2010; Schouten 2011; http://www.rspo.org.

Questions

1. RSPO is an example of a rule-setting partnership, and what has been called private or partnered governance.

   a. How does this approach to governance differ from conventional governance mechanisms?

   b. What are the key elements of its governance system?

   c. What are the strengths and weaknesses of multi-stakeholder partnerships as an approach to governance?

2. The partnership challenges of RSPO have evolved over time.

    a. Why were NGOs attracted to a demand-side led approach to begin with?

    b. Why did retailers and manufacturers doubt that this would work?

    c. Should NGO partners protect the palm oil industry from criticism by other civil society organizations?

3. RSPO has created a market for certified sustainable palm oil.

    a. How can it expand this market in emerging economies?

    b. Can it expand the area under cultivation for certified oil to more than 20 per cent of total production?

    c. What role can the different stakeholders play in increasing RSPO's legitimacy?

Endnotes

1. (Porter 1990)
2. Austin cited in Kolk (2011); Kjaer et al. and Rochlin et al. cited in Mouan (2010).
3. (Bulloch 2009)
4. (McPhail 2008)
5. (Berns 2009)
6. (Nelson 2007)
7. (Berns 2009)
8. (Harris 2010)
9. (Mouan 2010)
10. (Hamann 2008)
11. (Albareda 2008)
12. (Kourula 2008)
13. (Kourula 2008)
14. (E.g. Berns 2009; Johnstone 2010; Kourula 2008)
15. (Freeman 1984)
16. (Walsh 2004)
17. (Evan 1988)
18. (Goodpaster 2002)
19. (E.g. Polyani 1944)
20. (Manetti 2011; Wicks 2009)
21. (See, for instance, Henriques 2010; Husted & Allen 2011; Steger 2009; Werther 2011; Zadek 1997)
22. (Cummings 2001; Manetti 2011)
23. http://bao.publisha.com/articles/192617-conquering-a-deadly-disease, accessed 24 October 2011.
24. (Manetti 2011)
25. (Johnstone 2010)
26. (Marshall 2007, 2011)
27. (Harris 2010)
28. (Blowfield 2004; Idemudia 2007; Rajak 2008)
29. http://www.equator-principles.com/index.php/members-reporting/members-and-reporting, accessed 25 October 201.

30. Information in this section is from Pavlovich (2010).

31. http://www.greenmoneyjournal.com/article.mpl?newsletterid=22&articleid=220; http://ecosmagazine.com/paper/EC10027.htm; http://www.textileexchange.org/, all accessed 25 October 2011.

32. (Joule 2011); http://www.bettercotton.org/, accessed 25 October 2011.

33. (Vermeulen 2009)

34. (Harris 2010)

35. http://www.woolworthsholdings.co.za/downloads/The_Good_Business_Journey_Report_2010.pdf, accessed 30 October 2011.

36. http://www.engineeringnews.co.za/article/company-announcement-woolworths-ecoefficiency-award-2008-05-27, accessed 30 October 2011.

37. http://www.engineeringnews.co.za/article/wolworths-water-neutral-programme-2009-04-03, accessed 30 October 2011.

38. (Detomasi 2007)

39. (Trist, cited in Kolk 2011)

9 Next-generation competencies

Key terms

Hard and soft skills   Education
Sustainability frameworks   Limits to growth
Capabilities and competencies   Transformation gaps
Human resources   Business schools

Online resources

- Full-length version of Maxwell case study.
- Links to business education resources.
- Links to audio-visual resources for use in sustainability education.
- Ideas on additional case studies and education materials.

  http://www.oxfordtextbooks.co.uk/orc/blowfield/

Chapter in brief

This chapter examines the distinct competencies that business will require in order to address sustainability challenges. It explores how a company's interpretation of those challenges affects what competencies it needs, and the degree of change or modification required. It looks at evidence of demand for new competencies from companies and elsewhere. It then separates out the different types of competency, distinguishing between hard skills, capabilities, and new frameworks for transitioning to and prospering in the kind of world sustainability issues imply. It discusses the different kinds of organization that can deliver these new competencies, and pays particular attention to the role of business schools.

New competencies for what challenges?

Competencies to transition from a carbon-powered economy

What are the aspects of sustainability that require companies, their managers, their workforce, and their investors to acquire new skills, capabilities, and competencies? The answer depends very much on how one interprets the sustainability challenge. If you see it primarily as about energy substitution—the shift from reliance on fossil fuels to alternative sources—then the competencies you need will be different than if you are thinking in terms of transformation to a resource-constrained economy. Energy substitution assumes that the immediate challenge is to stabilize CO_2e emissions, preferably so that global average temperature does not rise by more than 2°C. At its simplest, this requires companies to be familiar with the basic science behind climate change, relevant legislation and policy at national and international levels, and what other companies are doing. Managers will need to be able to assess the merits of different technologies, and there may be new accounting practices to master if, for instance, the impacts of carbon intensive energy have to be internalized, or clean technology is accounted for differently in terms of taxation, depreciation, and amortization. They may need a deeper understanding of energy, including the advantages and disadvantages of energy efficiency and alternative energy, the functioning of carbon markets, and energy geo-politics. People on trading desks and others in finance will need to be familiar with carbon markets, green bonds, green investment banks, and other financial mechanisms (Chapter 7). The company might also want to address the vast untapped market of people who live off grid in emerging economies, and this will require new business models, different types of investment, and familiarity with partnership approaches (Chapter 8).

 Key concept 9.1   Capability and competency

Managers acquire the skills and experience they need to do their job in numerous ways throughout their careers. Much emphasis is put on the MBA, and since the mid-twentieth century this has certainly given managers a good overview of how companies are run and to some degree the role they play in society. However, on-the-job training, mentoring, peer group interaction, networking, and not least disciplinary training from engineering to design are some of the many other ways that managers build their capability and competence to manage organizations. Nonetheless, the game-changing nature some people attach to sustainability raises various questions about the need for additional capabilities, the application of existing ones, and the continued relevance of certain established ways of thinking.

A significant challenge will be getting the right balance between capability demand and supply. Timing is crucial in any investment decision, but especially when success or failure is to a large part dependent on natural deadlines (e.g. how quickly emissions need to be stabilized to avoid catastrophic climate change) and political ones (e.g. targets for emissions reduction). Companies do not want to find themselves in a situation similar to Y2K (year 2000) when IT skills demanded premium prices because of a shortage of supply. There are already signs of this: projections for nuclear power—probably essential for any switch from high carbon to low carbon energy without a drop in overall supply—do not take into consideration the availability of nuclear engineering expertise, and how long it would take to build a new generation of those skills; the failure of energy reduction policies in Australia (Chapter 6) was directly linked to inadequate skills amongst contractors, and the same situation could well happen in the building and electrical trades if there is inadequate investment in building up the competency levels of the huge pool of independent, skilled labour—what, in the UK, is collectively known as 'white van man'.

A smooth transition from a high carbon energy economy to a low carbon one might be analogous to other examples of well-managed shifts. In the 1980s and 1990s, manufacturing companies introduced what was then the radical idea of total quality management, and embedded its principles into their operations. In the 1980s also, companies of all stripes took IT to new levels, and built new systems that marked the difference between success and failure. Before then, in 1967 and 1968, Sweden then Iceland switched from driving on the left-hand side to the right-hand side of the road, a change by definition that had to happen overnight, but one that required an enormous amount of advanced planning, investment, public education, and inter-sector collaboration. Such examples offer important lessons for the types of competency required to successfully manage the energy transition.

However, they also show that seemingly straightforward (if profound) shifts requiring the right mix of technology and finance, need a wider range of competencies than it first appears. Changes in behaviour amongst the public will need to be managed, possibly with companies taking on a leadership role in the face of hostility and suspicion in some quarters. This type of behaviour change management leverages the experience of companies in marketing and management, but is quite different in character to the Four Ps of marketing in which the emphasis is on consumption (Chapter 5). Companies also have extensive experience of changing organizational behaviour, but the energy shift may require new competencies in this area. For example, the size of the increase in capacity for non-carbon sourced energy needed by 2020 and 2030 is enormous, requiring a redirection of skills and capital that by some measures is unprecedented outside of wartime (Chapter 2). We also know from current experience that political and economic events can significantly affect what commitments get made or kept, and how they are acted upon. Therefore, it is fair to conclude that the transition will not be seamless, and that there will be significant periods of uncertainty with targets not being met, energy prices fluctuating widely, geo-political instability, and supply and demand imbalances. Consequently, managing uncertainty is likely to be a key competency as the transition unfolds.

Competencies for transformation to a resource-constrained economy

Energy transition is only one story in the sustainability compendium. Others are all more complex, and each has its own implications for new competencies. For example, if the energy transition cannot be achieved, then we are left either managing an increased risk of climate change, or of trying to decouple economic prosperity from growth in energy usage. The challenges are compounded if alongside growing demand for energy, there is increased competition for food, water, land, and non-renewable natural resources as a result of population growth and demographic shifts. Companies will need to become much more skilled at managing their environmental footprints, and living within the Earth's carrying capacity (Chapter 3). The situation grows more complex still if we factor in human development as a right, and how nine billion people will experience improving standards of living in a world where there appears to be natural limits to economic growth.

Each of these interpretations of sustainability presents its own challenges in terms of what competencies will be required, but they share the underpinning belief that what companies are having to manage is a shift from a worldview where there are no limits on economic growth, natural resource exploitation, or population, to one that sees the world as a resource-constrained economy. This is a much more fundamental transformation than anything outlined in the previous section. Successfully shifting from high carbon to alternative, cleaner forms of energy involves mastering the competencies needed for a 'green business as usual' model: transforming from a high carbon, resource-intensive business model to one that creates prosperity in a RCE involves acquiring the competencies needed for a quite different and unprecedented business environment.

Some of the fundamental changes associated with a prosperous RCE are explained in other chapters, but are worth summarizing here. Short-termism by investors and executives is often blamed for decisions and behaviours that run counter to the requirements of a RCE; for instance, encouraging actions that boost short-term share price irrespective of any negative social or environmental ramifications. Therefore, the capability to manage companies for the long term, and to understand the long-term value of particular investments is an important shift that is often associated with sustainability (Chapter 7). Similarly, company performance as currently construed has been criticized for encouraging practices incompatible with sustainability. Management accounting measures such as return on investment and depreciation, the non-inclusion of externalities in company valuations, and the overwhelming emphasis on financial returns rather than social or environmental impacts are all aspects of current practice that might need rethinking in a RCE (Chapter 5).

Successful RCE multinational companies will need to resolve the seemingly competing pressures of resource constraint and rising demand from emerging economies and also from population growth. Products for the poor will be a part of this (Chapter 6), but such products (like all others) will need to be ones developed so as to internalize their social and environmental costs. The shift from competition to collaboration is another area that has been highlighted in relation to RCE prosperity. For several generations, company managers have been taught to focus on the competitive enterprise, but transforming successfully to a new business environment is often associated with effective collaborations and partnerships (Chapter 8). Effective collaboration involves certain hard skills (e.g. the negotiation of partnerships), but it also requires a change in mindset. The same is true of the fourth major shift implicit in building companies suited to a RCE. Economic growth is at the heart of current business models, and there are those who see growth itself as incompatible with a RCE (Chapter 3). However, in terms of business competencies, it is probably more appropriate to think in terms of a different kind of growth; a form of smarter growth that is supportive of, and not a threat to, the prosperous RCE (Chapter 12). How this evolves, and hence its implications for competencies, will depend greatly on the wider political economy and how sustainability challenges themselves unfold; but whatever scenario proves relevant, it has implications for the way innovation is managed (Chapter 6) and how companies are led (Chapter 4).

From short term to long term, from financial profitability to a triple bottom-line (3BL), from competition to collaboration, from externalizing to internalizing costs, and from growth to smart growth, each of these represents a fundamental shift in the way companies do business. Because they run counter to much conventional business management wisdom, they are seen by some as evidence that business can never adapt to the needs of a RCE. Equally, for the same reason, some people have preferred to put the known needs of business ahead of the less certain demands of a RCE, and thus dismissed the need for any change at all. Ultimately, it is for companies—investors, stakeholders, executives, and the wider workforce—to decide and be accountable for what competencies they need to tackle the challenges of sustainability; but unless one dismisses the evidence that those challenges are genuine (Chapter 1), there will be competency implications, and how they are addressed will be a determinant of future business success.

 Discussion points

The right mix of competencies is influenced by how companies interpret sustainability challenges.

- What kinds of new competencies are needed to transition to a low carbon economy?
- Where are there overlaps between transitioning from a carbon-powered economy, and transforming to a RCE?
- What are the main changes in outlook associated with success in a RCE?

Demand for new competencies

In 2010, Accenture and the UN Global Compact conducted a worldwide survey of CEOs, and found that 96 per cent believed sustainability should be fully integrated into the strategy and operations of their companies. Ninety-three per cent of respondents also believed sustainability is critical to their company's future success.[1] Eight-eight per cent pointed to the need for new competencies from business schools and other parts of the education system as necessary to reach a tipping point where sustainability is embedded within companies. Peter Lacy, Accenture's Managing Director for Sustainability in Europe, the Middle East, and Latin America, divides these competencies between execution and transformation. Execution competencies are knowledge of science, technology, and engineering, plus the management competencies described in 'Competencies to transition from a carbon-powered economy'. Transformation competencies are those that require a more fundamental shift in the way business helps society address sustainability challenges, and broadly equates to the new skills, capabilities, and mindsets described in 'Competencies for transformation to a resource-constrained economy'.

This distinction echoes the findings of a 2009 report, *Developing the Global Leader of Tomorrow*, which identified three sets of required competencies:

- **Context**: understanding and being able to respond to changes in the external environment.
- **Complexity**: having the skills to survive and thrive in situations of low certainty and low agreement.
- **Connectedness**: the ability to understand actors in the wider political landscape, and to engage and build effective relationships with new kinds of external partners.[2]

The overall interest in sustainability as an area for building new competencies is evident from a variety of studies, typically at senior management levels (Figure 9.1). For instance, the PwC 2011 CEO survey reveals a fairly common attitude towards sustainability in a range of

Survey	Description
PwC CEO Surveys (PwC 2011) http://www.pwc.com/ceosurvey	PwC surveyed 1,201 business leaders in 69 countries for their 2011 Global CEO Survey. Surveys were not focused on sustainability, but each industry report has a section devoted to the CEO outlook on sustainability and how it impacts on their business. Industries covered include Asset management, Automotive, Banking & capital markets, Chemicals, Communications, Consumer goods, Entertainment & media, Engineering & construction, Government, Insurance, Metals, Pharmaceuticals & life sciences, Retail, Technology, Transportation & logistics
Sustainability: The Embracers Seize Advantage (MIT Sloan/BCG 2011) http://c0426007.cdn2.cloudfiles.rackspacecloud.com/MIT-SMR-BCG-sustainability-the-embracers-seize-advantage-2011.pdf	MIT Sloan and BCG surveyed over 3000 business executives and managers around the world on their views regarding sustainability. They found that the habits of companies already embracing sustainability as a competitive advantage are providing a glimpse of the future of management
Fortune 1000: Despite Moral Obligation to Sustainability, Cash is Still King (Harris Interactive/ Schneider Electric 2011) http://www.schneider-electric.us/documents/news/corporate/fortune_1000_survey.pdf	Eighty-eight per cent of *Fortune 1000* senior executives feel business has a moral responsibility, beyond regulatory requirements, to make their companies more energy efficient, according to a poll by Harris Interactive and commissioned by Schneider Electric. At the same time, the vast majority (61 per cent) of respondents say that potential cost savings are their biggest motivator to save energy at the enterprise-level, outranking environmental concerns (13 per cent) or government regulations (2 per cent)
McKinsey Global Survey results: How companies manage sustainability (McKinsey & Co.2010) http://download.mckinseyquarterly.com/sustainability.pdf	This survey explored how companies define sustainability, how they manage it, why they engage in activities related to sustainability, and how they assess as well as communicate this engagement. McKinsey received responses from 1,946 executives representing a wide range of industries and regions. Energy companies, which are overall more engaged in sustainability activities than are companies in other industries (likely as a result of potential regulation and natural-resource constraints), were excluded from this group.
2010 Sustainability Survey (GlobeScan/SustainAbility 2010) http://www.sustainability.com/content/news/attachedfile/130/tss_media_release_sb10_june_2010.pdf	More than 1,200 experts were surveyed in February and March 2010 on a range of topics related to sustainability, including critical trends and issues, climate change, and the drivers of sustainability leadership. Respondents were drawn from corporate, government, NGO, academic, research, and service organizations, and span more than 80 countries globally. The Sustainability Survey is the largest global poll of the views of sustainability experts

Figure 9.1 Surveys of executive and senior management attitudes towards sustainability.

Source: data collected for this list by students at London Business School, Michael Kong and Lara O'Shea.

Survey	Description
Global Corporate Occupier Sustainability Survey (Jones Lang LaSalle 2010) http://www.joneslanglasalle.com/MediaResources/EU/Marketing/Netherlands/Presentatie%20Duurzaamheid%20Nieuwjaarsborrel%20JLL%202010.pdf	A global survey of 231 top level Corporate Real Estate (CRE) leaders undertaken in September/ October 2009 in order to: Gauge the importance of sustainability to CRE executives; assess what premium the industry is willing to pay for sustainability, and how strong the availability of sustainable space is; identify the opportunities and challenges of implementing sustainable strategies
Sustainability in business today: A cross-industry view Deloitte (2010) http://www.deloitte.com/assets/Dcom-UnitedStates/Local%20Assets/Documents/IMOs/Corporate%20Responsibility%20and%20Sustainability/us_es_sustainability_exec_survey_060110.pdf	A qualitative survey of sustainability leaders at the US headquarters of 48 large companies from late 2009 to early 2010. The objective was to paint a general picture of sustainability activity among respondents and to gather their views on several sustainability-related issues, including the way they defined sustainability, the impact of the American Recovery and Reinvestment Act (ARRA) on sustainability efforts, and their speculations on the future of sustainability in business.

Figure 9.1 (*continued*)

industries, and the 2011 survey of executives and managers by MIT Sloan & Boston Consulting Group concludes that companies that have embraced sustainability are demonstrating the kinds of competency that will be essential for successful businesses in the future. At the same time, one needs to be cautious about how to interpret these surveys. The Harris Interactive & Schneider Electric survey in Figure 9.1 shows that for many executives, the immediate bottom-line effects of sustainability are uppermost on their minds, rather than thoughts about transformational competencies. Furthermore, when sustainability is not the central focus of the survey, its importance can slip. For example, the 2010 IBM CEO survey into complexity found that sustainability was only seventh on the list of CEO priorities. However, just because a survey has a particular focus does not mean that respondent bias negates the whole exercise. In 2005, for instance, an *Economist* survey of attitudes to corporate responsibility found that under 35 per cent of managers ranked it as important, whereas by 2008 56 per cent saw it as a high priority.[3] A similar growth in interest is evident in repeated surveys such as that by GlobeScan and SustainAbility (Figure 9.1).

Sustainability in management education is a recent phenomenon, appearing as academic theory in the 1990s.[4] It appeared not because of any internal demand from business, but due to rising public awareness of environmental issues. NGOs that had targeted business since the 1980s, began to consider how to educate it on sustainability: for example, the World Resources Institute developed an online resource for relevant case studies, and initiated biennial social and environmental assessment of business schools' curricula and research. Both of these initiatives—subsequently called Caseplace.org and Beyond Grey Pinstripes—were influential, and there are now also publishing houses such as Greenleaf, Earthscan, and Island Press that have helped increase the amount and quality of teaching resources.

For an area to flourish in academia, it also needs good quality journals for academics to publish in because this is a significant element of their career progression. Gladwin, Kennelly, and Krause published a groundbreaking article in the prestigious *Academy of Management Review* in 1995, and there has been a trickle of articles in top-ranked journals since then. However, only a handful of journals in the influential *Financial Times* top 45 business journals regularly publish articles on sustainability (e.g. *Journal of Business Ethics*), and most articles on the business-sustainability relationship appear in smaller, specialist journals such as *Journal of Global Responsibility* and *International Journal of Sustainable Strategic Management*. As Starik et al. (2010) point out, there are many aspects of management, such as human resources, operations, supply chains, and accounting, which have only very recently paid attention to sustainability as it affects their disciplines.

Since the World Resources Institute's initial efforts, a number of initiatives have emerged aimed at effecting change in how companies are managed. These include the Global Foundation for Management Education, a joint initiative by the Association to Advance Collegiate Schools of Business (AACSB) and the European Foundation for Management Development (EFMD), the Aspen Institute's Business and Society Programme, the Graduate Management Admission Council's 'Team MBA' initiative, the European Academy of Business in Society (EABIS), the Global Responsible Leaders' Initiative, and the MBA network organization, Net Impact. The achievements and difficulties of these initiatives inspired the creation of the Principles for Responsible Management Education (PRME), organized by the United Nations. PRME signatories agree to six principles concerning the learning and educational activities

Signatories to PRME agree to the following six principles:

1. **Purpose:** to develop the capabilities of students to be future generators of sustainable value for business and society at large and to work for an inclusive and sustainable global economy.

2. **Values:** to incorporate into our academic activities and curricula the values of global social responsibility as portrayed in international initiatives such as the United Nations Global Compact.

3. **Method:** to create educational frameworks, materials, processes, and environments that enable effective learning experiences for responsible leadership.

4. **Research:** to engage in conceptual and empirical research that advances our understanding about the role, dynamics, and impact of corporations in the creation of sustainable social, environmental, and economic value.

5. **Partnership:** to interact with managers of business corporations to extend our knowledge of their challenges in meeting social and environmental responsibilities and to explore jointly effective approaches to meeting these challenges.

6. **Dialogue:** to facilitate and support dialog and debate among educators, students, business, government, consumers, media, civil society organizations and other interested groups and stakeholders on critical issues related to global social responsibility and sustainability.

Figure 9.2 Principles for Responsible Management Education.

Sources: Alcaraz & Thiruvattal 2010; http://www.unprme.org/the-6-principles/index.php. (2143 Alcaraz, Jose M. 2010) within business schools. The more than 400-strong signatories include INSEAD, Shantou University Business School, London Business School, and Babson College. Many of the top business schools in Europe are on that list, but few of their USA counterparts have endorsed the principles.

In assessing demand for new competencies, it is not enough to concentrate solely on the demand from companies, and certainly not just on the role of business schools in meeting that demand. Civil society pressure has over the past few decades played an enormous role in alerting companies to the significance of sustainability, and in alerting the public and government to the relationship between business and social and environmental challenges. In areas such as partnership and civil governance (Chapters 8 and 11), it is often civil society organizations that are creating demand and also defining best practice. It is certainly imprudent for management to ignore NGOs given the high levels of trust they enjoy with the public, and the distrust shown towards business.[5] Degrees of trust differ, however, depending on where one is in the world: for example, in Eastern Europe companies seem highly trusted compared to government, not only for providing goods and services, but also for their transparency and accountability.

Such geographical distinctions remind us that the types of competency the public demands of business vary dependent on the current and historical situation. For example, when people talk about their expectations of companies in emerging economies such as China or the Philippines, their definition of sustainability is often oriented towards issues such as pollution, health and safety, product safety, and accessibility. In OECD countries where there are strong norms and legal codes pertaining to these issues, people expect companies to show quite different, additional types of competency such as sustainability in supply chains, recalibrating corporate accounting systems, and managing the triple bottom-line.

The political drive for new competencies also differs from country to country and region to region. The European Union has created a demand for new corporate competencies in waste management and corporate reporting because of its directives in these areas. Governments in countries such as South Korea and China have, through their investments in green economic stimulus (Chapter 2), sent strong signals about where to invest, while conversely the mixed signals from countries such as Spain and the UK in areas such as renewable energy have made business wary about what competencies they will need.

Tools, processes, and hard skills

The competencies needed by companies that take a narrow if pragmatic view of sustainability challenges, emphasizing, for instance, the transition from a carbon-powered economy (see 'Competencies to transition from a carbon-powered economy'), overlap with but are not identical to those required by companies that believe the RCE presents a fundamentally different business environment (see 'Competencies for transformation to a resource-constrained economy'). The former are primarily focused on the 'execution gap' mentioned previously (see 'Demand for new competencies'), and are looking for tools, processes, and hard skills that will make the transition as efficient and smooth as possible.

Snapshot 9.1   Embedding sustainability inside the firm—Tata

The Tata Group comprises more than 90 operating companies in seven business sectors: communications and information technology, engineering, materials, services, energy, consumer products, and chemicals. It has operations in over 80 countries across six continents, and its companies export products and services to 85 countries. Although established and headquartered in India, most of its revenues now come from outside its historic homeland.

A challenge for a company of this size is how to enable the workforce to learn about sustainability. This is especially vexing if one recognizes, as Tata has, that sustainability cannot be the preserve of corporate leaders and senior managers. The company also recognizes that raising sustainability awareness needs to be cross-functional, and encompassing all business functions.

Within the Group, a distinction is drawn between individual learning and organizational learning. The former informs the possibilities for the latter: training an individual can change their mental models and maps to accommodate new information. This involves exposing the workforce to explicit information (e.g. codes of sustainability practice, technical standards, company policies), but also involves applied, experiential learning through, for instance, working on practical sustainability projects.

The company is also aware of non-explicit learning such as social learning, i.e. something that occurs through participation, observation, and interaction. Thus, for example, a worker can learn about sustainability from the way the firm's facilities take environmental factors into consideration, and equally, may question what he has gained from formal training if the facilities do not seem in line with sustainability best practice. Particularly relevant in the Indian context, where the majority of people still live below the poverty line, acceptable sustainability management cannot pay attention just to environmental issues, but must also recognize the different and sometimes competing claims of human development.

The foundation for Tata's approach to sustainability management is the company's Tata Business Excellence Model, first introduced in 1994 and intended to embed stakeholder engagement and sustainability into employees' perception of performance excellence. This was supplemented in 2003 with the Tata Index for Sustainable Human Development, now the Corporate Sustainability Protocol Index. These formal measures, together with the Group's structure and policies that bring together the CEOs of its companies, provide the formal basis for managing sustainability. Annual CEO events, online forums and trainings, events and competitions, and the dissemination of best practice examples are some of the ways sustainability is communicated across the Group and a dialogue facilitated. There are also training opportunities including experiential learning from the moment someone starts at Tata. For example, management trainees at Tata Chemicals spend up to eight weeks learning about sustainability on their induction programme, and business school graduates intended to be the next leaders of the company spend seven weeks living in rural areas or with poor communities. Visits to other companies in the Group are encouraged, as is employee volunteering to encourage people to get first-hand experience of sustainability issues.

Combined, these activities provide the individual learning basis for organizational learning about sustainability, and according to the Group this in turn gives it the capacity to change. 'As the construct of sustainability continues to evolve to reflect how different stakeholders interpret its meaning, the ability to learn becomes fundamental to organizational and employee development' (Alka Talwar, Tata Chemicals).

Sources: Haugh 2010; http://www.tata.com; http://www.tatainternational.com.

Questions

Tata is one of the world's largest conglomerates.

1. How has the company gone about developing competencies across the Group?

2. What does the company think is essential to develop organizational learning?

3. How does the Group encourage cross-learning between member companies?

For example, companies will require a better understanding of renewable energy, particularly as energy supply diversifies away from a dependence on OPEC countries. Understanding the advantages and disadvantages of energy efficiency and alternative energy (e.g. solar, nuclear), how different types of energy are developing, and what their true costs are will become an important capability. Similarly, understanding the ramifications of carbon markets, and the forms of carbon sequestration will be important as more attention is paid to offsetting emissions. The geopolitics of energy and how food and energy prices interact will also be relevant, as will a broad understanding of what are likely to be increasingly volatile global resource markets.

A sophisticated understanding of global supply chains, and where they present risks and opportunities is another new competency area. Since the supply chain revolution of the 1980s, OECD companies have concentrated on quality, price, and timeliness as the key elements of an efficient supply chain. The social and environmental risks in those chains became more apparent in the 1990s, and many of the companies considered to be front-runners in terms of good sustainability practice have a comprehensive understanding of their supply chains as part of their company's ecosystem. This includes whole supply chain and product life-cycle awareness, sustainability-oriented policies, supplier auditing, and the ability to build business cases that are convincing, flexible, and relevant to different scenarios.

One of the reasons supply chains are important is the risk they present to a company's reputation. Reputation tracking is a competency in itself, and one of the new competencies in marketing that are required. Marketing as something other than the traditional one-way street of selling more things is discussed in Chapter 5, and the skills associated with the changes of behaviour, product offerings, and company-consumer relations described there are new areas of competency needing to be built up.

Sustainability itself arguably is not a new competency: it is something to be integrated into many if not all of what a business does. For instance, if low carbon energy is the main concern of a company in retail, then awareness of it will affect product design, manufacturing, transport, packaging, display, marketing, and sales. It is incongruous to have energy efficient looms to make textiles if the carbon footprint of transportation or packaging remains high. The way that a sustainability issue can cut across many aspects of a company's operations means that strong project management skills are important. The right team, strong leadership, clear objectives, milestones, benefit, measurement, and monitoring are important, as are explicit incentives written into performance contracts.

The cross-cutting nature of sustainability issues lends itself to a systems thinking approach so that managers have a rounded view of their business decisions that takes account of sustainability risks and rewards. Adaptation of balanced score cards to include sustainability, and the introduction of 3BL reporting are aids to this, and are already being tried at companies such as Nike. Companies can decide how broad or narrow they wish to define these risks and rewards. The European Commission, for example, sums up the advantages as boosting brand, boosting sales, and motivating employees,[6] and it is quite possible to adopt a systems thinking approach that reflects this narrow, instrumental interpretation of a company's impacts.

A more expansive approach to systems thinking is discussed in the next section ('Transformation competencies'), but even for companies that want to make a conventional business case for addressing sustainability challenges, something more than including sustainability issues as an additional ingredient to tried and tested management recipes might be necessary. For example, as mentioned in Chapter 7, current accounting practices do not recognize the potential impact of fossil fuel reserves held by listed coal, oil, and gas companies, or the likelihood that if all of those reserves were used (as the valuations of those firms currently assume), global average temperatures would rise by more than 2°C. Alternatively, if those companies were prevented from using the reserves, investors would be exposed to the risk that a major part of the value of these companies could never be realized.[7] Doubts about how well established practices value companies at a time of sustainability-affected transition are something that could drive the creation of new accounting competencies even if one does not believe sustainability poses fundamental challenges for business.

 Discussion points

Managing sustainability is linked to an array of new competencies.

- Do you agree that sustainability itself is not a management competency?
- Why do some managers prefer to think in terms of hard skills rather than soft ones?
- How could the balanced scorecard be adapted to integrate sustainability?

Transformation competencies

Sustainability is more challenging to business than those who consider it to be a transition between two types of energy believe. At least that is the overwhelming impression one gets from the literature on business and sustainability. Underpinning any specific skills, tools, and processes, it is argued, is the need for a strong understanding of sustainability, its interconnectedness, and how it affects business in the short, medium, and long term. This knowledge in turn reveals the complexity of guiding companies through sustainability challenges, and this appears to demand new approaches to management, not least in terms of behaviour. Only when this knowledge of sustainability and its implications for corporate behaviour are understood, can the hard competencies be identified and worked on. Thus, for instance, there are calls for ecological intelligence to understand companies' impact on ecosystems, systems thinking to gain a holistic picture of inputs, outputs, and waste, appropriate technologies and design, and cultural literacy.[8] As Henriques (2010) highlights, it is impossible to imagine a successful form of transformation that is blind to the impacts companies have.

This line of reasoning has been evident in sustainability management theory since its early days. Gladwin, Kennelly, and Krause (1995) identify five principal components to sustainability in the business context:

- **Inclusiveness**: understanding the multiple driving forces of anthropogenic global environmental change such as technology, population change, economic growth, political and economic institutions, and attitudes and beliefs.
- **Connectivity**: understanding the interconnected and interdependent nature of the world's social and environmental difficulties (e.g. the relationship between poverty and ecosystem degradation).

- **Equity**: fair distribution of resources and property rights within and between generations.
- **Prudence**: maintaining the resilience of life-supporting ecosystems in order to avoid irreversible situations, and to keep the scale and impact of human activities within regenerative and carrying capacities.
- **Security**: ensuring the security of boundary conditions necessary for sustainability such as ecosystem health, critical stocks of natural capital, self-organization, carrying capacity, and human freedom.

According to these authors, the new competencies that the next generation of managers need will be ones that support these components. It is quite right to debate if this list is accurate or universal, but it has become the foundation stone for much subsequent thinking about what competencies companies will require. Moreover, it presents a clear challenge to the dominant technocentric view of the company that tends to treat the Earth as something inert and passive, and hence legitimately exploitable by humans. Technocentrism also regards nature as resilient, and any damage as reversible. These assumptions may not be explicit, but they are essential premises for technocentric ideas of economics which treat the economy as a closed linear system, isolated from nature. The primary objective of that system is to allocate resources efficiently so that human needs are met. Any scarcity is relative rather than absolute, and economic growth, productivity, and consumption can all increase without limits.

Gladwin, Kennelly, and Krause argue that technocentric management theory 'has evolved within a constricted or fractured epistemology, such that it embraces only a portion of reality . . . Sustainability shifts boundary constraints from plenitude to limitation and from efficiency to equity. It suggests that management theories must be framed as if the world is relatively full, rather than empty' (1995, p. 896). Much of what is presented as relevant to managing the transformation to a RCE is an alternative to technocentrism. As Gladwin and colleagues demonstrate, technocentrism is imbued with certain beliefs, assumptions and biases, and part of the new set of competencies is to reflect on the implications of these, and their alternatives.

The lack of awareness around sustainability issues, their importance, and how they should be approached noted in 1995, remain true today. Likewise, many of the changes in attitude identified then are still wanting now (e.g. an open-mindedness about social and environmental issues, and a willingness to treat them as something other than hype or a fad). The capacity for understanding needs to stretch beyond carbon footprints or any other single issue, to recognize the implications of finiteness and limitations, and the interconnectedness of issues such as deforestation, resource use, environmental systems, and biodiversity.[9] Therefore, ideas about new competencies often begin with questioning the social, cultural, and economic systems that have brought about the sustainability challenges that business now confronts. Thinking in new ways, it is argued, should be complemented by reflection on what kind of society is desirable, on what is important and worth protecting, and what humanity's ethical obligations are.[10]

Building on this comprehensive view of sustainability, those seeking new competencies for transformation argue that managers need to understand the role of sustainability within the business; to have a clear view of how sustainability fits into their structure similar to the understanding of climate change energy company managers have developed. Furthermore, individuals must understand what responsibility they have for sustainability in their role: for instance, when making decisions about a new retail store, the managers involved should understand the sustainability dimensions to its location, construction, use, economic consequences, and end of life. Similarly, managers should understand the different lenses through which the business case for sustainability can be viewed (e.g. impact on the bottom-line sustainability-related risk, efficiency, market opportunities), and also the limitations of quantitative cases where cause and effect can be hard to determine.

Soft skills

Books such as this one are intended to help managers build the knowledge they need about the business–sustainability relationship, and in areas such as innovation, marketing, strategy, and governance they should also give insight into some of the necessary hard skills. In addition to this, however, there are frequent calls made for an emphasis on 'soft skills'. Partnerships and collaboration are one aspect of sustainability management that demand an approach that seems at odds with established management behaviours (Chapter 8). Similarly, the modes of leadership discussed in Chapter 4 are somewhat different to those normally taught in business schools because it is claimed sustainability requires different behaviours. A frequently identified behaviour is the ability to build and sustain partnerships. For instance, collaborating with NGOs is often referred to as a good way of doing business in the sustainability context, and to do this effectively, business leaders require new competencies, not just to work with NGOs, but for engaging in operational improvement/supply chain optimization efforts. Likewise, new competencies are needed so that managers can collaborate with competitors in the kinds of best practice sharing partnership developed by Unilever, Coca-Cola, PepsiCo, and Walmart to eliminate CFCs from the manufacturing and storage of soft drinks. Partnership management includes the capacity and skill to know when a partnership is appropriate, how to make it happen, know when it is right to continue, and how to end it. As the examples in Chapter 8 make clear, managing complex stakeholder relationships is a quite different competency from what has been developed in the past.

A feature associated with a RCE is increased uncertainty, and hence managers will need to be comfortable with dealing with ambiguity, and making decisions when outcomes and options might be unpredictable. Agility, adaptability, and flexibility are valued qualities in this situation, as is the ability to manage for long-term rather than short-term goals. Likewise, as discussed in the chapters on leadership and innovation (Chapters 4 and 6), creativity and an entrepreneurial mindset are often cited as necessary qualities for transformation: this can take the form of conventional entrepreneurship, but also includes 'intrapreneurs'—champions of sustainability within companies. These people also need the capability to challenge mindsets and established ways of doing things. This in turn represents a substantial change management programme from the traditional way of doing things, and sustainability transformation can be considered as a large change management programme suited to the kinds of skills associated with other types of change management and business turnarounds (Figure 9.3).

The experience of companies strongly identified with sustainability such as Marks & Spencer demonstrates the important role managers play in implementing training programmes for operational and customer-facing staff (e.g. customer call centres, utility installers). While

Consideration and empathy: managers need to understand the culture of a business unit, company, industry, and country; to appreciate the association of an activity with an impact.

Integrity: companies can expect to be held accountable for their actions, and to make public commitments to action.

Negotiation, influence, and persuasion.

Communication: written and vocal.

Mentorship and managing people.

Emotional engagement: necessary to overcome cynicism and build project confidence.

Cross-cultural understanding, language skills.

Quality of listening, emotional awareness, sensibilities, and mutual respect.

Open-mindedness: preparedness to question the status quo.

Strength of character, conviction, tenacity, and ability to create a sense of urgency.
Positivity and passion.

Figure 9.3 Behaviours associated with sustainability transformation.

much attention is paid to the competencies corporate leadership requires, it is easy to overlook the skills needed by the staff and managers who represent the face of the company to the majority of people, and whose behaviour and knowledge not only affects how the company is perceived, but also represents an opportunity to affect the behaviour of customers.

Indeed, behaviour itself is one of the most commonly cited soft skills managers need as the extensive list in Figure 9.3 shows. Not all of these are unique to sustainability, and many are accepted elements of team-based approaches to modern international management. In fact, taken out of context, the behaviours can appear like a vanilla list copied from almost any book on behavioural change written in the last decade or so. This can be interpreted as heartening in that some of the skills required to manage transformation are already available, and simply need adapting to the sustainability context. However, the reliance on soft skills is uncomfortable for some managers who need to be persuaded of their efficacy. Furthermore, there is a noticeable reluctance, amongst sustainability theorists at least, to dwell on the significance of approaches that would be categorized as being on the tougher side of the soft skills package. For instance, cussedness, stubbornness, arm twisting, and sharp elbows are all qualities that have enabled individuals to make progress on sustainability within companies. Being the most liked person in the company is not necessarily a prerequisite for effecting change.

Moreover, we should not assume that the skills and mindsets that are most often mentioned are universally applicable or relevant. Although some authors associate these mindsets (and the competencies needed to manage sustainability more generally) with 'Eastern values',[11] they are better seen as reflecting the ideals of Western liberal democracy. Some of the world's most successful companies have adopted these values, but it is hard to argue that they are universal, and positive values and qualities in some very successful companies will be notably different.

This begs the question, what new competencies are essential for taking companies through sustainability transformation? There is a risk, very evident in the literature, that the appropriate competencies are informed more by particular ideals and assumptions, rather than by empirical evidence. Shrivastava has written extensively on the pedagogy of sustainability, and emphasizes the importance of passion in bringing about change.[12] Passion and knowledge are important in any change process, and many of the cases in this book show the significance of passionate people. However, many if not most people inside companies are not especially passionate about what they do, and certainly not about sustainability: indeed, the emphasis on work–life balance in recent management theory would suggest that too strong an identity with work is harmful and unsustainable. While the ability to inspire people is an important part of the new competency puzzle, as important (but much less mentioned) is to effect the necessary change amongst the large part of management and the wider workforce that simply wants to do its job. The specific soft skills for these people are rarely discussed, and there is a potential risk that all the attention given to positivity, emotional engagement, alternative values, and passion, while inspiring some, will alienate many without whom the transformation process is unlikely to succeed.

Prospering in a resource-constrained economy

Much of what has been described in this section so far concerns the process of shifting from an environment that business is familiar with to one that in many key respects will be different. That is the journey that companies addressing sustainability challenges are on, and inevitably some have invested more in building new competencies than others. This is reflected in the current state of play discussed in Chapter 3. From this experience, one can identify not only the competencies needed for transformation, but also gain an inkling of the ones that will be necessary to prosper in a RCE. It should be stressed that this is only an inkling because although many people have a vision of what a sustainable society would look like, these are ideal types that help frame how we think about transformation but do not necessarily portray any reality that will emerge from that process. In other words, visions of future sustainability help motivate companies to undertake a journey, but are not accurate portraits of their final destination.

Some of those visions are hard to imagine given where we stand today. For example, there is a strong current of oneness with nature in some sustainability ideas: '[transformation] could help people escape from the addiction and isolation of consumerism, gain a sense of belonging to a community, improve their mental and physical health through time spent working in and with nature, and reduce the risk of obesity and the many illnesses associated with a sedentary lifestyle' (Stibbe 2009, p. 10). Not everyone affected by the business–sustainability relationship would agree with this view, and one of the challenges for companies is to undertake meaningful action in the face of quite differing, frequently mutually hostile perspectives. However, whatever route one takes, the likelihood is that it will require a rethink of how we frame business success (e.g. macro-economics, enterprise, finance), how we evaluate that success (e.g. accounting, risk, performance measurement), and how we achieve it (e.g. strategy, investment, human resources, marketing).

The developments in these areas described, for instance, in Chapters 5, 6, and 7, all require complementary competencies. There are several existing frameworks that give an idea of how management might need to reorient itself to new measures of performance and success (Chapter 1). Interface, for example– a company that reinvented itself because of its CEO's awareness of sustainability challenges—has drawn on The Natural Step, a framework that sets out system conditions for human sustainability (Snapshot 9.2). The Natural Step has also influenced companies such as Nike, Rio Tinto, and IKEA, and many of its insights have been absorbed into other approaches to managing sustainability. It shares similarities with the Five Capitals model (Chapter 1) that explains the different types of capital a company draws upon, and needs to sustain and replenish.

 Snapshot 9.2 The Natural Step—a way of identifying new competencies

The Natural Step is the brainchild of Swedish scientist, Karl-Henrik Robèr. Launched in 1989 following the Brundtland Report two years earlier, and drawing on laws of thermodynamics, it sets out four systems conditions or principles for sustainability:

1. Eliminate mankind's contribution to the progressive build-up of substances extracted from the Earth's crust (e.g. heavy metals, fossil fuels).
2. Eliminate mankind's contribution to the progressive build-up of chemicals and compounds produced by society (e.g. dioxins, polychlorinated biphenyls [PCBs]; dichlorodiphenyltrichloroethane [DDT]).
3. Eliminate mankind's contribution to the progressive physical degradation and destruction of nature and natural processes (e.g. deforestation, loss of critical wildlife habitat).
4. Eliminate mankind's contribution to conditions that undermine people's capacity to meet their basic human needs (e.g. unsafe working conditions, less than living wages).

Although at first sight this might appear to be a recipe for halting economic activity, the framework's intention is not to end all extraction or to stop disturbing the natural environment. Rather, it is to prevent the over-exploitation of those resources and stop the indefinite build-up of substances damaging to the human ecosystem.

The Natural Step was not primarily targeted at business, but the framework was welcomed by some business leaders because it provided a way of thinking about what business could do rather than just what it could not. Ray Anderson of Interface was probably the most famous CEO to use The Natural Step as a way of rethinking his company, but the framework has also been used by companies such as Electrolux, Nike, and IKEA. It builds on a basic understanding of how the biosphere functions, and how humanity and business are part of the Earth's natural systems. As used in business, it aims to create proper understanding of ecological connections without reducing the whole to a collection of details, disagreements, and counterarguments.

Training employees in the framework provides the basis for a company to apply The Natural Step to its particular circumstances. For example, J.M. Bygg AB, a construction company headquartered in Sweden, applied The Natural Step with its employees and major customers, and this became the basis for the company's Guide For Environmentally Adapted and Sound House Construction. This in turn has become a framework for deciding what competencies need to be developed in order to operate in alignment with The Natural Step's principles.

(continued)

Employed in this way, The Natural Step offers a framework to enable long-range forecasting based on some generally accepted scientific principles. It does not tell managers what to do, but it sheds light on the conditions that will affect their success.

Sources: Hawken, Lovins, & Lovins 1999; Nattrass & Altomare 1999; http://thenaturalstep.org, accessed 10 November 2011.

Questions

The Natural Step is a sustainability framework that has been adopted by companies around the world.

1. Why is a framework of this kind important for developing new competencies?
2. Why is The Natural Step more acceptable to companies than some other sets of sustainability principles?
3. Do you think The Natural Step is a useful framework for business?

Triple bottom-line

In addition to frameworks such as The Natural Step which can help companies think strategically about new competencies, there are a number of alternative approaches to established management disciplines that have arisen because of sustainability concerns. For example, TRUEVA is an integrated measure of a company's off-the-books contingent environmental liabilities. It reveals the company's ability to finance this kind of exposure from operating surpluses. The name is short for 'true value-added', and it integrates economic value added (as defined by Stern Stewart) and a measure of economic damage done by environmental emissions and effluents (as developed by Trucost PLC).[13]

TRUEVA is part of a long-standing interest in new models of accounting that integrate sustainability-related costs. This includes largely theoretical work on social and environmental accounting (Chapter 3), and attempts to develop applied methods. The triple bottom-line (3BL) is probably the most well-known of these. It was initially developed by John Elkington, co-founder of the SustainAbility consultancy,[14] and is the basis for full cost accounting that has gained some traction in the public sector. 3BL accounting requires the accountable universe to be extended beyond financial measures to include social and environmental performance. Sometimes called 'people, planet, and profit', 3BL theory says that a company should calculate the contribution of its business practices to workers, local communities, regions, and other distinguishable social units. It should also calculate its contribution to environmental sustainability so that it increases the ecological benefits and limits any ecological damage. This type of accounting is evident in cradle-to-cradle life-cycle assessment (Chapter 6). Companies should of course also calculate their financial performance, but ultimately a company's profit is not the economic value to the company, but the value created for wider society.

3BL is an enticing concept in the sustainability context because it measures the performance of companies as integral members of society rather than as independent organisms. It also complements elements of stakeholder theory, and the emphasis on stakeholder rather than simply shareholder responsibility (Chapter 8). However, applying 3BL has been problematic for various reasons, not just because of resistance from the conventional accounting community. The requirement that companies demonstrate their benefit to society is problematic because companies interact at a broad range of levels. How does a company, for instance, weigh lost jobs in one country against ones created in another, or good relations with a local community against a record of tax avoidance? Nonetheless, it has stimulated action in the general area of valuing business' relationship with wider society. For example, Unilever's work on understanding its economic impact in Indonesia and South Africa reflects the concerns of 3BL with social and natural in addition to financial capital,[15] and it has influenced PwC's work on Total Tax Contribution intended to demonstrate companies' wider social and economic impacts, and to better monitor and manage tax risk.

However, the difficulties encountered in moving 3BL from concept to practice are also worth noting if we want to understand the challenges of building new competencies suited to a prosperous RCE. Some of the barriers are discussed further later in this chapter (see 'Barriers to business school change'), and it is true that 3BL reporting has been adopted in one form or another in many companies' sustainability report. However, 3BL has gained no more than a toe-hold in the accounting world, and is today best seen as a framing device to understand business relationships than the basis for a new type of accounting.

Surviving catastrophic change

There is something missing from the discussion about the competencies companies will need either to transform towards or thrive within a RCE. If sustainability challenges are not met, and the scientific predictions are correct, then companies will need competencies to manage an era of rapid, unpredictable, perhaps catastrophic climate change with all of the knock-on effects in terms of water accessibility, agricultural change, flooding, economic growth, and migration this implies (Chapter 1). Given the size of the challenges, and society's relatively poor performance in meeting them until now (e.g. the failure to reduce CO_2e emissions levels; Chapter 2), it would be imprudent to rule out some of the worst case scenarios.

The implications of the worst-case scenarios for business management have not received much attention. There has been plenty of discussion about how such scenarios would affect companies, not least in order to convince business to take action. However, the trends in building new competencies described in this chapter imply that companies and their stakeholders presume that somehow the negative predictions from people such as Lovelock and Gilding will not materialize.[16] This could be because some people prefer not to countenance this possibility, while others interpret it as an Armageddon-like situation which will make the concerns of business a side-show. Authors such as Hulme (2010), however, do not expect that there will be a moment when the fight against climate change will be won or lost, and therefore there will be a continual shift in conditions. Managers, therefore, will need the competencies that enable them to perform as well as possible in a world of constant and probably increasing uncertainty. More effort to date has gone into making the case for thinking in terms of uncertainty than into the practice of managing it, although there is a slowly expanding body of work on the use of scenarios, futures, and pathway tools, and the new competences they require.[17] Not surprisingly, some of this work has arisen out of Shell's long-term commitment to scenario planning, including its work on scramble and blueprints.[18]

Used in the context of energy, scramble provides a basis for understanding what kinds of competency would be in demand if there was a chaotic transformation, and blueprint does the same for an orderly one. A more recent Shell report, *Signals and Signposts*,[19] analyses which scenarios appear to be unfolding, and concludes that an orderly change is increasingly less likely with all of the implications for competencies that implies.

The role of deliverers

Whenever new competencies are required, a range of service providers emerge as the recent history with total quality management, information technology, and global supply chains bears out. As what is happening with companies acting on sustainability challenges shows, some competencies will be developed within firms, some will be provided (at least initially) by consultants, and some will be insourced. Peter White, a senior figure in sustainability at P&G, describes the extensive internal training programmes that his company has had to provide, and Chad Holliday, former DuPont CEO, points to the range of different deliverers his company had to call on.[20] Such examples also highlight the company's role as a provider of new competencies, not least with the public and government.

The role of business schools

Business schools fill only one part of the capability jigsaw, but rightly or wrongly they are often placed at the centre of any portrayal of what business is and can be. The one or two years spent at graduate business school are a small part of a manager's education, but there is a strong sense that what is taught here are the essential building blocks of managerial success: an impression not discouraged by the schools themselves who are some of the most expensive providers of higher education in the world. In many ways, business schools legitimate the proper approach to accounting, strategy, organizational behaviour, finance, ethics, economics, and marketing by what they include or exclude from their curriculum. They also add gravitas to a subject by including it in their core courses.

In recent years, business schools have come under fire for encouraging the wrong sort of management, the kind that is too focused on short-term financial returns, individualism, and harmful innovation. This in turn has led to demands that business schools focus more on the type and quality of leadership, and pay attention to subjects that were at best marginal to the curriculum such as business ethics, corporate responsibility, and increasingly sustainability.

'Beyond Grey Pinstripes' was the most well-known attempt to rank business schools according to how well they tackle these areas. Until it ended in 2012, it evaluated schools in four main areas: relevant coursework, student exposure, business impact, and faculty research. As well as what is taught on core courses, and what electives are offered, it tried to unpack how well the issues are integrated across different subjects, and how much they are treated as specialisms. The Ross School of Management (Michigan, USA) was a consistently well-ranked school in Beyond Grey Pinstripes: its students can take a joint MBA and MSc degree focused on integrating economic, social, and environmental interests, and all students receive a one-week leadership programme exploring ethical leadership and the business–society relationship. Smaller business schools have often been the most innovative in this respect: San Francisco's Presidio School of Management (California, USA), for example, and the University of Exeter (UK) have both created MBA programmes solely focused on sustainability management issues.

How much to integrate and how much to separate out sustainability issues is an ongoing debate amongst those responsible for curriculum development. Many people feel that integration should be the ultimate goal so that sustainability becomes the equivalent of a concept like globalization, i.e. present in every part of the curriculum but rarely mentioned explicitly, so strong is its normative power. Others, who might not disagree with this goal, argue that, for the time being, it is better to treat sustainability as a specialist area for fear that if it is integrated too quickly it will be lost beneath the conventions and wisdom of the disciplinary status quo.

There have been several efforts to increase the quality of business school offerings in areas such as ethics, governance, and corporate responsibility (e.g. European Academy of Business in Society; CSR Europe; Global Responsible Leadership Initiative), but these do not have a particular sustainability focus, and more to the point, they have done better at establishing new areas of academic activity than integrating their concerns into other disciplines. Tepper Business School at Carnegie Mellon (Philadelphia, USA) offers faculty a professional development programme on ethics and governance, and they also receive guidance on weaving sustainability into class projects. Teaching faculty at Brigham Young University (Utah, USA) have corporate responsibility and sustainability included in their annual reviews.[21]

Another question being asked in business schools is how much they should rely on the curriculum to enhance student awareness, and how much they should invest in creating a learning environment that also includes extra-curricular activities such as clubs, awards, guest speakers, conferences, and involving the student body in the school's own sustainability issues such as the design of new facilities, and the environmental impact of intercontinental teaching. However, for all the disagreements about approach, there is a sense of an emerging consensus about the goals. As Starik et al. (2010, p. 381) write:

> The need for dramatically expanding and increasing the effectiveness of management education for sustainability requires that business academics continually explore questions such as the following:
>
> What knowledge, values, attitudes, and skills do practitioners need to contribute to the creation of environmentally sustainable organizations?
>
> How well do various delivery mechanisms (residential, distance and hybrid models, and, degree, certificate, and major field programs) accomplish program goals?
>
> What is the relative effectiveness of interdisciplinary sustainability programs versus ones in which all courses are taught by business faculty with expertise in sustainability?
>
> What teaching materials and methods are most effective, and how can sustainability research best be incorporated into these tools?
>
> How do the various dimensions noted above interact, and are there more and less effective program configurations that emerge from these interactions?

These questions do not exist in isolation: rather, they are relevant to any attempts to improve management. Criticism of business schools has resulted in more attention being paid to leadership, change management, and risk management as part of better decision-making. Many of the competencies associated with sustainability are relevant to this shift (e.g. stakeholder engagement, managing uncertainty, collaboration), and there are signs that soft skills are becoming more accepted as essential to good management generally, not just in a sustainability context. Joseph Wharton, founder of the first business school, wanted business to be as honourable a profession as medicine, the law, or theology, and its practitioners to be equipped to address the social problems of civilization. More recently, Roger Martin, dean of Rotman School of Management (Toronto), blamed business schools in part for promoting self-interest to the point where employees are being paid to bet on 'the high-stakes game' of modern capitalism.[22] INSEAD Dean, Dipak Jain, says that the role of business schools should be to turn students 'from success to significance'.[23]

Barriers to business school change

Business schools constantly face the dichotomy of what to do, how much, and when. They are one part of a person's education, and are typically short, intensive experiences that people encounter as the last part of formal learning. Students have varying expectations, but they are willing to pay high fees because they will give a strong return on investment in a fairly short space of time. The link between high fees and high remuneration packages is only made possible by companies' accepting that what students learn at business school is worth having. Company expectations of the competencies management graduates possess is therefore a key determinant of what business schools offer.

Companies are constantly reassessing this situation, and are well-represented on the governing bodies of schools as well as providing the funding for a significant (if declining) proportion of the graduate class of any given year. Some companies have criticized the established curriculum, but it is hard to detect a strong groundswell for major change. Business schools have come under attack during the ongoing global financial crisis, not least because of the role of financial institutions staffed by many masters in finance and business administration. Some prominent schools (e.g. Harvard) are paying more attention to business ethics as a result of this, but it is hard to discern major changes in what is taught in finance, accounting, or economics—all disciplines that have been blamed in one way or another for what has happened.

Is it, therefore, a case of business schools being resistant to change, or reflecting the demands of their market? In the past, they have changed; for instance, in the shift from Wharton's vision of a professional institution (see 'The role of business schools') to something akin to a vocational college teaching the essential tools of management practice.[24] There are calls (perhaps growing) for business schools to rediscover their social purpose, and this reflects the debate about the new competencies needed to manage sustainability challenges. This raises the question of how much business schools should lead in the rethinking of business rather than disseminate accepted best practice. There are many instances where business school research has led to innovative business ideas (e.g. in the areas of finance, accounting, and marketing), but they do not have a monopoly on innovation. Indeed, their role has often been to legitimize others' ideas so that they become the norm. For instance, MacKenzie (2006) has shown how ideas at the margins of economics were mainstreamed through business schools to become the primary way of understanding financial markets.

The chances of legitimizing an idea depend to a significant degree on how it relates to established disciplines and knowledge frameworks. For example, if an idea can be accommodated in an established discipline, its chances of acceptance are greater than otherwise would be the case. As noted from the earliest reflections on business and sustainability, schools are divided into disciplinary silos such as organizational behaviour, finance, and macro-economics. There is a long-standing debate about whether sustainability is a cross-cutting issue that should be integrated into each of these silos, or a stand-alone area of management that needs to be established as a new discipline. Equally, it has been argued that the current silos need to be broken up, and schools restructured to reflect their social purpose.[25] Probably, most people favour the former, but in the business school context this raises an immediate issue. A budding academic needs to publish in well-respected journals in order to progress. At present, an economist is less likely to be published in prestigious journals if s/he specializes in sustainability, and the same is true of someone building a career in strategy, accounting, or other business school disciplines. Similarly, a sustainability specialist, even if employed in the first place, would struggle to find a well-ranked journal interested in his/her work.

The various initiatives given in previous sections show that there is recognition of this problem, but it is far from being resolved. Centres dedicated to areas such as sustainability, corporate responsibility, ethics, social enterprise, and socio-management are one way forwards, and have been established in a number of schools. Nonetheless, there have been no attempts to date to systematically measure the effectiveness of the different approaches on offer. Furthermore, addressing structure by itself may leave other barriers untouched. For example, Audebrand (2010) has pointed out the vast array of war metaphors that are commonplace in the day-to-day-language and the concepts of business schools. The 'state of war' is a basic metaphor for business taught in Porter's influential competitive enterprise model (Chapter 8). Target, attack, capture, victory, deploy, defend, engage, campaign, strike, and take a shot are all part of the everyday lexicon of management teaching, and concepts such as logistics and strategy all have their origins in military thinking. Many business school students will have been introduced to Sun Tzu's *The Art of War*, and some business school texts draw directly on military literature (e.g. Ries and Trout's *Marketing Warfare* which makes use of the works of Prussian military thinker, von Clausewitz). Even advocates of sustainability education have absorbed this mindset: for example, Shrivastava equates the separation of management theory and the natural environment with 'castration'.[26]

These are very different metaphors and mindsets than the ones associated with sustainability such as health, stewardship, family, community, and cooperation. 'In a worldview structured by competition and antagonistic relationships, mutual and reciprocal relationships are marginalized and denaturalized' (Hamington 2009, cited in Audebrand 2010, p. 417). This begs the question how much sustainability can be embedded into business schools if the root metaphors are incompatible.

 ## Discussion points

Various types of organization have been associated with delivering next-generation competencies.

- How important will in-house delivery by companies be?
- Why are business schools important in this context?
- What is the biggest barrier to business schools becoming champions of sustainability?

Summary

Addressing the business–sustainability relationship implies the need for all manner of new competencies in order to ensure continued business prosperity. The exact nature of these competencies varies according to how one interprets the sustainability challenge: for instance, whether it is about transitioning to low carbon energy, or transforming to a RCE. In either case, however, new competencies will be needed, and in some cases these will be quite different to what have been developed in the past.

The competencies can be divided between hard skills (e.g. understanding renewable energy; building sustainable facilities), new capabilities (e.g. collaborative innovation; new approaches to risk), and changed mindsets (e.g. a sustainability-based understanding of society). Executives express a strong degree of interest in sustainability and how to incorporate it into their companies, but it is less clear what exactly they want, how much they are willing to invest in it, and the timeframe for any action. This situation is exacerbated by the mixed signals they receive from governments and investors.

There are different ways of delivering these new competencies, and provision currently comes from a mix of in-house teams, executive education, consultancy firms, and specialist organizations. Business schools have been singled out as key to the development and delivery of sustainability competencies, and this has often been linked to a wider criticism about management education's perceived failure to produce managers who are stewards of the public good. Needless to say, this criticism is rejected by many, but that is not the only reason business schools are struggling to address new competencies, and decide how much they should take on a leadership role in this area. There are many innovative initiatives at different schools, but for the most part they are not supplying nor creating the demand for new competencies that sustainability challenges seem to demand.

 Further reading

Carpenter, M.A. & Carpenter, M. 2009, *An executive's primer on the strategy of social networks*, Business Expert Press, New York, NY.
Primer for senior managers on how to manage sustainability relationships.

Landrum, N., Landrum, N.E., & Edwards, S. 2009, *Sustainable business: An executive's primer*, Business Expert Press, New York, NY.
Primer for senior managers on how to manage sustainability.

Nattrass, B.F. & Altomare, M. 1999, *The Natural Step for business: Wealth, ecology, and the evolutionary corporation*, New Society Publishers, Gabriola Island, BC.
Introduction to The Natural Step framework and its implications for business.

Ramirez, R., Selsky, J.W., & Van der Heijden, K. (Eds) 2010, *Business planning for turbulent times: New methods for applying scenarios*, 2nd edn, Earthscan, London.
A collection of papers on how companies will need to improve their ability to manage uncertainty, and the competencies this involves.

Wankel, C. & Stoner, J.A.F. 2009, *Management education for global sustainability*, Information Age Publishing, Charlotte, NC.
Ideas on how to include sustainability in management education.

Case study 9   Sustainability dichotomies in business schools

Professor Marquez had been dean of Maxwell School of Management for less than a month. He had made his name for his research into equity derivatives, although later on he had distanced himself from trends he saw as confirming Warren Buffet's view that they can turn into 'financial weapons of mass destruction'. He had also published a couple of papers on liquidity and exit strategies for investors in social enterprises.

That all seemed a long time ago; before he became more famous as a 'turnaround dean' coming to the rescue of struggling business schools. However, he had been reminded of some of those ideas by an email from an eminent Maxwell graduate whom the school was trying to get to be more active on campus. The person in question was a senior executive at a very reputable private bank, and an active promoter of young entrepreneurs. She had emailed Dean Marquez in her typically abrupt style. She wanted to know what Maxwell was doing to teach its students about sustainability. She said she was shocked at the lack of awareness some senior managers had of social and environmental trends, even when they appeared to have material consequences for their operations. Moreover, she was horrified at the very different levels of knowledge amongst her clients on these issues, ranging from panic to obliviousness. Why, she asked, weren't these issues at the heart of the school's curriculum?

Maxwell is a small school, well regarded by its students, but stuck in the middle of the business school rankings. The appointments committee had made no bones about why they wanted Dean Marquez: they wanted to see the school grow, in terms of student numbers, campus size, revenues, and reputation. They had agreed to give him a free hand about how to achieve these goals, and in turn he had agreed to link his performance to Maxwell's showing in the all-important rankings. Since then, the size of the challenge had become yet more obvious. The plans for a new block of lecture theatres and student accommodation could not be paid for without an increase in student numbers; without more students the school would not have enough income for future developments and would struggle to improve.

Dean Marquez had every sympathy for the alumnus's message. A senior faculty member had mentioned Beyond Grey Pinstripes, and it was rumoured that the government (which provided research funding and also validated Maxwell's charitable status) was testing a sustainability ranking system for higher education generally. Her 'suggestion' that she survey the alumni on sustainability issues for business schools could not be taken lightly. He was also vaguely aware, as she had pointed out, that several schools were developing sustainability electives, trying to integrate sustainability into the core courses, perhaps even create a core course or a capstone on sustainability. However, were these the leading schools that Maxwell aspired to stand amongst? A few of the top-ranked schools in Beyond Grey Pinstripes were also prominent in the *Financial Times* rankings, but most were not, and the Harvards, Whartons, and London Business Schools were noticeable by their absence. Was it going to help Maxwell grow if it was associated with Hixville Little Pixie School of Administration?

Dean Marquez's PA stuck her head round the door: five minutes to the management committee meeting. Maxwell's new vision was on the agenda. A few of the longest-serving faculty were quite happy with the old vision, but he sensed there was an appetite for change: most faculty seemed unhappy with Maxwell's old strategy that Marquez summarized as 'adequacy without excellence': the school did a lot of things fairly well, but did not stand out in anything. This was reflected in two key indicators for students: their salary on leaving the school, and how quickly they got a job. A Maxwell MBA seemed even less in demand now there was a recession on: it stood for competence but not irreplaceability.

There had already been some suggestions about new directions. One faculty member was very keen on social enterprise, and Dean Marquez himself was patron of a children's charity he had set up in his youth. But to put it bluntly what kind of fees would budding social entrepreneurs be willing to pay, and how would the salaries of even senior managers of NGOs affect the rankings? Maxwell ran

(continued)

programmes with a neighbouring engineering department, and one of its strengths over the years had been producing good manufacturing managers. Perhaps there was something that could be developed further here. Finance was the backbone of top schools, and there was plenty of opportunity for increasing Maxwell's reputation in that area (although finance professors were not cheap).

Whatever route the school took, it would need to help put the school on a firmer financial footing in terms of fees, corporate donations, and alumni gifts. But the good news was that in the short term there was a reasonable investment fund that could be used to recruit people, establish new programmes, and promote them. At least for now, finances were not a big item on the management's agenda, although that would change if Maxwell did not rethink itself. The PA knocked on Dean Marquez's door again.

NB Maxwell and Little Pixie are entirely fictitious institutions, as is Dean Marquez and anyone else in this case study. However, the situation is a real one for many business schools today.

Questions

1. Maxwell is under pressure to change.

   a. What are the incentives to change?

   b. What are the risks of not changing?

   c. What are the different areas the school has available to it to make changes?

2. A prominent alumnus says sustainability is an opportunity for Maxwell.

   a. Why is sustainability an opportunity?

   b. What are the disadvantages of focusing on sustainability?

   c. What are some of the ways Maxwell could address sustainability as part of its curriculum?

3. Dean Marquez is about to set to work on creating a new vision for the school.

   a. What are the arguments for putting a focus on sustainability at the centre of that vision?

   b. What are the arguments against?

   c. Based on this case and relevant information from elsewhere in Chapter 9, decide what the new vision will be, and three of its key features.

 ## Endnotes

1. (United Nations Global Compact 2010)

2. (Ashridge, United Nations, & EABIS 2009)

3. (Blowfield 2011)

4. (Starik 2010)

5. See, for instance, the Edelman Trust Barometer, http://www.edelman.com/trust/.

6. (Henriques 2010)

7. (Campanale & Leggett 2011)

8. (Stibbe 2009)

9. I am grateful to two of my London Business School students who conducted work on understanding and behaviour competencies as part of their Second Year Project, and whose ideas and findings have been incorporated in this section.

10. (Stibbe 2009)

11. (E.g. Gladwin 1995; Stibbe 2009)

12. (Shrivastava 2010)

13. (Thomas 2007)

14. (Elkington 1997)

15. (Clay 2005; Kapstein 2008)

16. (Gilding 2011; Lovelock 2010)

17. (E.g. Heifetz 2009; Ramirez 2010; van der Heijden 2010)

18. http:// www.shell.com/scenarios, accessed 5 October 2011.

19. http://www-static.shell.com/static/aboutshell/downloads/aboutshell/signals_signposts.pdf, accessed 5 October 201.

20. (Holliday 2010; White 2009)

21. (Christensen 2007)

22. (Martin 2011)

23. Dipak Jain, opening remarks at EABIS colloquium, Fontainebleu, October 2011.

24. (Khurana 2007)

25. (Gladwin 1995)

26. (Gladwin 1995)

Section 3

The external environment

10 Governance

Key terms

Universal owner   Government
Civil economy   International negotiations
Civil governance   Path dependence

Online resources

- Resources on non-climate change governance.
- Case study on integrated transport.
- Case study on multi-stakeholder governance and sustainable living environments.
- Links to policy advice for business.

  http://www.oxfordtextbooks.co.uk/orc/blowfield/

Chapter in brief

This chapter looks outside of business at how other sections of society are attempting to govern sustainability issues. It begins by identifying the different sectors of society, their governance roles, and some of their achievements. It then looks in more detail at government initiatives at the international, regional, national, and local level. It discusses the phenomenon of multi-stakeholder governance, and how different sectors are collaborating to address sustainability challenges. Climate governance is dealt with in considerable detail, both because of the importance of the climate change challenge, and for the lessons it offers for other sustainability governance initiatives. The chapter concludes with a look at the future of sustainability governance.

Sustainability and governance

Government

Sustainability is a governance problem. This at least is the view of some people who having assessed issues such as energy, water, and biodiversity, and the solutions on offer from innovation, corporate leadership, and sustainable consumption and production, reach the conclusion that a strong governance system is essential to meet our various sustainability challenges. By this, some people mean that government has the primary responsibility in tackling climate change, biodiversity, demographic change, etc. Historically, governments have been charged with forging a social consensus and rallying support for existential crises such as wars and combating natural disasters. Only government, for instance, can mobilize the power of the state to tackle fundamental contradictions at the core of sustainability such as that between the long-term interests of society that require us to pay now for future benefits that will go to people we will never know, and the short-term biases of people today who attach more importance to personal experience than objective facts (proximity bias), prefer to keep what they have rather than jeopardize it by pursuing greater rewards (risk aversion), and place a higher value on immediate benefits than future ones.

One of government's main roles has been to mediate between the myriad interests in a society to reach a consensus about the common good. This at least is a principle of democratic government which is imbued with checks and balances to prevent any single interest group forcing through its will. There are different forms of democracy, and as we will see these have resulted in different sustainability policies around the world. Some democracies are weaker than others, and there are also various non-democratic forms of government, including countries such as Russia and China which are important from a sustainability perspective. In terms of the business–society relationship, all governments in all countries in which there is capitalist enterprise must negotiate a consensus around two apposite quandaries. On the one hand, business is asking how it can make a profit from and while contributing to sustainability: on the other hand, society is wondering what can be done if money cannot be made from sustainability, or more profoundly, what will happen if sustainability cannot be achieved by making money.

As we will see throughout this chapter, governments have invested considerable amounts of financial and political capital to try and resolve sustainability's governance challenges. However, for reasons we shall also explore, there is a sense that sustainability is a governance failure. This could be because in some parts of the world that have only recently emerged from dictatorship, there is an inherent distrust of government, and a sense that business and civil society offer a brighter future. In some countries, there is apathy about the democratic process reflected in low voter turnout, and more trust in civil society organizations as champions of key societal issues. Governments have not covered themselves in glory in the way they have conducted international negotiations on themes such as global warming, and have contributed to a climate of uncertainty amongst business and the general public because of U-turns and mixed messages in areas such feed-in tariffs, product labelling, and the materiality of sustainability in relation to corporate reporting (Snapshot 10.1). Britain, Italy, and especially Spain, for example, have offered, then reduced or withdrawn renewable energy subsidies, leaving households and businesses confused and financially out of pocket.

Even without this hesitancy about government, however, many sustainability challenges are difficult to resolve within the current international political system. Following the Second World War, there was great enthusiasm for international governance, finance, and collaboration. This led to the setting up of the United Nations, and the so-called Bretton Woods Twins (the International Monetary Fund and the World Bank Group). The Cold War, soon after, showed that international governance would always have to serve national interests, and although important conventions and resolutions have been passed on issues from biodiversity to atomic energy to the law of the sea, from women in development, to renewable energy, international governance has struggled to address the global and trans-boundary issues that affect business. The UN Conference on Trade and Development (UNCTAD), for instance, was set up in 1964 to improve the benefits of trade for developing economies, but it has been criticized for failing to develop an alternative to the neo-liberal agenda, and it is now overshadowed by the World Trade Organization as the focal point for international business decisions.[1] The World Trade Organization in turn is now in crisis because of the failure of the Doha Development Round of trade negotiations which have been stalled since 2008.

 Snapshot 10.1   Unintended consequences—Tate & Lyle Sugars

Mention Tate & Lyle, and one does not immediately think of renewable energy. The sugar and agribusiness giant, responsible for products such as SPLENDA, is however engaged in renewable energy generation, in particular CoCHP technologies (co-firing of biomass with combined heat and power).[2] As such, the company was affected by the British government's Renewable Obligations Certification (ROC) scheme, introduced in 2002 and obliging UK electricity suppliers to source a portion of their energy from renewable sources. Suppliers demonstrate they are in compliance by presenting certificates that can be acquired by generating renewable energy directly or buying it from other suppliers.

In order to encourage certain renewable energy technologies, in 2009 the government introduced banding so that some sources of energy earn more ROC than others. In the process of deciding the bands, the government noticed errors in the original cost assessments of CoCHP, and an upshot was that Tate & Lyle went from receiving 1.5 ROC per megawatt hour, to one ROC. Fearful that other suppliers would get greater subsidies because they were not included in the review, the company sought a judicial review (which failed), and a subsequent appeal.

The company argued that it was unfair to single out its technology, and subject it to a review that its competitors did not undergo. It said that the subsidy to other technologies was based on older, incorrect information, and that the error in the original assessments should not be used to reduce the CoCHP subsidy to the company which had made investments on the basis of the government's figures.

Tate & Lyle Sugars lost in the courts because it was held that the review of the figures was in the public interest, and that the company was not being treated unfairly. Other technologies might also warrant review, the courts said, but that had no relevance in this case. The company was now receiving an appropriate subsidy given the costs of developing CoCHP; all they were being denied was a windfall that they might have had if the original errors had not been discovered.

Sources: http://ukhumanrightsblog.com/2011/06/03/roc-sugar-keep-the-swings-and-ignore-the-roundabouts/; http://cleanenergyblog.eversheds.com/all-briefings/the-law-of-unintended-consequences/; http://www.freshfields. com/publications/pdfs/2011/sep11/31165.pdf, all accessed 18 February 2012.

Questions

The case of Tate & Lyle Sugars Ltd. versus Secretary of State for Energy and Climate Change is an example of the often heated debate about subsidies for renewable energy.

1. Why are some governments cautious about subsidizing renewable energy?

2. Was the court's decision unfair to Tate & Lyle Sugars?

3. Is this an instance of governments 'moving the goalposts', something companies have pointed to as a disincentive to making sustainability-related investments?

Civil governance

Our earlier examples show the shortcoming of international government to government collaboration, and are part of the backdrop for the emergence of civil governance. Some of the most significant developments related to sustainability have started outside of government. Carson's *Silent Spring*, the non-government organization Greenpeace, and the Sierra Club (Chapter 2) all demonstrate how the media, communities, and organizations of like-minded people can influence business and government behaviour. Over the past 100 years, governments in the USA, the UK, and elsewhere have gone from staying well clear of economics, to becoming deeply involved following the depressions of the 1920s, to championing free markets with minimal government interference.[3] The latter of these periods coincided with the rapid expansion of civil society organizations, often focused on single issues or the concerns of a particular group of citizens. Some of the main contributors to sustainability debates—and organizations that business is often keen to partner with (Chapter 8)—came to prominence during the pro-business periods associated with Margaret Thatcher, Roger Douglas, and Ronald Reagan. NGOs filled some of the gaps left by government's partial retreat from social welfare, and appeared to be more knowledgeable and trustworthy on a range of issues such as international development, conservation, and ethical consumerism.

In this respect, NGOs were continuing a long tradition of civil engagement in policy reform. The eighteenth-century anti-slavery groups in London and Philadelphia spawned a mass movement that was to outlaw the slave trade worldwide in less than a century despite government and business opposition. Trades unions throughout the nineteenth and twentieth centuries forced changes on business owners, changed the face of government, and were often behind the overthrow of colonial powers. One thing that was different this time, however, was that rather than operating largely in geographical isolation with limited contact and even less liaison with similar groups elsewhere, civil society was increasingly the beneficiary of global interconnectedness, not least through the internet. In 1990, when companies were learning how ICT advances could help them create global supply chains, NGOs and trades unions were discovering how easy it was to send news about labour or environmental abuses in that same supply chain to like-minded organizations worldwide. At first through faxes and then through emails, civil governance was able to by-pass local press censorship and corporate disinformation campaigns to explain the situation in factories, mine-towns, forest communities, and other hitherto sheltered outreaches of global trade.

In a relatively short space of time, companies began to realize the importance of teaming up with civil governance actors. While Nike was trying to whitewash claims of labour abuses in factories in the early 1990s,[4] B&Q was working with the WWF to establish the UK Buyers' Group that would become the basis for the Forest Stewardship Council.[5] Often these partnerships would ignore government, something that was met by government with a mixture of annoyance at being supplanted, and quiet gratitude that it would not have to try and legislate or enforce complex transboundary issues. The idea of multi-stakeholder governance as a way of addressing issues arising because of global supply chains is now an important element of sustainability as it is of corporate responsibility generally.[6] The FSC, the International Federation of Organic Agriculture Movements (IFOAM), and the ETI are examples of multi-stakeholder governance initiatives, each offering a voluntary means for companies to conform to particular social or environmental production standards, regulated through the combined power of the commercial value chain and civil society organizations.

At times feeding into this, at times isolated from it, have been local movements reacting to sustainability issues.[7] It seems likely that poor people in developing economies will be amongst the most susceptible to negative consequences of climate change, water shortages, and competition for ecosystem services, and already rural communities in parts of Africa and South Asia are having to *adapt* to climate change rather than mitigate it. (See Case study 10.)

 Key concept 10.1 Civil society

In analysing democratic societies, it is common to distinguish between government, the private sector, and civil society. Civil society refers to that part of a democracy that provides a counterweight to the other sectors, and thereby adds balance to the process of governance. Civil society organizations include trades unions, NGOs, the media, and community groups, as well as informal networks of groups and individuals that form around a particular issue.

Civil economy

An aspect of civil governance that can get overlooked is what Davis, Lukomnik, and Pitt-Watson (2006) call the civil economy. Civil society organizations have a history of using their position as shareholders to put pressure on companies. Organizations such as the Interfaith Center on Corporate Responsibility have used the power of faith-based organizations' pension funds to advocate on a range of environmental and human rights issues. In 2002, the pension funds of several Catholic religious orders backed a resolution by nuns asking that GE report on GHG emissions. CEO Jeff Immelt dismissed the resolution and asked that it be rebutted, but 23 per cent of GE's investors supported the nuns' case. Arguably, that was the turning point that led Immelt to integrate sustainability issues into GE's strategy called ecomagination (sic). Similarly, Marks & Spencer executives were surprised when their shareholders, after what had been a tough financial year, applauded the company for winning a handful of sustainability awards, and within a year the retailer had launched its Beyond the Label initiative (see Appendix 1, Extended case study A).

Civil economy refers to the vast number of people who, through their savings, hold the majority of stock in the world's largest corporations. This shift in ownership is relatively recent: previously, a fairly small number of rich investors owned the majority of shares. The rise in pension funds, college tuition funds, and other funds that allow people to hedge for the future means that half of all stocks in the USA, and 75 per cent of those in the UK are owned by financial institutions acting for small investors. Sovereign wealth funds have added to what Peter Drucker long ago predicted would be a revolution in share ownership.[8]

Although pension funds may not seem to be a hotbed of revolutionary zeal, and despite the antagonistic relations funds such as USS have provoked by trying to downgrade members' benefits, there are two important points about the way they are run. First, their investment policies cannot favour any particular member: they must serve the common good. Second, they are universal owners: because of their size, they own a slice of the entire economy through their portfolios (Chapter 7). Unlike small investors who look to profit from the performance of particular companies or industries, and are therefore happy to take short-term gains regardless of wider consequences, universal owners only prosper when the economy as a whole flourishes. If they focused too narrowly on a particular section of the investment universe, they would be accused of holding high-risk, unbalanced portfolios. In theory at least, the universal owner wants companies to create real value, and to allocate capital to where real value is being created. It does not want companies to damage society, and it does not want them to hold on to capital or waste it by investing in non-value adding acquisitions. As Davis, Lukomnik, and Pitt-Watson point out, '[universal owners] can have no interest in abetting behavior by any one company that yields a short-term boost while threatening harm to the economic system as a whole' (2006, p. 18).

Furthermore, the universal owner must represent the interest of the millions of citizens who entrust their savings to it. Hermes is a pension fund manager that has a reputation for applying the universal owner hypothesis (see Chapter 7, Snapshot 7.1). It claims that by taking a position as an activist fund manager, it has created a surplus for its investors, and released billions of dollars in value from companies that were being managed in the interests of their executives. It argues that it is not in the interests of citizens as investors to have companies that lock up capital or waste it on mergers and acquisitions that are rewarded in executive bonuses but fail to add value to the company. Moreover, it is not in the interests of those same citizens as workers or as members of society to have companies that fail to add jobs, pay good wages, or be good custodians of their products.

⊙ Discussion points

In the light of what we have discussed so far, consider the following:

- Is sustainability a governance challenge?
- What is the difference between civil society and the civil economy?
- What are the strengths and weaknesses of government in the sustainability governance context?

Government initiatives

There has been no shortage of government initiatives to do with some aspects of sustainability. In India, for example, shocked at the levels of city pollution, the Kolkata Government is pursuing a policy of scrapping high emissions vehicles, and promoting compressed natural gas alternatives. In North America, a coalition of states and provinces has banded together to develop a carbon trading system under the title, the West Coast Initiative. South Korea was the most aggressive government in making green development part of its economic stimulus package in the late 2000s (Chapter 2). TEEB has been funded by the European Commission and countries such as Japan and Sweden (Chapter 3), and through the United Nations many of the world's countries have signed up to resolutions on biodiversity, water management, and renewable energy. In 2008, the Climate Change Act made Britain the first country to adopt a legally binding framework to tackle the dangers of climate change. China's twelfth five-year plan (2011–2015) includes aggressive targets to reduce energy intensity, and identifies clean energy, energy conservation, and clean energy vehicles as strategic sectors for the national economy that will grow from being three per cent to five per cent of GDP.

As demonstrated in the example of the international climate change negotiations explored later in this chapter, sustainability has been hugely challenging for governments. However, it can be a mistake to rush too quickly to the conclusion that governments are doing a 'bad job'. On issues such as transboundary water issues, for instance, although there is potential for conflict, it is noteworthy how little conflict there has actually been.[9] However, there have certainly been failures and governments in countries such as Australia have been ousted because of their sustainability policies.

The examples of success and failure show the kinds of option available to government at local, national, and international level. Broadly, there are six main options available.[10]

Option 1. Surmounting sustainability challenges through growth: based on the premise that sustainability challenges lend themselves to technological solutions (Chapter 6), governments can pursue policies to encourage faster economic growth because this will generate increases in wealth required to invest in sustainability solutions. This is the option that characterizes federal government policy in the USA, and some European countries.

Option 2. Autocratic, centralized command and control: although fewer in number than 50 years ago, there are various countries that adopt a scientific approach to government exemplified, for instance, in state socialism. Such countries are reliant to a considerable degree on the private sector to deliver their targets, but government sees its role as engineering the economy, not just through trade and fiscal policies, but by investing in particular industries. This option is exemplified by China's approach to sustainability such as the aforementioned five-year plan, and its renewable energy plan (Chapter 2).

Option 3. Green growth version 1: social democratic governments have long sought a halfway house between free enterprise and social engineering, and this is being carried over into their policies on sustainability. Unlike Option 1, they do not trust economic growth and technology to deliver the necessary solutions in a timely fashion, and in marked contrast to some neo-liberal economists, they believe markets have to be encouraged to take timely action. The Netherlands with its policy of promoting a 'cradle-to-cradle' society with a minimal environmental footprint is one country pursuing this version of green growth, and broadly speaking it characterizes the policies of the European Commission.

Option 4. Green growth version 2: some governments hold that sustainability can be incorporated into a successful capitalist economy (cf. Option 3), but are reluctant to go too far down the route of coordinated markets because they do not believe governments make wise investment decisions. Thus, for example, the UK led the world in setting legally binding targets for CO_2 emissions reductions (see earlier), but successive right- and left-wing governments have been reluctant to interfere as the market decides how best to achieve these goals.

Option 5. Prosperity without growth: some people argue that sustainability challenges can only be met if we decouple prosperity from economic growth (Chapter 3). Alternative measures of societal well-being to GDP are being tried in countries such as Thailand and Bhutan, and there is a growing (though still marginal) interest in including happiness in national statistics (Chapter 11).

Option 6. Plutocratic growth: few politicians would ever stand up and say they wanted more wealth for the rich, and did not care about the poor. However, one could argue that a possible outcome of weak sustainability policies now and worst case scenarios in the future will be an exacerbation of the current wealth divide that separates developed and developing economies, and is characteristic of countries such as the USA, the UK, and Brazil (Chapter 2). In a variation of Option 1, plutocratic growth similar to that described by Ajay Kapur (Chapter 2) would see wealthy sections of the population investing in the means to flourish in a resource-constrained economy, and poorer sections struggling to deal with the consequences of ecosystem degradation, water and energy shortages, and increases in global average temperatures of more than 2°C. Governments today do not recognize this option, but it is one that given some interpretations of the present sustainability situation, needs to be taken seriously in the coming years.

These different Options are part of the context within which any business decisions about sustainability need to be considered. The Options themselves do not exist in a vacuum: they are positions that have been reached because of a long history of negotiation, dispute, and consensus, and this represents a path dependency that cannot simply be discarded (Chapter 12). Von Hayek (1944) talks of society being created over time like a footpath through a field: it is not a deliberate act, but the outcome of innumerable, largely forgotten acts that culminate in the present, and are determinants of future possibility. Thus, for example, governments with a long tradition of favouring supply side policies (e.g. Options 1 and 4) will face considerable system inertia if they suddenly plump for demand-side policies such as changing consumer behaviour.

Path dependence is one of the factors that contributes to an impression of government inertia when it comes to tackling sustainability issues. This is not universally true, and the progress made in some countries is often cited with envy as a criticism of what is happening in one's own region. The USA has been called 'a failed state' when it comes to climate change, even though the Kyoto Protocol that it refused to ratify is itself now often seen as a failure.[11] Developed economies have been blamed by developing ones for taking unreasonable positions in international negotiations, even as the former have tried to implement the ideas of Ted Hanisch to increase investment in climate change mitigation in poorer countries (Chapter 6). While some politicians—at times funded by corporate leaders—have spoken vociferously against the idea of sustainability being an issue for governments, overall disappointment with government achievements is often a matter of realpolitik as politicians try to mediate the demands of different policy objectives such as economic growth, financial recovery, energy security, international trade, land use, and managing the global commons. Thus, for instance, at its first conference since resuming power in 2010, Britain's Conservative Party—which had promised in its manifesto it would be the greenest government ever—had to cancel its green growth day in favour of debates about child benefits, welfare reform, and motorway infrastructure.

National and local government

Discussion about sustainability governance tends to focus on major national, regional, and international initiatives. However, local government often led the way in acting on agreements at the 1992 Rio Summit, and in countries such as the USA where there has been relatively little federal government progress, state and city governments have continued to be innovative. The C40 Cities Climate Leadership Group, for example, brings together large cities from around the world to tackle climate change. It was founded in 2005 by London Mayor, Ken Livingstone, and in 2006 merged with Bill Clinton's Climate Initiative. It is currently chaired by New York Mayor, Michael Bloomberg, and includes cities such as Berlin, Hong Kong, Jakarta, Johannesburg, Los Angeles, Sao Paulo, Seoul, and Tokyo.

Through planning policy, building regulations, and programmes for 'zero-carbon' housing, local and national governments can influence the direction of sustainability. In the UK, companies pay a surcharge on their energy bill (the Climate Change Levy), and this funds the activities of the Carbon Trust, an organization set up to help the private and public sectors cut carbon emissions and save energy. Municipal governments have not only had local impacts, but have also influenced national policy. For instance, the London Borough of Merton was the first to expect all new developments to integrate renewable energy technologies on site which would reduce carbon emissions by ten per cent. This policy has been widely copied, and is now part of national planning policy. Cities such as Stockholm and Malmö (Chapter 6) pride themselves on their comprehensive sustainable planning policies, and others such as Bogota and Curitiba have won praise for integrated planning and transport.

However, not all such initiatives are a success. In 2009, France's President Sarkozy promised to 'lead a battle' to introduce a carbon tax on imports from countries that did not abide by international targets on carbon emissions, but had to back down when China proposed including an emissions charge at the site of production.[12] For many years, researchers such as Tony Allan (1998) have highlighted the issue of virtual water, referring to the water embedded in traded products (Chapter 2). For example, when a country imports a tonne of wheat, it effectively saves itself 1,300 cubic metres of water, i.e. the amount of water needed to grow that amount of wheat. If this is not taken into account, countries can hide the consequences of their trade for other nations, particularly those that are water stressed. However, virtual water is one of the many aspects of sustainability that has had very little impact on government policy.

Furthermore, any policy advances have to be considered in the context of wider policy trends. We have mentioned how renewable energy is increasingly framed in some countries as an aspect of energy security (Chapter 2). Some countries are adopting strident policies of resource nationalism.[13] This can take the form of governments taking direct control of economic activity to do with their own natural resources (e.g. controlling gas reserves, forests, land), or foreign governments (including sovereign wealth funds) securing their access to other countries' resources. For example, Mali handed over large tranches of land to Libya for industrial agriculture in a project called Malibya, and this is part of a wider worldwide trend that has uncertain consequences for sustainable development (Chapter 12).

 Discussion points

There has been a host of initiatives on sustainability governance.

- Which governance option most closely reflects the policies of your country? Which one least reflects them?
- How are the policies in your country path dependent?
- Why are local governments sometimes more active in tackling sustainability than national ones?

Alternative governance

Whenever solutions to sustainability challenges are discussed, fingers are pointed at government, sometimes for interfering too much, sometimes for doing too little. Business through initiatives such as the Prince of Wales's Corporate Leaders Group on Climate Change has asked for governments to establish sensible, rigorous policies to combat climate change. At the same time, if governments are judged at fault in the sustainability context, this cannot be divorced from the conscious intentions of the surge in business lobbying activity in many democracies which according to some observers has seriously weakened the capacity of governments to develop coordinated policies and regulations.[14]

Another interpretation is that the way government perceives the world has changed in ways that affect its outlook on sustainability. It has been argued, for instance, that a feature of modern democracies is their reliance on scientific evidence rather than previous appeals to political ideology. Government policy, it is claimed, is typically based on the evidence of technical experts that is then subject to some kind of discussion with special interest groups representing the citizenry.[15] Thus, the Millennium Development Goals, for example (Chapter 2), were compiled by human development and poverty alleviation experts, and assessed by international development NGOs before being adopted as international targets. Governments are keen to engage citizens to give their policies legitimacy, especially if electoral turnouts are in decline. However, the typical engagement has been criticized for the same reasons stakeholder management by companies has (Chapter 8): citizens may not feel NGOs represent them, or if they are consulted directly, they feel more like an audience than participants. This criticism became a central thread of the participatory school of policy and management that was influential in the 1980s and 1990s,[16] and is evident in the various United Nations consultative processes about sustainability.

Participation, and associated themes such as accountability and transparency are now central to sustainability discourses, and are championed as self-evident goods by civil society organizations, business, and government (Chapter 8). However, the notion that multi-stakeholder approaches built on such common principles are an effective form of governance has also been questioned. Their effectiveness against alternatives is rarely tested, but more fundamentally the values they champion can have some perverse outcomes in the sustainability context. For example, participation is designed to achieve a consensus that in turn is considered efficient (i.e. the optimal outcome given the parties and information involved). Hence, participation is utilitarian-based, and like all such approaches runs the risk of discounting, marginalizing, or ignoring other facts and points of view that may be significant in the longer term. Similarly, accountability and transparency is only useful if what is counted is important in the sustainability context. This can generate highly complex data that are difficult for any but technical experts to interpret, and thus runs the risk of giving a democratic sheen to what is ultimately a technocratic decision. Furthermore, accountability validates quantitative explanations, something that Mike Hulme, for instance, blames for some of the missteps in climate change policy.

Hulme observes that as the scientific data on climate change grew in volume and consensus, so the scientific community, environmentalists, and policy-makers began to talk in terms of global findings and implications (Hulme 2009, 2010). This served the purpose of presenting combating climate change as a global project, one in which the international community and its multiple sectors needed to unite to avert unacceptable rises in global average temperatures. Whereas in the past the world had been described in terms of local climates, now there was a global climate measurable through a single index. This was useful for scientists, politicians, and some environmental campaigners: it made climate change a unitary concept around which different actors could gather. These actors in turn made the concept the focus of particular initiatives such as the United Nations Framework Convention on Climate Change (see 'The UN process'). These initiatives serve as what political scientists call field configuring events, i.e. prominent forums that have the power to influence how a field like climate change is thought about and addressed.[17]

However, the framing of climate change as a unitary concept has also had negative consequences for governance. First, it has helped alienate people from the fundamental issue: 'no-one experiences or witnesses global mean temperature and it requires extraordinary efforts of the imagination for it to acquire purchase in the practices of everyday living' (Hulme 2010, p. 560). Second, it has encouraged policy-makers to think in terms of narrow goals to be achieved within specific timeframes, something that can stifle the way we think about climate change and its solutions (Chapter 2). Third, it has made international policy insensitive to local variables, preventing people from considering how climate change's impacts differ from place to place.

Ironically, civil society organizations have contributed to this alleged misframing of the governance challenge. Many of the non-government (sic) governance organizations see their role as keeping government and business honest, alerting them to overlooked dimensions to the sustainability challenge at hand. Their commitment to this is very evident during field configuring events to the point where Copenhagen city welcomed a 2009 climate change summit there as a tourist attraction.[18] However, in order to perform this function, NGOs have to take a very conventional view of politics and the private sector because to question the legitimacy of these sectors would risk alienating themselves from the processes they wish to influence.

Climate governance

Many of the examples in this chapter so far are connected to climate change. Climate change is, of course, only one dimension of sustainability, and companies would be mistaken to be myopic about viewing all social and environmental challenges through this one lens. However, in the governance context it is very informative in multiple ways. It has propitiated the most sophisticated responses we have seen to the governance of global commons. These responses comprise government, private sector, and multi-stakeholder initiatives developed through international processes involving countries with widely diverging interests. They comprise legally-binding commitments, voluntary agreements, market-based interventions, and collaborations that range from finance to technology transfer to capacity building of government and civil society. Taken as a whole, they offer examples of how history and path dependence affect the development of sustainability solutions, and offer lessons for the governance of other sustainability challenges in the future.

Snapshot 10.2   Alternative governance—private equity and NGOs collaboration over coal-fired power

Kohlberg Kravis Roberts's (KKR's) 1989 acquisition of RJR Nabisco became infamous as an example of hard-headed, shareholder value-driven capitalism in Burrough and Helyar's *Barbarians at the Gate* (1990). Two decades on and KKR's record-breaking private equity deal to purchase the energy utility, TXU, has made headlines for different reasons.

TXU had been under attack from environmental groups because of its plans to build 11 old-technology, coal-fired power plants in Texas. The plans became bogged down in a swamp of public outcry, political manoeuvring, and litigation. Texas governor, Rick Perry (a recipient of TXU campaign donations), applauded TXU's plans, and signed an executive order fast-tracking the permitting process so that what once took up to four years could now be done in six months.

In what some are holding up as a landmark collaboration between private equity and environmental activists, two environmental NGOs, the Natural Resources Defence Council and Environmental Defense, negotiated a deal whereby, in return for their backing the purchase, KKR agreed to suspend developments of eight of the power plants, pilot a 'clean coal' plant, cut GHG emissions, invest in alternative energy, and back government climate change legislation.

For the NGOs involved, it is another example of how to collaborate with business to achieve environmental objectives, although this, in turn, has led to criticism from other environmental groups that the KKR–NGO agreement contained too many loopholes. For KKR, the support of these multi-million-dollar NGOs reduces the risk that the purchase might otherwise represent and, it hopes, will strengthen TXU's licence to operate. It also signifies a new development in private equity strategy, under which firms bet on the profits to be made from social and political change.

Sources: Paulden 2009; Smith & Carlton 2007; *The Economist 2007*.

Questions

The purchase of TXU is an example of alternative governance by business and civil society upsetting government plans.

1. Although it is portrayed as a 'win–win agreement' between KKR and the NGOs, what do you think were the advantages for the former?

2. What do you think were the risks and potential disadvantages for the NGOs?

3. Why were the NGOs more credible than the governor?

The UN process

Scientists and politicians had been aware of the climate change phenomenon for a long time before collective action started to be considered. The increasing amount of research led the World Meteorological Organization and the United Nations Environment Programme to commission a review to identify any consensus amongst scientists in 1988. The IPCC produced its first report in 1990, and its findings spurred the beginning of international climate change negotiations in 1991.[19] Initially, the negotiations acted to establish a governance framework which took the form of the United Nations Framework Convention on Climate Change (UNFCCC) which was adopted in 1992 and entered into force two years later (Figure 10.1).

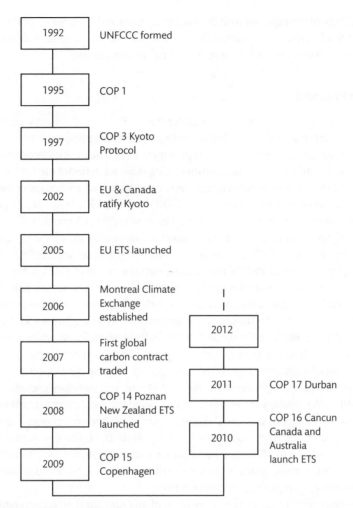

Figure 10.1 Climate change policy's evolution.

One of the first actions under the UNFCCC was to set up the Kyoto Protocol (see 'Kyoto Protocol') under which signatory governments committed to particular actions to combat climate change. The negotiations took two years, the Protocol was adopted by member states in 1997, and rules of implementation were finalized in 2001 in Marrakesh. The Marrakesh meeting was the seventh Conference of Parties (COP), the senior body under UNFCCC which meets annually. Over the period since the adoption of the UNFCCC thousands of negotiators, meeting at least twice a year, have formed themselves into a negotiating community. In the intervening years, the science of climate change has become considerably more sophisticated, and there is general agreement amongst climate change experts on the need to defossilize the global economy by the middle of the twenty-first century. Furthermore, over the same period, a group of nations representing a very large proportion of the world's population has formed a new category of emerging powers. China, India, Brazil, Mexico, South Africa, and Indonesia can no longer sensibly be placed in a category of 'non-Annex 1' countries together with the likes of Ethiopia and Haiti. Some of these countries are amongst the highest overall GHG emitters, with China, for instance, matching the USA, and Indonesia ranked the fourth largest emitter by some measures.

The Kyoto Protocol

The Kyoto Protocol is a key achievement under the UNFCCC, and is highly prized by many governments—notably in the EU—for providing a rules-based system to tackle climate change. It set out GHG emissions reduction targets for 37 developed economies and the European community, this group of countries being referred to under the Protocol as Annex 1 countries. The individual emissions targets were intended to reduce emissions by developed countries by five per cent over the period 2008–2012 against 1990 levels. No targets were set for developing economies which were referred to as non-Annex 1 countries.

Under the Kyoto Protocol, market-based mechanisms were established to help countries reach their targets in a cost-effective way. The major instruments are the Emissions Trading Schemes, inspired by the success of the SO2 trading schemes in the USA (Case 1); the Clean Development Mechanism; and Joint Implementation (Chapter 7). Since the Bali COP in 2007, the negotiations have focused on policy for the post-2012 period when the Kyoto Protocol's first commitment period ends. These negotiations proceeded along two tracks. The first track, known as the Ad hoc Working Group on Further Commitments for Annex I Parties under the Kyoto Protocol (AWG-KP), was intended to negotiate improvements in the Kyoto Protocol and a second set of emissions targets. This track covers only the developed countries signed up to the first commitment period of the Kyoto Protocol, and therefore excludes the USA.

The second track launched at the Bali COP, was called the Bali Action Plan. Its purpose was to work towards an 'agreed outcome' under the UNFCCC and was charged to the Ad hoc Working Group on Long-Term Cooperative Action (AWG-LCA). The Bali Action Plan would agree mitigation actions for developed economies, nationally appropriate mitigation actions by developing economies, financial arrangements, adaptation, technology transfer, and a system for monitoring, reporting, and verification.

There has been much debate about the form of any emissions reduction agreement for the post-2012 period; principally, whether or not there should be a single instrument that would replace the Kyoto Protocol, or two instruments, one to extend the Kyoto Protocol and the other under the UNFCCC. Since Bali, enormous effort has been put into reaching an agreement. COP 14 in Poznan set the ground for what was intended to be major agreement at the Copenhagen Summit (COP 15), although ironically of greater long-term significance was the EU countries' independent agreement to cut emissions by 20 per cent by 2020 announced in the run-up to the Poznan meeting.[20] Prior to Copenhagen, expectations amongst civil society were raised to a very high level, and the frenzy increased when Climategate erupted. Just as the summit was about to begin, emails inferred as saying that some of the science behind climate change had been rigged were released to the media: the summit's launch was therefore accompanied be a resurgence in climate change scepticism. Climategate cast a shadow over the whole summit, which ended with a sense of failure because no major breakthrough had been achieved.

One can see how this heightened sense of expectation can occur at such meetings from a snapshot of a single event (Box 10.1). Thousands of people representing government, civil society, and business come together for an intense two-week period during which they exchange information, present their different viewpoints, haggle over details, and eventually make announcements about the future. Government representatives are under pressure from other nations, and also from other sectors because ultimately all decisions are made on behalf of signatory governments.

The meetings are well-documented and involve high-level officials, and are closely scrutinized by the media as well as other parties. In many ways, negotiations around the Kyoto Protocol reflect many people's idea of governance best practice because they are transparent, participatory, and inclusive. Yet the 2008-2012 phase of the negotiations was unsuccessful in its aim to produce a new legal instrument for the period beyond 2012, and the Kyoto process is now seen by many people as a failure. Some of the reasons for this are discussed in the next section.

Why sustainability governance can fail

The UNFCCC was not conjured out of thin air: three previous examples of international governance in particular influenced the climate change governance regime.[21] One was the International Stratospheric Ozone Regime set up under the UN's auspices because of fears that the protective ozone layer was being damaged by CFC from aerosols, refrigeration, and air conditioning. This culminated in the 1987 Montreal Protocol that established targets and a timetable for limiting the production of CFCs and their eventual banning. Features of the ozone regime all found their way into the international climate change governance regime including an intergovernmental panel of experts to advise on science and policy, targets for reducing emissions, and a framework convention.

Box 10.1   Climate negotiations from the inside

Conference of Parties are attended by organizations from government, business, civil society, and the scientific community. Participation is restricted to organizations registered by the UN, and they are divided into four groups, identifiable by the colour of badge they wear. Country governments wear a red badge and can attend any of the negotiations. Blue badges signify members of international agencies such as the World Bank. Most participants wear yellow badges, and they come from NGOs and business. At COP 14, there were 4,000 red-badge wearers, and 4,500 yellow-badge wearers. The press has its own coloured badge.

The conference is divided into two main areas: negotiations take place in plenary and breakout rooms, and are attended by red-badge wearers; there are side events held by NGOs, industry bodies, and governments; and there are trade shows. Away from the main site, companies and international agencies hold their own events on topics such as finance and energy policy. Events take place over a two-week period, culminating in ministerial discussions, national statements, and closing ceremonies. Ministers set out their governments' positions, but many of the negotiators are civil servants who have attended many previous COP meetings.

Although a COP is attended by invited organizations from different sectors, only governments are involved in decision-making. Negotiations can run long into the night, especially during the final days, but even then the outcomes are uncertain. Bill Clinton famously signed the Kyoto Protocol but the US Senate refused to ratify it, and announcements about countries' interpretations of what has been agreed carry on months after the COP meeting ends.

The USA's Acid Rain Programme which established a cap-and-trade mechanism to limit emissions was also influential (Chapter 3). Thirdly, the Strategic Arms Reduction Treaty (START) negotiated between the USSR and the USA between 1982 and 1991 influenced the climate change governance regime because many of the people who became involved in climate change negotiations in the 1990s (e.g. Al Gore) learned about international negotiations through involvement in this treaty process. Amongst the key learnings from START that found their way into the UNFCCC was that targets, timetables, and mutually verifiable reductions were important elements.

The problem with these three examples is that none of them addressed the unique features of climate change.[22] As a result, the design of the UNFCCC—including the Kyoto Protocol—has been open to criticism that it has:

> locked the world into a framing of the climate change challenge based on plausible analogies that have the painful dual characteristics of being superficially proximate but structurally misleading on deeper inspection. Ozone depletion, acid rain and nuclear arms control were all complicated problems, but compared to climate change they were relatively simple to solve.
>
> (Prins & Rayner 2007, p. 17)

For instance, the path dependence created by these earlier initiatives meant that climate change was viewed as a discrete global commons problem that could only be settled through an international consensus to achieve common targets through emissions trading. However, it could also have been argued that a handful of countries were responsible for most of the emissions, and if they cooperated, other countries would have to fall in line. Similarly, as seen in Chapters 1 and 2, it is odd to treat climate change as something discrete from other sustainable development challenges, and failure to address these other issues was always likely to be met with resentment and resistance. Furthermore, the assumption that international coordination was required—reinforced by the experience with START—overlooked the fact that the degree of cooperation needed would be historically unprecedented, something predicted by some academics:

> Historically, there simply is no precedent for the co-operative, top-down creation of an international market of the sort that is envisaged for carbon by the architects of the climate regime. On past performance, it is more likely that radical technological change will be achieved by genuine international competition once there is a firm consensus that national security is at stake. After all, competition led to the stockpile of American and Soviet warheads in the first place. The competition will come not only from nations trying to protect themselves against climate impacts, but also from pursuit of profit deriving from more efficient energy production. It will also be greatly to the West's geostrategic advantage when it can reduce dependence on oil and gas supplies held by autocratic regimes.
>
> (Prins & Rayner 2007, p. 19)

Indeed, appeals to energy security have been effective in prompting government action amongst countries that have resisted global agreements. Clean energy is no longer just seen as a means of tackling global warming; it is now part of the arsenal in the mounting war for energy security, something that has gained traction in North America, parts of Europe, and the Far East due to concerns about being held an energy hostage by particular countries.

The architects of the UNFCCC, some say, also failed to recognize that effective climate change governance (as with many areas of sustainability) relies heavily on reaching an agreement between developed and developing economies (and also incorporating a mechanism for graduating countries from developing to developed status over time).[23] There are few examples of rule-making, monitoring, and enforcement at an international level that deal adequately with this problem. Indeed, some of the resistance by developing economies to proposals made through the UNFCCC process stems from a history of being forced to adopt decisions from the wealthier countries responsible for most of the historical emissions.

> Many developing countries are concerned and sceptical about the prospect of new regulatory arrangements. They do not wish to become 'rule-takers' in yet another sphere of global politics which leaves them vulnerable to rules, monitoring, and enforcement which they see as having asymmetric impact to their disadvantage.
>
> (Ghosh & Woods 2009, p. 455)

It can be argued that more progress on climate change governance has been made outside the UNFCCC process through what has been termed 'muscular bilateralism'. For example, the British government took a leading role in 2003, unilaterally declaring its intention to reduce CO_2 emissions by 60 per cent by 2050, and introducing an internal trading system in 2004, a year before the European Union's ETS. Britain also decided to place climate change at the top of its international agenda, initiated by an international conference on the impacts of climate change in 2005, and followed by successive meetings of G20 science, energy, and environment ministers.[24] At the 2005 Gleneagles G8 summit, the heads of states of China, India, Brazil, Mexico and South Africa were also invited for the top agenda item, climate change, thus creating the G8+5 grouping. In subsequent years, the G8+5 format has been continued, and climate change has been maintained as the lead agenda item.

Individual governments have also spent considerable political capital on climate change. Partly in response to the UK's 'aggressively competitive' announcements, Brazil declared it would halt all deforestation by 2025. The Chinese opened the door to low-emission technology, and the EU ETS embraces all 27 member states. In the years since COP 15 in Copenhagen, 90 countries—together responsible for 85 per cent of the world's emissions—have announced voluntary climate commitments.

With the European ETS inaugurated in 2005, a new factor emerged. Once this new trading market was established in London, the financial community and the business community became engaged in the issue of global warming, with important consequences. The CEOs of many major international companies became champions of the need for action on climate change.

Climate change governance directions

Even before the Copenhagen Summit, there were calls for a less ambitious, integrated multi-track approach to governance. The distinction between Annex 1 and non-Annex 1 countries would be abandoned, and major emitters of whatever economic status would commit to emissions reductions, but would have the flexibility to devise their own approaches.[25] The top-down emphasis of the Kyoto Protocol would be replaced with a more bottom-up approach allowing individual governments to decide how they were to contribute to the common goal of emissions reduction.

The final stages of the Copenhagen Summit opened up the possibility for this new direction. Faced by the prospect of criticism at failing to deliver a major outcome, a political agreement was negotiated by 28 countries in the final days of the conference. This was called the Copenhagen Accord, and was only two and a half pages long. It was developed at the next COP in the Cancun Agreement. This agreement incorporates targets and actions from countries responsible for 85 per cent of total emissions, including China and the USA. It commits developed economies to providing new finance for mitigation and adaptation in developing economies, and lays the ground for better monitoring, reporting, and verification. However, it does not address doubts about whether a global target is useful in the first place, and important aspects of mitigation such as deforestation were left unresolved (Chapter 7).

The following COP in Durban in 2011 was meant to flesh out the details of implementation and resolve some of the outstanding issues. It was a much more low-key event than COP 15, and even efforts to reignite the Climategate scandal fizzled out very quickly.[26] The Kyoto Protocol was kept alive with an agreement to a second commitment period running from 2013 until 2020, and signatory countries promising to reduce emissions to 25–40 per cent of their 1990 levels. This is good news for those who believe that a rules-based system of governance is essential. Others argue that the AWG-LCA (see 'The Kyoto Protocol') charged with longer-term strategy achieved mixed results in terms of finance, periodic review, transparency, and reporting.[27] However, even this has been welcomed in by those who do not think the top-down governance approach of UNFCCC is effective, and that the flourishing of independent initiatives around the world such as the low carbon trading schemes adopted by 32 countries around the world,[28] will eventually result in a genuine global governance agreement.

Box 10.2   Government pledges

China

As the largest carbon emitter in the world, China's actions towards climate change are particularly important. China has pledged to reduce its emissions per unit of GDP by up to 45 per cent by 2020 compared to 2005: a target the government calculates can be met without constraining economic growth. China's pledge also includes other actions: to increase the share of non-fossil fuels in primary energy consumption to around 15 per cent by 2020, and actions on reforestation.

In 2009, China had the greatest aggregate investment in clean energy, with investment levels of US$34.6 billion. It has the world's largest manufacturing capacity for solar collectors and solar cells and is likely to reach the same status for wind turbines. The Loess Plateau reforestation project, initiated some 12 years ago, has resulted in the greening of an area the size of Belgium, and once completed by 2020 will be the equivalent of reforesting an area the size of France. China has pledged to increase forest coverage by 40 million hectares and forest stock volume by 1.3 billion cubic meters by 2020 from 2005 levels.

Europe

The EU has pledged a target of 20 per cent GHG emission reductions by 2020 compared with 1990 levels, and this will be increased to 30 per cent if other major economies commit to significant reductions. The EU ETS will clearly play a significant role in achieving these goals, but in addition each of the 27 nations comprising the EU will need to introduce obligations and regulations required to meet the national objectives.

A considerable scaling up of effort will be required to improve the energy intensity of the economy and the carbon intensity of the energy mix. The EU's 2020 objectives need to be set within an overall target for 2050, so large-scale energy infrastructure (e.g. coal-fired power stations) in all member states needs to be replaced with energy efficient, low CO_2 energy systems as they come up for renewal. In the UK, for example, the opportunity is immediate since about £200 billion worth of energy infrastructure will need to be replaced over the coming decade. This infrastructure will be productive until mid-century and beyond, and will need to be fit for a defossilized economy.

Due to the impact of the financial crisis upon the levels of CO_2 emitted by the EU, the move to the more ambitious target of 30 per cent emissions reductions by 2020 is being considered irrespective of the actions of other countries.

USA

The USA has pledged an emissions reductions target of 17 per cent by 2020 relative to 2005 levels. This equates to a three per cent decrease by 2020 compared to 1990 levels, less than the total five per cent target of the developed countries in the Kyoto agreement. The biggest downside of the USA's pledge, however, is that the proposal was based upon anticipated legislation which did not materialize. There is therefore great uncertainty over the future actions of the USA, particularly at federal government level.

The passage of climate and energy bills in the USA has long been seen as key to the development of climate negotiations at the international level. By 2012, these seemed to be hostage to the outcome of the next Presidential elections, and through legislation such as the Keystone Pipeline Bill, Congress seemed to be adopting a policy of carbon intensive energy security. Although the USA's climate change negotiation team felt it had forced countries such as China and India to embrace emissions reduction, other people feel that there is sufficient consensus amongst nations to enable progress to be made regardless of the USA's position.

Sources: Klimasinska 2012; Pew Charitable Trusts 2010; SSEE 2011.

 Discussion points

The governance of climate change is important not only in its own right, but for the lessons it offers for the future of sustainability governance.

- What are the main achievements of the UNFCCC, and where has it failed?
- What are the main shifts in the direction of governance since the Copenhagen Summit?
- How does business influence the direction of climate change governance?

Summary

Sustainability issues are often referred to as governance challenges, but there is considerable disagreement about whether this means they are the concern of government, or whether they require non-conventional approaches involving actors from a cross-section of society. There is considerable frustration about the achievements of government so far, although accusations of inertia, over-ambition, misguidedness, and conceit in many ways are a reflection of wider social attitudes. Moreover, there are examples of significant achievements from around the world, and it should be borne in mind that much of what government is wrestling with is a new type of global challenge for which established governance models are of limited usefulness.

Business is increasingly seen as part of the governance solution, not least through collaboration with civil society and the state. However, these alternative governance approaches are still largely framed and legitimized by government, and this has led to questions about not only if challenges are being addressed adequately, but whether we are misunderstanding what needs to be done and how to set about it. In part, this is because there is a strong tendency to draw on past experiences rather than see new problems afresh. Path dependence accounts for some of the mistakes made in tackling climate change, and there is a risk that this will be repeated as new sustainability governance issues come to the fore.

 ## Further reading

Bulkeley, H. & Newell, P. (Eds) 2010, *Governing climate change*, Routledge, London.
Introduction to climate change governance.

Gough, I. 2011, *Climate change and public policy futures*, British Academy, London.
Concise introduction to governance options in climate change.

Kaletsky, A. 2010, *Capitalism 4.0: The birth of a new economy*, Bloomsbury, London.
Analysis of the governance challenges of different phases of capitalism, and why the current era is different.

Prins, G. & Rayner, S. 2007, *Wrong trousers: Radically rethinking climate policy*, Institute for Science, Innovation and Society, Oxford.
Challenging critique of the UNFCCC and how climate change has been managed since the 1990s.

Žižek, S. 2011, *Living in the end times*, Verso Books, New York, NY.
Arguments for why capitalist democracy is approaching the end of its natural life, and the implications of this.

 ## Case study 10   Rwanda—sustainability governance in a developing economy

Rwanda is an African state that has spent much of its post-colonial existence embroiled in civil war, but which is now enjoying a degree of sustained economic development. Ecotourism is popular, agricultural production has doubled since 2007, there is an increasing number of off-farm jobs, and although the public sector dominates the formal economy, there is a growing private sector.

The country is admired for having the highest percentage of women in government in the world (60 per cent), and over 95 per cent of children are enrolled in primary school. However, it is highly dependent on foreign aid, and aid-workers are an everyday sight in the capital, Kigali. Moreover, the country is land-locked, making imported items expensive; a situation worsened because of the hilly terrain and problems with land transportation. It has the highest population density of any country in Africa, and the population is expected to reach 26 million by 2050 compared to 11 million today. This puts pressure on land and encourages urbanization. Handled correctly, it could result in high-density, resource-efficient towns supporting a skilled workforce; but it could also increase the risk of slums and their attendant health and welfare problems.

Rwanda has some of the lowest GHG emissions in the world (0.4 tonnes CO_2e/ person compared to a global average of 6.7 tonnes), but it is at risk from climate change. Its domestic crops and exports of tea and coffee are reliant on rainfall, and its main indigenous source of power is hydro. Oil accounts for 39 per cent of energy and all transport fuel, and shifts in oil price have a significant impact on GDP. It is anticipated that precipitation will rise because of climate change: average temperatures have already risen 1.4°C since 1970, and are expected to rise a further 1.1°C by 2050, increasing flooding, landslides, crop losses, and the impact of water-borne disease. It has been estimated that climate change could result in annual economic costs of about one per cent of GDP by 2030.

The challenge for Rwanda, therefore, is how to continue its economic development, not just while wrestling with its sustainability challenges, but where possible by using them to its advantage. Vision 2020, the government's economic development plan, aims to transform the country from a largely subsistence agricultural economy to a knowledge-based society with average incomes of at least US$900 per capita. Now climate resilience and low carbon development need to be integrated into that strategy. As the government sees it, Rwanda will be a country:

> where agriculture and industry have a minimal negative impact on the environment, operating in a sustainable way, and enabling Rwanda to be self-sufficient regarding basic necessities.
>
> By 2050, development will be achieved with low carbon domestic energy resources and practices, reducing Rwanda's contribution to climate change while allowing it to be independent of imported oil for power generation. . . . Rwanda will have the robust local and regional knowledge to be able to respond and adapt to changes in the climate and the resulting impacts, supporting other African countries as a regional services hub to do the same.

In order to achieve this, the government has identified certain 'big wins' that would have a significant impact on adaptation, mitigation, and economic development. These include geothermal power generation, better soil fertility management, and high-density walkable cities. They also involve investing in irrigation, road networks, agroforestry, and knowledge networks. There are also 'quick wins' necessary to inspire interest and further action, including accessing international climate finance, implementing resource-efficient design into the special economic zones already agreed, and ensuring sustainability is incorporated into current capacity building projects. The main determinants of success will be building human capacity and getting access to finance, but the government feels it is well positioned to make use of the various sustainability-financing opportunities offered by the international community.

Sources: King 2011; Republic of Rwanda 2011; http://uk.oneworld.net/guides/rwanda/climate-change, accessed 20 February 2012.

....

Questions

1. Rwanda is an example of a poor country that has low historical emissions, but which will nonetheless experience negative impacts as the climate changes.

   a. What are wealthy countries doing to assist such countries?

   b. How will climate change affect Rwanda?

   c. Is the UNFCCC fair to Rwanda?   *(continued)*

2. The Rwanda government is treating climate change as an opportunity in the context of its overall development strategy.

    a. What risks does climate change pose for the country?

    b. What opportunities does the government envisage?

    c. How can the government finance low carbon development?

3. Look at Rwanda government's full green growth strategy, http://www.smithschool.ox.ac.uk/wp-content/uploads/2011/03/Rwanda-Green-Growth-Strategy-FINAL.pdf.

    a. What are the government's strategic objectives, and what programmes of action does it have planned to meet them?

    b. What are the main opportunities for the private sector in the strategy?

    c. Evaluate the strengths and weaknesses of the strategy, and its utility as a model for other countries?

 ## Endnotes

1. (Bello 2002; Sitkin 2010)

2. Tate & Lyle Sugars Ltd., the topic of this snapshot, is now a separate entity trading under the name Taste and Smile.

3. (Kaletsky 2010)

4. (Ballinger & Olsson 1997)

5. (Elliott & Center for International Forestry Research 2000)

6. (See, for instance, contributions to *Journal of Business Ethics* 2010, 94, 17–19; Albareda 2008; Scherer, Palazzo & Baumann 2006).

7. (Bulkeley & Newell 2010)

8. (Drucker 1976)

9. (Shen et al. 2010)

10. (Gough 2011)

11. http://www.guardian.co.uk/environment/georgemonbiot/2009/jun/26/us-obama-climate-monbiot, accessed 19 February 2012.

12. http://www.ft.com/cms/s/0/a5fb6084-9e32-11de-b0aa-00144feabdc0.html#axzz1mv74whZu, accessed 19 February 2012.

13. (Ward 2009)

14. (Blowfield 2005)

15. (Rayner 2003)

16. (Berkhout, Leach & Scoones 2003; Chambers 1983, 1994; Leach, Scoones, & Wynne 2005)

17. (Lampel & Meyer 2008)

18. (Sterk et al. 2007; Wittneben 2007; Wittneben et al. 2006)

19. Data from SSEE (2011) is drawn on throughout this chapter, with permission.

20. http://www.guardian.co.uk/environment/2008/dec/13/carbon-emissions-eu, accessed 19 February 2012.

21. (Prins & Rayner 2007)

22. (Hulme 2009; Prins & Rayner 2007)

23. (Depledge & Yamin 2009)
24. G20 and G8 refer to groupings of leading economic countries.
25. (Bodansky & Diringer 2007)
26. (Nature 2011)
27. See, for instance, http://insights.wri.org/news/2011/12/reflections-cop-17-durban, accessed 19 February 2012.
28. (King 2011)

Sustainable consumption and production

11

Key terms

Consumption   Ethical consumers
Behavioural economics   Product life cycles
Consumer behaviour   Choice editing
Resilience   Dematerialization

Online resources

- More information on sustainability awards.
- Links to specialists in life-cycle management.
- Sources on alternative measures of well-being.
  http://www.oxfordtextbooks.co.uk/orc/blowfield/

Chapter in brief

Striking a balance between production, consumption, and resource efficiency is a trichotomy that affects multiple facets of the business–sustainability relationship. This chapter explains the background to the rising interest in sustainable consumption and production, and identifies the major trends. It then examines sustainable production: its meaning, its drivers, the types of approach being adopted, and the challenges for further progress. That is followed by an exploration of sustainable consumption: the main areas of consumer behaviour, the principles for effective action, the strengths and weaknesses of behavioural economics, and lessons from initiatives to date. The chapter concludes with a discussion of different types of consumption, and how this links to alternative definitions of well-being.

The sustainable consumption and production trichotomy

Historically, resource usage and GHG emissions have increased commensurate with economic growth. A major challenge in the sustainability context is decoupling these phenomena so that economies can prosper without increasing material throughput (Chapter 3). Decoupling is central to sustainable consumption and production. It is a topic that, as we will see, generates often heated debate because it gets to the heart of what we mean by wealth, prosperity, and well-being.

Production refers to the creation, manufacture, and marketing of goods and services. In the sustainability context, it can also include product reuse and disposal as part of cradle-to-cradle life-cycle management (Chapters 5 and 6). Consumption is probably a more emotive topic (Key concept 11.1). Consumerism and over-consumption are just two of the negative phenomena associated with consumption, and which for some are characteristic of contemporary capitalism (see 'Sustainable consumption'). However, consumption is not only about shopping: it is also about how we use things and get around; the ways in which we use the Earth's resources in our daily lives. Moreover, the challenge of sustainable consumption is not simply that we consume too much—over-abundance—but that much of the world consumes too little, in terms of either meeting their aspirations—under-consumption—or fulfilling their basic needs—human development. To offer two simple examples: in wealthier countries, persuading consumers to use low-energy compact fluorescent light bulbs is often cited in case studies of sustainable consumption, but in countries such as Indonesia, Pakistan, or Nigeria, the consumption challenge is to provide most of the population with affordable, reliable electric lighting. Likewise, in the West, meat-protein diets are often considered damaging to the environment, but finding ways to feed the bulk of the world's population without increasing methane emissions from rice cultivation could be a more important challenge than persuading people to become vegetarians (Chapter 3).

 Key concept 11.1   Consumption

Consumption refers to the choices made by the individual consumer to fulfil their own needs. A company consumes goods and services, but only as part of production for others. The consumer acts out of need, self-gratification, desire, obligation, generosity, and all manner of motivations that are cultural, psychological, and social as much as economic.

In wealthy economies, consumption is associated with shopping, and is celebrated in advertising and the media for helping people lead richer lives. It is also subjected to hostile moral and ecological assault because of its associations with gluttony, alienation, avarice, and waste. However, consumption is not just about shopping—be it in shopping malls or charity shops: it includes all of the ways that consumers as end users of the production chain use the Earth's resources as part of their daily lives. Hence, mobility, holidays, and sports, for instance, are all part of consumption.

The rise in production and consumption

Since the Second World War, production and consumption globally have risen enormously. GDP—a measure of throughputs and economic activity (Chapter 3)—has grown faster than at any time in the past, and economies such as South Korea, China, and India have doubled GDP in less than 16 years despite high population rates. By contrast, the largest economies of the nineteenth century took between 53 and 154 years to achieve the same feat despite having much lower populations.[1] There are many factors behind this, and no single explanation.[2] However, there is one counterintuitive factor that appears linked to GDP growth: there has been a real-term decline in resource prices with average commodity prices falling by almost 50 per cent between 1900 and 1999.[3] This is odd because if GDP growth is coupled to greater resource usage as asserted earlier, then the laws of supply and demand should mean average commodity prices rose. However, while resource usage grew during the twentieth century, the productivity associated with commodities from grain to oil, oranges to copper oxide also grew. Furthermore, resource-intensive consumption (e.g. food, energy) tends to account for a smaller proportion of household income once incomes reach US$15,000–20,000 in terms of purchasing power parity. Indeed, as countries such as Germany, France, and Australia have increased their per capita GDP, their per capita energy consumption has remained static or declined.[4] Therefore, there appear to be countries at certain stages of economic development where GDP growth is unaffected by average commodity prices. Moreover, since the Second World War, significant increases in end-use productivity of resources have meant that the demand for commodities has grown more slowly than GDP.[5]

This picture suggests that the rapid growth anticipated in emerging economies is not unfeasible, even if one uses commodity price or decoupling criteria. The historical record suggests that material-intensity declines with GDP growth, and commodity prices are less influential once a particular level of per capita GDP is reached. Whether we are talking about energy, materials, food, or water, there are documented precedents of new supplies, techno-logical advances, and reduced resource-intensity enabling the decoupling of economic growth and resource usage.

The global middle class

If these trends were to continue, then arguments that the growing body of new middle class will want to emulate their Western forebears would deserve attention. However, as the next section shows, past trends do not seem to be repeating themselves today. If this break with the past continues, then there are consumption implications, not least for the booming middle class in emerging economies who will account for a significant part of the anticipated 90 per cent rise in real global GDP from US$ 50 trillion today to US$95 trillion by 2030.

An estimated five billion people will join the middle class by 2030 in addition to the two billion middle-class people today. This means they will have expenditures of US$10–100 a day, and although once they achieve middle-class status their resource intensity will proba-bly stabilize, and technological advances mean that resource intensity will be less than in the past, rising standards of living nonetheless could drive an overall rise in energy demand of 40 per cent, in food of over 25 per cent, and in water of about 40 per cent (Figure 11.1).

Is the past old news?

> Unless the present link between growth and consumption of scarce resources is severed, our resource base, governance and policy structures are unlikely to sustain the standard of living societies have grown accustomed to and aspire to.
>
> (World Economic Forum [WEF] & Accenture 2012, p. 5)

Given the reasonably weak historical link between commodity demand and commodity prices, the evidence of improved resource intensity associated with increased GDP, and

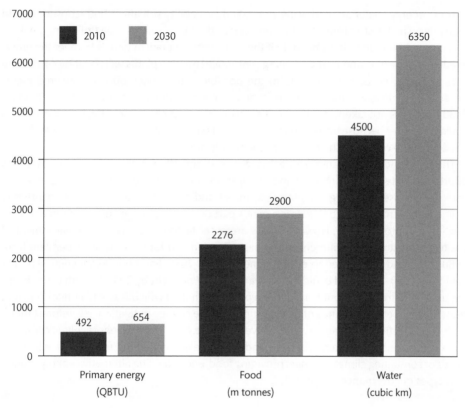

Figure 11.1 Predicted commodity demand growth 2010–2030.

the likelihood that the new middle classes will have access to more resource-efficient technologies than was the case hitherto, why should the WEF paint such a gloomy picture? Its
report reflects a more widely held belief that for much of the industrial era, we have enjoyed
a prolonged bubble during which the price of assets has been divorced from their fundamental value.[6] Thus, commodity prices were unduly low, companies did not internalize the
true costs of production, and material gains were achieved without proper consideration of
their social or environmental costs. Environmental economists have long made this point,[7]
but it is one increasingly shared in mainstream business.

This conclusion emerges from several analyses. For instance, low average commodity
prices already seem to be a thing of the past, with rises since 2000 wiping out the previous
century's price declines. According to the Indexmundi Commodity Price Index, prices
which in 2000 were as low as at any time since the Great Depression, had risen 160 points
to an all-time high by 2010;[8] energy prices were up 190 per cent, food prices by 135 per
cent, and materials prices by 235 per cent. Furthermore, for some of this period, the richest
countries were experiencing recession, depressing overall demand. In addition, commodity
prices have become increasingly volatile with prices for agricultural commodities such as
cotton, palm oil, and cocoa fluctuating 75, 230, and 246 per cent respectively over the past
decade.[9]

Food, energy, materials, and water prices and availability will affect both consumers and industries. The latest commodity to come under the 'peak' microscope (following peak oil and peak gas) is metals. It is uncertain if there are sufficient raw materials to meet the growing demand for steel and iron, and energy-intensive smelting plants will be hit by continuing rises in energy costs, not least due to the possible cutting back on coal-powered plants because of emissions concerns. A peak metals scenario could jeopardize US$2 trillion by 2030 if action is not taken. This is equivalent to 1.7 per cent of GDP, and the knock-on effects could be greater because under a business as usual scenario, steel costs could account for 2.3 per cent of the output of the consumer goods industry.[10]

The rising price and volatility of steel as well as several other commodities is in part due to efforts associated with climate change mitigation and adaptation. These are discussed at some length elsewhere (e.g. Chapters 2, 3, and 6), and our failure to reduce carbon intensity in line with climate change targets is a major part of the sustainable consumption and production trichotomy today. However, there are other factors that make the environment of the twenty-first century different to the past. The demand for water rose 41 per cent from 1980–2010, and is expected to do the same again by 2030. Food demand increased 59 per cent from 1980–2010, and could increase a further 27 per cent by 2030. In both cases, keeping up with demand will put considerable pressure on land which is already under pressure from the competing demands of urbanization, climate change mitigation (e.g. reforestation), biofuel production, land-hungry alternative energy (e.g. wind farms, photovoltaic cells). It is an exaggeration to talk in terms of peak land, but there is an emerging 'trilemma' in which the needs of combating climate change, providing food, and providing alternative energy require new types of governance (Chapter 12).

Consumer attitudes

Trends affecting sustainable production will inevitably affect consumers. Consumers have variously been vilified for their uncaring, unsustainable patterns of consumption, and deified for the leadership role they have played in influencing company behaviour. It is often a highly subjective, personalized debate: the 'evil' consumer is typically a member of a group the accuser has little contact with, and most of the implicit changes demanded will affect the perceived culprit; the consumer hero, on the other hand, is more likely to be someone 'like us', and the changes they make are ones we can understand and aspire to.[11] Hence, pejorative terms such as chavs, treehuggers, and even climate change nazi are flung about the sustainable consumption arena.

A more level-headed approach has been adopted by some companies. Retailers such as Marks & Spencer (M&S) and Tesco have conducted consumer surveys on attitudes to sustainability. M&S, for example, divided its consumers into four types based on attitude. Ten per cent were those who consciously incorporated sustainability issues into their purchasing decisions, and would broadly accept the title 'green consumer' (Figure 11.2). Thirty-five per cent said they were interested providing it was easy (e.g. the company clearly labelled sustainably-sourced products, and they were readily available), and a similar amount said they cared about sustainability but did not think there was much they could usefully do. The final group were those who did not care about sustainability (19 per cent).

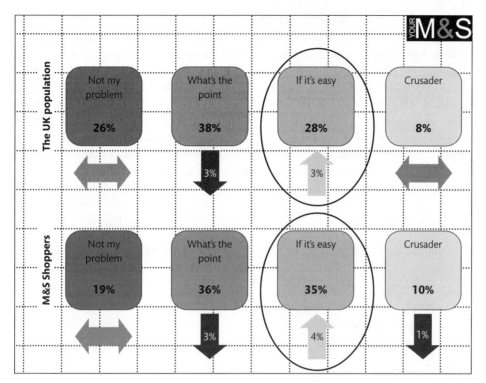

Figure 11.2 Consumer attitudes towards sustainability.
© Marks & Spencer 2012.

There are four things to note about the attitudes revealed in this survey. First, although M&S is highly-regarded for its sustainability reputation, the majority of its consumers do not appear to factor sustainability into their purchasing decisions. However, compared to the British population as a whole, M&S has less consumers who are disinterested (19 per cent versus a national average of 26 per cent), and a higher number who will think about sustainability in making their choices (45 per cent versus 36 per cent). Third, despite an economic downturn that has made consumers more cost-conscious, M&S customer attitudes have not changed greatly, and if anything people have become more interested in sustainability. Finally, although retailers rank quite low in terms of consumers' attitudes about sustainable industries, M&S is amongst the highest ranked companies.

The M&S example shows that although there is not an overwhelming demand from consumers for companies to act sustainably, in industries such as fast moving consumer goods and retail it would be dangerous to risk alienating a significant number of people, especially given that so few people object to it. There has been a rise in the LOHAS consumer group who factor health and sustainability into decision-making (Chapter 5), and in China as much as OECD countries, middle-class consumers are expressing a willingness to pay a premium for demonstrably green products.[12] However, there is a 'value-action gap' between what people say matters and what accounts for their ultimate purchasing decisions, so that, for instance, the European Commission found 72 per cent of people surveyed wanted to buy green products, but only 17 per cent had done so in the previous month.[13] In another survey, the majority of respondents said they favoured greater energy efficiency at home, but because of cost savings rather than environmental impacts.[14]

Value-action gaps, mixed messages about consumer motivations, and uncertainty about the size and behaviour of the sustainability consumers mean that consumer attitudes are not easy to understand. Companies such as GoodGuide.com have built their success on uniting ethical consumers, but increasingly sustainable consumption is framed more in terms of changing consumer behaviour than getting companies to respond to consumer pressure. The limits of the first generations of green or ethical consumer may have been reached, and as we will see later, sustainable consumption is taking new directions (see 'Sustainable consumption').

 Discussion points

Sustainable consumption and production poses all kinds of dilemma for business and for wider society.

- Should the world consume more?
- Why is it so difficult to change consumer behaviour?
- Is over-consumption the fault of business?

Sustainable production

Drivers of sustainable production

Consumers are one driver of sustainable production. Early on, ethical consumers created a market for sustainably produced goods and services, and played an important part in the success of companies such as Green & Black, innocent (sic), and Alter Eco. However, as already mentioned, consumers alone have not been a sufficient driver. This is not just because the ethical consumption market is relatively small; it is also because consumer expectations are not always a reliable compass for determining the course of sustainable production. Consumer behaviour is often emotional rather than rational, and can send signals, for instance, that protecting the orangutan is as important in sustainability terms as saving peat forests, or that saving pandas is important for biodiversity conservation when it might make more sense to let them become extinct.[15]

However, consumer attitudes are no longer considered the only driver of sustainable production. Meeting the needs of three billion new members of the middle classes will require more careful stewardship of resources if the sharp rise in and volatility of commodity prices in recent years is to be stabilized. In the past, commodity supply expanded and the costs of production were kept low: now, there are fewer new sources of commodity supply, and exploitation is becoming harder and more expensive. For instance, the average real cost of establishing oil wells doubled during the first ten years of this century, and high-quality arable land is being lost to urbanization.

There is considerable excitement about hydraulic fracturing (fracking) to extract oil, coal bed methane, and gas from impermeable rock formations. This is better seen as a contribution to energy security than one to sustainability, not least because oil and coal-bed methane in particular have negative consequences for global warming.[16] In the sustainable production context, however, fracking shares with other new technologies the fact that it is resource intensive. For example, four times as much steel is required for the horizontal drilling in extracting tight gas, than in conventional vertical drilling, in the same way that wind generation consumes more steel than conventional power plants. Other alternatives associated with sustainability are also energy intensive (e.g. desalination). Companies are therefore driven to consider sustainable production from a cost perspective, and also how the transition from one set of technologies will affect price, supply, and risk.

A further driver is the trend for companies to be responsible for the social and environmental dimensions of value chains. The Roundtable for Sustainable Palm Oil and the Marine Stewardship Council (Chapter 8) are examples of how companies from different parts of the value chain are introducing new forms of governance and creating shadow markets in order to aid sustainable production. This has happened for commodities where particular parts of the value chain face reputational damage or a supply risk because of what others in the chain do, and in cases in which some form of transboundary action is required.

Value chains have proved vulnerable to online campaigns which create stakeholders out of geographically and ideologically disparate people. The 2011 Arab Spring has already entered folklore as an example of how quickly movements can be mobilized through communications technology that is penetrating deeply into what were previously considered fairly isolated locations. The Arab Spring has been linked to commodity price volatility with abnormally wet weather in North America causing a spike in grain prices in the Middle East creating a sense of social unrest that was ignited when a Tunisian trader killed himself after the police confiscated his wares. Similar political disruption remains a possibility if food prices, land clearances, drought or flooding, and corruption continue on a large scale, providing fuel for new forms of political action. In the last six months of 2010, 44 million people were pushed into poverty because of rises in food prices,[17] and companies that find themselves negatively associated with such events risk becoming targets for protesters, while those that earn a positive reputation could earn brand loyalty.

Meeting future demand

There are three ways to meet future demand for products without relying on the resource-intensive model of the twentieth century.

Expanding supply

The first possibility is to expand the supply of inputs by, for example, increasing land productivity and the supply of water. In the 1960s to 1970s, the scourge of famine was greatly diminished by the Green Revolution that led to major improvements in the yields of some staple crops. Land reform in countries such as Japan has also increased food supplies.

However, the next great technological leap forwards is hard to predict, and supply solutions in the foreseeable future will be dependent on incremental improvements. The gains made are unlikely to be as impressive overall as those in the past (although there are regions where productivity can be raised significantly), and moreover they could exacerbate certain challenges. For example, converting land to agriculture could lead to further deforestation, increased pressure on water supplies, and greater GHG emissions.

Moreover, expanding supply has significant social implications in terms of land ownership, possible forced displacement of communities, and tensions over access to common resources such as water, forests, and grazing land. Furthermore, investments in increased commodity supply will be costly, and according to McKinsey & Company estimates, expanding the supply of steel, water, agriculture, and energy will require capital investment of US$3 trillion per annum, a third higher than in recent history, and exclusive of additional investments in climate change adaptation.[18]

Increasing productivity

The second possibility is to drastically increase resource productivity at the extraction, conversion, and end-use stages. Resource intensity has improved considerably in recent years, and, as noted, beyond a certain level it becomes decoupled from per capita GDP. Cars are but one example: in the 1960s, a car would typically emit 100 grams of CO_2 and nitrogen oxides for every mile driven, but in OECD countries today the figure is about two grams per mile. Improvements such as the catalytic converter have led to an absolute decline in US emissions by more than 30 per cent since the 1970s, even as vehicle mileage has increased by 38 per cent.

According to McKinsey & Company, a step change in resource productivity could lead to US$2.9 trillion in annual savings, and this figure would rise if the price of carbon reached US$30 per tonne.[19] However, the productivity option is US$100 billion per annum more capital intensive than the aforementioned expansion of supply, and represents a US$1.2 trillion increase on historical expenditure in the same sectors. Furthermore, the internal rate of return (IRR) is often unappealing. Although over 70 per cent of investment opportunities in land and water offer ten per cent or more IRR (more if prices are adjusted for subsidies and a US$30/tonne carbon price), over 50 per cent of opportunities in energy—a vital area for sustainability investment—offer less than ten per cent IRR, a figure that improves slightly once prices are adjusted.[20]

There is, however, a wide range of productivity opportunities (Figure 11.3), and this diversity may appeal to investors. Furthermore, some of these opportunities lie in problematic industries such as steel, iron, and cement, all of which are large users of energy, manufacturing products that are not substitutable on a large scale (Box 11.1).

As with expanded supply, it would be misguided to treat increasing productivity as simply a technological challenge. Every major technological advance has had a profound social dimension to it. The backdrop to famous Victorian novels by Dickens, Eliot, and the Bronte sisters was often the upheaval caused by new technologies, and more recently the ICT revolution has created and made redundant entire professions, brought about geographical shifts in the location of white-collar jobs, and altered the balance between work and personal lives. Anthropologist Clifford Geertz observed how relatively small changes in technology can have profound consequences for social and economic organization,[21] and it has been widely observed that new technologies and new economic opportunities more broadly are appropriated by men to the detriment of women.[22] The Green Revolution (see 'Expanding supply') had profound social consequences in terms of land ownership and labour, to the

Energy efficient buildings	Reduced food waste
Increased agriculture yields	Reduced water waste
Increased urban density	Reduced land degradation
Increased transport fuel efficiency	Improved oil and coal recovery
Adoption of electric and hybrid vehicles	Less road freight
Improved end-use efficiency of steel	Improved power plant efficiency
Improved efficiency in high-energy industries (e.g. iron, steel, cement)	Improved irrigation

Figure 11.3 Investment opportunities related to increased productivity.

Box 11.1   Peak steel

When we think of commodities peaking, we tend to think of non-renewables such as oil and gas. But there are other basic materials that may be less available in the future. Looked at in terms of global market size, the availability of substitutes, and its significance to the production process, steel is an at risk material that is vital to the global economy. Steel accounts for 40 per cent of the value of the market for non-energy materials (e.g. iron ore, nickel, and zinc), and steel production uses five per cent of global energy.

Emerging market demand means that steel production could rise by 80 per cent by 2030. This will primarily be for construction, machinery and engineering, and transport. Although iron ore and coking coal—two of the main materials used in steel—are not at risk, the predicted rise in demand could lead to shortages in other materials important to production (e.g. lead, tin). This is especially true of materials for which there are no ready substitutes (e.g. platinum, rare earth), or ones for which there is demand from other sectors (e.g. phosphate, potash). Furthermore, clampdowns on the use of the fossil fuels that since Bessemer's innovations in the nineteenth century have been essential to the production of cheap, mass produced steel, increase the chances that there will be at least short-term shortages of energy for steel mills.

Sources: Diamond 1998; Fisher 1963; McKinsey Global Institute 2011

---

point where in some regions it is remembered as the cause of social revolution.[23] These social dimensions are typically absent from cost–benefit calculations such as those cited in this section, but there is ample evidence that we should think of technology in the sustainability context not only as technological innovations, but as socio-technological phenomena, the success, failure, and especially the evolution of which is affected by the uncertain, largely unpredictable interplay of social, political, economic, and cultural factors.[24]

A sustainability response

The third way of addressing product demand is to alter the nature of demand itself. Instead of asking the question, How can we produce enough steel? or How can we meet the demand for meat?, the sustainability response requires us to rethink what kinds and levels of demand are acceptable given the carrying constraints imposed by climate change and other facets of sustainability. In addition, it could also involve us reconsidering how to meet universal demands such as access to clean, reliable, affordable energy, water, food, and housing. The expanding supply and increasing productivity responses are analogous to a person who tries to find the smallest pair of trousers to fit their waist; the sustainability response is more like slimming down to fit the trousers we have.

To take climate change in isolation, it has been estimated that carbon emissions now need to be reduced at a rate of 4.8 per cent annually to stay within the 450-ppm ceiling associated with a 2°C change in global average temperature.[25] This is achievable if highly challenging and expensive from a technological standpoint. Aggressive investment programmes for renewable energy, biofuels, and carbon capture and storage, along with better land-use management would by some estimates stabilize emissions. However, this would need investments in renewable energy to be 30–50 per cent higher by 2030 than they were in 2010, and even then renewables would only account for 25 per cent of power generation. The total cost has been put in the region of US $3.4 trillion per annum: US$370 billion more than under the productivity option, and well over a third more than investments in recent history.[26] However, it would cut emissions by 13 gigatonnes a year; far more than the other sustainable production options.

It is easy to get lost in such figures, especially when the assumptions built into any estimates are debatable. US$3.4 trillion is about five per cent of the global economy, making it significantly higher than Stern's initial estimate that tackling climate change would cost about one per cent of GDP (Chapter 1). Depending on one's point of view, this can be considered relatively expensive or cheap, but it is almost certainly inaccurate. It represents the costs of technologies, and assumes a relatively smooth deployment pathway: it therefore excludes the cost of changes in lifestyles, and takes no account of the impact of social, cultural, and political interference or inertia. Yet, it is exactly these excluded dimensions that will affect the outcomes of a sustainability response. If it delivers what is accepted as an improvement in livelihoods (including, for instance, providing four billion more people with access to modern energy services), then it would be welcomed. However, if it means less energy per capita at higher cost and an overall perception of a worsening of living standards, then it will lose the support of consumers. Moreover, given the unfavourable IRR associated with many of the technologies, and the possibility of a prolonged government and private debt crisis in wealthier countries, significant portions of the sustainability response may well struggle for investment.

How companies are tackling the production challenge

There are numerous ways that production can be made more sustainable, and they are not limited to large-scale investments in energy or infrastructure. Leaking water pipes in European cities, petrol generators in developing country slums, and food waste in shops and at home are just some areas where inputs can be reduced to deliver sustainability benefits. Recycling is taken for granted in many businesses, and reduces costs as well as resource use. The profitability of consumer goods companies in industries such as clothing and food is dependent on how well they manage the gap between raw materials costs (e.g. cotton, oil, wheat) and product prices. The former have risen in recent years as noted previously, providing an extra incentive for firms to rethink inputs. In addition, a favourable sustainability image can protect companies to some degree from pressures to slash the retail price. Furthermore, this image can be enhanced if the company is innovative in areas such as waste (e.g. packaging, recycling, reuse), delivering the double benefit of lower costs and enhanced reputation.

Snapshot 11.1   Sharing intellectual property—GreenXchange

Collaboration, partnership, and knowledge sharing are frequently mentioned qualities when talking about business and sustainability. One area where it offers value is the exchange of ideas so that rather than companies replicating each other's efforts, and being restricted to incremental progress, they can share their experiences and innovations.

Building on the idea of open innovation that has come to the fore in industries such as software and publishing in recent years, Nike and the NGO, Creative Commons, decided to develop GreenXchange, a digital platform and system that promotes the creation, sharing and adoption of technologies that have the potential to solve important global or industry-wide sustainability challenges.

GreenXchange was launched at the World Economic Forum in Davos in 2010. It enables patent owners to make parts of their intellectual property portfolio available under a set of terms that sits between the normal choices of 'all rights reserved' and 'no rights reserved'. Its patent licensing tools are intended to stimulate research, development, and the commercial roll-out of relevant ideas. Patent users receive the rights they need to innovate, and patent owners receive credit for their works and the option of annual licensing payments. In some cases, the technologies are ones that are not mainstream to the company that developed them, but are useful for others working on sustainability. In these cases GreenXchange helps unlock ideas that would otherwise languish in corporate vaults. Rather than deprive innovators of earnings from their ideas, it is hoped GreenXchange will provide steady, uncomplicated revenue streams while making more ideas available to enhance sustainable production.

Sources: http://www.nikebiz.com/crreport/content/environment/4-4-0-case-study-greenxchange.php; http://greenxchange.cc/; http://www.businessweek.com/the_thread/techbeat/archives/2010/01/davos_nike_and.html, all accessed 30 January 2012.

Questions

GreenXchange is an attempt to stimulate sustainability innovation.

1. What is the main problem it addresses?
2. What are the incentives for participating in GreenXchange?
3. Has it been a success? Why?

Although the amounts required to fund a shift to renewable energy are large (see 'Meeting future demand'), companies have plenty of opportunities to enhance their energy efficiency. If energy costs rose by 50 per cent by 2030, then companies would only have to reach the same levels of efficiency that Canadian consumer goods companies achieve today in order to save US$33–55.5 billion a year.[27] This is an example of 'dematerialization': reducing material intensity by cutting back on inputs. It is made more beneficial by increasing the contribution of renewable energy, and taken together dematerialization and clean energy are two of the main ways companies can make progress on sustainable production.

Another route being tried by some firms is creating rentalized markets and fractional ownership. In some ways, this is a return to bygone decades when goods were too expensive to own, and people rented televisions, washing machines, and radios. Nowadays, the motivation is a combination of dematerialization, the rising cost of raw materials, and concern about life-cycle product responsibility (Chapter 9). Sun Microsystems was an early mover in taking back and reusing components from its computer hardware (Chapter 6), and Xerox has

Benefit	Trends	Examples
Cost avoidance	Growing competition for resources Rising cost of externalities	Price volatility greater than at any time since 1970s
Cost reduction	Product resource-efficiency Operational and supply chain resource-efficiencies	Xerox saved US$ 400 million in 2009 by remanufacturing parts in product lines (85 per cent of net revenue)
Revenue growth	Emerging environmental goods and services markets Consumer pull for innovation	Global market for low carbon environmental goods and service estimated at £3 trillion in 2007–2008
Revenue protection	Changing consumer attitudes Tightening up the social contract	Fast-moving consumer goods companies risk 47 per cent of pre-tax earnings if they do not mitigate against environmental risks

Figure 11.4 Benefits of sustainable production.

Sources: WEF & Accenture 2012; WEF & Deloitte 2011; Worldwatch Institute 2010.

reported significant savings from designing the use of remanufactured parts in its product lines (Figure 11.4). Similarly, WhipCar and ZipCar have introduced alternative approaches to renting and sharing rather than buying cars.

A different approach to taking responsibility for product life cycle is the use of voluntary standards that require different elements of a commodity's value chain to adhere to resource management criteria as a condition of trade. The Roundtable on Sustainable Palm Oil, the Forest Stewardship Council, and the Marine Stewardship Council are examples of this approach (Chapter 8). RSPO launched its certified palm oil in 2008 which has now reached four million tonnes (ten per cent of total production). FSC certified forests cover 144 million hectares, and MSC has made some inroads into the world's largest fisheries including China and Russia.[28]

Getting to scale

There are various approaches companies can adopt to tackle sustainable production, and many of the companies mentioned throughout this book are not just implementers but also communicators of their chosen routes. There are also a number of different awards in recognition of sustainability achievements such as the Corporate Knights Most Sustainable Corporations in the World list, the Ethical Corporation Awards, and the national Association of Certified Chartered Accountants reporting awards in Portugal, the Netherlands, Hong Kong, and elsewhere.[29]

The prize for sustainable production is not just cups and medals. Resource efficiency can deliver new markets, industries, and jobs at the national level. For example, South Korea's Green New Deal is expected to create 960,000 jobs, and its policy of extending producer responsibility for products such as paper, glass, and tyres, could have an economic benefit of US$1.6 billion. Brazil has invested heavily in recycling which already generates returns of US$2 billion while avoiding 10 million tonnes of GHG emissions.[30] In a single industry such as consumer goods, volatile energy prices are a significant risk, but there are opportunities to cut energy costs by 20–50 per cent with a payback period of less than three years.[31]

However, despite the opportunities that exist and the models of how to improve the sustainability of production, change at the present time is incremental rather than rapid or radical. More sustainable options exist for consumers, but not at the necessary scale to energize a shift in consumer behaviour. Renewable energy, product labelling, dematerialized goods, and the option to rent rather than own goods are all available, but for the most part they are novelties. The WEF has identified what it calls a serious case of 'pilot paralysis' in which innovative ideas such as forest certification or short term car rentals fail to dominate their own industries and are not imitated by other industries, meaning that the overall management of water, carbon, energy, and biodiversity remains unresolved.[32]

There are various reasons why sustainable production is affected by incrementalism. Insufficient technological or infrastructural investment, the complexity of global supply chains (resulting in difficulties in tracking components), and perverse subsidies (e.g. for oil) and limited trade incentives are some of the most commonly cited factors. However, one of the most widely discussed aspects is the role of consumers, and how their pull and engagement affects company decisions. It is this we turn to now.

 Discussion points

There are different ways of achieving sustainable consumption but they do not appear to have been widely enough employed so far.

● What are the relative advantages and disadvantages of the three approaches to meeting future demand?

● What is meant by pilot paralysis, and why do you think it occurs?

● What products are suited to a rentalized market approach?

Sustainable consumption

Sustainability has often been presented as a consumption problem. Eighty per cent of household impact on the environment in developed economies stems from the way we run our homes, what we eat, how we get around, and our holiday travel.[33] Equally, there is a strong moral and spiritual dimension to consumption. Anyone who knows about Joel Osteen, the Yoido Full Gospel Church, or the Paula White Ministries will be aware of the 'prosperity gospel' that links spiritual and physical health with economic prosperity. At the other end of the spectrum, there is robust criticism of consumption. According to this, not only are certain forms of consumption a drain on natural resources, they are unfair and do not improve people's lives. Authors such as Schor (2010) and Frank (1999, 2000) highlight how the quest for ever greater consumption does not bring personal satisfaction and lies behind a host of social problems from economic, to psychological, to the erosion of natural capital.

Attention has been paid in recent years to non-economic measures of well-being and happiness. It is argued that happiness rather than wealth is the primary human desire, and that financial wealth or levels of consumption are not good indicators of human satisfaction.[34] Thailand is trying to establish what it calls a 'sufficiency economy' in which economic

OECD Better Life Index	An online tool to help visualize and compare some key factors well-being in OECD countries
Sustainable Competitiveness Index	The World Economic Forum's complement to the Global Competitiveness Index, factoring in elements such as changing demographics, social cohesion, and environmental stewardship
UK Happiness Index	Long-term government programme started in 2010 to assess national well-being
Happy Planet Index	Measures the ecological efficiency at which human well-being is being achieved
Genuine Progress Indicator	An addition to a national system of accounts to show what is claimed to be the 'true cost' of economic growth
Genuine Wealth Assessment	A private initiative offering alternative metrics to GDP

Figure 11.5 Alternatives to GDP as a measure of prosperity.

stability and human development take precedence over simple economic growth. Bhutan famously measures prosperity by 'gross national happiness' rather than GDP. The OECD has developed a 'better life index' to compare well-being across countries[35] (Figure 11.5).

These developments are the result of two trends that have come to prominence since the mid-twentieth century. First, as noted, there is the apparent disconnect between wealth and happiness. This is not true across the board, and people clearly feel better about their lives if they have health, security, education, food, and other basic needs. However, at a certain level of GDP (US$10,000–15,000), the benefits begin to tail off, and the well-being of those in the wealthiest countries (over US$30,000) is not significantly better. On the contrary, by some measures such as unemployment, mental health, education, physical health, crime, and social mobility, it could be that well-being depends more on equality than overall wealth.[36]

This is in stark contrast to the predominant view of the late twentieth century, encapsulated in Galbraith's idea of the 'affluent society': that period in the 1950s and 1960s when the majority of Americans went beyond meeting their basic needs, and became the mass consumers who drove the economy forwards.[37] However, the demands placed on people to maintain this consumption-oriented lifestyle had consequences across society, and these were neatly captured in Putnam's *Bowling Alone* (2000) which described how community life in the USA was changing. Today, addressing sustainability is presented by some people as an opportunity to redress the imbalances of modern social life through, for instance, providing people with more secure livelihoods, more meaningful opportunities, and a closer connection with communities and families.[38]

The second trend that has influenced current debates about sustainable consumption is one about distribution and fairness. For much of the twentieth century, a major economic and political concern was how to create systems so that poorer countries could ultimately enjoy similar standards of living to wealthier ones. Much effort was put into understanding why poor countries are poor, what needs all humans were entitled to, and how to increase wealth or create more even wealth distribution. In the 1960s and 1970s, much emphasis was put on equality, but since the 1980s it has been widely propounded that by focusing on economic growth and increasing the overall wealth of society, poor people will benefit from what is commonly portrayed as a tide that lifts all boats. One can argue about which point of view is right, and what can be concluded from the fact that we inhabit a world which has seen unprecedented numbers of people lifted out of poverty, but has more poor people in it than ever before.[39] However, from a sustainability perspective, the oft-expressed concern is that the Earth does not have the carrying capacity to support a population of nine billion people if they are to enjoy the same levels of consumption as developed economies (Chapter 3).

Changing behaviour

Under sustainable production (see 'Drivers of sustainable production'), we have examined some of the technological challenges related to balancing consumption and production. Sustainable consumption lends itself more to a psychological and ethical interpretation. A basic premise in a consumer society is that consumers have the right to choose, and moreover that they make rational choices. It is often said by companies that the customer decides, and it is not for business to say what people can or cannot have. Companies, however, spend enormous sums of money on influencing those choices, and although consumers ultimately decide what products are a success, their decisions are affected by numerous factors firms have control over. Indeed, the biggest successes are often when a company anticipates what people want long before consumers know they want it: it was Apple that gave people the iPod, not the consumers who demanded it.

For a long time it was assumed that consumers made rational choices: their consumption was based on conscious decisions based on information about price, attributes, and performance. Psychologists, however, demonstrated that people often made what to an economist would seem the wrong choice, and their insights have given rise to the field of behavioural economics. Behavioural economics concerns influencing behaviours so that people amend their 'wrong' choices, and persuading or inducing behaviours that are closer to 'right choices'.[40] Thus, for example, people might be encouraged to respond to incentives to buy electric vehicles if charging outlets were nearer to the exits in shopping car parks, or they might be discouraged from speeding by a buzzer attached to their speedometer. Under the term 'nudge', retailers have encouraged consumers to donate to charity at check-out time, or promoted healthier diets by placing certain foods at eye level.[41]

In behavioural economics, the right choice is typically the one that is economically rational according to normative economic theory. This is a highly value-laden view of rationality, especially given that the rationale of mainstream economics can be critiqued in the sustainability context (Chapter 9). For example, behavioural economics can show us why it is irrational to speed if all it means is we use more fuel to get to the next traffic jam, but it cannot explain why it is irrational in a sustainability context to use gasoline in the first place even if petrol is cheaper and more readily available than alternative fuels. As Simon pointed out long before the recent surge of interest in behavioural economics, a more appropriate focus is not the quest for conformance with objective rationality, but how it explains 'approximate rationality' (Simon 1955). Approximate rationality is not about a set of wrong decisions that can be rectified with reference to normative economic theory: it is a non-judgemental approach to understanding what decisions people actually make when—as they normally do—they have limited knowledge and ability.

These decisions are often emotional and contextual. We buy in part because of our beliefs (e.g. that a product is good for us), emotions (e.g. retail therapy), image (e.g. how a brand will affect our sense of self); habits (what we have bought before); and social influences (e.g. what our friends do). Seventy per cent of weekly purchases are repeat purchases, with no consideration given to other options.[42] Furthermore, we typically only change our habits because of price or promotions. Changes over the longer-term are influenced as much by the context of consumption as about emotions. Retailers go to great lengths to manage the shopping environment, and consumer goods companies compete for prime locations within stores. A consumer who makes the decision to shop at what is perceived as a higher quality store, may be more amenable to paying a higher price for a product more closely aligned with personal values, and equally may have higher expectations of that store to guarantee its social and environmental standards. Similarly, consumption is affected by the social and cultural context in which decisions are made, something that ultimately determines the acceptability or not of our behaviour as consumers.

Ethical consumption

Some social groups comprise a social context in which ethical consumption is now the norm. This means that a variety of social and environmental criteria is factored into one's purchasing decisions across an array of consumer goods. Ethical consumption grew in popularity in the 1990s, and an array of guidebooks, magazines, and introductions were published to explain the choices consumers had available to them.[43] Fairtrade, organic agriculture, certified timber, and responsible tourism were all part of the panoply of goods and services on offer to ethical consumers, and in certain product categories such as bananas, coffee, and some cosmetics products, the values originated by the ethical consumer movement made significant inroads into the mainstream consumer goods industry.

Today, ethical consumption is alive and well. Consumers can get advice on how to consume from organizations such as Ethical Consumer and GoodGuide, and badged ethical choices are widely available, even from mainstream retailers.[44] However, ethical consumption has never reached the market share that some predicted of it.[45] There are several reasons for this: early problems of product quality have largely been resolved, but there are still difficulties with availability. For some products, there may not be an obvious ethical choice, and when there is the options can be blurred because of competing ethical labels and claims. New consumers can find entering the ethical market place daunting, and those who understand it exhibit similar emotional behaviours to conventional ones (i.e. basing their decisions on habit, image, belief, etc.).[46] There is, as we saw in the discussion of consumer attitudes, the problem of value action gaps, and why expressed beliefs do not manifest themselves in actual purchasing decisions. Figure 11.6 illustrates the rationale used in defraying sustainability-based choices.

More fundamentally, ethical consumption is ultimately a framework for consuming, and in the sustainability context, it is consumption itself that is problematic. Philosopher Peter Singer (1972) has argued that it is morally indefensible to allow suffering on the grounds that it happens in far-off places, and that those fortunate enough to have enough for a reasonable standard of living, should redistribute their wealth for the benefit of others even if we do not know who they are. In other words, he implies that consumption cannot be ethical if it does not help relieve the suffering of others. Proponents of fairtrade and ethical sourcing

The average person in the UK is responsible for 9.6 tonnes of carbon emissions each year. That needs to come down by 50–80% by 2050. Here are some of the behaviour changes that could help achieve that, and some of the reasons we might be reluctant to act.

Consumption area	Behaviour change	Excuses for inaction
Managing our homes	Increase the use of all-renewable green-energy tariffs	Too costly; do not trust the energy firms; need government incentives
	More energy efficient habits such as home insulation	Council-sponsored insulation schemes have struggled because tenants do not like government intrusion
Food and drink	Cut down on meat and dairy produce	Rice is more environmentally harmful; resistance to being told what to do; animal protein fast food is cheaper
	Eat more in-season produce	Harmful to health; maintaining living standards
Mobility	Use choice editing to increase share of energy efficient cars	Large cars are important for status; cars are a part of the right to personal freedom
	Reduce the number of cars used in commuting (e.g. by home working, car pooling, train use, etc.)	Public transport is expensive, inconvenient, and unpleasant; homes are too small to work in
Holiday travel	Holiday in Britain	The weather is terrible; too expensive
	Increase carbon offsetting for air journeys	There are too many additions to ticket prices already; distrust of offsetting schemes

Figure 11.6 The logic behind ignoring sustainability in consumer decision-making.

contend that engaging in ethical consumption gives wealthier consumers an avenue to help poorer people, even if it is at the cost of encouraging consumption.[47] However, this does not take into account some of the main concerns about sustainable production, and therefore makes consumers an unreliable arbiter of sustainable consumption. This can leave the ethical consumer torn between the benefits to developing country producers of receiving a fair return for producing for world markets, and the carbon and water intensity of that product. Similarly, an ethical consumer might choose their holiday based on its benefits for local economies, but in sustainability terms overseas travel for pleasure might be unacceptable because of the carbon and water impacts. Ethical labels and brands are at best blunt tools for measuring the complexity of sustainable consumption, and although they have pioneered some of the rethinking about the responsibilities and possibilities of business, different approaches are needed to meet the dilemmas at the heart of sustainable consumption.

Approaches to sustainable consumption

Discussion of sustainable consumption is split between two camps: on the one hand are those such as Singer and Jackson who argue we should break away from a culture of consumption; on the other hand are those who say we should consume differently and less. The former are part of a long historical tradition of people who treat material wealth with suspicion and abhorrence, and it is a great irony that such beliefs were shared by the early Europeans who became the founders of what was to become the citadel of consumption, the USA.[48] The resilience movement and transition towns are two modern-day examples of how such thinking has been incorporated into sustainability. These are small-scale, local responses to global challenges such as climate change, poverty, and affordable energy, and rely on creating resilient local systems that can sustain communities in the face of global events. The possibility of such communities has particular implications for business (Chapter 12), but as yet there has been little thought given to how a wide-reaching shift to a more localized economy of this kind would take place.

One of the underlying psychological drivers for rejecting consumption is the belief that it is a manifestation of greed, avarice, vanity, and inequality. Even before we knew over-consumption could harm the planet, consumption was viewed as immoral: now that view is further validated because the Earth cannot sustain the current rates of resource use. Those who argue that we should consume less and differently would accept this latter point even if they would reject the moral interpretation. They do not necessarily believe that consumption is wrong, but they say that there are numerous ways to reduce the impact of consumption, and to make it fairer. For instance, we can reduce the energy intensity of many consumer goods, and at the same time invest in providing a reliable electricity supply for poor communities (see 'Sustainable consumption'). As already mentioned, dematerialization is possible if we design for modularity and reuse, and closing recycling loops and improving material input decisions can be encouraged by making companies responsible for the life-cycle ownership of their products. We have also looked at open innovation, fractional ownership, and renting as ways of changing the nature of consumption.

The earlier are examples of how the offerings of producers can open up new options for consumers. Consumer choice editing is an approach that has been shown to achieve significant changes in behaviour on a large scale. Given that only a small number of consumers seem willing to choose the sustainable or ethical option (see 'Ethical consumption'), it is argued that consumers should be edited out of the product selection process. In the same way that retailers would not choose to sell unsafe televisions, for instance, they should not give consumers the option of unsustainably produced goods. When energy efficiency ratings were introduced for domestic appliances, some retailers soon began to stock only the most efficient product lines. Similarly, do it yourself store B&Q decided in the 1990s to only sell certified timber. Both of these are examples of choice editing: denying consumers the chance to buy poorer quality goods. Although initially regarded as an unwarranted infringement on the consumers' right to choose, the fact is that choice editing is a common feature of modern retailing because retailers do not have the space or capital to stock all of the products available. Not many retailers stock 20 types of apple: in other words, they have reduced consumer choice to about 0.25% of the varieties available.[49] In recent years, Nestlé, Cadbury, and Mars have all removed ingredients that do not meet ethical criteria from major product lines, and companies such as Starbucks and Dunkin' Donuts deny their customers the choice of non-fairtrade coffee in many products.

Choice editing is attractive in the sustainability context because it addresses the challenge of getting to scale (see 'Getting to scale'). As we have seen, consumers make decisions quickly and emotionally in most cases, and choice editing provides a way of circumventing this. Another direction that relies more on consumers than producers or retailers is a shift in people's focus from consuming physical things to consuming experiences.[50] For instance, the experience of travel, different cultures, and ways of thinking are by some measures becoming valued as an alternative to simply owning 'stuff', and such attitudes are discernible amongst certain sections of younger generations. Part of these experiences relates to different means of consumption such as the use of the Cloud to store and swap information rather than physically owning films, music, or books. It is possible to imagine a world where YouTube, Netflix, and Twitter were simply the early, primitive services in an era of heightened interconnectedness that in turn altered the nature of consumption.[51]

 Snapshot 11.2   Choice editing—energy-efficient refrigerators

A mandatory labelling scheme to show the relative energy efficiency of fridges and freezes was introduced in the EU in 1995. In its early years, it had little effect on consumer behaviour, and A-rated models accounted for less than three per cent of the market. In 1999, the most inefficient categories were outlawed, and two years later price incentives were introduced through energy suppliers as part of an EU-wide energy efficiency programme.

The price incentives led to a growth in A-rated models from 10 per cent to 70 per cent of the market. Consequently, retailers began to stock only the most energy-efficient appliances, and by 2004 manufacturers had instigated a voluntary agreement to cut out C-rated fridges entirely. Moreover, they engaged in a programme of further innovation, introducing A+ and A++ models that went beyond the standards set by government. Today, these are the only grades on offer, and are 23 and 46 per cent more energy efficient than the original A-grade machines.

This approach to choice editing was not detrimental to consumers because over time A-rated machines were sold at the same price point as less efficient models, and offered performance improvements. Other factors in consumer decision-making such as brand, quality, aesthetics, and utility were unaffected. However, the longer-term energy benefits are less clear. In some countries, the trend for families to own more than one fridge meant that the total energy used for chilling and freezing foodstuff cancelled out efficiency gains. This is an example of the Jevons paradox in which improvements in material intensity per unit are offset by overall increases in material usage because of production and consumption growth.

Sources: Sustainable Consumption Roundtable 2006; http://www.which.co.uk; http://www.bbc.co.uk/bloom/actions/aratedappliances.shtml, accessed 30 January 2012.

....

Questions

Fridges and freezers are an example of choice editing.

1. What were the main factors that led to the success of this initiative?

2. What was the role of regulation?

3. Can you find other examples of the Jevons paradox?

Lessons on sustainable consumption

There have been some notable successes in relation to sustainable consumption despite the problems of behaviour and scale noted previously. The market share of A-rated energy efficient washing machines grew to 85 per cent within seven years of their introduction, and the global market for FSC-certified forest products is worth more than five billion dollars. Once agreement had been reached through the Montreal Protocol on ozone-depleting chemicals, they were phased out in Europe inside five years. In the early 2000s, the paint industry underwent a major shift as volatile organic compounds were reduced, and the market share for water-based paints rose to about three-quarters. Condensing boilers, recycled paper, and lightweight packaging are other success stories, and it is easy to forget that advances we now take for granted such as catalytic converters and unleaded petrol were major leaps forward when they were first introduced.

These examples succeeded for a combination of different reasons, but the key lessons are set out in Box 11.2. They include actions by regulators, manufacturers, retailers, and consumer groups.

Box 11.2   Lessons on changing consumer decisions

1. Ethically aware consumers can play a role as early adopters of new ideas, but they are not a big enough market on their own to change major product markets.

2. Products must perform in line with consumer expectations: even ethical consumers do not accept lower-standard items.

3. Choice editing has often been a major driver, and can be done by regulators, retailers, or manufacturers.

4. Labelling is an important enabler of choice editing, but it needs to be done in parallel with consumer awareness campaigns so that customers understand the advantages.

5. Consumer decisions become less reflective if they are confronted by too many choices.

6. Consumer information is largely ignored in preference to the habit, intuition, and emotion that inform most choices.

7. Lasting behavioural changes depend on establishing decisions as social norms.

8. Women are responsible for the majority of consumer choices including electronic items.

9. Early legislation setting minimum standards can drive a virtuous circle of rapid innovation and further choice editing as manufacturers and retailers compete to exceed the statutory requirements.

10. Any fiscal incentive needs to close the price gap with conventional products, or deliver significant tax benefits.

11. Consumers prefer up-front benefits rather than the promise of future savings.

12. Consumer action can create an emotional drive for change (e.g. related to food scares, animal welfare), and some companies have benefited from predicting or responding quickly to such events.

Sources: Sustainable Consumption Roundtable 2006; Tischner 2010; WEF & Deloitte 2011

These lessons reveal that a break is needed with certain common practices regarding consumer behaviour. Typically, efforts to affect behaviour take place either at the point of purchase (e.g. special offers, in-store promotions) or during the pre-purchase phase. Because in-store behaviour tends to be transactional and price driven, messages about sustainability need to be received before the moment of purchase. Values can have a decisive effect on consumer decisions, but they are relatively hard to create or change having often been instilled early on in life. This, of course, has not prevented elements of the value chain such as advertising from trying, and one approach in recent decades has been to disaggregate individual consumers through a process of perpetual market segmentation, aided by ever-more sophisticated ways of understanding and reaching consumers. It is ironic, therefore, that sustainability is often presented as an appeal to rebuild community, and to treat people as citizens rather than atomized consumers, suggesting the need for a return to mass marketing.

However, this is unlikely to be the mass marketing of the past. Trust, co-creation, and authentic engagement with consumers have all been cited as prerequisites for future marketing (Chapter 5). Specific attention is being given to the demands of the next generation of consumers. It is often claimed that they are more acutely aware of global social and environmental issues, and feel in a state of higher alert about the uncertainties they pose.[52] At the same time, they respond better to positive language; perhaps preferring resource-efficient economies to the term resource-constrained economies used in this book. There are identifiable social leverage points to reach this group presented by sport, music, art, film, and design. Solar-powered showers and stages are a feature at many festivals, as are recycling schemes run by local charities that get to sell the aluminium and other recyclable materials they collect. The Olympics has become a showcase for sustainability innovation. Beijing's National Aquatics Centre built for the 2008 games showed the potential of ethylene tetrafluoroethylene, a type of plastic that increases light and heat penetration, and significantly reduces energy usage. The London 2012 games promised to be the 'greenest games ever', and organizers claim that alongside increased interest in sport, increased interest in sustainability will be the major legacy of the event.[53]

Although the so-called next generation are probably more brand-aware than any in the past, they have an ambivalent attitude towards brands that is laced with suspicion and cynicism as much as self-identity and image. The next generation continues to communicate through brands, but they use them to convey quite complicated messages about values and beliefs, and in order to justify such consumers' trust, companies need to be transparent about their own values, genuine in what they communicate and where they choose to lead, and be open to engagement and co-creation as a break with the Four Ps (product, price, place, and promotion) marketing model of the past (Chapter 5). This at least is the message that one repeatedly hears from people involved in sustainable consumption.[54] Some of the claims made about next-generation consumers seem to echo those once made about an earlier generation of ethical consumers who subsequently proved a more fragmented and less influential group than originally imagined. However, the demands of a resource-constrained economy could mean that the choices facing future consumers are fundamentally different to those of their predecessors in that the imperative for action could be much greater. As Princen (2005) argues in explaining the need to shift from efficiency to sufficiency, the choice for consumers will not be about denial, sacrifice, or going without. Rather, due to resource depletion and the consequences of over-consumption, he argues, in future sufficiency will define what it means to be doing well, and goods are only good to a point.

Consuming differently; consuming less

The Earth's carrying capacity is a recurring concept throughout this book, and it has been estimated that if everyone in the world consumed as much as people in Europe, we would need the equivalent of three planet's worth of natural resources. This highlights the very geographically skewed nature of modern consumption, but in order to redress it requires that we either consume much less (i.e. put an end to rampant consumerism), or consume very differently than we do at present.[55] Both points of view are highly emotive because they require fundamental changes in the way we live our lives. A more nuanced view is that it is not consumption per se that is problematic, but what we consume. For example, there are resource-light products such as MP3 tracks that can be consumed with less energy and material intensity. Sustainable consumption, therefore, requires us to consume less of certain things; not to reject consumption outright.

The difficulty here is that at present, we measure individual, corporate, and national well-being by overall consumption, not the type of consumption. Consumption equates with economic stability, and vigorous consumer spending is synonymous with full employ-ment, higher tax revenues, buoyant industries, and a booming economy in general. When North American and European politicians have called out for more economic growth since the financial collapse of 2008, what they want to see is more consumption, and until that is achieved, they seem to argue, sustainable consumption is not a priority. The ethical con-sumer, as already noted, is still a consumer, and the power to consume in recent years has become a form of political power. For example, purchasers of fairtrade produce feel they are helping the poor, and consumers of organic fruit and vegetables have a sense of improving the planet's health as well as their own. Shareholder activism, consumer boy-cotts, and consumer rights advocacy are all legitimate forms of citizen protest in a world where citizenship is at times equated with the act of consumption. Indeed, many govern-ments are happy to champion consumer rights, even as they try to rein in other rights to do with freedom of association, employment law, and public protest. Many governments have shown themselves prepared to react to sustainability challenges with policies that imply major changes in consumption, but few have proved themselves willing or able to tackle the inconsistencies a consumption driven sense of well-being present for such policies.

For the most part, governments of the wealthiest economies have readily accepted that people's relationship to material things is enmeshed in social and psychological goals, and have not been prepared to address ways of fulfilling those goals in ways involving less mate-rial consumption. Community groups, consumer groups, and others who say that material aspirations should be tempered by concerns about family, security, and the future show that there are genuine concerns and tensions about what consumption means if we transition to a resource-constrained economy,[56] but they sit on the outside of a social and political consensus that consumption is an essential activity and a worthy goal.

 Discussion points

Consumption and sustainability are often portrayed as being at odds with each other.

- Can sustainability be made a rational choice for consumers?
- Why do value action gaps exist?
- Do you believe there is a shift towards consuming experiences rather than products?

 Summary

The sustainability of production and consumption is a central issue in the business–sustainability relationship. There has been a rise in the use of materials in production, and a growth in mass consumption in wealthy economies, especially since the Second World War. However, the conditions that enabled this to happen such as falling commodity prices, leaps in productivity, and rising real wages can no longer be taken for granted. Wealthy economies have done well at producing more with less, but this has not brought about an absolute decoupling in economic growth and material throughput. Furthermore, the burgeoning middle classes in emerging economies are driving an unprecedentedly rapid increase in the demand for consumer goods.

Expanding supply and increasing productivity are the conventional responses to this kind of situation, but they each have their weaknesses in the sustainability context. A sustainability response is different nature, but it is also more expensive than the alternatives, and in important areas the rates of return on financial capital are low. There is plenty of innovation connected to sustainable production, but new ideas have not been scaled up. Similarly, there has been plenty of activity to do with sustainable consumption, but the basic premise of modern capitalist society that consumption is a right and a sign of well-being seems as strong as ever. Even amongst sustainability aware consumers, there is a value action gap that is evident in emerging economies as well as developed ones.

 Further reading

Dauvergne, P. 2008, *The shadows of consumption: Consequences for the global Environment*, The MIT Press, Cambridge, MA.
An overview of the social and environmental consequences of over-consumption.

Frank, R.H. 2011, *The Darwin economy: Liberty, competition, and the common good*, Princeton University Press, Princeton, NJ.
The case for a less market-driven, more regulated approach to managing consumption.

Lebel, L., Lorek, S., & Daniel, R. 2010, *Sustainable production consumption systems: Knowledge, engagement and practice*, Springer Verlag, Berlin.
Case studies of specific sustainable production and consumption systems.

Trentmann, F. 2012, *The Oxford handbook of the history of consumption*, Oxford University Press, Oxford.
A guide to the history of the role consumption has played in human society through the ages.

Wilkinson, R.G. 2010, *The spirit level: Why equality is better for everyone*, Penguin, London.
Highly graphical analysis of the disconnect between wealth and well-being.

Case study 11   PUMA's valuation of ecosystem services

PUMA has become the first company in the world to put a value on the eco services it uses to produce its sports shoes and clothes, signalling a radical change in the way business will account for its use of natural resources.

This was the opening paragraph of a newspaper article in *The Guardian* announcing the launch of PUMA and its parent company, PPR's, environmental profit and loss account (E P&L) in 2011. Building on conventional profit and loss accounts, PUMA claims it is the first global business to put a true value on the natural resources used, and the environmental impacts caused, by providing products to its customers. It is intended to give the company a detailed understanding of the implications of its decisions on the environment, enabling actions to be taken that combine commercial benefits and safeguarding the natural assets it depends upon.

It began by quantifying its GHG emissions and water consumption in its business and supply chain operations. It then applied values so that it could account for the associated economic impacts. This addresses a commonly voiced problem of conventional accounting, that it allows companies to externalize their social and environmental costs. The E P&L sets out in monetary terms the scale of its reliance on natural capital, and provides a platform to determine what can be done to manage its impact. It also helps to prioritize issues because it reveals where the biggest impacts lie.

TruCost along with PwC helped develop the methodology. Its chief operating officer, Richard Mattison describes it as a way for companies to minimize the risk of sustainability-related commodity volatility by increasing sustainability in the value chain. He says, 'Reporting a company's use of natural capital and impacts on ecosystems and biodiversity is vital as these costs are already impacting businesses; natural resources are becoming scarcer and more costly, and natural systems are not providing the protection from floods, storms and droughts that they once did'.

For example, if one takes the example of water used in cotton production, it is a business risk if growers pay only a small part of the true value of the resource (e.g. in water-scarce areas) because the crop can fail if water is mismanaged. Equally, the current price put on carbon emissions does not yet reflect the economic impact of climate change. Overall, the analysis looks at impacts ranging from raw material production (e.g. cotton farming, oil drilling) to processing (e.g. leather tanneries, the chemical industry, oil refining).

The E P&L puts a value on the social cost of GHG emissions based on the impact of current and future climate change. In the first account, a value of £57 was calculated for each tonne of CO_2, meaning that the company's overall GHG emissions value was £41 million for 2010. Water availability is a more localized issue, and so assessing impact requires location-specific values. When these variables were accounted for, the value of water consumption was estimated at £41 million in 2010. The greatest impacts related to the production of raw materials such as cotton cultivation and cattle ranching. These account for 35 per cent of the company's total GHG emissions (£14.3m) and 43 per cent of its water consumption (£21.2m). In other words, the highest water intensity in producing a t-shirt occurs right at the beginning of the supply chain.

PUMA has committed itself to making half of its international collections according to its internal sustainability standard within four years, using more sustainable materials such as recycled polyester, as well as ensuring its suppliers develop more sustainable materials and products. In launching the account, the company said: '[We] will look to play a catalytic role in raising awareness that the current business model is outdated and needs decisive reforms, forging partnerships and collaborations to explore new and innovative ways to differentially attribute the responsibilities and equitably share the costs of these, while building capacity at suppliers' factories and developing new materials and products'.

Sources: http://safe.PUMA.com/us/en/category/key-performance-indicators/; http://www.guardian.co.uk/
sustainable-business/PUMA-value-environmental-impact-biodiversity; http://about.PUMA.com/wp-content/
themes/aboutPUMA_theme/media/pdf/2011/en/PwC_Trucost.pdf; http://www.marketingweek.co.uk/sectors/sport/
PUMA-introduces-%E2%80%9Cgame-changing%E2%80%9D-environmental-report/3026438.article, all accessed 30
January 2012.

Questions

1. E P&L has been praised for putting PUMA and PPR brands such as Gucci and Stella McCartney
ahead of their apparel industry peers when it comes to tackling sustainable production.

   a. What is innovative about E P&L?

   b. How does it help PUMA management?

   c. What do you think will be different about PUMA products as a result of E P&L?

2. PUMA says it will tackle the social dimensions of its impact later on.

   a. Why is it taking a staggered approach?

   b. What are some of the social impacts it will need to measure?

   c. Should it include consumer behaviour as a social impact?

3. E P&L is the latest sustainability-oriented management innovation to come out of the apparel
industry.

   a. How does PUMA's approach compare to what peers such as Gap, Pentland, and Nike are doing to
   improve sustainability production?

   b. How might PUMA achieve its aim of playing a catalytic role?

   c. How could PUMA strengthen its impact on sustainable consumption?

 Endnotes

   1. (McKinsey Global Institute 2011)

   2. For contrasting explanations, see, for instance Chang (2002), Collier (2007), Easterly (2006), Maxwell
      (2005).

   3. (McKinsey Global Institute 2011)

   4. International Energy Agency figures.

   5. (McKinsey Global Institute 2011)

   6. (Senge 2008, chapter 3)

   7. (E.g. Cabeza Gutés 1996; Mander & Goldsmith 1996; Meadows & Meadows 2004; Turner 1994)

   8. http://www.indexmundi.com.

   9. (WEF & Accenture 2012)

   10. (McKinsey Global Institute 2011; WEF & Accenture 2012)

   11. (Shove 2010; Stern 2011; Whitmarsh, O'Neill, & Lorenzoni 2011)

   12. (WEF & Accenture 2012)

   13. (Sustainable Consumption Roundtable 2006); http://ec.europa.eu/public_opinion/archives/ebs/
       ebs_295_en.pdf, accessed 23 January 2011.

   14. (WEF & Accenture 2012)

   15. (Thompson 2010)

16. See, for instance, reports of Wood Mackenzie's Unconventional Gas Service, http://www.woodmacre-search.com.

17. http://www.worldbank.org/foodcrisis/, accessed 23 January 2012.

18. (McKinsey Global Institute 2011)

19. (McKinsey Global Institute 2011)

20. (McKinsey Global Institute 2011, p. 17)

21. (Geertz 1963)

22. (Barrientos, Dolan, & Tallontire 2003; Braun et al. 2010; Holden, Deininger, & Ghebru 2011; Jonvallen et al. 2009; Wajcman 2010)

23. (Bell, Chilvers, & Hillier 2011; Freebairn 1995; Pinstrup-Andersen & Hazell 1985)

24. (Bell, Chilvers, & Hillier 2011)

25. (PwC 2011)

26. (McKinsey Global Institute 2011)

27. (WEF & Accenture 2012)

28. All data from the organizations' respective websites.

29. For a fuller list, see http://www.enviroreporting.com/detail_page.phtml?page=awards.

30. (WEF & Accenture 2012)

31. (McKinsey Global Institute 2011)

32. (WEF & Accenture 2012)

33. (Sustainable Consumption Roundtable 2006)

34. (Haidt 2006; Wilkinson 2010)

35. http://oecdbetterlifeindex.org/

36. (Wilkinson 2010)

37. (Galbraith 1958)

38. (E.g. Ehrenfeld 2008; Leonard 2010; Soper, Ryle, & Thomas 2009)

39. See Blowfield (2011) for a discussion of these issues.

40. (Kahneman & Tversky 1979)

41. (Sunstein & Thaler 2008; Thaler & Sunstein 2003)

42. (WEF & Deloitte 2011)

43. (E.g. Brower, Leon, & Union of Concerned Scientists 1999; Brown & Dacin 1997; Harrison, Newholm, & Shaw 2005; Jackson 2006)

44. (Grande 2007)

45. (Nicholls & Opal 2005; Zadek et al. 1998)

46. (Belz & Peattie 2009; Bhattacharya & Sen 2004)

47. (Lehmann & Lehmann 2010)

48. Ehrenreich (2001) offers an interesting explanation of this evolution.

49. There are 7,500 varieties of apple. http://www.dralanknight.com/my-narrative/choice-editing-versus-informed-consumer-choice, accessed 31 January 2012.

50. (Morewedge et al. 2010)

51. (Scholte 2000)

52. (WEF & Deloitte 2011)

53. http://sd.defra.gov.uk/2010/03/sustainable-olympics-oxymoron-or-reality/, accessed 31 January 2012.

54. (E.g. Jackson 2006; Worldwatch Institute 2010)

55. (CPI 2007; Dauvergne 2008)

56. (Sustainable Consumption Roundtable 2006)

12 Looking to the future

> **Key terms**
>
> Transition   Plutonomy
> Justice   Catastrophic change
> Land   Resilience

Chapter in brief

This chapter is about the future of the business–sustainability relationship. It draws together the major issues raised in previous chapters, and looks at where we stand at present. It then explores the transition process, and what we can expect to happen if we shift to a RCE. It highlights some of the new challenges that are on the horizon, and discusses some of the breakthroughs that could alter our current thinking. It concludes with a discussion of the importance of including sustainability into future thinking about the direction and purpose of business, both for the good of companies and for society as a whole.

Surmising the situation today

Throughout the 11 previous chapters of this book, we have examined different perspectives on whether, why, and how business is addressing sustainability issues around the world. Given the evidence, what can we conclude about the business–sustainability relationship? Is business addressing the major sustainability challenges, or is it exacerbating them? Is it winning the public's trust or generating animosity? How does it view sustainability, and what actions is it taking? Before we look too far into the future, how does that future look to business right now?

In order to answer these questions, let us consider some recent points of view.

We are now well into the second decade of the twenty-first century, and the role of business in society is as contentious as it ever was. As a reaction to corporate crime, high unemployment, abuses of power, and failure to deal more aggressively with unsustainable practices, the Occupy movement sprang up to do what its name implies—occupy sites at the bastions of capitalism such as Wall Street, the City of London, and La Défense in Paris. In response, the self-proclaimed richest one per cent of the population have fought back. Bank CEO, John Allison, told other business leaders under pressure to disclose the gap between their salaries and those of their employees, 'Instead of an attack on the 1 percent, let's call it an attack on the very productive'.[1] The debate about whether the richest one per cent are essential to creating wealth or an unnecessary luxury has split the business community itself, putting, for instance, hedge-fund manager John Paulson and Berkshire Hathaway CEO, Warren Buffett, at loggerheads with each other over how much tax the rich should pay.

This argument between business leaders and others in society, and amongst business leaders themselves underpins how business' relationship to sustainability will move forwards. It is a muddled debate, often fuelled by hyperbole, political grandstanding, and vitriol on all sides. But beneath the posturing and hot air are fundamental questions about business' role and how it is to be fulfilled. How important, for instance, are the very rich in shaping the course of sustainability? Are they greedy and exploitative, uncaring of anything except how to increase their own wealth regardless of the harm this can cause? Or are they magnanimous benefactors who will use their wealth wisely to create employment and preserve the world's natural capital because it is in their interests to do so? Might it even be that plutonomy—economic growth fuelled by the spending and consumption of the wealthy—can deliver better outcomes in sustainability terms because targeting the top of the pyramid rather than the bottom requires less inputs, and offers a way of decoupling economic activity from the overuse of finite resources?

Or is it simply misleading to confuse business with wealth? Worldwide, most jobs are created by smaller companies and have little or nothing to do with the richest one per cent. Innovation rarely comes from major corporations, and conventional capital is seldom suited to technological breakthroughs.[2] Is it perfectly logical to be suspicious of wealth, and yet supportive of business as a way of tackling sustainability challenges? Starbucks founder, Howard Schultz, has said:

> Despite the mistrust that . . . businesses have engendered as of late, history suggests a different truth: that while government can create a framework and conditions that will support positive economic change, it is . . . business that will turn things around, and deliver the prosperity and sustainable economic stability and security that can follow.
>
> But today, an increasingly challenging economic climate around the world and a historic decline in consumer confidence at home are combining to cause many business leaders to stop leading their businesses forward. They have become fixated on the short term. And when short term results alone drive or unduly influence management decisions, the temptation to push off sound longer-term investments, those that will fuel innovation and strengthen the enterprise for the future, can become overwhelming.
>
> With that mindset comes the false belief that investments in people and training can wait; that corporate social responsibility can be put on the back burner.
>
> (Schulz 2008, http://www.huffingtonpost.com/howard-schultz/
> yes-business-can_b_141969.html, accessed 22 December 2011)

Martin Chilcott, CEO of the business sustainability platform 2Degrees, compared the progress of government sustainability interventions and business activities, and concluded that large corporations are:

> getting on the sustainable business bus, even if big government and the UN wasn't providing a properly qualified driver.
>
> Unilever, Tesco, Nike, Toyota and a host of others are more concerned about resource scarcity, impact and cost reduction, the disruption of new markets and reputation management than they are about talks in Durban. (Particularly, as the outcome is only 'to start negotiating about a legally binding agreement'.) Furthermore, these corporations see real opportunity to meet a new generation of consumer needs and develop new business

models that will give them a real sustainable competitive advantage as the economic revolution gets underway.

(Chilcott 2011, http://www.2degreesnetwork.com/groups/all-2degrees-members/resources/
did-sustainable-business-go-mainstream-2011/, accessed 22 December 2011)

Chilcott and Schultz are amongst the many who are less concerned about the leaders of companies than about the leadership provided by business as a whole. From their perspective, business is an essential institution in contemporary society, and part of its implicit social contract is that it helps solve the major challenges society confronts. The Occupy movement believes business has broken that contract, and Schultz seems to agree. Others more optimistically argue that business is becoming more comfortable exhibiting leadership in a sustainability context, and point to an array of areas where companies are active (Figure 12.1).

Corporate carbon strategies

Initiatives to explore corporate carbon management and offsetting and identify appropriate strategies.

Energy efficiency

Initiatives to explore how to gain competitive advantage from developing and implementing a distinctive sustainability strategy.

Energy policy and strategy

Initiatives to analyse emerging and existing energy policies and consider corporate energy strategies.

Finance and corporate sustainability

Initiatives to examine and explain the role of financial services in sustainability, with conversations covering environmental and social risk management and investment opportunities.

Green communications

Initiatives to investigate the issues surrounding effective communications regarding sustainability to consumers.

Resource efficiency

Initiatives to accelerate resource efficiency by identifying related strategic opportunities for major companies. How to demonstrate the resource efficiency and security opportunities for business, and to value current efficiency initiatives.

Sustainable technology performance

Initiatives to explore how businesses use renewable and other sustainable technologies to power their operations and reduce their environmental impact.

Sustainable supply chains

Initiatives to understand what the supply chain sustainability consists of, the business case for pursuing it, and ways to go about creating it.

Figure 12.1 Examples of current types of business initiative to address sustainability.

Sources: adapted from http://www.2degreesnetwork.com; http://www.greenmondays.com.

Arguably, these types of effort may be laudable in their own right but are too little too late given the challenges some foresee. If one attends conferences of innovators such as EmTech,[3] one quickly gets the impression that technological solutions are scurrying up the pipeline to meet the greatest challenges. 'In this crowd, the world's most pressing problems, like climate change, famine, and disease are seen as opportunities – and even better, lucrative opportunities – and what could generate more optimism than that?' (Halpern 2011, p. 37). However, as Siemens CEO, Greg Sorenson, points out, 'Unless products can save money, meaning make somebody some money somewhere, innovations don't make it across the desert from the idea stage into actually helping people' (Halpern 2011, p. 37). Thus, although there is plenty of optimism that human genius can conjure up solutions to sustainability's challenges, it remains to be seen if those ideas will win out in the market place, or whether we have the mechanisms in place to evaluate sustainability innovations against, for instance, the new smart phone enabling TV viewers to buy whatever is on their screen without leaving their armchair.

Pessimists—what some would call realists—such as scientist James Lovelock, say that it is effectively too late to avoid major catastrophic events associated with sustainability.[4] For example, it could be too late to avoid average global temperatures rising by less than 2°C, and therefore our focus now should be on dealing with the consequences of that. The possibility that adaptation is becoming a more realistic play than mitigation is one that many politicians, environmentalists, and business people have been hesitant to take seriously. However, missed targets, evidence on the ground, increased understanding, inertia, and false starts all give cause to question whether even our best efforts will bring challenges such as climate change under control. Might the most important innovations, therefore, not be the ones that substitute coal with hydrogen, but ones that enable humanity to thrive on an unprecedentedly hotter planet, or even offshore our more damaging activities to another part of the solar system? If we have gone too far to turn back, what questions should business be asking about the future: about its role in adaptation to change as opposed to mitigating change; about its investment strategies; about its research and development pipelines?

It is tempting when trying to answer these questions to conjure up visions of the world copied wholesale from sci-fi books. Less sensational and alluring, but no less profound in terms of the scale of change, is the idea that to be sustainable we need to live on less and be smaller with our footprints. Schumacher declared that 'small is beautiful', and his idea of sustainable societies has informed various authors cited in this book such as Porritt, McKibben, and Shiva.[5] Visions of a sustainable future can crudely be divided between those that foresee a global technological revolution, and those that see a social revolution with a society comprising much smaller communities, each resilient to the shocks caused by unsustainable lifestyles in the past. This is what Rob Hopkins calls the 'transition model', characterized by a strong localized economic base, more connected local communities, and people trained in the skills of what he refers to as a 'power-down' life (i.e. a lifestyle that uses less oil, gas, electricity, and less energy overall).[6]

Neither the technological revolution nor power-down lifestyles are inherently business friendly or unfriendly, but the type of business that succeeds, and the nature of business success will look very different in each. Technological revolutions (especially ones that happen rapidly) have often been linked to government intervention, and leaps forward in geo-engineering or desalination are as likely to hinge on public investment as the expansion of the German railways or the creation of the US internet did in the past. History also tells us that the private sector can thrive without globalization and the mega-corporation. While the temptation is to ask whether business will survive and prosper in what we have been calling a RCE, the more salient question is 'What kinds of business will prosper?'. Despite the array of viewpoints discussed in this section so far, none of them really addresses this question. Some make a case for business as it is as if what exists today is the zenith of economic evolution, and something to be preserved at all costs. Equally, others treat the present state as the nadir of human endeavour, to be displaced with something better-aligned with the human spirit. In between, there are those who would encourage business to reconsider its role in society, or who praise the steps it has taken in a generally unfavourable environment. Things become less clear, however, if we consider what steps it should be taking next, in what direction, and to what end. It is this we turn to now.

 Discussion points

We all have ideas about companies that are green and ones that are not.

- In what ways does Howard Schultz appear to agree with the Occupy movement that business has broken its social contract?
- Do you agree that plutonomy could help to create a more sustainable world?
- What might a successful company in a power-down world look like?

What happens now?

Companies spend significant resources trying to envision the future, yet Howard Schultz is not alone in saying that business leaders plan for the short- not the long-term (see 'Surmising the situation today'). Industrial giants of the past such as Dunlop, Kodak, and Olivetti, might all wish that they had had better foresight than they did, but the time horizons attached to sustainability can seem too long even for the most forward looking company. After all, history seems to tell us that it is not companies that predict the future that do well, but ones that adapt to it in a timely and effective fashion.[7] Therefore, in this section, rather than try to look too far out at what is a highly complex landscape, we will examine some of the factors that will affect if, how, and when business changes.

Transitions

A passing or passage from one condition, action, or place, to another.

This definition from the *Oxford English Dictionary* captures the essential elements of *transition*—the idea of a passage from one condition to another. To avoid the impression that transition is a series of stepping stones where we leap from one to the next, wait for a while as if playing statues, and then leap to a third and so on, it is helpful to think of each condition as dynamic and volatile in itself. In other words, transition is: 'a shift from one dynamic equilibrium to another dynamic equilibrium' (Kemp & Rotmans 2005).

Transition, therefore, is something different to change. Change is a constant feature of life, but transition is something more momentous than that. One can change one's hair by cutting it, dying it, letting it grow and so on, but losing one's hair is a transition: it is an irreversible shift from one condition to another. A bald person can continue to change their hair, but not in the same way as they could when they were hirsute. Invention, modification, and improvement will still be a feature of a RCE, but the world in which they occur will be fundamentally different to the one that preceded it, and therefore what counts as useful or worthwhile will also be different.

Transitions are typically described in terms of three types of driver: economic, political, or technological innovation. These drivers were brought together in the work of Joseph Schumpeter whose theories of business cycles and creative destruction attempted to explain dynamism in the capitalist economy.[8] Although he was politically aware (e.g. he considers innovation to ultimately be part of an inevitable shift from capitalism to socialism),[9] creative destruction emphasizes the role of technology in driving transition. If we look at previous major transitions such as the early Industrial Revolution, the Railway Age, the IT Revolution, transitions, they are all associated with technological shifts, and have a number of common features.[10] Each plays out over a period of roughly 50 years (Chapter 5), during which time there are distinct phases (Figure 12.2). For example, there is a gestation period when new ideas are formulated and experimented with without gaining much financial, social, or political attention. Then comes a period of 'irruption' (sic), the abrupt intrusion of the new ideas into the socio-economic sphere. This is when great fortunes are made and lost, and when a new infrastructure is put in place: it is a time of technological but also financial innovation

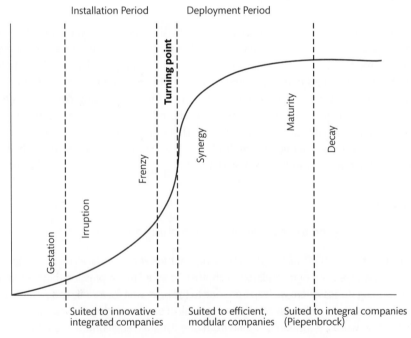

Figure 12.2 Phases of technological transition.

and installation. However, as the bursting of the dot.com bubble at the end of the twentieth century or the collapse in railway company shares in the 1840s demonstrated, irruption leads to frenzy and in turn to collapse. This 'installation' phase plays out over 20–30 years, and the economic crash at the end of it creates an opportunity for recomposing the institutions of society so that what follows is a more stable period of deployment during which the benefits of the new ideas are more widely felt.

Another feature of these grand transitions is that different elements affect the process not only at different moments but at different speeds. For example, technological innovation moves fast, and one of the reasons it can fail is that entrepreneurs cannot find enough capital. As the potential of a new swathe of innovations becomes apparent, financial innovation by both the private and public sectors makes risk capital available in the form of new instruments as happened with the rise of joint-stock companies during the early Railway Age, and the growth of venture capital to fund the IT Revolution. Financial innovation outpaces the speed at which government can regulate it, and also the speed at which government and other social institutions can remediate any negative consequences of rapid increases in wealth, changes in employment, and a sense of injustice and inequality. Eventually, these elements at the regime level exert an ever more powerful moderating influence on the faster moving ones, although by that time (i.e. during the deployment period) many of the social and environmental consequences of the new ideas have become accepted as the norm, and much of what was originally radical and alternative comes to be regarded as the new common sense.[11]

The Schumpeter-based transition model highlights other common features. First, transition is irreversible: one cannot revert to the previous state. Second, transitions take place at multiple levels. If we imagine carriage-makers confronting the railway age, for example, we can imagine the vision statements and strategies they could have come up with to make the transition as comprehensible and controllable as possible, but the real changes that would ultimately drive them out of business were happening at levels beyond the firm or their industry.

Kemp (1994) divides the world into three levels, the interplay of which affects transition. These are hierarchical; *niches* which are the hotbed of innovative new ideas feed into *regimes* (i.e. the established elements of society such as infrastructure, knowledge, policy) that in turn shape the *landscape* (i.e. norms and slower moving trends such as culture, demographic change, and political change). When an organization talks about managing transition it is often referring to managing its part in a niche, but it will have no influence over whether that niche breaks through or not at the regime level: 'Radical innovations [only] break out of the niche-level when ongoing processes at the levels of regime and landscape create a 'window of opportunity' (Geels 2002, p. 1262).

Consequently, seemingly promising innovations to do with sustainability will succeed not on their merits alone, but also on the circumstances they exist within. For example, the compact fluorescent lamp (CFL) was first marketed in the 1980s, but it did not take off as a commercial technology until concern about climate change at the landscape level began to influence sectoral policy, consumer practices, and corporate strategy at the regime level. Subsequent alignment at the regime level opened the windows of opportunity for CFL to succeed as a technological niche, and in time the technology opened up new regime level possibilities (e.g. profitable ecoefficiency strategies, government promotion of energy efficiency, green consumerism) that in turn opened new windows for other technologies.

Path dependence

Attention to how the regime and landscape levels affect technology show that transition is influenced by context and boundary conditions. This is the realm of path dependence which in its simplest form reminds us that history matters. More importantly, it encourages us to consider how much pre-existing conditions influence the transition pathways that are possible or not. For example, it has been argued that the Kyoto Protocol mechanism (Chapter 10) was heavily influenced by the experiences of its framers in areas as diverse as acid rain and nuclear treaties, and it was this body of knowledge that was applied in confronting the quite different issue of GHG emissions reduction. As it turned out, those experiences were inappropriate and in part account for the limited impact of the Protocol,[12] but the path dependence created by those previous instruments, treaties, and mechanisms meant that it was always likely that they would influence subsequent international agreements even if some more appropriate approach was on offer.

Path dependence is evident in many aspects of sustainability. For example, the success of biofuels and flex-fuel vehicles in Brazil in the 2000s is in part a consequence of that country's long history of using ethanol as a gasoline additive dating back to the 1930s, and the well-established existence of alternative markets for sugar (the source of ethanol) in case the biofuel market slumped.

The path dependencies that will affect how we respond to sustainability challenges over the coming decades are already in place. At present, society as a whole seems set on a course of moderate transition in the face of certain sustainability challenges. If we think of mobility, for example, there is a degree of acceptance that carbon fuels will need to be substituted with alternative ones so far as is feasible in terms of cost, technology, and practicality. The hybrid electric vehicle is with us, and electric cars are being marketed: the internal combustion engine is being made ever more fuel efficient, hydrogen fuel cells are in development, and biofuels are becoming a serious part of the energy mix. Yet, for all of these developments, we seem orientated to a future where mobility increases with economic growth, per capita mobility in developed economies does not significantly change, and economic activity itself is unaffected. (If anything, the shift to low carbon mobility is considered to be a stimulus to economic growth.)

From an optimal sustainability perspective, other orientations might be more desirable. For example, some might argue that better outcomes will be achieved if mobility decreases along with less use of carbon fuels (e.g. because changes in lifestyle make it unnecessary to travel so much), thereby decoupling carbon and mobility from economic growth. A third orientation might be that we learn to live with less economic growth itself, and that this reduces the demand for mobility and energy. Each of these orientations would affect business in distinct ways, but path dependence means that the first orientation is much stronger than the others. As we will discuss in the next section, this does not mean that radical transitions are impossible, but all other things being equal society has a preference for gradual, incremental change. In a number of areas of sustainability, the evidence that this approach is working is far from convincing, and as deadlines for action are shifted further and further backwards for political rather than any clear scientific reasons, so there is a risk of solutions taking the form of 'hail Mary passes', the long, last-minute kick or throw that will hopefully save the game.

Shifts or tipping points?

The multi-faceted nature of transition raises the question of in what sense can transitions be said to be manageable. Executives are used to setting goals, and managers are used to achieving them: together they share a belief that change is something controllable, and anything less is a management failure. In management studies, transition theory and behavioural change from Lewin onwards has concentrated on controlling the change process. Although the chaotic multi-faceted nature of transition is recognized, it is treated as a problem, a cause of inertia, and ultimately something that has to be overcome if transition is to go ahead as it should. Consequently, whether one is considering Lewin's unfreezing, moving, and refreezing model of change, or Kotter's coalition, vision, and institutionalization model,[13] the central idea is that transition involves bringing order out of chaos, and then embedding the outcomes of that change into organizational practices. Even when the role of forces beyond the organization in shaping its actions is recognized (cf. stakeholder management), those external parties are regarded as something to be identified, known, and ultimately controlled.

However, the relevance of this kind of model has to be questioned in the sustainability context. First, it is a model developed for individual organizations, not for sectors or industries. Sustainability transition, by contrast, calls for change at different levels including the inter-organizational, inter-sectoral, and inter-industry (see 'Transitions'). Second, it is a linear model based on the assumption that managers can predict and explain transition, and the organization can shift from one condition to another by setting and achieving predefined outcomes through consciously undertaken actions.

Contemporary transition theory is sceptical of this idea, even if it remains prevalent in much management literature. Linearity and the transition from one equilibrium to another is at odds with the ideas of non-linearity and disequilibrium that not only inform contemporary physics,[14] but also new economics,[14] scenario planning,[15] and innovation.[16] The latter are connected with concepts such as turbulence and uncertainty that are seen as part of the contemporary management challenge. This in turn reflects a wider discourse on sustainability and prosperity, a central theme of which is that we are moving from an era of relative congruence (cf. equilibrium, fit, alignment) amongst society's main institutions and their pursuit of a common purpose (i.e. economic growth) to an era of incongruence (cf. disequilibrium, bifurcation, chaos) when there is much more disturbance, disruption, and unpredictability in the environment organizations exist within, and along with that a reappraisal of the common purpose and how to achieve it.

In this kind of a situation, transition is best seen as an uncertain journey that needs to be navigated rather than a roadway to be designed and constructed. One's journey can be managed, but it cannot be controlled any more than, say, a whitewater raft can be said to control the river it is racing down. Furthermore, there is a genuine risk that sustainability transition will not be gradual, but could be prompted by sudden, hard to predict changes more akin to lurches than shifts. In scientific circles, these are typically referred to as catastrophic events associated, for instance, with increases in global average temperatures of more than 2°C or rises in population beyond ten billion. All major sustainability issues have possible catastrophic events associated with them. What marks them out is that they threaten changes to our social and natural environment so profound and so rapid that conventional responses may not only be inappropriate, but also highly damaging.

There has not been much thought given to the managerial consequences of catastrophic change despite the level of scientific interest it has engendered, and the nascent interest from mainstream economists.[17] One can speculate about why this is, but to date what insights have been offered have either come from natural disasters or international wars and peacemaking,[18] and have tended to emphasize the role of government rather than how business might react.

 Discussion points

Transitioning to a RCE could prove one of the major managerial challenges in the coming decades.

- What are the key features of technologically-driven transitions?
- Why do some feel a linear model of transition is inappropriate in a sustainability context?
- What do you think are some of the reasons managing catastrophic changes associated with sustainability have not been widely considered in a business context?

New challenges

Justice

The diversity of issues that fall under the sustainability umbrella already appear overwhelming, but looking ahead the challenges will continue to shift or at least be reshaped. For instance, it is noticeable that as emerging economies have grown in wealth and political power, they have succeeded in getting sustainability issues considered from a justice perspective, ensuring principles such as 'common but differentiated responsibilities'[19] are put into practice. Justice is at the heart of 'burden sharing', the issue of how the costs and other consequences of sustainability-related changes such as climate change are to be divided. The ethics of burden sharing have been an important part of sustainability from the earliest days of international policies. The very notion of sustainability (cf. the Brundtland Report; Chapter 1) has been tied to intergenerational justice, evident in the idea that the needs of the present generation should be met without compromising the ability of future generations to meet their own needs. Today, the ethical dimension to sustainability has been extended to include geographical justice, including the principle that tackling sustainability issues should be accomplished in ways that do not impede poorer economies' development. Geographical justice and international burden sharing have been central themes in recent international debates to resolve sustainability challenges, and failure to resolve the resultant difficulties has been one reason these negotiations have stumbled (Chapter 10).

Sustainability justice is already relevant to business, not least because until it is resolved companies confront a policy vacuum that makes for an uncertain business environment. However, the situation could worsen if, because of sustainability challenges, business cannot deliver prosperity in line with people's expectations. Even though there has always been unease about capitalism as a system—and we are going through a phase of discontent in some of the most advanced capitalist countries at present—overall the wealthiest nations have accepted that capitalism equates with justice and enables a more just society than would otherwise be the case. Business clearly benefits from this because although its contract with wider society is continually subject to renegotiation, its purpose and outcomes are broadly aligned with the accepted good of capitalist society.

However, this general acceptance of business is in jeopardy if sustainability challenges are not met in a way that sees a satisfactory transition to a prosperous RCE. Business comes under greatest scrutiny when it is seen as unfair, unable to ensure general prosperity, and incongruent with social reality. In such circumstances, companies cannot justify their actions by appealing to economic laws; rather, they are susceptible to an explicit justice-based agenda that in the past has resulted in industrial unrest, capital flight, and nationalization.

The trilemma of land

Major sustainability challenges do not exist in isolation: there are water and biodiversity aspects to climate change, for example, just as the depletion of natural resources is connected to habitat loss, poverty, and urban migration. Nonetheless, sustainability issues have tended to be siloed; hence the specific initiatives about climate change, biodiversity, deforestation, water management, and so on mentioned in other chapters of this book. An indication that sustainability is being accepted as marking a fundamental shift in the nature of the world's economy might be when the interconnectedness of issues are more evident in policies and business strategies.

Land offers a good example of how such thinking might look. Land as a global resource is becoming the focus of intensive competition.[20] For most of history, it has been treated as a common good, and although usage at the local level has been regulated in some countries, and much blood has been shared to protect national boundaries, globally there have been no attempts to restrict its use any more than there have to regulate the use of air, freshwater, or the sea. This situation could change, not just because an unprecedentedly large global population will put pressure on land use, but also because it is uniquely important for food, energy, and managing the environment. This has been called a 'trilemma'[21] in which one set of problems (e.g. land to produce sufficient and affordable food) requires solutions that undermine resolution of another set (e.g. land to produce biofuels for cleaner energy; land to host forests to absorb CO_2). Agriculture and land conversion, for instance, account for two and a half times greater GHG emissions than global transport, and future increases in production for food and energy will need to be achieved without exacerbating climate change.[22] Given that agricultural production may have to double to meet the estimated demand to feed nine billion people and to fuel unprecedented numbers of bioethanol- and biodiesel-driven vehicles, this is a profound challenge, and one that could reshape thinking on sustainability issues such as climate change, ecosystems, and biodiversity.[23] Furthermore, failure to resolve any one of the issues makes solving the others more difficult: for example, increased land use would most likely exacerbate climate change which in turn would reduce the availability of highly productive lands.

It has been argued that the urgency and radical changes needed to address this trilemma mean that conventional business and innovation solutions are insufficient. One possibility is that the political governance of market economies will alter significantly (perhaps along lines similar to China's regulated economy). This could involve, for instance, sustainability regulation affecting all land-based production and consumption. It could also include more overtly strategic, government-directed investment in areas such as agriculture intensification, biorefinery, and industrial biotechnology.[24] Calls for greater government intervention are a common theme in sustainability, but the idea that government has a command and control leadership capability is an outdated oversimplification. In reality, a government cannot lead change unless the danger of the problem confronted is perceived by society's citizens and main institutions as greater than the threat it poses to what is regarded as normal. This is the current situation with climate change where any government leadership has had to battle against the idea that tackling global warming is an unwarranted threat to our lifestyles, and it is the likely case with the land trilemma.

The feasibility or infeasibility of government intervention of the type outlined earlier have their respective implications for business (e.g. greater government intervention, or an uncertain business environment due to a governance vacuum). However, tackling the trilemma shows yet another way business could be affected by sustainability. Until now, the general trend in innovation has been towards universalization meaning that an idea—be it a technology, a management innovation, or an ideology—expands out from the place it was invented to become a global presence. This is as true of the internal combustion engine as it is of the green revolution in farming, and it is something taken for granted in many industries in which success is determined by how well companies do at turning their products into global brands. It is also something that was made possible by transportable energy, in particular coal, oil, and gas, which have allowed manufacture to be physically decoupled from the site of energy production. Tackling the trilemma means sharply reducing dependency on fossil fuels and petro-chemicals, and turning to more localized alternatives. This is true of alternative energy where wind power may be suited to some regions, for instance, and solar suited to others. It is also true of biofuels because agricultural conditions mean that ethanol is more viable in zones able to produce wheat, sugarcane, corn, and beet, while biodiesel is suited to zones producing rapeseed and palm oil. Geo-politically this means that the best technologies for Europe, South-East Asia, North America, and Latin America could all be different and regionally specific because of the needs of regulated land use. It is also a sign that successful companies in a RCE may be ones able to manage diversity rather than promote uniformity.

Breakthroughs and opportunities

As with most of society's major challenges, sustainability thinking often veers between alarmism and over-optimism. We have seen throughout this book that sustainability issues affect business in fundamental ways, but it is still to be decided if the upshot as a whole will be positive or negative for companies. It is easy to get caught up in a vortex of gloom, especially when many of sustainability's naysayers rely more on wishful thinking and populist rhetoric than on rigorously constructed evidence. However, it can be too tempting to consider only the worst-case scenarios, and there are indications that breakthroughs are on the horizon that will moderate the effects of some sustainability issues.

Breakthrough technologies

Major technological innovations are one area where some people believe significant breakthroughs can be made. We have looked at geoengineering, and the impact that CO_2 reduction and solar radiation management technologies could have (Chapter 6). To date, none has been shown to be effective at an affordable cost or with acceptable side effects. CO_2 Reduction techniques are more attractive because they do not permanently alter the climate

Snapshot 12.1   ITC e-Choupal—efficient supply chains

e-Choupal was the future in the past. Established in 2000, it is the largest Internet initiative in rural India, covering over four million farmers. Choupal means gathering place in Hindi, although e-Choupal is a multilingual service spread across ten states. It was the brainchild of the ITC (Indian Tobacco Company) Agribusiness Division, one of India's largest exporters of agricultural commodities. Its aim is to tackle key challenges in Indian agriculture, such as fragmented farms, a weak infrastructure, and the involvement of numerous intermediaries (middle-men).

Although the primary objective of the project was to bring efficiency to ITC's procurement process, an important by-product is the increased empowerment of rural farmers where e-Choupals have been established. In the view of ITC and the World Bank, this unshackles the potential of Indian farmers who were otherwise trapped in a cycle where low risk-taking ability led to low investment, low productivity, low value addition, and low margins.

An e-Choupal is a local choupal converted by setting up a computer and Internet connection. The centre gives farmers accessed to information such as crop prices, weather, farming practices, farmer peer groups, and soil-testing services. The farmer can also get quotes for his produce, and if he accepts he can take it to collection centres, getting payment within two hours rather relying on the uncertainty of middle-men.

e-Choupal cost about Rs 100,000 to set up and up to Rs 8,000 annually to run. (Rs 100 = US$1.90.) Farmers have attributed the centres with improved incomes resulting from higher prices, better transport, less waste, quicker payment, and higher yields. ITC benefits from direct access to farmers, sales of inputs through the e-Choupal, and more consistent product quality.

Sources: Annamalai & Rao 2003; Rao 2008; http://www.itcportal.com, accessed 17 January 2012.

Questions

e-Choupal is an example of how IT is being used to help poor people.

1. What are the advantages of this system for farmers?
2. What sustainability challenges does it help address?
3. What other examples can you find of this type of solution?

system's natural state, but they are costly and their impact is slow. Solar radiation management techniques are probably less expensive and promise a faster impact. However, not only are they a long way from realization, they create an artificial balance between increased GHG concentrations and reduced solar radiation, and this would need to be managed and maintained potentially for centuries.

For the inventors and entrepreneurs who gather at events such as EmTech (see 'Surmising the situation today'), these breakthroughs represent an exhilarating challenge. Perversely, the more society fails to meet the targets it has set itself for sustainably managing the environment, the more appealing these solutions become, serving as life rafts if the alternatives fail.

Population decline

Demographic change was one of the first sustainability issues highlighted in this book (Chapter 1). During the months it has taken to write this book, estimates of the world's population have gone from six billion to seven billion, and by some estimates the world's population will reach ten billion by 2050. If true, this will put unprecedented pressure on the Earth's ecosystems, and it is estimated that people will have 80 per cent less land to meet their needs than they did 150 years earlier.

However, some claim we are already doing quite well at defusing this perceived population time bomb.[25] World fertility has roughly halved since 1960, and women on average have half as many babies as their grandmothers did. For a period, the decline in child mortality rates because of vaccines and healthier environments initially meant that populations grew fourfold, but now higher survival rates mean women have less children. This trend is boosted by urbanization because, unlike on farms, children are less of an economic asset in cities. The high and seemingly fast growing population figures we see today may therefore be an anomaly: the legacy of a population bulge caused by a lag between declining child mortality and the number of children born. It would be historically unprecedented for lower death rates not to affect birth rates: yet, the replacement rates used in population projections assume that this will be the case.[26]

None of this means that the population will not grow, but it could mean that the peak happens sooner and at a lower level than current projections anticipate. Any growth in population poses a threat to major ecosystems, and it is frequently highlighted how increased populations in poorer economies will be accompanied by heightened expectations about standards of living with implications for water shortages, GHG emissions, land, and so on. However, in fast growing economies such as China and Brazil, the population is relatively stable, and increased resource usage will be due to growing prosperity rather than growing populations. In parts of Africa, which experiences the highest rates of population growth, it would take unimaginable levels of economic growth for per capita emissions and overall resource use to come anywhere near the levels of advanced economies. In the view of environmental journalist Fred Pearce, the real sustainability challenge is not population growth amongst the poor, but consumption by the rich:

> We must not . . . blame the world's poor for the environmental damage caused overwhelmingly by . . . the rich. The truth is that the population bomb is being defused round the world. But the consumption bomb is still primed and ever more dangerous.
>
> (Pearce, 15 March 2010, http://authorsplace.co.uk/fred-pearce/blog/, accessed 4 January 2011)

Privatizing resources

There is a well-established, if controversial, tradition of claiming that privatized goods are better managed and hence more sustainable. This is the claim that underpins Hardin's 'tragedy of the commons' theory[27] (Chapter 2), and it has become a central tenet of resource management policy around the world.[28] Nowadays, the idea that land or other resources can be bought and owned not just for security, private use, or speculation, but because it is part of a strategy for managing sustainability issues is growing worldwide. The environmental NGO, The Nature Conservancy, has pioneered land acquisition as a way of conserving natural resources, a model that has been copied in various regions of the world.[29] However, the largest acquisitions have been by the private sector. For instance, almost 2.5 million hectares of land have been acquired in Ethiopia, Ghana, Mali, Sudan, and Madagascar since 2004, and similar trends can be witnessed in the developing economies of Africa, South and Central Asia, and Latin America. Russia, Ukraine and Australia have also offered large tracts of farmland to foreign investors.[30]

Many of the major acquisitions (over 1,000 ha) are for conventional commercial reasons, but some are directly related to sustainability. Deals have been struck for a 452,500-ha bio-fuel project in Madagascar, and a 100,000-ha irrigation project in Mali. For all of the land acquisitions for tourist resorts in countries such as Cambodia and Vietnam, there are others in places such as Pakistan, Brazil, and Argentina that relate directly to sustainability concerns. Foreign investment dominates, although domestic investment is important in some markets. Foreign investors are often driven by food security concerns in their own countries due, for instance, to shortages of water and arable land. Increased demand for biofuels and other non-food agricultural commodities is another driver. From both demand and rates of return perspectives, land acquisition for agricultural production appears attractive, and major agri-business companies such as Cargill and ADM are pursuing vertical integration strategies to enter into direct production. Moreover, demand for land is likely to increase with demand for carbon credits linked, for instance, to avoided deforestation and to aforestation. As a United Nations briefing notes, 'It is no longer just the crops that are commodities: rather, it is the land and water for agriculture themselves that are increasingly becoming commodified, with a global market in land and water rights being created'.[31]

This trend has been criticized, e.g. for its impact on local farmers and the unclear benefits for local communities. However, for companies and other investors such as sovereign wealth funds, acquiring a portfolio of resources around the world is an attractive proposition even if for some it represents a shift from an era of outsourcing risk to more vertical integration.

 Snapshot 12.2   Rainbow Nightfreight—small and medium-sized enterprises

According to some people, a RCE will inevitably become more localized than the economy we know now. This will remove some of the competitive advantages of large corporations, and open up new opportunities for SMEs. Yet it has also been argued that addressing sustainability issues is a burden that smaller firms can ill-afford. Moreover, many SMEs are in industries where the opportunities to behave more sustainably seem few and far between.

Rainbow Nightfreight is a fairly small logistics company in Britain. You will not find sustainability mentioned on its lorries or storage facilities, and it is difficult to find the corporate responsibility section on its website. The business it is in means that Rainbow creates carbon emissions and uses large amounts of packaging materials. It is also in a highly competitive, cost-conscious industry in which there is little room for investments that do not feed directly to the bottom-line. In other words, Rainbow Nightfreight is typical of thousands of other SMEs.

Rainbow's business model relies on a multi-user nightfreight service that enables it to provide high levels of vehicle capacity usage, and reduce the distance of travel on journeys. This gives it an advantage over its larger competitors because it results in fewer empty journeys. It was awareness of this distinction that led the company to focus on sustainability, and give it a unique selling point compared to companies such as FedEx and UPS. According to the company's Finance Manager, Rob

(continued)

Smith, 'Outgoing vehicles and return vehicles can be full. Compared to a dedicated company with its own fleet, we can do fewer miles and use less fuel and, therefore, produce fewer emissions for each item we deliver'.

Building on this initial awareness, Rainbow has made a conscious effort to identify other sustainability-related opportunities. It runs driver training programmes that include fuel efficiency, reducing brake wear, tyre pressure, and efficient journey planning. It has engaged with government to promote sustainability within its industry, including, for example, explaining the benefits of its business model to the Department for Transport's Low Carbon Supply Chain Steering Group. It is part of the European Regional Development Fund's Future Factory project through which it has explored reusable transit packaging, and it has incorporated environmental considerations into its latest depot. Fleet efficiency is another area it is concerned about, and as its current fleet reaches the end of its life, the feasibility of electric and hybrid vehicles is being explored. Underpinning all of these investments is a programme of monitoring and measuring against defined environmental metrics. This allows Rainbow to provide the same sort of information to customers as they get from DHL and other multinational competitors.

The programme falls under the remit of the finance manager who has been able to develop an increasingly sophisticated argument as to why sustainability-related investments pay. One of the advantages of being an early-mover in this area has been that as sustainability has become an issue for the whole industry, Rainbow is well placed compared to its peers. As well as fully recognizing the links between sustainability, efficiency, and cost savings, it has the knowledge and networks to keep abreast of the latest research on how to improve sustainability in key areas of its business, and how to devise appropriate metrics and monitor performance on key parameters for internal and customer use. It also knows about the environmental expertise it needs when designing new capital projects, and has the experience to decide what are realistic goals.

Sources: http://rainbownightfreight.com/SustainableWorkshop.html; http://rainbownightfreight.com/index.html?ifrm_2=CSR.html; http://www.cica.ca/research-and-guidance/sustainability/item52804.pdf, all accessed 18 January 2012.

Questions

Rainbow Nightfreight is one of the millions of smaller companies that will be involved in the future of business and sustainability.

1. What is the relationship between Rainbow's sustainability activities and its competitive advantage?

2. What are the main lessons of the company's experience for other SMEs?

3. What can encourage SMEs to think strategically about sustainability?

Coda

In his foreword to *The New Capitalist Manifesto*, Gary Hamel argues that the fundamental tenets of business need challenging.[32] He questions money-making as the primary objective of business, and argues that executives should be rewarded based on overall value creation, not simply short-term profitability (Figure 12.3). He also points to the changing nature of customers, and the standards to which they hold companies to account. His views are significant because of his position as an influential mainstream business strategist, but they echo the views expressed by many corporate responsibility thinkers since the 1990s.

Old tenet	New tenet
The primary objective of the company is to make money	The primary objective is to enhance well-being in economically efficient ways
Company leaders are only accountable for the immediate consequences of their actions	Company leaders are also accountable for the second- and third-tier consequences of the pursuit of growth and profitability
Executives should be compensated based on the short-term performance of their companies	Executives should be compensated based on the company's long-term value creation
Brands are built with marketing dollars	Brands are socially constructed by all of a company's constituents
A company's customers are the people who buy its products	A company's customers include anyone influenced by its actions
Customers only care about product performance and price	Customers care about the values honoured or defiled in the making and selling of a product
Angry customers will nurse their anger in private	Angry customers will join forces to shame corporate culprits
Workers are human resources	Workers are human beings
Business is about competitive advantage, focus, differentiation, superiority, and excellence	Business is about love, joy, honour, beauty, and justice

Figure 12.3 Past and future tenets of business.

Sources: adapted from Hamel (2011) and Haque (2011).

Corporate responsibility as a theory has influenced management practice in numerous ways,[33] but it has nibbled at rather than devoured the established dogmas of business.

However, if we look again at those tenets through a sustainability lens, they relate less to business values, and more to what is required to stay in business. For example, advocates of greater corporate responsibility might want executives to be more accountable for the consequences of their actions; but in the context of a RCE, second- and third-tier effects of company actions are likely to be under serious scrutiny because business is being conducted in a finite rather than infinite environment. Likewise, sensitive ecosystems and constraints on land and water exploitation mean that making money without showing that this demonstrably enhances human well-being is unlikely to be palatable either to citizens or their political representatives. At the same time, sustainability concerns have already revealed that 'customers' are no longer just the people who consume, and as noted in Chapter 5, the social construction of brands is already happening for reasons closely associated with sustainability challenges.

The nature of a RCE poses fundamental challenges, not only to the way business is managed, but the acceptable purpose of business itself. Throughout this book, we have seen examples of how sustainability issues are being treated as opportunities that can be taken up by applying conventional business wisdom. Yet, we have also seen that conventional wisdom can exacerbate the situation, and is being blamed by some people for the inadequate responses in spheres such as climate change and biodiversity.

It is not that opportunities do not exist, but identifying them requires a different way of thinking if resource constraint is taken seriously as a condition of future social and economic prosperity. It is understandable to think that as yet undiscovered technological innovations will solve issues from global warming to food shortages to peak oil, just as given the false alarms of the past, it is reasonable to treat the often overwhelming scientific evidence with caution. However, in both cases, such stances can amount to no more than wishful thinking and denial. The truth is that although it might be brave for someone to deny the existence of gravity, it would be foolhardy in the extreme to build a business on their beliefs. There are aspects of sustainability for which the scientific evidence is no more contestable than that for gravity, and yet business continues to operate in a social and political environment unable to accept this fact.

If we accept that a RCE will be fundamentally different to any we have experienced to date, and that this has implications for the basic premises of the unconstrained econo- mies represented in nearly all economic theory (including economic growth and the effi- ciency of markets in determining value), then we can address the questions that in the long run will be most important for business. Instead of asking whether business can sur- vive and prosper in a RCE, we can pay more attention to 'What kinds of business will prosper?'.

There are many people who see business as a spectre at the feast of sustainability, but the private sector—in terms of its role, its wealth, its qualities, its creativity—is too established and too important a part of society to treat it as anything other than a contributor to a sus- tainable future. Equally, there are people who say business should not involve itself in sus- tainability leadership. That too seems a questionable point of view: it increases the chances of creating a regulatory regime that might insulate society from capitalism's vices, but would also deny us its virtues. Regulation might help steer companies away from an age of 'thin value', but it is hard to see how it would generate alternative forms of prosperity. By thin value, we mean 'the real-world expression of overproducing bads and underproducing goods' (Haque 2011, p. 19). Thin value is artificial (e.g. McMansions), unsustainable (goods produced without reference to foregone benefits in the future), and meaningless (goods that do not make society tangibly better off, and would benefit nobody if everyone con- sumed them—the Big Mac has been cited as an example).[34] Ultimately, it is only business that can reject thin value and replace it with goods and services that are sustainable and meaningful.

At present, it is fashionable to portray capitalism as something endangered.[35] Sustainabil- ity is not synonymous with the collapse of capitalism, but the implications are that business will need to be different. Transitioning to a RCE will be traumatic for many companies and filled with uncertainty: some companies, even entire industries will fail. The notion of good business practice will be put under the microscope, and areas of management from market- ing to risk, from finance to accounting may well have to change. All of these possibilities have been discussed in this book, as has the role of leadership and business models. Business will find itself operating in a different kind of society than the one it has grown used to: one where production and consumption is no longer the preserve of market forces. It will also find itself operating in a very different governance environment in which the rules of the game are decided by multiple forces, and in which government has yet to reassert its capacity for leadership.

It is by no means clear what sort of company will be fit for purpose in this changing environment. Much of this book has focused on the actions of large companies, in particular multinationals, because along with some entrepreneurs this is where much of the action around sustainability is situated. However, the future of such companies in the new type of economy we are referring to is far from certain. Historically, incumbent companies have not done well during periods of major transition, yet at present they are the ones with the greatest resources at their disposal and the greatest self-interest in taking a global perspective. The example of diverse, locally appropriate energy solutions mentioned earlier in this chapter (see 'Trilemma of land') challenges the ideas of scale and universal technologies and brands that multinationals typically rely on. Local appropriateness is not restricted to energy: the historically unprecedented speed at which some economies are growing means that they can leapfrog stages in technology installation so that, for instance, mobile telephony makes telephone poles unnecessary in countries such as China and Kenya, and the healthcare systems in places such as India or Vietnam could look very different to ones in OECD countries (e.g. an infrastructure built more on outpatient care than hospitals). In other words, companies will need to be very attuned to local conditions if they are to succeed, and it may be that multinationals are at a disadvantage compared to local firms in this situation.

In many cases, awareness of local conditions will include being in tune with the needs of poor people. Not only are they a vast potential market as spelled out in 'bottom-of-the-pyramid' theory (Chapter 2); they are people who are particularly prone to the consequences of ecosystem change and other sustainability challenges as, for instance, the recent droughts in East Africa testify. Throughout this book, we have seen that sustainability is about people as much as it is about the environment, and the way humans are treated will significantly affect how effectively sustainability challenges are met. It is exciting to see intrapreneurship and human ingenuity within companies encouraged as a way of dealing with the business–sustainability relationship, but if employers fight for the right to lay-off workers as they please, restrict real-term pay increases to a handful of senior managers, and continually seek out ways to undermine employee relations, it is unrealistic to expect loyalty from the workforce. Furthermore, even in high growth economies such as China, unemployment is increasingly cited as a problem both for skilled and unskilled people.

Poverty may not be a sustainability issue as such (Chapter 2), but there is a poverty dimension to much of sustainability, and if companies are looking to rebuild the business–society relationship as part of their sustainability strategies, then poverty and marginalization are a part of that. The balancing act between resource-constraint, fairness, human development, and prosperity for business and society will require something quite different from company managers, investors, customers, and employees than has been the case in the past. The preceding chapters of this book were intended to offer an insight into some of the main areas of difference, and why they are significant. Looked at in the round, there is as much opacity as there is clarity, and as much turbulence as there is certainty. All told, it could add up to the turnaround challenge of twenty-first century business, presenting the defining moments of future success.

 ## Summary

It is enticing to predict the future, but perhaps more useful to understand how it might unfold. Previous chapters have offered all sorts of suggestions, clues, and alternatives concerning how the world business finds itself in, and how business itself might change. Comprehending the process of transition, its features, constraints, and determinants is a useful step in anticipating what will happen next as sustainability issues emerge. There are particular models of transition that are relevant, and that recognize the technological, political, cultural, and social factors that influence how any transition unfolds. The past has shaped our present, and has created a path dependence that will affect our future decisions. Radical transitions only happen quickly when crises are acknowledged, and without catastrophes we are reluctant to accept we have reached a tipping point.

The future will comprise new challenges, although some of these can be predicted now. While many of the scenarios are frightening, not least because of their complexity, breakthroughs could also diminish some of the risks as well as creating new opportunities. Without wishing to downplay the seriousness of some of the challenges, an unremittingly bleak picture is unjustified. However, the picture that emerges from the sketches in this chapter is one of an environment that is different from any that business has had to prosper within in the past. We have seen throughout this book that sustainability issues affect business in fundamental ways, but it is still to be decided if the upshot as a whole will be positive or negative for companies. Resolving this uncertainty will be one of the principle features of business management for the foreseeable future.

 ## Further reading

Kaletsky, A. 2010, *Capitalism 4.0: The birth of a new economy*, Bloomsbury, London.
An accessible account of the different forms capitalism has taken over the years, and why we are now entering a new period.

Lovelock, J. 2010, *The vanishing face of Gaia: A final warning*, Penguin, London.
The most recent book by a pioneering climate change scientist responsible for some of the most important discoveries since the 1960s. It stresses the urgency of action, and argues that current predictions underestimate the changes that will happen in the next 30 years.

Lynas, M. 2008, *Six degrees: Our future on a hotter planet*, National Geographic Society, Washington, DC.
A popular book on how we are underestimating the potential social and environmental damage of unresolved sustainability challenges.

McAnany, P.A. & Yoffee, N. (Eds) 2010, *Questioning collapse: Human resilience, ecological vulnerability, and the aftermath of empire*, Cambridge University Press, Cambridge.
Asking the question how often do societies collapse, and how resilient they are? It is a comprehensive riposte to arguments in Jared Diamond's 2005 book, *Collapse: How societies choose to fail or survive*.

Turney, J. 2010, *The rough guide to the future*, Rough Guides, London.
A readable look at all manner of events, changes, and innovations that could be in our future.

Case study 12   How did we get here? An exercise in backcasting and scenario building

It is 2050 and we are living in a prosperous low carbon economy.

....

Questions

1. The mid-twenty-first century looks different to 2000.

   a. What are the main changes that have taken place?

   b. Has the meaning of prosperity changed?

   c. What are some of the most notable ways that people's lives have changed?

2. Addressing sustainability challenges implies significant shifts.

   a. What were the milestone events that happened between 2015 and 2050?

   b. What are the most successful industries of 2050 and why?

   c. Has the role of business changed since 2015?

3. Scenario planning is a widely used method for long-term planning.

   a. Create scenarios that help analyse the journey of a fictional company in an industry of your choosing to reach a prosperous resource constrained economy by 2050.

   b. What are the biggest risks that emerge from these scenarios?

   c. What are the biggest opportunities that emerge from these scenarios?

 Endnotes

1. http://www.bloomberg.com/news/2011-12-20/bankers-join-billionaires-to-debunk-imbecile-attack-on-top-1-.html, accessed 22 December 2011.

2. (Perez 2002)

3. http://www.technologyreview.com/emtech/11/.

4. (Lovelock 2010)

5. (McKibben 2010; Porritt 2005; Schumacher 1973; Shiva 2002)

6. (Hopkins 2008)

7. (E.g. Collins 2001)

8. (Schumpeter 1939/1982, 1947)

9. (Schumpeter 1939/1982, 1947)

10. (Perez 2002)

11. (Perez 2002)

12. (Ghosh & Woods 2009; Hulme 2009)

13. (Kotter 1995; Lewin 1946)

14. (Beinhocker 2007)

15. (Ramírez, Selsky, & Van der Heijden 2008)

16. (Geels 2002)

17. (E.g. Weitzman 2011)

18. (de Sherbinin et al. 2011; Mainka & McNeely 2011; Pielke et al. 2007; Yasuhara et al. 2011; You & Howe 2011)

19. From the 1992 UN Framework Convention on Climate Change.

20. (Harvey & Pilgrim 2011)

21. (Tilman et al. 2009)

22. (Harvey & Pilgrim 2011)

23. (Godfray et al. 2010)

24. (Harvey & Pilgrim 2011)

25. (Bardi 2011; Pearce 2010)

26. (Pearce 2011)

27. (Hardin 1968)

28. (Deinlnger & Binswanger 1999; Sjaastad & Bromley 2000)

29. (Fairfax et al. 2005); http://www.nature.org/aboutus/privatelandsconservation/index.htm, accessed 3 January 2012.

30. (Cotula et al. 2009); http://www.un.org/esa/dsd/resources/res_pdfs/publications/ib/no8.pdf, accessed 3 January 2012.

31. http://www.un.org/esa/dsd/resources/res_pdfs/publications/ib/no8.pdf, accessed 3 January 2012.

32. (Haque 2011)

33. For a detailed discussion, see Blowfield (2011).

34. (Haque 2011)

35. (Bower, Leonard, & Paine 2011; Harvey 2010; Kaletsky 2010)

Extended case study A: Marks & Spencer—how serious is sustainability?

The challenge

Plan A was launched in January 2007. It is retail giant Marks & Spencer's flagship programme to make itself the greenest multiple retailer, and comprises 100 commitments on issues such as climate change, waste, human health, trading, and natural resource utilization. Plan A has placed it amongst the most respected companies when it comes to tackling sustainability challenges, and it has achieved this while lifting its share price above the industry average.

However, Plan A was due to end in 2012. It has decided to invest in a period of integration from 2012–2014 to ensure that Plan A commitments are embedded across the company's business lines. For CEO Marc Bolland, who inherited his place at the head of the M&S Plan A committee when he took over from Stuart Rose in 2010, the question is 'What next?' The differentiating power that Plan A had when it was first launched has been diluted as other retailers such as Walmart and Tesco have developed their own sustainability programmes. The value proposition in terms of corporate reputation is now well-established, and makes it less urgent that the company invest in sustainability innovation. Competitors such as Aldi, Lidl, Asda, and Primark are continually trying to drive down prices, making M&S's higher cost items less attractive. Evidence from the high street shows that tackling human rights, sustainable agriculture, and carbon footprints is not going to get most customers to come through the shop doors.

Context

Marks & Spencer was founded in 1884 in Leeds, England. A long-time fixture of British and Irish high streets, it has over 750 stores around the world and is the 43rd largest retailer. In the UK, it has 35,000 product lines and 75,000 employees, and serves 21 million customers a week. Ninety-nine per cent of its products are own-brand, sourced from 2,000 independently-owned factories, and 20,000 farms that between them employ over a million workers. The company is publicly traded, and has a large number of small investors who were especially hit when pre-tax profits fell from over £1 billion in 1997–1998 to £145 million in 2000–2001. Historically, the company prided itself on long-standing relations with British manufacturers, but during the 1990s this put M&S at a disadvantage compared to competitors that sourced from countries with lower production costs. As part of restoring its competitiveness, M&S now has a global supply base, and in 2007–2008 was once more able to declare pre-tax profits in excess of £1 billion. During the financial downturn of 2009–2011, the company still reported pre-tax profits in excess of £700 million.

The background to Plan A

It is 1999, and a period of rapid earnings growth has come to a screeching halt for British retail icon M&S. The strategy of chasing higher margins by raising prices, reducing costs, and putting pressure on suppliers is no longer working. Sales are falling, and profits collapsing as the company's reputation for customer service and good quality has turned into a reputation for high prices, poor products, and indifference to both consumers and suppliers. Business analyst John Kay concluded, 'The magic of Marks & Spencer had gone, probably forever'.

Fast forward to 2007 and the headline to an article in the *Harvard Business Review* reads, 'Back in fashion: How we're reviving a British icon'. M&S is consistently profitable and seeing strong growth in its key food and clothing segments. Profits are up 173% from 2004/2005, and the share price has more than doubled. According to Stuart Rose, CEO, 'We've gained back our confidence, and the media and investors seem to be championing our achievements. We've gone from zero to hero more quickly than we fell in the first place'. The company's 2007 annual review and financial summary states, 'We've a long way to go before we are truly a world-class retailer again, but we are on the right track'.

Evolution not revolution

There are several parts to M&S's rejuvenation: Rose emphasizes the importance of improving products, the shopping environment, and service. But sustainability has been one of the threads running throughout the change story—one first started before Rose came on board in 2004, but which the CEO readily acknowledge 'will shape everything about the way we do business'.

Thread is an apt metaphor. Sustainability did not burst onto the M&S agenda; the centenarian company certainly did not have an epiphany that changed it overnight. Rather, the emergence of sustainability as something important to the company's strategy of improving product, service, and shopping environment happened gradually through a mix of forward thinking, fortune, opportunism, and patience. To understand that evolution, it helps to break the story into phases.

Phase 1, 2000–2002: guerrillas in their midst

In 2000, M&S was experimenting with various ways to restore the company's reputation amongst consumers, investors, and the media. Onlookers saw all manner of consultants coming in to give advice on how to fix the brand. The company had found itself caught up with other major retailers in allegations of poor labour and environmental conditions in food and clothing production, and had joined the Ethical Trading Initiative and begun to explore organic foodstuffs. But sustainability was not high on the company's must-do list, and few onlookers would have noticed the recruitment of a new environmental manager as Group Finance Director Alison Reid's assistant with responsibility for the environment. Reid, a long-time M&S employee, had become increasingly aware that the environment was becoming an issue for retailing, and had an inkling it would be a problem the company would need to address. Without knowing what needed to be done, she recognized there would be a need for change.

The environmental manager's role was to bring clarity to a murky debate that rambled between issues such as the demand for organics, ISO14000 certification for stores, child labour, and integrated pest management: to provide a basis for prioritization. He was linked up with two senior M&S staffers, David Gregory—then head of food technology—and Krishan Hundel—head of technology for general merchandise. They were given free range to find out what was happening across the business. The environmental manager, Mike Barry, had no line manager, and recalls the first two years as being like 'a guerrilla war'.

The team discovered early on that at the corporate level M&S had become very arrogant: it was out of touch with both society and its stores, and had no awareness of what was happening in its supply chains or amongst its consumers. While this was a problem that cut across the company's operations, two telling examples were to do with sustainability. First, in the late 1990s, the company was taken unawares by British consumer backlash against genetically modified (GM) foods. Although subsequently in 1999 it announced it would be the first high street retailer to become non-GM, the issue showed how out of touch M&S had become with consumer sentiment. Then in 2001, Friends of the Earth hit the front page of *The Independent* newspaper with its report on pesticide residue in food—including the finding that M&S had higher residue levels than any other retailer. There was no suggestion of illegality—M&S was within acceptable residue limits—but this was a poor defence in the court of public opinion. The experience brought home to M&S that complying with the law was no longer an adequate defence: the company had to be on the front foot to defend its reputation. In both the GM and pesticide cases, the company was taken unawares, and consequently powerless to calm the media frenzy or prevent itself from getting a bloody nose.

While it was apparent to some that M&S needed to change, the time was far from right for outright revolution. Instead, in keeping with the spirit of a guerrilla war, a number of low-profile or off-the-radar actions were taken. The first was to build alliances with those across the business who had related interests. It was not that everyone in M&S was disinterested in social and environmental issues: on the contrary, in different parts of the organization you could find people addressing issues such as sustainability, human rights, working conditions, responsible timber sourcing, personal ethics, and more, but more often than not they were working in isolation or failing to join the dots with potential allies in other parts of the business. The small team began building alliances below the board level and corralling people from across the company in a common sense of purpose. Most members came from Gregory and Hundel's departments who had intimate knowledge of where M&S sourced from, but there were also some buyers and people from Public Relations and Communications.

The team also began to combat the company's image of arrogance. Organizations such as Greenpeace, Friends of the Earth, RSPCA, WWF, and Forum for the Future that had given up trying to talk to M&S or had been brushed aside, now found they had an ear inside the company: people prepared to listen to what they had to say. Much of what they heard was critical, and not coincidentally brought home the wider message that M&S was out of touch on consumer tastes from the environment to ethics to fashion to the shopping experience. In hindsight, some of the most difficult conversations in the company about sustainability happened early on, and were to do with getting management to listen to stakeholders.

But the first two years were not only spent on finding out what others were doing and thinking. A formal Head of Corporate Social Responsibility position was created overseeing two environmental specialists and two philanthropy specialists. As it became more apparent that M&S could not avoid the public's expectations of corporate responsibility, it was clear the company needed to improve its systems in areas such as risk management. But the scope of what the company needed to manage was daunting, and while the board were informed of some of what was taking place, they were never shown the whole picture for fear that this would scare them and undermine the process. However, as they learned more about what was happening inside the company, they were also increasingly exposed to what other companies were doing, and how M&S stacked up against its peers.

Phase 2, 2003–2006: riding the wave of upheaval

By 2003, it was increasingly clear that M&S's recovery was stalling badly. The array of new product lines and the plethora of initiatives introduced by external consultants had diluted the brand's identity and reputation, and seemed to be alienating consumers and staff alike. Profits which had exceeded £1 billion in 1998 were down to £145 million. According to Stuart Rose, 'The problem was, M&S lost its customers' trust; it lost sight of what had made it great for more than 100 years'.

Against a bleak backdrop, corporate responsibility provided some of the few highlights. When M&S won a handful of awards in areas such as pesticides and timber, it was some of the few pieces of good news in a bad-news year. This in turn increased confidence internally that sustainability was something the company could actually do properly. It was also something that had emerged from within the company at a time when external consultants seemed to have a monopoly on new ideas, much to the chagrin of some long-time staffers who valued the company's tradition of risk taking and innovation from the inside. '[There] were 31 "strategic projects" being run by these consultants', explains Rose. 'There was constant change. The company was lurching from one strategy to another. If a strategy didn't work by Friday, a new one was initiated on Monday. The staff became demoralized by the onslaught of ever-shifting, unclear messages and strategies, which led to more bad decisions about product and further damaged the way M&S dealt with customers. It was a rapid downward spiral.'

In May 2004, the company's chair and CEO were removed, replaced by Paul Myners and Stuart Rose respectively. Before the new CEO had even been announced, Philip Green announced he was launching a hostile takeover bid for the company. The takeover battle lasted six weeks, and in no small measure depended on who won over the relatively large number of small shareholders, many of whom valued the company's history and reputation. At the shareholders' meeting, one of the news items Myners announced was that the M&S had won the Business in the Community award for the most responsible company in Britain. The news was greeted with a spontaneous round of applause.

The following day, Green pulled out of the takeover, but the way the small shareholders had responded to the news of the Business in the Community award seemed to resonate with Rose. If they were in many ways a proxy for consumers, Rose figured, then sustainability, corporate responsibility, call it what you will, seemed to be something consumers wanted and expected of M&S. Rose met the corporate responsibility team. He explained that his first year in post would be focused on sorting out the company's fundamental problems, but that they should keep the corporate responsibility alliance alive, and be ready for when the time was right to raise the stakes on sustainability.

That moment came in September 2005 when Rose approached the corporate responsibility alliance, and set in train what became the 'Behind the Label' campaign to inform consumers about the way M&S sources its products. By then the company was well aware of the importance its shoppers attached to how its goods were produced. A M&S-commissioned survey had shown almost a third of shoppers had put clothes back on the rails amid concerns about their origins, and one in five had avoided food items because of concerns about where they had come from or how they were made. The survey also found that 78 per cent of shoppers wanted more information about the way clothes were made, including use of chemicals and conditions in factories producing the goods.

The campaign was launched with in-store publicity and a series of full page adverts run in major newspapers over a five-day period in early January 2006. The adverts talked about M&S's commitment to fairtrade (including the launch of fairtrade-certified cotton products) and non-GM food, as well as moves to cut salt and fat in M&S foods, promote sustainability, recycle packaging, and protect animal welfare. They received a strong positive response, and the campaign marked a significant step in restoring the company's image in the public's eye.

Publicly, the products and promoting the values M&S was keen to associate with them were treated as a toe in the water: 'We'll see how it goes', said Stuart Rose to the BBC. 'It's a bit like the introduction of organic foods some years ago—let's test the market.' But at corporate HQ, Behind the Label's success was not underestimated, and while it might have been possible to think the campaign's mission had been accomplished, it became clear this was just the start. Any sense of smugness by the increasingly confident corporate responsibility team disappeared when Rose told them Behind the Label was already 'old news'. As Barry, who was now Head of Corporate Social Responsibility, recalls it, Rose told the team they would be out of a job if in three months' time they were still doing Behind the Label: it was time to move on.

Phase 3, 2006–2012: Plan A

One reason for moving on from Behind the Label was that M&S's competitors quickly began to imitate it, and with their own good stories to tell, it was difficult to distinguish what was different about M&S. Moreover, as competitors responded to the challenge of the raised bar, so consumers began to make more demands of M&S. They made it clear they wanted a more complete story about how M&S did business, and they also wanted the company to make a long-term commitment, and set out its vision of where it wanted to go in the future.

In September 2006, Rose asked for 'a Behind the Label version 2': something bolder; something that didn't smack of complacency. The alliance of guerrillas that had come together in 2001 had become more formalized, commissioned by the CEO and containing the directors of technology and communications, and the head of marketing. But the members were essentially the same, and it was they who brainstormed about the social and environmental dimensions to M&S's operations, and what the company could do to have a positive impact. They came up with 200 things the company could be doing in the belief that the company had to tackle everything it could. However, they soon realized this was too ambitious and there was a lot of overlap. They whittled the list down to 100 priority items that included estimates of the cost of taking action, and an assessment of what the competition was doing about these issues. For many of the items, nobody at M&S knew what the solution would look like, but this was considered unimportant: it was more important to know what needed to be done than to know if it could be done. According to Barry, the risk taking that he sees as part of M&S's culture meant that the corporate responsibility team was not expected to have all of the answers. This in turn meant the company could act more quickly.

The 100 challenges became the 100 commitments contained in what was called Plan A. Plan A's launch in January 2007 attracted enormous media and public attention. In part this was because in addition to full-page adverts and in-store promotion, but it also mattered that Stuart Rose was willing to tell the Plan A story to anyone who would listen: that M&S was committed to becoming 'The greenest—genuinely the greenest—retailer in the UK by 2012'. Timing also played its part, as Rose himself stressed: 'No one had announced a big initiative up until then, and we wanted to be the first. We were the first out of the pack. I'm not crowing, but it's important. It does, I'm not going to deny, if you get it right, give you a competitive advantage.' (As an article in *The Observer* noted, Stuart Rose is unapologetically competitive in his efforts to save the planet.)

Part of that competitive advantage was also Plan A's boldness: a list of commitments that the company would be accountable for delivering by 2012. Two days after the Plan A launch, Tesco, Britain's biggest grocery chain, announced its climate change strategy. It was applauded for moving in the right direction, but also criticized for being less ambitious than M&S. While Plan A had climate change as one of its five pillars for sustainability-related action (including a commitment to be carbon neutral by 2012), it gave equal attention to waste, sustainable raw materials, health, and being a fair partner. (See Figure 1.) Arguably, no other retailer has been able to match Plan A, and Barry believed that it would continue to influence what constitutes the industry's benchmark for a while: 'The five pillars cover what the industry needs to cover. Anyone else will have to take the same pillars and try to better our performance. But

Climate change	Waste	Sustainable raw materials	Fair partner	Health
Making our operations in the UK and Republic of Ireland carbon neutral and helping customers and suppliers reduce their emissions too	Stop sending waste to landfill from our UK and Irish stores, offices and warehouses; reduce our use of packaging and carrier bags	Ensuring our key raw materials come from the most sustainable sources available to us	Improving the lives of hundreds of thousands of people in our supply chain and local communities	Helping thousands of customers and employees choose a healthier lifestyle

Figure 1 Plan A headline commitments.

the 100 targets are already challenging enough: going beyond them right now would be commercial suicide'.

According to M&S managers, the public's response to Plan A's content is evidence of its robustness. Only two of the 100 commitments have been subject to challenge—the increasingly controversial area of biofuels, and the commitments on labour standards which some unions and NGOs feel could be bolder—and for the most part they appear to meet the public's expectations of comprehensiveness. However, figuring out which commitments are most important and to whom is not straightforward, and M&S now ranks them based on a stakeholder engagement process that is verified using AA1000 AS and ISAE 3000 standards (Figure 2).

Responsibility for Plan A has undergone various changes since 2008, and since 2009 has been coordinated through the How We Do Business Committee. The Committee is chaired by Marc Bolland, CEO, and comprises directors and senior managers who hold direct responsibility for key aspects of M&S' social, environmental, and ethical performance (Figure 3). Its work is supported by a small team of social, environmental, and ethical specialists, headed by Richard Gillies, Director of Plan A. His team is in charge of policy and solution development, stakeholder relationships, and risk management.

The objective is that Plan A is implemented throughout the business lines: not by the team members themselves, but as part of everyday operations. Plan A is treated not as a sustainability strategy, but as a business plan. It is one part of a five-pronged business strategy that also includes building the M&S brand, developing trading property, international expansion, and Internet expansion. There are 560 Plan A champions located in every store and office, and responsible for local coordination of Plan A activities.

The company produces an annual report documenting its sustainability performance called 'How we do business', and progress with Plan A has been included in the company's annual report since 2007.

		LOW: part of Plan A relevant for a small part of M&S operations	MEDIUM: part of Plan A relevant to strategy of specific M&S operations	HIGH: part of Plan A relevant to strategy for a large part of M&S operations
Importance to stakeholders	HIGH: as judged by frequency in media, mentions by key stakeholders, and sustainability benchmarks			
	MEDIUM: sometimes mentioned in media, by stakeholders, and in benchmarks			
	LOW: infrequently mentioned by above groups			
		Importance to M&S		

Figure 2 Comparison of importance of Plan A's commitments using a stakeholder engagement process.

Marc Bolland, CEO	Dominic Fry, Director of Communications
Steven Sharp, Executive Director, Marketing	Richard Gillies, Director of Plan A and Sustainable Business
Alan Stewart, CFO	Krishan Hundal, Head of Sourcing and Technology, General Merchandise
Kate Bostock, Executive Director, General Merchandise	Paul Willgoss, Head of Technology, Food
John Dixon, Executive Director, Food	Mike Barry, Head of Sustainable Business
	Adam Elman, Head of Plan A Delivery

Figure 3 How We Do Business Committee members 2011.

Lessons from implementing Plan A

Approaching the end of Plan A's intended lifespan, the company recognized that it was probably only ten per cent of the way towards creating a sustainable business. As Mike Barry puts it, a momentum has been created that will give the company a fighting chance to tackle the sustainability challenges that lie ahead. For instance, it has learned practical lessons such as the importance of continually reviewing what is being done, and of the support and commitment of the CEO in making things happen. With Stuart Rose, it was not only his endorsement that made a difference, but his in-depth knowledge of how the company works, acquired from his 17-year stint with the firm long before he was hired back as CEO. He was also prepared to make decisions and take risks (e.g. deciding to go ahead with charging for carrier bags), and give permission to others to take a chance and make mistakes. That commitment has carried on with the arrival of Marc Bolland: a M&S outsider but with retail experience as CEO at Morrison's supermarket chain.

Strong commitment at the highest level does not necessarily translate into buy-in from senior management. In introducing Plan A, a key lesson was not to approach managers with a message about why they should adopt Plan A, but to ask them how Plan A could help them meet their current challenges. For example, a director might say he needed a point of differentiation with a key competitor, and another might be charged with building a new business and needed to know how sustainability would affect its prospects. Externally, a lesson was that commitments alone are not enough to engage with consumers: they want to be involved in tangible activities. For example, the introduction of a charge for disposable plastic carrier bags in February 2008 was a highly visible, widely discussed manifestation of Plan A commitments to reduce waste. Another initiative was the launch of the Clothes Exchange with Oxfam a month earlier whereby consumers can help reduce the amount of clothing going to landfill by taking M&S clothes to Oxfam shops, in return for a £5 M&S discount voucher to spend on purchases of £35 or more.

A further important lesson is that an ambitious programme need not cost the earth. Initially, M&S planned to spend £200 million on Plan A over five years, and allocated £40 million for the first year. In reality, the actual cost of Year 1 was much less than expected, and in

2012 the company calculated that it delivered £70 million in net benefits (ten per cent of pre-tax profits). Moreover, the savings are to a degree hypothecated, one portion going to the bottom-line and another available for further investment into the development and implementation of Plan A. Plan A is therefore to a degree a profit centre, and no longer receives 'special treatment' in the form of subsidies and similar incentives. Investors have been comfortable with this, not least because they see M&S as a strong performer overall. Indeed, it is probably no coincidence that while the company's commitment to sustainability emerged from a period when it was in trouble, Behind the Label and Plan A were launched when the company was doing well.

Phase 3, 2012–2014: integration

It should not be inferred from the earlier described lessons that M&S has mastered sustainability strategy. As noted, the company believes it has covered about ten per cent of the journey it needs to. Integration is the theme for the next phase. The data and processes required to measure and monitor performance have proved a challenge, not least because in contrast to industries such as aviation or automotives the systems required are not part of retail's culture. By 2014, it is hoped that managers will have access to a live database showing information on Plan A commitments for all stores, product lines, and suppliers.

Significant progress has been made in linking Plan A to the commercial plan, but this needs to be driven further throughout the operational levels of the firm. Plan A is linked to top managers' bonuses, and there is internal coaching on commitments across the company. The company has said that by 2020, all of the 2.7 billion items sold annually will be Plan A compliant, and every Director's performance bonus is connected to their progress against this target. However, Plan A is ultimately a project management challenge, and that part of the integration challenge means that Adam Ellman's role as Head of Plan A Delivery is crucial.

The final aspect of integration is engaging with consumers. Not all of the Plan A commitments resonate with the public, and consumers have very different attitudes towards sustainability. Ultimately, price and style are what matter most, and if consumers do not understand why sustainability makes M&S's products different, Plan A will not have an effect on consumer behaviour, and may negatively affect M&S's sales.

Sources

BBC 1999, 'M&S first to go GM free', http://bbc.co.uk, 30 June 1999.

BBC 2006, 'M&S set to launch fair-trade range', http://bbc.co.uk, 30 January 2006.

Frith, M. 2004, 'Exposed: how M&S uses wood from rainforests', *The Independent*, 10 July 2004.

Kay, J. 2003, *The truth about markets: why some nations are rich but most remain poor*, Allen Lane, London.

M&S 2007, *Annual review and summary financial statements 2007*, Marks & Spencer, London.

M&S 2008/2010/2011, *How we do business*, Marks & Spencer, London.

M&S 2011, *Annual review and summary financial statements 2011*, Marks & Spencer, London.

Mesure, S. 2007, 'Tesco follows M&S with climate change move.' *The Independent*, Business, January 16, p. 36.

Presentations over the period 2007–2012 by Mike Barry at London Business School, University of Cambridge, and University of Oxford.

Rose, S. 2007, 'Back in fashion: how we're reviving a British icon', *Harvard Business Review*, May, 51–7.

Vernon, P. 2007, 'Stuart Rose is the UK's greenest grocer. His mission: to turn Marks & Spencer carbon neutral by 2012', *The Observer, Observer Woman*, 15 April 15, p. 30.

Extended case study B: Unilever—evolution of a sustainability strategy

Introduction

Rizwan was delighted to be invited to interview for a vacant position as facility manager for one of Unilever's detergent manufacturing facilities in South East Asia. He had been with the company for five years, and he saw his selection as recognition for his hard work and achievement. He knew that the other candidates would be likely to have several years more experience than him, but he also knew he had a good record of improving older, underperforming plants in the region. It was a great opportunity and he had talked it through with a longstanding colleague who had taken over a similar plant a year earlier. The colleague agreed Rizwan should be excited, and was up to the task. Rizwan asked him what it had been like running a plant, and was unsurprised by any of the answers except for one. Category managers and regional managers were, as ever, keeping a close eye on productivity and costs, but now they were starting to ask how facilities were contributing to Unilever's Sustainable Living Plan (USLP; Exhibit 1).

Rizwan was thrown. He knew that the company had a long-standing interest in its social, economic, and environmental performance—someone had even asked about palm oil at his first interview with the company: but listening to his colleague sharing his experience, he realized the company was thinking more seriously than ever about how to execute a sustainability strategy. What was more, there was a real possibility that this would come up at his interview, leaving him to ponder just how does a manufacturing facility contribute to the Sustainable Living Plan and still meet all of its other business targets?

Background

Unilever, along with Nestlé and P&G, is one of the pantheon of world-leading fast-moving consumer goods companies. Its brands include Wall's, Omo, Brooke Bond/Lipton, Dove, Lynx, Ben & Jerry's, Vaseline, and Sunsilk. The company operates in 280 markets—more countries than there are members of the United Nations. It operates over 270 manufacturing plants around the world—more than are owned by the top three car manufacturers combined. It has a global turnover in excess of €46 billion, and sells 170 billion items a year.

Its manufacturing facilities are highly diverse, manufacturing everything from ice cream to detergents, from tea bags and instant coffee to shampoo and mayonnaise. Every plant has its own challenges: not just because its products are different, but equally because of the wide

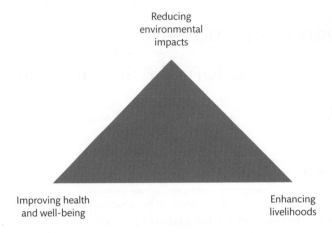

EXHIBIT 1 Three prongs of USLP.

array of locations. A liquid detergent plant has different challenges to one producing mustard, but the same type of plant in Pakistan also faces different challenges to its counterpart in the Netherlands in terms of water, energy, waste, and carbon emissions.

Early initiatives

At the same time, although in general Unilever is a respected blue chip company, and its Sustainable Living Plan had been well received by various stakeholders, it was far from being an overachiever in the eyes of the financial markets. In the late 1990s, when Unilever first began paying explicit attention to sustainability, it was a struggling giant. Its strategy of growth through mergers and acquisitions had left it with an enviable portfolio including Birds Eye, Wall's, Hellmann's, and Lipton, and a strong worldwide presence, not least in emerging markets. But markets were not inclined to reward this strategy, and the share price underperformed industry rivals who were able to beat Unilever to the top spot in categories such as shampoo, washing powder, instant coffee, and frozen food. Then CEO Niall Fitzgerald recognized social and environmental issues as something relevant to Unilever, and during his tenure the company produced its first social and environmental reports, became a co-founder of the sustainable fisheries initiative, the Marine Stewardship Council, and also of what was to become the Ethical Tea Partnership. The Sustainable Agriculture Initiative Platform was an early example of multi-company partnerships to tackle sustainability issues, and was established in 2002 by Nestlé, Unilever, and Danone to share knowledge on sustainable agricultural practices (Exhibit 2).

A similar approach was adopted in a more goal-driven partnership following the discovery that chlorofluorocarbons (CFCs) used as refrigerants, were linked to ozone depletion. With products such as frozen foods and chilled drinks amongst its main products, Unilever was under the spotlight to provide a way of substituting CFCs. Through a partnership with

- Refrigerants, Naturally!

- Marine Stewardship Council: Certified sustainable seafood

- RSPO: Roundtable on Sustainable Palm Oil

- SAI Platform

- Ethical Tea Partnership.

EXHIBIT 2   Selected sustainability initiatives involving Unilever.

Coca-Cola, PepsiCo, and Walmart it had developed the technology to eliminate CFCs from the manufacturing and storage of soft drinks, and thereby contributing to the success of the Montreal Protocol to phase out CFCs.

Roundtable on Sustainable Palm Oil

Unilever, which is a major buyer of palm oil used in its food and personal care products, was also amongst the first to recognize the environmental and reputational dangers associated with the rapid expansion of oil palm production in Malaysia and Indonesia, often resulting in the deforestation of tropical forests. Palm oil is a major global commodity used in foodstuffs, soaps, cosmetics, and now biofuels. It is produced from the fruit of oil palms that grow in tropical regions on plantations and smallholdings. The Roundtable on Sustainable Palm Oil (RSPO) was formed in 2002, and Unilever was one of its founding members along with palm oil processors and traders, financiers, retailers, food manufacturers, and industry bodies such as the Malaysian Palm Oil Association. Unilever and Migros had already set standards for sustainable palm oil, but it was felt that retailers and manufacturers working together would be able to put more pressure on producers to conform to the new standards. Moreover, by involving NGOs, it was felt that the demand-side could build consumer awareness and support, and reduce what sometimes felt like ill-informed campaigns by advocacy groups.

Over 5.1 million metric tonnes of certified palm oil has now been sold on the international market, accounting for approaching ten per cent of global production, although there are major energy and food markets where non-certified oil can be sold (e.g. China and India), and the European market represents no more than 20 per cent of world demand. Nonetheless, RSPO has demonstrated to Unilever the value of a partnership model in addressing sustainability challenges.

A growing reputation

The previously described initiatives were typically examples of intrapreneurship with individuals such as Chris Pomfret, Mandy Cormack, and Jan Kees Vis championing aspects of sustainability they were concerned about from very different functions within the company.

Their work was not connected by a coherent strategy, and there were a lack of formal channels to enable them to work efficiently together. This raised questions about how much the success of their early efforts were restricted by the lack of a sustainability mission, and the disconnect between corporate strategy and the evolving understanding of sustainability issues.

Not that this was necessarily obvious outside of the company. Unilever was developing a reputation in corporate responsibility circles, not least for its award-winning social and environmental reports. Although Fitzgerald's 'path to growth' strategy became less and less trusted by investors, and the continual restructuring that strategy required led some initiatives to stall, it was also apparent that there were important overlaps between corporate strategy and sustainability. For example, the company believed that developing and emerging markets offered its biggest opportunity for growth, and it had the advantage of 35 per cent of its revenues already coming from those markets. Its Indian subsidiary, Hindustan Lever, believed that success in such markets would require distinct approaches to product development, marketing, and retailing, and in 2000 began pilot projects that would eventually form the basis for Project Shakti. Shakti saw Hindustan Lever work with local NGOs to create a network of female entrepreneurs providing rural consumers with products that met their ideas of convenience and affordability. Over ten years, it aimed to reach 500,000 villages through 100,000 micro-entrepreneurs, in what became a high-profile case of bottom-of-the-pyramid enterprise.[1]

Project Shakti complemented another element of the 'path to growth' strategy, winning with customers which required the company to build stronger bonds with consumers, distributors, and retailers. Its network of entrepreneurs not only sold Unilever's products; they provided continual marketing intelligence that was fed into product development and other business operations. Moreover, Shakti was only one of a number of sustainability-relevant initiatives that Unilever could draw on in executing its corporate strategy.

It is also noteworthy that Unilever kept flagging its sustainability achievements despite turbulent times within the company. 'Path to growth' was ultimately judged a failure, and Fitzgerald was replaced by Patrick Cescau in 2004. In his first year, the company issued its first ever profits warning. But in 2007, he reiterated the importance of sustainability to the company:

> The agenda of sustainability and corporate responsibility is not only central to business strategy but will increasingly become a critical driver of business growth . . . I believe that how well and how quickly businesses respond to this agenda will determine which companies succeed and which will fail in the next few decades.[2]

An array of new initiatives were rolled out. Although the company's involvement with MSC ended when it sold off Birds Eye, it certified its Brooke Bond tea products to Rainforest Alliance social and environmental standards, and became a founding partner in WSUP (Water and Sanitation for the Urban Poor), a partnership tackling inadequate access to water and sanitation in developing country cities. It funded ground-breaking work on understanding a company's economic impact in Indonesia and South Africa[3]; studies that helped operationalize triple bottom-line accounting theory, and subsequently influenced PwC's work on Total Tax Contribution and the social and environmental profit and loss account work by

PUMA and other PPR brands. Increasingly, the company was recognized as a thought-leader on matters relating to the business-sustainability relationship, and had the ear of government and civil society actors.

Sustainable living

In 2008, Cescau was replaced as CEO by Paul Polman. There was nothing obvious in his background to say if he would continue on the path trodden by Fitzgerald and Cescau: the company was in healthier financial shape than it had been going into the new millennium, but its reputation with the financial markets was still not stellar. Like many companies, it was cutting jobs and it was severing some of its historical relations as it sought out tax havens. The situation became gloomier—although not for Unilever alone—when some of its major markets went into recession in 2008, with little prospect for significant growth for many years to come.

Yet, Polman has shown himself to be at least the equal of his predecessors when it comes to sustainability. Unilever announced its Sustainable Living Plan in November 2010. It sets out the company's sustainability commitments and targets until 2020, and according to Polman, is more than a sustainability plan, more than a business strategy—it represents a new business model:

> Growth at any cost is not viable. We have to develop new ways of doing business which increase the positive social benefits arising from Unilever's activities while reducing our environmental impacts. We want to be sustainable in every sense of the word.

The Plan promises three headline outcomes:

- Helping over a billion people to improve their health and well-being.
- Decoupling company growth from its environmental impact.
- Enhancing the livelihoods of people in the company's supply chain.

Moreover, this will be achieved while doubling the company's sales. By 2020, Unilever's environmental footprint will be the same as it was in 2008 while sales will have doubled. Achieving these goals involves addressing social, economic, and environmental challenges relating to all of Unilever's product lines and brands. The Plan also applies to the company's entire value chain: from the cultivation and sourcing of raw materials to consumer use and waste disposal.

The Sustainable Living Plan marks the clearest statement of the company's ambitions to go beyond what was largely a compliance approach to sustainable sourcing, to thinking of itself as part of a complex ecosystem in which all of its actions affected ecosystem prosperity. Hence, the Plan includes stretch targets such as halving the environmental footprint of its products, sourcing all of its agricultural raw materials sustainably, and linking over 500,000 smallholder farmers and small-scale distributors to its supply chain.

One could argue that it is simple business sense to target a billion new consumers with products such as soap, toothpaste, and safe drinking water, because beneficial though these may be, Unilever has a strong brand presence in these areas. However, Unilever argues that its strategy is not just to sell more products, but to help people to change their behaviour so that healthy habits such as brushing teeth twice a day become part of every-day living. For example, Lifebuoy soap is a strong brand in many developing and emerging economies where diarrhoeal disease and respiratory infections are two of the biggest killers of children under five. Handwashing with soap would be good for Lifebuoy, but could also potentially reduce diarrhoeal disease by 25 per cent, and increase school attendance by up to 40 per cent.

Actions beyond the factory walls are crucial to achieving the Plan's goals. The company will only be able to halve its GHG emissions, for instance, if it can have an impact on consumers whose behaviour accounts for 68 per cent of emissions relating to the company. Manufac-turing and transport are relatively straightforward areas of intervention compared to chang-ing people's behaviour when it comes to showering, hair-washing, and doing laundry. To succeed, Unilever will have to provide consumers with more products that use less water, and readily admits that it doesn't yet know how it will achieve its target.

Reading the Plan's smallprint, it is apparent that Unilever's environmental footprint will be no smaller in 2020 than it is today, but the company itself will be twice the size meaning that it is committed to zero environmental growth. At present, the emphasis is on how to achieve this by changing sourcing, production, marketing, and consumer behaviour, but it will be interesting to see how it affects other strategic decisions.

Integration

Polman has challenged his company, its industry peers, and governments to think seriously about what a sustainable business means. He has set out three big goals for 2020: sustainable sourcing for all of Unilever's agricultural raw materials; halving the environmental impact of its products; and reaching a billion poor people to improve their health and well-being. He is open in saying that the company's brands should have a social mission, and is outspoken in acknowledging the constraints financial analysts put on long-term company thinking: 'Unilever recognises that growth at any cost is not viable. We have to develop new ways of doing business which will increase the positive social benefits arising from our activities while at the same time reducing our environmental impacts'.

Thanks to the relatively consistent approach to social and environmental reporting the company has adopted, it is possible to track how well the company has been doing in some of the main areas where it has an impact. For example, on the company's website at http://www.unilever.com/sustainability/news/publications/previous/, there are social and environ-mental reports dating back to 2000, and a full set of its annual sustainability reports pub-lished since 2006. One can also analyse the company's overall GHG, waste, and water challenge using the product analyser at http://www.sustainable-living.unilever.com/ this also shows the resources used in selected individual products. For instance, in India distribution and retail account for 61 per cent of the GHG emissions associated with a wafer cone ice cream, whereas for the same product in the Netherlands the figure is 74 per cent.

Those within the company have much more comprehensive data at their fingertips. A factory manager, for example, should know the waste, energy, water, and GHG intensity of products coming off his/her production line. People working on supply chains should know the amount of inputs going into packaging, storage, and distribution. Moreover, with a worldwide marketing spend in access of €5 billion designed to put as much product as possible into consumers' hands, sustainability performance criteria have to be embedded into product design and innovation. In some cases, this kind of data has been monitored for nearly two decades, and in the main areas listed earlier there have been reductions of between 50 and nearly 80 per cent.

Gains are easier to achieve in some circumstances compared to others. For instance, building a state-of-the-art factory enables the company to incorporate the latest technologies from the outset, and increases the likelihood that sustainability will be a factor in the siting and design of the facility. However, most factories are legacy plants built many years ago: not only are these technological challenges, but improvements are accounted for differently than they are in new-builds. Moreover, because of continual improvement over the years, most of the low-hanging fruit in terms of sustainability performance has already been plucked: in many areas of operation, managers are restricted to smaller, incremental gains. Furthermore, in terms of life-cycle analysis, much of Unilever's occurs either before raw materials are bought by the company, or after they have been sold to consumers. If carbon emissions are taken as an example, manufacturing and distribution are far smaller elements than producing the raw materials, consumer activity, and disposal (Exhibit 3).

Rizwan's challenge

The more Rizwan thought about his upcoming interview, the more he realized that sustainability would need to be part of his preparation. Like many others, he was familiar with the emails, internal communications, publicity releases, and PR campaigns the company

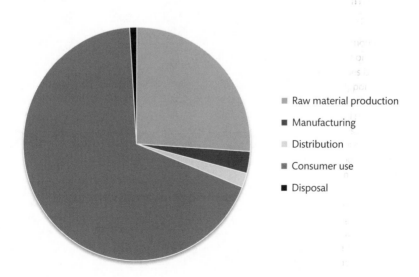

- Raw material production
- Manufacturing
- Distribution
- Consumer use
- Disposal

EXHIBIT 3 Relative causes of carbon emissions in Unilever products.

had put out over the years. Maybe he was too familiar and he had stopped treating the messages seriously. Now it seemed—at least according to his colleague—sustainability performance was no longer something that took place at corporate headquarters or was lost in a stack of data: it was something that was important for an aspiring factory manager to have a handle on; it was something that could affect whether or not he became factory manager at all.

 ## Endnotes

1. (Neath & Sharma 2008)
2. http://www.wbcsd.org/plugins/DocSearch/details.asp?type=DocDet&ObjectId=MjQ3ODI, accessed 11 August 2011.
3. (Clay & Jason 2005; Kapstein 2008)

Glossary

behavioural economics A strand of economic and psychological theory investigating why people make choices that are irrational from an economic viewpoint. Has been developed to propose ways of making consumer behaviour more economically rational.

Brundtland Commission (formally, the World Commission on Environment and Development) Convened in 1983 by the United Nations and widely known by the name of its chair, Gro Harlem Brundtland, the Commission proved to be a highly influential enquiry into environmental deterioration and the challenge of sustainable development. Its definition of sustainable development—development that meets the needs of the present without compromising the ability of future generations to meet their own needs—is frequently cited in discussions about the role of business in sustainability.

carrying capacity The maximum population of a species that can be sustained within a given environment. It has been estimated that humanity's needs are now 2.3 times greater than the carrying capacity of the Earth.

civil society A sector of society that is outside of formal government institutions and the private sector, and which in a democracy helps provide a balance in the process of governance. Civil society organizations include trade unions, non-government organizations, the media, and community groups, as well as informal networks of groups and individuals that form around a particular issue.

climate change Significant change in measures of climate, such as temperature, or precipitation, that last for an extended period (i.e. decades or longer). These changes can be the result of natural factors and processes, such as alterations in ocean circulation, or of human activity, such as deforestation and burning fossil fuels. (*See also* global warming.)

climate change mitigation Actions taken to prevent global average temperatures rising by more than 2°C.

climate change adaptation Actions taken in response to irreversible changes that happen due to climate change, e.g. because global average temperatures are rising by more than 2°C.

choice editing Deliberate restriction of the range of goods on offer by a manufacturer or retailers. An approach to fostering sustainable consumption by limiting choices to products with the best energy ratings or least material intensity. (*Also called* consumer choice editing.)

consumption End-user choices to fulfil their needs. Consumption is driven by need, self-gratification, desire, obligation, generosity, and all manner of motivations that are cultural, psychological, and social as much as economic. (*See* sustainable consumption.)

corporate responsibility Theory and practice related to the multiple aspects of business' relationship with the rest of society. It includes the nature of the relationship, how it is negotiated, and how it is managed.

cradle-to-cradle design *See* life-cycle management.

decarbonization Reducing the amount of hydrocarbons used in economic activities.

dematerialization Reducing the amount of material used in production. For instance, the advent of MP3 players has led to considerable dematerialization in the production of music.

developing economy A national economy in which the majority of the population are at or below the poverty line. (*Compare* developing economy.)

ecological carrying capacity *See* carrying capacity.

eco-efficiency Achieving efficiencies through the reduced use of natural resources and energy, fewer harmful emissions, greater recycling and reuse, increased lifespan, and the increased use of renewable resources in the design, manufacture, and consumption/use of products.

emerging economy A country that, based on GDP and indicators of human development, is considered to be on a path towards being included among the wealthy/developed nations in the foreseeable future. (*Compare* developing country.)

environmental auditing The evaluation of an organization to ascertain the validity and reliability of information about that organization's claims concerning its performance in relation to the environment (e.g. emissions, waste management).

environmental ethics Enquiry into the ethical relationship of human beings to the environment and non-human entities, and into the value and moral status of these.

environmental impact assessment Assessment of a company or facility's environmental consequences, normally focusing on inputs and outputs within a particular geographical location.

environmental, social, governance (ESG) Commonly used term that captures the areas of non-financial performance with which corporate responsibility management practice is often concerned.

ethical consumption The factoring of ethical criteria into consumer decision-making.

ethical sourcing A company's recognition of its responsibilities for the social and environmental conditions under which products are manufactured/grown within its supply chain. Typically, this involves the application of a code of practice as a condition of doing business with suppliers, although it may also involve engaging with suppliers to improve their capacity to meet that standard.

ethical trade An umbrella term for a variety of approaches under which companies take responsibility for the conditions under which products are manufactured/grown within their supply chains. Includes ethical sourcing, fairtrade, and sourcing from sustainably managed forests and fisheries.

fair trade A trading partnership established as a contribution to achieving greater equity in international trade through, for example, ensuring a price paid to the producer that is greater than the cost of production, a surplus paid to the producer group (not the individual) for investing in social development activities, and a long-term relationship between producer and buyer. Originally intended to help small producers in developing countries, larger producers are now included, and, for these, the emphasis is on worker rights. Fair trade takes different forms, but is most widely associated with the Fairtrade label, which certifies that an item has been produced and traded according to the principles set out by the Fairtrade Labelling Organizations International (FLO International).

financing sustainability An emerging facet of corporate responsibility, dealing with the interrelationship between companies' corporate responsibility objectives and the behaviour of the finance community (investors, analysts, fund managers, etc.). At its core is the perceived mismatch between the long-term nature of sustainability and the short-term orientation of much investment activity.

fractional ownership A new concept of ownership fostered by sustainable consumption whereby consumers use a product when they need it, but do not fully own it. For instance, fractional ownership of cars has increased in popularity with users able to borrow a car for a few hours and drop it off at given locations once they have finished.

global commons Natural assets important to human well-being that are outside national jurisdiction (e.g. the oceans, outer space, the atmosphere).

Global Reporting Initiative The custodian body behind an international effort to create a common framework for the voluntary reporting of the economic, environmental, and social impact of business' and other organizations' activities. This framework is set out in the GRI guidelines.

global warming The average increase in atmospheric temperature near the earth's surface and in the troposphere, which can contribute to changes in global climate patterns. (*See also* climate change.)

human rights Basic entitlements accorded to all human beings. There are significant differences of opinion as to what these rights should be, although the most commonly mentioned ones in a corporate responsibility context concern legal, civil, and political rights, especially those set out in the Universal Declaration of Human Rights.

Industrial Revolution The historical period, lasting throughout most of the nineteenth century, during which the economies of the USA and many European nations shifted from an agricultural to a manufacturing base, with an accompanying strengthening of the capitalist economic system.

international development The policies and programmes undertaken by government and non-government agencies in developed and developing economies, with the intention of alleviating poverty and creating sustainable livelihoods for people in developing countries.

Jevons paradox The paradox whereby improvements in material intensity per unit are offset by overall increases in material usage because of production and consumption growth.

liberal economics A theory of economics that is rooted in the belief that individuals' economic actions based largely on self-interest ultimately make the greatest contribution to the common good. Some see globalization as synonymous with economic liberalism, particularly its free flow of capital, goods, services, and (more contentiously) labour with minimal government or other non-market interference.

libertarian A political philosophy based on the belief that individual liberty is the basis for prosperity and well-being, and that government/the state is an unwarranted constraint on people's liberty to choose. It is important in the sustainability context because of its influence on certain economic thinkers, and on political discourse, especially in the USA.

licence to operate The right granted to a company (or other organization) to carry out its business. In the sustainability context, licence to operate usually refers to the licence granted by a community or other stakeholder group, rather than by a formal regulatory authority.

lifecycle management The process of managing and taking responsibility for a product throughout its life cycle (e.g. invention, design, manufacture, use, disposal). Has received particular attention in the sustainability context because it encourages companies to consider the social and environmental impacts of a product throughout its life, and make optimal choices about materials, energy, water, packaging, waste, distribution, etc.

Millennium Development Goals (MDGs) A set of eight targets (including eradicating extreme poverty and hunger, improving maternal health, and ensuring environmental sustainability) that were adopted by all countries represented in the UN General Assembly, and which are to be achieved by 2015. The targets commit countries to a particular vision of international development and are widely used as a framework for measuring development progress.

non-financial performance Aspects of business performance not normally addressed in financial reporting and auditing, including wider environmental, social, and governance indicators.

non-government organization (NGO) A loose term distinguishing a range of organizations that are concerned with particular social and environmental objectives from profit-making organizations and government agencies. Commonly called 'non-governmental organizations', some actually perform a governmental function by way of their role in influencing the process of governing. (*See also* civil society.)

path dependence Pre-existing conditions that influence current and future options, and help determine whether a transition is possible or not.

resource-constrained economy An economy within which human activity (including commercial activity) is knowingly constrained by an awareness that natural resources are finite, and need to be managed so as to sustain the Earth's carrying capacity.

rentalized markets *See* fractional ownership.

reputation management The aspect of management practice that is concerned with understanding perceptions of an organization's reputation, and the actions necessary to protect or enhance it. Reputation management has been identified as a significant driver of defensive approaches to sustainability.

resilience The capacity of a community or society to respond to global challenges associated with sustainability. Often contrasted with modern management theory's emphasis on efficiency because it puts extra value on local resources, and encourages a degree of 'excess capacity' or 'redundancy' as a safeguard against external events.

rights Powers, privileges, or other entitlements that are assured by custom or law.

Rio Earth Summit A meeting, in Rio de Janeiro in June 1992, of over a hundred heads of state, plus representatives of non-government organizations, business, and local government, which was the summit of an international discussion of environmental and development issues of the kind raised by the Brundtland Commission. It was the first time that a multi-sectoral dialogue had been conducted to address these issues, and resulted in leaders signing a number of important agreements, including the United Nations Framework Conventions on Climate Change (UNFCCC) and the Convention on Biological Diversity (CBD), the Rio Declaration on Environment and Development, and Agenda 21 (an international plan of action for achieving a more sustainable pattern of development in the twenty-first century). The meeting is highly significant in the history of contemporary corporate responsibility, because it recognized the importance of business–government–civil society cooperation in achieving sustainable development goals—something that was developed further at the 2002 World Summit on Sustainable Development.

risk management The aspect of management practice that is concerned with understanding and acting upon the degree of risk presented to an organization by political, social, environmental, and economic factors. Risk is often seen as a driver of defensive approaches to sustainability and is evident, for example, in the support of food companies for sustainable agriculture and fisheries.

self-regulation This refers to the practice of a company or other organization voluntarily putting constraints on what it does—e.g. through the adoption of a code of practice or adherence to voluntary guidelines—even though the constrained policy or action might be legal. Some see voluntary self-regulation as a defining feature of corporate responsibility.

small and medium-sized enterprises (SMEs) A classification of company that is normally based on number of employees (or, occasionally, on turnover). In the EU, a small enterprise employs fewer than 50 people and a medium one, fewer than 250; in the USA, the figures are higher, but still not more than 100 and 500 respectively. SMEs comprise the vast majority of businesses in the world (99 per cent in the EU) and account for the bulk of private sector employment generation.

smart grid Energy transmission infrastructure to intelligently manage flows of electricity so as to enable better load management and control. Smart grids, which are probably essential to the scaling up of renewable energy, allow utility companies to manage supply and demand using stored power, including that from distributed generation sources such as solar power. They also enable more efficiency, and open the possibility of tweaking voltage levels. All of these measures would reduce consumption, and it has been estimated that despite the high costs of installing smart grids, they could reduce the overall cost of investment in energy in the long run by 12 per cent.

social and environmental ratings The rating of companies for investment purposes, according to defined criteria for their social and/or environmental performance. Examples include the Domini 400 Social Index, the KLD Climate Change Index, the FTSE4Good Index series, and the Dow Jones Sustainability Indices.

social contract The implied agreement between members of a society that defines and puts limits on the duties, responsibilities, and obligations of each member. Social contract theory is associated with the ethical theory of John Locke and underpins ideas about the company's *licence to operate*.

social entrepreneurship An imprecise term used to refer to a wide range of organizations—both profit-making and non-profit—for which the primary purpose is to deliver social and/or environmental value in contrast with financial value.

socially responsible investment (SRI) An approach to investing that considers the social, environmental, and ethical consequences of investments within the context of financial analysis.

stakeholder An entity with a stake in another organization, by virtue of the fact he, she or it is affected by, or has influence over, that organization. In sustainability terms, 'stakeholder' usually refers to the stake that an individual or organization has in a company, and includes employees, local communities, shareholders, customers, and clients.

stakeholder dialogue The convening of a discussion between a company and (all, or some of) its stakeholders.

stakeholder engagement The managed process of interaction between a company and its stakeholders.

stakeholder management The application of stakeholder theory to management practice. It includes stakeholder engagement, stakeholder dialogue, and stakeholder partnership.

stakeholder partnership A partnership between a company and its stakeholders, intended to capitalize on their combined capabilities in pursuit of a particular purpose.

state An organized political community, occupying a definite territory and governed by a sovereign government. In some sustainability literature, the term 'state' is used interchangeably with government—but the terms are distinct.

steady-state economics Economic theory relating to the management of an economy of stable or mildly fluctuating size. Like many economic theories it seeks legitimacy in physics, in this case Fred Hoyle's steady state theory.

sustainability Referring to those forms of human economic and cultural activity that can be conducted without long-term degradation of the resources that are used. The term is often used interchangeably with *sustainable development*.

sustainable consumption and production Continuous economic and social progress that respects the limits of the earth's ecosystems, and meets the needs and aspirations of everyone for a better quality of life—now, and for future generations.

sustainable development According to the Brundtland Commission, which is the most widely known definition, this is human development to meet the needs of the present generation without compromising the ability of future generations to meet their own needs.

The Natural Step An approach to sustainability that is based on four systematic principles relating to people's capacity to meet their needs, and aspects of the interaction between humanity and the earth. Karl-Henrik Robèrt first proposed the approach in 1989, following the publication of the Report of the Brundtland Commission.

triple bottom-line A framework for measuring company performance and added value, in terms of economic, social, and environmental parameters. Triple bottom-line accounting is an extension of the conventional financial accounting framework to measure these additional areas of performance.

United Nations A supranational organization founded in 1945, with the purposes of: (a) maintaining international peace and security; (b) developing friendly relations among nations; (c) cooperating in solving international economic, social, cultural, and humanitarian problems, and in promoting respect for human rights and fundamental freedoms; (d) acting as a centre through which nations can work jointly to attain those ends. It comprises member States, as well as bodies such as the General Assembly, Security Council, and the International Court of Justice, and it administers programmes to achieve its purpose through agencies such as the UN Development Programme, UN Environment Programme, and the International Labour Organization.

United Nations Global Compact A UN-convened initiative to promote concrete and sustained action by business participants, to align their actions with broad UN social and environmental objectives, the Compact's ten principles, and the international Millennium Development Goals (MDGs). It aims to achieve this through: (a) learning forums to analyse case studies and examples of good practice; (b) global policy dialogues on the challenges of globalization; (c) multi-stakeholder collaborative development projects to further the MDGs; (d) support for new national networks, such as those in India and South Africa.

Universal Declaration of Human Rights A 1948 UN Declaration—signed and ratified by most of the world's countries—which sets out a basic definition of universal human rights. The Declaration is often referred to in human rights and worker rights codes of conduct.

World Commission on Environment and Development *See* Brundtland Commission.

Bibliography

Albareda, L. 2008, 'Corporate responsibility, governance and accountability: from self-regulation to co-regulation', *Corporate Governance*, 8(4), 430–9.

Alcaraz, J.M. & Thiruvattal, E. 2010, 'An interview with Manuel Escudero: The United Nations' principles for responsible management education: a global call for sustainability', *Academy of Management Learning & Education*, 9(3), 542–50.

Allan, J.A. 1998, 'Virtual water: A strategic resource global solutions to regional deficits', *Ground Water*, 36(4), 545–6.

Allen, M.R., Frame, D.J., Huntingford, C., Jones, C.D., Lowe, J.A., Meinshausen, M., & Meinshausen, N. 2009, 'Warming caused by cumulative carbon emissions towards the trillionth tonne', *Nature*, 458(7242), 1163–6.

Allen, R.C. 2002, *Guiding change journeys: A synergistic approach to organization transformation*, Jossey-Bass/Pfeiffer, San Francisco, CA.

Alvesson, M. & Sveningsson, S. 2007, *Changing organizational culture: Cultural change work in progress*, Routledge, New York, NY.

Andriof, J., Waddock, S., Husted, B., & Rahman, S.S. 2002, *Unfolding stakeholder thinking 1: Theory, responsibility and engagement*, Greenleaf, Sheffield.

Annamalai, K. & Rao, S. 2003, *What works: ITC's E-choupal and profitable rural transformation–web-based information and procurement tools for Indian farmers*, A World Resources Institute Digital Dividend Case Study, World Resources Institute, Washington, DC.

Ashridge, United Nations, & EABIS 2009, *Developing the global leader of tomorrow*, European Academy of Business in Society, Brussels.

Audebrand, L.K. 2010, 'Sustainability in strategic management education: The quest for new root metaphors', *Academy of Management Learning & Education*, 9(3), 413–28.

Austin, R.D., Nolan, R.L., & Harvard Business School 2000, *IBM Corporation Turnaround*, Harvard Business School Publishing, Cambridge, MA.

Automotive World 2010, *Automotive World – Research: The electric car report (2nd edition)*, Automotive World, London.

Baer, P. & Mastrandrea, M. 2006, *High stakes: Designing emissions pathways to reduce the risk of dangerous climate change*, Institute for Public Policy Research, London.

Ballinger, J. & Olsson, C. 1997, *Behind the swoosh: The struggle of Indonesians making Nike shoes*, Global Publications Foundation, Uppsala.

Barbier, E. & United Nations Environment Programme 2010, *A global green new deal: Rethinking the economic recovery*, Cambridge University Press, Cambridge.

Bardi, U. 2011, *The limits to growth revisited*, Springer Verlag, New York, NY.

Barnea, A. & Rubin, A. 2010, 'Corporate social responsibility as a conflict between shareholders', *Journal of Business Ethics*, 97, 71–86

Barrientos, S., Dolan, C., & Tallontire, A. 2003, 'A gendered value chain approach to codes of conduct in African horticulture', *World Development*, 31(9), 1511–27.

Bass, B.M. & Avolio, B.J. 1994, *Improving organizational effectiveness through transformational leadership*, Sage, Thousand Oaks, CA.

Bateman, M. 2010, *Why doesn't microfinance work?: The destructive rise of local neoliberalism*, Zed, London.

Baumol, W.J., Litan, R.E., & Schramm, C.J. 2007, *Good capitalism, bad capitalism, and the economics of growth and prosperity*, Yale University Press, New Haven, CT.

Beinhocker, E.D. 2007, *The origin of wealth: Evolution, complexity, and the radical remaking of economics*, Random House Business, London.

Bell, S., Chilvers, A., & Hillier, J. 2011, 'The socio-technology of engineering sustainability', *Proceedings of the ICE-Engineering Sustainability*, 164(3), 177–84.

Bello, W. 2002, *Deglobalization: Ideas for a new world economy*, Zed Books, London.

Belz, F. & Peattie, K. 2009, *Sustainability marketing: A global perspective*, John Wiley and Sons, Hoboken, NJ.

Bendell, J., Collins, E., & Roper, J. 2010, 'Beyond partnerism: toward a more expansive research agenda on multi-stakeholder collaboration for responsible business', *Business Strategy and the Environment*, 19(6), 351–5.

Bennis, W.G. 1989, *On becoming a leader*, Addison-Wesley, New York, NY.

Bennis, W.G. 2007, *Leading for a lifetime: How defining moments shape the leaders of today and tomorrow*, Harvard Business School Press, Boston, MA.

Benson, K.L., Brailsford, T.J., & Humphrey, J.E. 2006, 'Do socially responsible fund managers really invest differently?', *Journal of Business Ethics*, 65(4), 337–57.

Benyus, J.M. 1997, *Biomimicry: Innovation inspired by nature*, Morrow, New York, NY.

Berkhout, F., Leach, M., & Scoones, I. 2003, *Negotiating environmental change: New perspectives from social science*, Edward Elgar Publishing, Cheltenham.

Berners-Lee, M. 2010, *How bad are bananas?: The carbon footprint of everything*, Profile, London.

Berns, M., Townend, A., Khayat, Z., Balagopal, B., Reeves, M., Hopkins, M., & Kruschwitz, N. 2009, 'The business of sustainability: what it means to managers now', *MIT Sloan Management Review*, 51(1), 20–6.

Bhattacharya, C.B. & Sen, S. 2004, 'Doing better at doing good: when, why, and how consumers respond to corporate social initiatives', *California Management Review*, 47(1), 9–24.

Birkinshaw, J., Hamel, G., & Mol, M.J. 2008, 'Manage-ment innovation', *The Academy of Management Review*, 33(4), 825–45.

Birney, A., Salazar, C., & Morgan, J. 2008, 'How do we enable systems change for a one planet future?', *Journal of Corporate Citizenship*, Summer 2008, 23–36.

Bitzer, V. & Glasbergen, P. 2010, 'Partnerships for sustainable change in cotton: an institutional analysis of African cases', *Journal of Business Ethics*, 93, 223–40.

Blackburn, W.R. 2007, *The sustainability handbook: The complete management guide to achieving social, economic and environmental responsibility*, Earthscan, London.

Bloom, D.E., Canning, D., & Sevilla, J. 2003, *The demo-graphic dividend: A new perspective on the economic consequences of population change*, Population Matters Monograph MR-1274, Rand, Santa Monica, CA.

Blowfield, M.E. 2004, 'Implementation deficits of ethical trade systems: lessons from the Indonesian cocoa and timber industries', *Journal of Corporate Citizenship*, (13), 77–90.

Blowfield, M.E. 2005, *Does society want business leadership? An overview of attitudes and thinking*, Center for Corporate Citizenship at Boston College, Chestnut Hill, MA.

Blowfield, M.E. 2010, 'Business and poverty reduction' in P. Utting & J.C. Marques (Eds), *Corporate social responsibility and regulatory governance: Towards inclusive development?*, pp. 124–50, Palgrave Macmillan, New York, NY.

Blowfield, M. & Dolan, C. 2010a, 'Outsourcing governance: Fairtrade's message for C21 global governance', *Corporate Governance*, 10(4), 484–99.

Blowfield, M.E. & Dolan, C. 2010b, 'Fairtrade facts and fancies: What Kenyan fairtrade tea tells us about business' role as development agent', *Journal of Business Ethics*, 93, 143–62.

Blowfield, M.E. & Murray, A. 2008, *Corporate responsibility: A critical introduction*, Oxford University Press, Oxford.

Blowfield, M.E. & Murray, A. 2011, *Corporate responsibility: A critical introduction*, 2nd edn, Oxford University Press, Oxford.

Bodansky, D. & Diringer, E. 2007, *Towards an integrated multi-track climate framework*, Pew Center on Global Climate Change, Arlington, VA.

Bokalders, V. 2009, *The whole building handbook: How to design healthy, efficient, and sustainable buildings*, Earthscan, London.

Boltanski, L. & Chiapello, E. 2005, 'The new spirit of capitalism', *International Journal of Politics, Culture, and Society*, 18, 161–88.

Bornstein, D. 2004, *How to Change the World: Social Entrepreneurs and the Power of New Ideas*, Oxford University Press, New York, NY.

Bower, J.L., Leonard, H.B., & Paine, L.S. 2011, *Capitalism at risk: Rethinking the role of business*, Harvard Business Review Press, Boston, MA.

Boyle, G. 1996, *Renewable energy: power for a sustainable future*, Oxford University Press, Oxford.

Boyle, G. (Ed) 2007, *Renewable electricity and the grid: The challenge of variability*, Earthscan, London.

Bracking, S. 2009, *Hiding conflict over industry returns: A stakeholder analysis of the extractive industries transparency initiative*, Brooks World Poverty Institute Working Paper 91, Brooks World Poverty Institute, Manchester.

Braun, B., Whatmore, S.J., Stengers, I., & Bennett, J. 2010, *Political Matter: Technoscience, Democracy, and Public Life*, University of Minnesota Press, Minneapolis, MN.

Brower, M., Leon, W., & Union of Concerned Scientists 1999, *The consumer's guide to effective environmental choices: Practical advice from the Union of Concerned Scientists*, 1st edn, Three Rivers Press, New York, NY.

Brown, T.J. & Dacin, P.A. 1997, 'The company and the product: corporate associations and consumer product responses', *Journal of Marketing*, 61, 68–84.

Brueckner, M. & Pforr, C. 2011, 'Western Australia's short-lived 'sustainability revolution'', *Environmental Politics*, 20(4), 585–9.

BSR & GlobeScan 2010, *State of sustainable business poll 2010*, Business for Social Responsibility and GlobeScan, San Francisco, CA.

Bulkeley, H. & Newell, P.E. 2010, *Governing climate change*, Routledge, New York, NY.

Bulloch, G. 2009, *Development collaboration: None of our business?*, Accenture, London.

Burton, T., Jenkins, N., Sharpe, D., & Bossanyi, E. (Eds) 2011, *Wind energy handbook*, 2nd edn, Wiley, Oxford.

Cabeza Gutés, M. 1996, 'The concept of weak sustainability', *Ecological Economics*, 17(3), 147–56.

Calthorpe, P. 2010, *Urbanism in the age of climate change*, Island Press, Washington, DC.

Campanale, M. & Leggett, J. 2011, *Unburnable carbon: Are the world's financial markets carrying a carbon bubble?*, Carbon Tracker, London.

Carney, W.J. 1998, 'Limited liability', in B. Bouckaert and G. D. Geest (Eds), *Encyclopedia of law and economics*, pp. 659–91, Edward Elgar, Cheltenham.

Carpenter, M.A. & Carpenter, M. 2009, *An executive's primer on the strategy of social networks*, Business Expert Press, New York, NY.

Carson, R., Darling, L., & Darling, L. 1962, *Silent spring*, Houghton Mifflin, Cambridge, MA.

Carter, R.M., De Freitas, C., Goklany, I.M., Holland, D., Lindzen, R.S., Byatt, I., Castles, I., Henderson, D., Lawson, N., & McKitrick, R. 2006, 'The Stern Review: a dual critique', *World Economics*, 7(4), 165–232.

CCC 2005, *Going global: How U.S.-based multinationals are operationalizing corporate citizenship on a global platform*, Center for Corporate Citizenship, Chestnut Hill, MA.

Chaffin, J. 2012, 'Cheap and dirty', *Financial Times*, 13 February.

Chambers, R. 1983, *Rural development: Putting the last first*, Longman London.

Chambers, R. 1994, 'The origins and practice of participatory rural appraisal', *World Development*, 22(7), 953–69.

Chang, H. 2002, *Kicking away the ladder: Development strategy in historical perspective*, Anthem, London.

Chang, H. 2010, *23 things they don't tell you about capitalism*, Allen Lane, London.

Cheung, D.K.K., Welford, R.J., & Hills, P.R. 2009, 'CSR and the environment: business supply chain partnerships in Hong Kong and PRDR, China', *Corporate Social Responsibility and Environmental Management*, 16(5), 250–63.

Chick, A. 2011, *Design for sustainable change: How design and designers can drive the sustainability agenda: Required reading range course reader*, Ava Publishing, Lausanne.

Christensen, L.J., Peirce, E., Hartman, L.P., Hoffman, W.M., & Carrier, J. 2007, 'Ethics, CSR, and sustainability education in the Financial Times top 50 global business schools: baseline data and future research directions', *Journal of Business Ethics*, 73(4), 347–68.

Clay, J. 2005, *Exploring the links between international business and poverty reduction: A case study of Unilever in Indonesia*, Oxfam, Oxford.

Club of Rome & Natural Edge Project 2009, *Factor five: transforming the global economy through 80% improvements in resource productivity: A report to the Club of Rome*, Earthscan, London.

Coca-Cola Company 2010, *2009/2010 sustainability review*, Coca-Cola Company, Atlanta.

Collier, P. 2007, *The bottom billion: Why the poorest countries are failing and what can be done about it*, Oxford University Press, Oxford.

Collier, P. 2010, *The plundered planet: How to reconcile prosperity with nature*, Allen Lane, London.

Collins, J.C. 2001, *Good to great: Why some companies make the leap – and others don't*, HarperBusiness, New York, NY.

Collins, J.C. & Porras, J.I. 1994, *Built to last: Successful habits of visionary companies*, 1st edn, HarperBusiness, New York, NY.

Convery, F.J. 2009, 'Reflections—the emerging literature on emissions trading in Europe', *Review of Environmental Economics and Policy*, 3(1), 121–37.

Costello, A., Abbas, M., Allen, A., Ball, S., Bell, S., Bellamy, R., Friel, S., Groce, N., Johnson, A., & Kett, M. 2009, 'Managing the health effects of climate change', *Lancet*, 373(9676), 1693–733.

Cotula, L., Vermeulen, S., Leonard, R., & Keeley, J. 2009, *Land grab or development opportunity?: Agricultural investment and international land deals in Africa*, IIED/FAO/IFAD, London/Rome.

CPI 2007, *Sustainable consumption and production*, Cambridge Programme for Industry, Cambridge.

CPSL 2006, *Facing the future: Business, society and the sustainable development challenge*, Cambridge Programme for Sustainable Leadership, Cambridge.

CPSL 2011, *A journey of a thousand miles: The state of sustainability leadership in 2011*, Cambridge Programme for Sustainability Leadership, Cambridge.

Crane, A., Matten, D., & Crane, A. 2007, *Business ethics: Managing corporate citizenship and sustainability in the age of globalization*, 2nd edn, Oxford University Press, Oxford.

Cummings, J. 2001, 'Engaging stakeholders in corporate accountability programmes: A cross-sectoral analysis of UK and transnational experience', *Business Ethics: A European Review*, 10(1), 45–52.

Daft, R.L. & Weick, K.E. 1984, 'Toward a model of organizations as interpretation systems', *Academy of Management Review*, 9, 284–95.

Daly, H.E. 1996, *Beyond growth: The economics of sustainable development*, Beacon Press, Boston, MA.

Dasgupta, P. 2008, 'Discounting climate change', *Journal of Risk and Uncertainty*, 37(2), 141–69.

Dauvergne, P. 2008, *The shadows of consumption: Consequences for the global environment*, The MIT Press, Cambridge, MA.

Davis, S.M., Lukomnik, J., & Pitt-Watson, D. 2006, *The new capitalists: How citizen investors are reshaping the corporate agenda*, Harvard Business School Press, Boston, MA.

Davis, S.M., Lukomnik, J., & Pitt-Watson, D. 2006, *The new capitalists: How citizen investors are reshaping the corporate agenda*, Harvard Business School Press, Boston, MA.

de Sherbinin, A., Castro, M., Gemenne, F., Cernea, M., Adamo, S., Fearnside, P., Krieger, G., Lahmani, S., Oliver-Smith, A., & Pankhurst, A. 2011, 'Preparing for resettlement associated with climate change', *Science*, 334(6055), 456–7.

Dees, J.G. 1998, 'The Meaning of "Social Entrepreneurship"', Comments and suggestions contributed from the Social Entrepreneurship Funders Working Group.

Deinlnger, K. & Binswanger, H. 1999, 'The evolution of the World Bank's land policy: principles, experience, and future challenges', *The World Bank Research Observer*, 14(2), 247–76.

Deming, W.E. 2000, *Out of the crisis*, 1st edn, MIT Press, Cambridge, MA.

Depledge, J. & Yamin, F. 2009, 'The global climate-change regime: A defence', in D. Helm & Hepburn, C. (Eds) *The economics and politics of climate change*, pp. 433–53, Oxford University Press, Oxford.

Desai, M. 2012, 'The incentive bubble', *Harvard Business Review*, 90(3).

Detomasi, D.A. 2007, 'The multinational corporation and global governance: modelling global public policy networks', *Journal of Business Ethics*, 71(3), 321–34.

DFID 2008, *Degrees of separation: Climate change, shared challenges, shared opportunities*, DFID, London.

Diamond, J.M. 1998, *Guns, Germs and Steel: A short history of everybody for the last 13,000 years*, Random House, London.

Doppelt, B. 2010, *Leading change toward sustainability: A change-management guide for business, government and civil society*, updated 2nd edn, Greenleaf, Sheffield.

Dreher, R. 2006, *Crunchy cons: How birkenstocked burkeans, gun-loving organic gardeners, evangelical free-range farmers, hip homeschooling mamas, right-wing nature lovers and their diverse tribe of countercultural conservatives plan to save America (or at least the Republican Party)*, Crown Forum, New York, NY.

Drucker, P.F. 1946, *Concept of the corporation*, The John Day Company, New York, NY.

Drucker, P.F. 1976, *The unseen revolution: How pension fund socialism came to America*, Heinemann, London.

Drzik, J. 2011, 'Price volatility is here to stay', *Financial Times*, 23 May.

Easterly, W.R. 2006, *The white man's burden: Why the West's efforts to aid the rest have done so much ill and so little good*, Oxford University Press, Oxford.

Efstathiou, J. 2008, 'Carbon trading can raise billions of dollars to save forests', *The Independent* (Ireland), 8 April 8.

Ehrenfeld, J. 2008, *Sustainability by design: A subversive strategy for transforming our consumer culture*, Yale University Press, New Haven, CT.

Ehrenreich, B. 2001, *Nickel and dimed: On (not) getting by in America*, Metropolitan Books, New York, NY.

Eichholtz, P., Kok, N., & Quigley, J.M. 2009, *Doing well by doing good? Green office buildings*, Berkeley Program on Housing and Urban Policy, Working Paper Series qt507394s4, Berkeley, CA.

EITI 2005, *Extractive industries transparency initiative source book*, Extractive Industries Transparency Initiative, London.

Eliatamby, A. 2010, *Principled leadership for sustainability: A guide for our tomorrows*, Grosvenor House Pub, Guildford.

Elkington, J. 1997, *Cannibals with forks: The triple bottom line of 21st century business*, Capstone, Oxford.

Elkington, J. 2001, *The chrysalis economy: How citizen CEOs and corporations can fuse values and value creation*, Capstone, Oxford.

Elkington, J. & Hartigan, P. 2008, *The power of unreasonable people: How social entrepreneurs create markets that change the world*, Harvard Business School Press, Boston, MA.

Ellerman, A.D., Buchner, B.K., & Carraro, C. 2011, *Allocation in the European emissions trading scheme*, Cambridge University Press, Cambridge.

Elliott, C. & Center for International Forestry Research 2000, *Forest certification: A policy perspective*, Center for International Forestry Research, Bogor, Indonesia.

Ellsworth, R.R. 2002, *Leading with purpose: The new corporate realities*, Stanford Business Books, Stanford, CA.

Epstein, M.J. 2008, *Making sustainability work: Best practices in managing and measuring corporate social, environmental and economic impacts*, Greenleaf, Sheffield.

Esty, D. 2011, *The green to gold business playbook: How to implement sustainability practices for bottom-line results in every business function*, John Wiley, Hoboken, NJ.

Esty, D.C. & Winson, A. 2009, *Green to gold: How smart companies use environmental strategy to innovate, create value, and build a competitive advantage*, Rev. and updated edn, John Wiley, Hoboken, NJ.

Evan, W.M. & Freeman, R.E. 1988, 'A stakeholder theory of the modern corporation: Kantian capitalism', *Ethical Theory and Business*, 3), 97–106.

Fairfax, S.K., Gwin, L., King, M.A., Raymond, L., & Watt, L.A. 2005, *Buying nature: The limits of land acquisition as a conservation strategy, 1780–2004*, MIT Press, Cambridge, MA.

Fairhead, J. 1996, *Misreading the African landscape: Society and ecology in a forest-savanna mosaic*, Cambridge University Press, Cambridge.

Farr, D. (Ed) 2008, *Sustainable urbanism: urban design with nature*, John Wiley, Hoboken, NJ.

Fildes, N. 2011, Going green is seen as 'the' issue, *Business News, Business – The Independent*, 28 February.

Fisher, D. 2009, 'The enlightened shareholder-leaving stakeholders in the dark: Will section 172 (1) of the Companies Act 2006 make directors consider the impact of their decisions on third parties', *International Company and Commercial Law Review*, 20(1), 10–16.

Fisher, D.A. 1963, *The epic of steel*, Harper & Row, New York, NY.

Fisher, R. 1981, *Getting to yes: Negotiating agreement without giving in*, Houghton Mifflin, Boston, MA.

Fletcher, K. 2008, *Sustainable fashion and textiles: Design journeys*, Earthscan, London.

Ford, J.D., Ford, L.W., & D'Amelio, A. 2008, 'Resistance to change: The rest of the story', *The Academy of Management Review (AMR)*, 33(2), 362–77.

Frame, D. & Hepburn, C. 2011, *Emerging markets and climate change: Mexican standoff or low-carbon race?* Centre for Climate Change Economics and Policy Working Paper No. 58, London and Leeds.

Frank, R.H. 2000, *Luxury fever: Money and happiness in an era of excess*, new edn, The American College, Bryn Mawr, Pennsylvania.

Frank, R.H. 2011, *The Darwin economy: Liberty, competition, and the common good*, Princeton University Press, Princeton, NJ.

Freebairn, D.K. 1995, 'Did the Green Revolution concentrate incomes? A quantitative study of research reports', *World Development*, 23(2), 265–79.

Freeman, R.E. 1984, *Strategic management: A stakeholder approach*, Pitman, Boston, MA.

Friedman, A.L. & Miles, S. 2006, *Stakeholders: Theory and practice*, Oxford University Press, New York, NY.

Friedman, M. 1962, *Capitalism and freedom*, University of Chicago Press, Chicago, IL.

Friel, H. 2011, *The Lomborg deception: Setting the record straight about global warming*, Yale University Press, New Haven, CT.

Galbraith, J.K. 1958, *The affluent society*, Penguin Books, London.

Galea, C.E. 2004, *Teaching business sustainability*, Greenleaf, Sheffield.

Gauthier, A., Link, W., Corral, T., & Network, G.L. 2008, 'Developing generative change leaders across sectors: An exploration of integral approaches', *Integral Leadership Review*, June.

GE 2005, *Solving big needs: GE corporate citizenship report 2005*, General Electric, Fairfield, CT.

Gearty, M. 'Achieving carbon reduction: Learning from stories of vision, chance and determination', *Journal of Corporate Citizenship*, 30, 81–94.

Geels, F.W. 2002, 'Technological transitions as evolutionary reconfiguration processes: a multi-level perspective and a case-study', *Research Policy*, 31(8–9), 1257–74.

Geertz, C. 1963, *Agricultural Involution. The process of ecological change in Indonesia. [With maps.]*, University of California Press, Berkeley & Los Angeles, CA.

Gerstner, L.V. 2002, *Who says elephants can't dance?* HarperBusiness, New York, NY.

Gertner, J. 2008, 'Capitalism to the rescue', *New York Times*, 5 October.

Ghosh, A. & Woods, N. 2009, 'Governing climate change: lessons from other governance regimes', in D. Helm & C. Hepburn (Eds), *The economics and politics of climate change*, pp. 454–77, Oxford University Press, Oxford.

Gilding, P. 2011, *The great disruption: How the climate crisis will transform the global economy*, Bloomsbury, London.

Gitsham, M. 2011, 'CEO perspectives: management education in a changing context', *Corporate Governance*, 11(4), 501–12.

Gladwell, M. 2000, *The tipping point: How little things can make a big difference*, 1st edn, Little, Brown, Boston, MA.

Gladwin, T.N., Kennelly, J.J., & Krause, T.S. 1995, 'Shifting paradigms for sustainable development: Implications for management theory and research', *Academy of Management Review*, 20(4), 874–907.

Glasbergen, P. 2011, 'The politics of partnerships: A critical examination of nonprofit-business partnerships', *Journal of Integrative Environmental Sciences*, 8(2), 139–40.

Godfray, H.C.J., Beddington, J.R., Crute, I.R., Haddad, L., Lawrence, D., Muir, J.F., Pretty, J., Robinson, S., Thomas, S.M., & Toulmin, C. 2010, 'Food security: the challenge of feeding 9 billion people', *Science*, 327(5967), 812–18.

Goodpaster, K.E. 1991, 'Business ethics and stakeholder analysis', *Business Ethics Quarterly*, 1(1), 53–73.

Goodpaster, K.E. 2002, 'Stakeholder thinking: beyond paradox to practicality', in J. Andriof, S.A. Waddock, B. Husted, & S.S. Rahman (Eds) *Unfolding stakeholder thinking: Theory, responsibility and engagement*, pp. 43–64, Greenleaf, Sheffield.

Gough, I. 2011, 'Climate change and public policy futures', The British Academy, London.

Grande, C. 2007, '*Ethical consumption makes mark on branding*', Financial Times, 20 February.

Gray, R. & Bebbington, J. 2001, *Accounting for the environment*, 2nd edn, Sage Publications, London.

Gray, R.H. & University of Glasgow 2003, *Social and environmental accounting and reporting: from ridicule to revolution? From hope to hubris?*, University of Glasgow, Glasgow.

Gray, R.H., Kouhy, R., & Lavers, S. 1996, 'Corporate social and environmental reporting: a review of the literature and a longitudinal study of UK disclosure', *Accounting Auditing and Accountability Journal*, 8(2), 47–77.

Grayson, D. & Dodd, T. 2007, *Small is sustainable (and beautiful!): Encouraging European smaller enterprises to be sustainable*, Doughty Centre for Corporate Responsibility, Cranfield.

Green, S. 2009, *Good value: Reflections on money, morality and an uncertain world*, Allen Lane, London.

Greenwald, R. 'The Koch brothers' campaign to kill social security', *The Guardian*, 22 June. Accessed 10 July 2011 at http://www.guardian.co.uk/commentis-free/cifamerica/2011/jun/22/koch-brothers-social-security [2011, 7/10/2011].

Gunther, M. 2008, 'Merrill Lynch's carbon bet: Why a Wall Street firm wants to save a forest in Sumatra', *Fortune.com*, 18 April.

Haanaes, K., Arthur, D., Balagopal, B., Kong, M., Reeves, M., Velken, I., Hoppins, M., & Kruschwitz, N. 2011, 'Sustainability: The "embracers" seize advantage', *MIT Sloan Management Review Report* Winter 2011.

Haidt, J. 2006, *The happiness hypothesis: Putting ancient wisdom and philosophy to the test of modern science*, Arrow, London.

Halpern, S. 2011, 'Over the high-tech rainbow' *The New York Review of Books*, November 24. Accessed 3 January 2012 at: http://www.nybooks.com/blogs/nyrblog/2011/oct/24/over-high-tech-rainbow/.

Hamann, R. & Boulogne, F. 2008, 'Partnerships and cross-sector collaboration', in R. Hamann, S. Woolman, & C. Sprague (Eds), *The Business of Sustainable Development in Africa: Human Rights, Partnerships, Alternative Business Models*, pp. 54–82, Unisa Press, Pretoria.

Hamann, R., Woolman, S., & Sprague, C. (Eds) 2008, *The business of sustainable development in Africa: Human rights, partnerships, alternative business models*, Unisa Press, Pretoria.

Hamburger, T., Hennessey, K., & Banerjee, N. 2011, 'Koch brothers now at heart of GOP power', *Los Angeles Times*, 6 February. Accessed 10 July 2011 at http://articles.latimes.com/2011/feb/06/nation/la-na-koch-brothers-20110206.

Hamel, G. 2000, *Leading the revolution*, Harvard Business School Press, Boston, MA.

Hamel, G. 2007, *The future of management*, Harvard Business School Press, Boston, MA.

Hammer, M. & Champy, J. 1993, *Reengineering the corporation: A manifesto for business revolution*, HarperBusiness, New York, NY.

Hankins, M. 2010, *Stand-alone solar electric systems: The Earthscan expert handbook for planning, design, and installation*, Earthscan, London.

Hansmann, H. & Kraakman, R. 2000, 'End of history for corporate law, *Georgetown Law Journal*, 89, 439–68.

Haque, U. 2011, *The new capitalist manifesto: Building a disruptively better business*, Harvard Business Press, Cambridge MA.

Hardin, G. 1968, 'The tragedy of the commons', *Science*, 16(1), 1243–8.

Harris, C. & Centre for Alternative Technology (Great Britain) 2005, *The whole house book: Ecological building design & materials*, 2nd edn, Centre for Alternative Technology, Machynlleth.

Harris, D.L. & Twomey, D.F. 2010, 'The enterprise perspective: a new mind-set for competitiveness and sustainability', *Competitiveness Review: An International Business Journal incorporating Journal of Global Competitiveness*, 20(3), 258–66.

Harrison, R., Newholm, T., & Shaw, D. 2005, *The ethical consumer*, Sage, London.

Hart, S.L. 2010, *Capitalism at the crossroads: Next generation business strategies for a post-crisis world*, 3rd edn, Wharton School, Philadelphia, PA.

Harvey, D. 2010, *The enigma of capital: And the crises of capitalism*, Oxford University Press, Oxford.

Harvey, L.D.D. 2010, *Energy and the new reality*, Earthscan, London.

Harvey, M. & Pilgrim, S. 2011, 'The new competition for land: Food, energy, and climate change', *Food Policy*, 36, S40–S51.

Haugh, H. 2006, 'Social enterprise: beyond economic outcomes and individual returns' in J. Mair, J. Robinson, & K. Hockerts, *Social entrepreneurship*, pp. 180–206, Palgrave Macmillan, Basingstoke.

Haugh, H.M. & Talwar, A. 2010, 'How do corporations embed sustainability across the organization?', *The Academy of Management Learning and Education (AMLE)*, 9(3), 384–96.

Hawken, P. 1995, *The ecology of commerce*, Phoenix, London.

Hawken, P. 2004, *Socially responsible investing. How the SRI industry has failed to respond to people who want to invest with conscience and what can be done to change it*, Natural Capital Institute, Sausalito.

Hawken, P., Lovins, A.B., & Lovins, L.H. 1999, *Natural capitalism: Creating the next industrial revolution*, 1st edn, Little, Brown and Co., Boston, MA.

Hawley, J.P. & Williams, A.T. 2000, *The rise of fiduciary capitalism: How institutional investors can make corporate America more democratic*, University of Pennsylvania Press, Philadelphia, PA.

Head, P. 2008, *Entering the ecological age: The engineer's role*, Institution of Civil Engineers, London.

Heifetz, R.A. 2009, *The practice of adaptive leadership: Tools and tactics for changing your organization and the world*, Harvard Business Press, Boston, MA.

Heinberg, R. 2004, *Power down: options and actions for a post-carbon world*, New Society Publishers, Gabriola Island, BC.

Helm, D. 2008, 'Climate-change policy: why has so little been achieved?', *Oxford Review of Economic Policy*, 24(2), 211–38.

Helm, D. & Hepburn, C. 2009, *The economics and politics of climate change*, Oxford University Press, Oxford.

Henriques, A. 2010, *Corporate impact: Measuring and managing your social footprint*, Earthscan, London.

Heyerdahl, T. 1996, *The Kon-Tiki expedition: By raft across the South Seas*, New edn, Flamingo, London.

Hickman, L. 2010, 'James Lovelock: Humans are too stupid to prevent climate change', *The Guardian*, 29 March. Accessed 10 May 2011 at http://www. guardian.co.uk/science/2010/mar/29/james-lovelock-climate-change.

Hinkley, R. 2002, 'How corporate law inhibits social responsibility', *The Humanist*, 62(2), 26–6.

Hoekstra, A.Y. 2011, *The water footprint assessment manual: Setting the global standard*, Earthscan, London.

Holden, S.T., Deininger, K., & Ghebru, H. 2011, 'Tenure insecurity, gender, low-cost land certification and land rental market participation in Ethiopia', *The Journal of Development Studies*, 47(1), 31–47.

Holliday, S. 2010, 'An interview With Chad Holliday, (Former) CEO & Chairman, DuPont: The relationship between sustainability education and business', *Academy of Management Learning & Education*, 9(3), 532–41.

Holmes, I. & Mabey, N. 2010, *Accelerating the transition to a low carbon economy*, E3G, London.

Holt, D.B. 2004, *How brands become icons: The principles of cultural branding*, Harvard Business School, Boston, MA.

Hopkins, R. 2008, *The transition handbook: From oil dependency to local resilience*, Chelsea Green Publishing, White River Junction, VT.

HSBC 2011, *Energy in 2050: Will fuel constraints thwart our growth projections?*, HSBC, London.

Hulme, M. 2009, *Why we disagree about climate change: Understanding controversy, inaction and opportunity*, Cambridge University Press, Cambridge.

Hulme, M. 2010, 'Problems with making and governing global kinds of knowledge', *Global Environmental Change*, 20(4), 558–64.

Hulme, M.E. 2010, *Making climate change work for us: European perspectives on adaptation and mitigation strategies*, Cambridge University Press, Cambridge.

Husted, B. & Allen 2011, *Corporate social strategy: Stakeholder engagement and competitive advantage*, Cambridge University Press, Cambridge.

IATA 2009, *Aviation and Climate Change: Pathway to Carbon Neutral Growth in 2020*, The International Air Transport Association, Geneva.

IBM 2010, *Capitalizing on complexity: Insights from the global chief executive officer study*, IBM.

Idemudia, U. 2007, 'Community perceptions and expectations: reinventing the wheels of corporate social responsibility practices in the Nigerian oil industry', *Business and Society Review*, 112(3), 369–405.

IEA 2008, *Energy technology perspectives 2008*, International Energy Agency, Paris.

IEA 2010a, *Key world energy statistics 2010*, International Energy Agency, Paris. Accessed 6 March 2011 at: http://www.iea.org/textbase/nppdf/free/2010/ key_stats_2010.pdf.

IEA 2010b, *World energy outlook 2010*, International Energy Agency, Paris.

IEA 2011, *Clean energy progress report*, International Energy Agency, Paris. Accessed 3 June 2011 at http:// www.iea.org/papers/2011/CEM_Progress_Report. pdf.

Institution of Mechanical Engineers 2010, *Population: One planet, too many people*, Institution of Mechanical Engineers, London.

IPCC, 2007, *Fourth Assessment Report: Climate Change 2007*, United Nations Intergovernmental Panel on Climate Change, New York, NY.

ISSP 2010, *The sustainability professional: 2010 competency survey report*, International Society of Sustainability Professionals, Portland, OR.

Jackson, T. 2009, *Prosperity without growth: Economics for a finite planet*, Earthscan, London.

Jackson, T.E. 2006, *The Earthscan reader in sustainable consumption*, Earthscan, London.

Jaeger, C.C., Paroussos, L., Mangalagiu, D., Kupers, R., Mandel, A., & Tabara, J.D., 2011, *A New Growth Path for Europe: Synthesis Report*, European Climate Forum, Potsdam. Accessed 5 May 2011 at http://www.european-climate-forum.net/fileadmin/ecf-documents/Press/A_New_Growth_Path_for_Europe__Synthesis_Report.pdf.

James, O. 2007, *Affluenza*, Vermilion, London.

James, W. 1918/1950, *The principles of psychology*, authorized edn, Dover Publications, New York, NY.

Jenkins, H. 2009, 'A "business opportunity" model of corporate social responsibility for small-and medium-sized enterprises', *Business Ethics: A European Review*, 18(1), 21–36.

Jewson Associates Research report on ethical investment for Oxford University, *The costs of ethical investing*, Jewson Associates, London.

John, R. 2006, *Venture Philanthropy: The evolution of high engagement philanthropy in Europe*, Skoll Centre for Social Entrepreneurship, Saïd Business School Publications, Oxford.

Johnstone, S., Wilkinson, A., & Ackers, P. 2010, 'Critical incidents of partnership: five years' experience at NatBank', *Industrial Relations Journal*, 41(4), 382–98.

Jones, T. 2010, *Future Agenda: The World in 2020*, Infinite Ideas, Oxford.

Jonvallen, P., Olofsson, J., Wamala, C., & Mellström, U. 2009, *Current strands of thought and work in progress at the division of gender and technology*, Division of Gender and Technology, Luleå University of Technology, Luleå.

Joule, E. 2011, 'Fashion-forward thinking: Sustainability as a business model at Levi Strauss', *Global Business and Organizational Excellence*, 30(2), 16–22.

Kahneman, D. & Tversky, A. 1979, 'Prospect theory: An analysis of decision under risk', *Econometrica: Journal of the Econometric Society*, 47, 263–91.

Kaletsky, A. 2010, *Capitalism 4.0: The birth of a new economy*, Bloomsbury, London.

Kapstein, E.B. 2008, *Measuring Unilever's economic footprint: The case of South Africa*, Unilever, London.

Kapur, A. 2005, *Plutonomy: Buying luxury, explaining imbalances*, Citigroup, New York, NY.

Kats, G. 2010, *Greening our built world: Costs, benefits, and strategies*, Island Press, Washington, DC.

Kelly, M. 2001, *The divine right of capital: Dethroning the corporate aristocracy*, Berrett-Koehler Publishers Inc., San Francisco, CA.

Kemp, R. & Rotmans, J. 2005, 'The management of the co-evolution of technical, environmental and social systems', in M. Weber & J. Hemmelskamp (Eds) *Towards environmental innovation systems*, pp. 33–55, Springer, Heidelberg.

Kemp, R. 1994, 'Technology and the transition to environmental sustainability 1: The problem of technological regime shifts', *Futures*, 26(10), 1023–46.

Khurana, R. 2007, *From higher aims to hired hands: The social transformation of American business schools and the unfulfilled promise of management as a profession*, Princeton University Press, Princeton, NJ.

Kiernan, M. 2006, 'Sustainable investment research: Innovest Strategic Value Advisors' in R. Sullivan & C. MacKenzie (Eds) *Responsible investment*, pp. 122–31, Greenleaf Publishing, Sheffield,

Kiernan, M.J. 2009, *Investing in a sustainable world: Why GREEN is the new color of money on Wall Street*, Amacom Books, New York, NY.

King, D.A. 2011, December, *Kings Comment: Voluntary agreements and country actions: the way forward on climate change* [Online]. Accessed 19 February 2012 at http://www.static-ubs.com/global/en/investment-bank/sir-david-king/_jcr_content/par/textimage.1044212239.file/dGV4dD0vY29udGVudC9kY-W0vSW52ZXN0bWVudEJhbmsvZG9jdW1lbnRzL-1NES19kZWNlbWJlcjIwMTEucGRm/SDK_december2011.pdf.

Klimasinska, K. 2012, 'Keystone pipeline bill passes house, lacks match in U.S. senate', *Businessweek*, 22 February. Accessed 22 February 2012 at http://www.businessweek.com/news/2012-02-19/keystone-pipeline-bill-passes-house-lacks-match-in-u-s-senate.html.

Kolk, A. & Pinkse, J. 2008, 'Business and climate change: emergent institutions in global governance', *Corporate Governance*, 8(4), 419–29.

Kolk, A. & Pinkse, J. 2011, *The climate change-development nexus and tripartite partnerships*, The Partnerships Resource Center, Rotterdam.

Kotler, P. 2008, *Principles of marketing*, 12th edn, Pearson/Prentice Hall, Harlow.

Kotler, P., Kartajaya, H., & Setiawan, I. 2010, *Marketing 3.0: From products to customers to the human spirit*, Wiley, Hoboken, NJ.

Kotter, J.P. 1995, *Leading change: Why transformation efforts fail*, Harvard Business School Publication corporation, Cambridge, MA.

Kotter, J.P. 1996, *Leading change*, Harvard Business School Press, Boston, MA.

Kourula, A. & Halme, M. 2008, 'Types of corporate responsibility and engagement with NGOs: an exploration of business and societal outcomes', *Corporate Governance*, 8(4), 557–70.

Kramer, M. & Kania, J. 2006, 'Changing the game: leading corporations switch from defense to offense in solving global problems', *Stanford Social Innovation Review*, Spring 2006, 20–7.

Kreander, N., Gray, R.H., Power, D.M., & Sinclair, C.D. 2005, 'Evaluating the performance of ethical and non-ethical funds: A matched pair analysis', *Journal of Business Finance & Accounting*, 32(7-8), 1465–93.

Krosinsky, C. 2008, 'Sustainable equity investing: the market-beating strategy' in C. Krosinsky & N. Robins (Eds), *Sustainable investing: The art of long-term performance*, pp. 19–30, Earthscan, London

Krosinsky, C. & Robins, N. 2008, *Sustainable investing: the art of long-term performance*, Earthscan, London.

Krupp, F. 2008, 'The making of a market-minded environmentalist', *Strategy and Business*, 51, 18.

Kubler-Ross, E. & Kessler, D. 2005, *On grief and grieving: Finding the meaning of grief through the five stages of loss*, Simon & Schuster, London.

Kurokawa, K. (Ed) 2003, *Energy from the desert*, Earthscan, London.

Lampel, J. & Meyer, A. 2008, 'Field-configuring events as structuring mechanisms: how conferences, ceremonies, and trade shows constitute new technologies, industries, and markets', *Journal of Management Studies*, 45(6), 1025–35.

Landrum, N., Landrum, N.E., & Edwards, S. 2009, *Sustainable Business: An Executive's Primer*, Business Expert Press, New York, NY.

Lang, T. 2009, *Food policy: Integrating health, environment and society*, Oxford University Press, Oxford.

Laszlo, C. 2003, *The sustainable company: How to create lasting value through social and environmental performance*, Island Press, Washington, DC.

Leach, M., Scoones, I., & Wynne, B. 2005, *Science and citizens: Globalization and the challenge of engagement*, Zed Books, London

Lebel, L., Lorek, S., & Daniel, R. 2010, *Sustainable production consumption systems: Knowledge, engagement and practice*, Springer Verlag, New York, NY.

Lecacheur, X. 2010, *What model for a Green Investment Bank? Can we learn from European examples?*, Climate Bonds Initiative.

Lee, I. 2005, *Corporate law, profit maximization and the 'responsible shareholder'* The Berkeley Electronic Press (bePress Legal Series) [Online]. Accessed 9 July 2011 at http://law.bepress.com/cgi/viewcontent.cgi?article=2 238&context=expresso&sei-redir=1#search='company law profit'.

Lee, L. 2011, 'Business-community partnerships: understanding the nature of partnership', *Corporate Governance*, 11(1), 29–40.

Lehmann, F. & Lehmann, J.E. 2010, *Peace and prosperity through world trade*, Cambridge University Press, Cambridge.

Lehmann, S. 2010, *The principles of green urbanism: Transforming the city for sustainability*, Earthscan, London.

Leipziger, D. 2003, *The corporate responsibility code book*, Greenleaf, Sheffield.

Leonard, A. 2010, *The story of stuff: How our obsession with stuff is trashing the planet, our communities, and our health - and a vision for change*, Free Press, New York, NY.

Lewin, K. 1946, 'Action research and minority problems', *Journal of Social Issues*, 2(4), 34–46.

Lewin, K. 1963, *Field Theory in Social Science Selected Theoretical Papers*, Tavistock Publications Ltd, London.

Litan, R.E. & Wallison, P.J. 2003, 'Beyond GAAP', *Regulation*, 26(3).

Lomborg, B. 2001, *The skeptical environmentalist: Measuring the real state of the World*, Cambridge University Press, Cambridge.

Lomborg, B. 2007, *Cool it!: The skeptical environmentalist's guide to global warming*, Cyan: Marshall Cavendish, London.

Lomborg, B. 2010, *Smart solutions to climate change: Comparing costs and benefits*, Cambridge University Press, Cambridge.

Long, J.C. 2008, 'From Cocoa to CSR: Finding sustainability in a cup of hot chocolate', *Thunderbird International Business Review*, 50(5), 315–20.

Lovelock, J. 2000, *Gaia: the practical science of planetary medicine*, rev. edn, Gaia, London.

Lovelock, J. 2006, *The revenge of Gaia: Why the earth is fighting back - and how we can still save humanity*, Allen Lane, London.

Lovelock, J. 2010, *The vanishing face of Gaia: A final warning*, Penguin, London.

Lukes, S. 1974, *Power: A radical view*, Macmillan, Basingstoke.

Lydenberg, S.D. 2005, *Corporations and the public interest: Guiding the invisible hand*, 1st edn, Berrett-Koehler Publishers, San Francisco, CA.

Lynas, M. 2008, *Six degrees: Our future on a hotter planet*, National Geographic Society, Washington, DC.

MacKay, D.J.C. 2009, *Sustainable energy - without the hot air*, UIT, Cambridge.

MacKenzie, D.A. 2006, *An engine, not a camera: How financial models shape markets*, MIT Press, Cambridge, MA.

Mainka, S.A. & McNeely, J. 2011, 'Ecosystem considerations for postdisaster recovery: Lessons from China, Pakistan, and elsewhere for recovery planning in Haiti', *Ecology and Society*, 16(1), 13.

Mair, J. & Noboa, E. 2006, 'Social entrepreneurship: How intentions to create a social venture are formed', in J. Mair, J. Robinson, & K. Hockerts (Eds) *Social entrepreneurship*, pp. 121–35, Palgrave Macmillan, New York, NY.

Makower, J. 2009, *Strategies for the green economy: Opportunities and challenges in the new world of business*, McGraw-Hill, New York.

Mander, J. & Goldsmith, E. 1996, *The case against the global economy: And for a turn toward the local*, Sierra Club Books, San Francisco, CA.

Manetti, G. 2011, 'The quality of stakeholder engagement in sustainability reporting: empirical evidence and critical points', *Corporate Social Responsibility and Environmental Management*, 18(2), 110–22.

Mannell, J. 2010, 'Are the sectors compatible? International development work and lessons for a business–nonprofit partnership framework', *Journal of Applied Social Psychology*, 40(5), 1106–122.

Margulis, L. & Lovelock, J.E. 1976, 'Is Mars a spaceship, too', *Natural History*, 85, 86–90.

Marshall, J. 2007, 'The gendering of leadership in corporate social responsibility', *Journal of Organizational Change Management*, 20(2), 165–81.

Marshall, J. 2011, 'En-gendering notions of leadership for sustainability', *Gender, Work & Organization*, 18(3), 263–81.

Martin, R.L. 2011, *Fixing the Game: How Runaway Expectations Broke the Economy, and how to Get Back to Reality*, Harvard Business School Pub.

Mather, G., Denby, L., Wood, L.N., & Harrison, B. 2011, 'Business graduate skills in sustainability', *Journal of Global Responsibility*, 2(2), 188–205.

Mawson, A. 2008, *The social entrepreneur: Making communities work*, Atlantic, London.

Maxwell, S. 2005, *The Washington Consensus is dead! Long live the meta-narrative*, Working paper 243, Overseas Development Institute, London.

McAnany, P.A. & Yoffee, N. (Eds) 2010, *Questioning collapse: Human resilience, ecological vulnerability, and the aftermath of empire*, Cambridge University Press, Cambridge.

McDonough, W. & Braungart, M. 2002, *Cradle to cradle: Remaking the way we make things*, North Point Press, New York, NY.

McKibben, B. & McKibben, B. 2007, *Deep economy: The wealth of communities and the durable future*, Times Books, New York, NY.

McKibben, B. 2010, *Eaarth: Making a life on a tough new planet*, Henry Holt, New York, NY.

McKinsey & Co 2005, *The impact of aging*, McKinsey & Company, New York, NY. Accessed 6 May 2011 at http://www.mckinsey.com/mgi/reports/pdfs/demographics/The_Impact_of_Aging_Executive_Summary.pdf.

McKinsey Global Institute 2011, *Resource revolution: Meeting the world's energy, materials, food, and water needs*, McKinsey & Company, New York, NY.

McPhail, K. 2008, 'Contributing to sustainable development through multi-stakeholder processes: practical steps to avoid the "resource curse"', *Corporate Governance*, 8(4), 471–81.

MEA 2005, *Ecosystems and human well-being: our human planet: Summary for decision-makers*, Island Press, Washington, DC.

Meadows, D.H. & Meadows, D.L. 2004, *Limits to growth: the 30-year update*, Earthscan, London.

Medeiros, M. 2007, 'Now, the rich', *Poverty in focus*, June, 18–19.

Mill, J.S. 1848, *Principles of Political Economy: With some of their applications to social philosophy*, John W. Parker, London.

Miller, D. 2009, *Selling solar: The diffusion of renewable energy in emerging markets*, Earthscan, London.

Millstone, E. 2008, *The atlas of food*, 2nd edn, Earthscan, London.

Ministry of Fisheries 2009, *Fisheries 2030: New Zealanders maximising benefits from the use of fisheries within environmental limits*, Ministry of Fisheries, Wellington.

Mintzberg, H. 1994, *The rise and fall of strategic planning: Reconceiving roles for planning, plans, planners*, Free Press, New York, NY.

Mirvis, P.H. 2000, 'Transformation at Shell: Commerce and citizenship', *Business and Society Review*, 105(1), 63–84.

Mitchell, L.E. 2001, *Corporate irresponsibility: America's newest export*, Yale University Press, New Haven, CT.

Monitor 2009, *Investing for social and environmental impact*, Monitor Group, Boston, MA.

Morewedge, C.K., Gilbert, D.T., Myrseth, K.O.R., Kassam, K.S., & Wilson, T.D. 2010, 'Consuming experience: Why affective forecasters overestimate comparative value', *Journal of Experimental Social Psychology*, 46(6), 986–92.

Morris, N. 2009, *Biomass power*, Franklin Watts, London.

Morsing, M. & Perrini, F. 2009, 'CSR in SMEs: do SMEs matter for the CSR agenda?', *Business Ethics: A European Review*, 18(1), 1–6.

Mouan, L.C. 2010, 'Exploring the potential benefits of Asian participation in the Extractive Industries Transparency Initiative: The case of China', *Business Strategy and the Environment*, 19(6), 367–76.

Murillo, D. & Lozano, J.M. 2006, 'SMEs and CSR: an approach to CSR in their own words', *Journal of Business Ethics*, 67(3), 227–40.

Murray, J. 2008, 'Merrill Lynch throws weight behind avoided deforestation credits: Investment bank predicts strong demand for credits that it claims will deliver biodiversity benefits alongside carbon reductions', *BusinessGreen*, 17 April.

Murray, S. 2011, 'Delivering change', *Special Reports – Financial Times*, 27 October.

Nattrass, B.F. & Altomare, M. 1999, *The natural step for business: Wealth, ecology, and the evolutionary corporation*, New Society Publishers, Gabriola Island, BC.

Nature 2011, 'A poor sequel: muted media response to the release of more climate e-mails shows science's strength', *Nature*, 480(6), 5.

Neale, J. 2008, *Stop global warming: Change the world*, Bookmarks Publications, London.

Neath, G. & Sharma, V. 2008, 'The Shakti revolution', *Development Outreach*, 10(2).

Nelson, J. 2007, *Building linkages for competitive and responsible entrepreneurship*, Harvard University John F Kennedy School of Government & UNIDO, Cambridge, MA.

Newell, P. & Paterson, M. 2010, *Climate capitalism: global warming and the transformation of the global economy*, Cambridge University Press, Cambridge.

Nicholls, A. & Opal, C. 2005, *Fair trade: Market-driven ethical consumption*, Sage, London.

Nicholls, A.E. 2008, *Social entrepreneurship: New models of sustainable social change*, 2nd edn, Oxford University Press, Oxford.

Nikoloyuk, J., Burns, T.R., & de Man, R. 2010, 'The promise and limitations of partnered governance: the case of sustainable palm oil', *Corporate Governance*, 10(1), 59–72.

Nordhaus, W.D. *The challenge of global warming* [Online]. Accessed 9 May 2011 at http://nordhaus. econ.yale.edu/dice_mss_072407_all.pdf.

Nordhaus, W.D. 2006, *The 'Stern Review' on the economics of climate change*, National Bureau of Economic Research, Cambridge, MA.

Novak, M. 1982, *Spirit of democratic capitalism*, Simon and Schuster, New York, NY.

NPR 2011, 'The Koch brothers & big political money', *On Point with Tom Ashbrook*, 8 February. Accessed 7 October at http://onpoint.wbur.org/2011/02/08/ koch-brothers-money-politics.

Oh, W.Y., Chang, Y.K., & Martynov, A. 'The effect of ownership structure on corporate social responsibility: Empirical evidence from Korea', *Journal of Business Ethics*, 104, 283–97.

Oreskes, N. & Conway, E.M. 2010, *Merchants of doubt: How a handful of scientists obscured the truth on issues from tobacco smoke to global warming*, Bloomsbury Press, New York, NY.

Ostrom, E. 1990, *Governing the commons: The evolution of institutions for collective action*, Cambridge University Press, Cambridge.

Pacala, S. & Socolow, R. 2004, 'Stabilization wedges: solving the climate problem for the next 50 years with current technologies', *Science*, 305(5686), 968–72.

Palazzo, G. & Richter, U. 2005, 'CSR business as usual? The case of the tobacco industry', *Journal of Business Ethics*, 61, 387–401.

Parker, C. & Lewis, R. 1981, 'Beyond the Peter Principle—Managing Successful Transitions', *Journal of European Industrial Training*, 5(6), 17–21.

Patricof, A. & Sunderland, J. 2006, 'Venture capital for development' in L. Brainard (Ed) *Transforming the Development Landscape: The Role of the Private Sector*, pp. 74–84, Brainard, Brookings Institution, Washington DC.

Patterson, W.C. 2007, *Keeping the lights on: Towards sustainable electricity*, Earthscan, London.

Paulden, P. 2009, *TXU LBO 'disaster' punishes bondholders with offer*, online edn, Bloomberg, New York.

Pavlovich, K. & Akoorie, M. 2010, 'Innovation, sustainability and regional development: the Nelson/ Marlborough seafood cluster, New Zealand', *Business Strategy and the Environment*, 19(6), 377–86.

Pearce, F. 2010, *The coming population crash: And our planet's surprising future*, Beacon Press, Boston, MA.

Pearce, F. 2011, 'Dubious assumptions prime population bomb', *Nature*, 473(7346), 125.

Peattie, K. & Belz, F. 2009, *Sustainability marketing: A global perspective*, John Wiley & Sons, Hoboken, NJ.

Peattie, K. 2011, 'Towards sustainability: achieving marketing transformation-a retrospective comment', *Social Business*, 1(1), 85–104.

Perez, C. 2002, *Technological revolutions and financial capital: The dynamics of bubbles and golden ages*, Edward Elgar Publishing, Cheltenham.

Pew Charitable Trusts 2010, *Who's winning the clean energy race?*, Pew Charitable Trusts, Washington, DC. Accessed 3 June http://www.pewtrusts.org/ uploadedFiles/wwwpewtrustsorg/Reports/Global_ warming/G-20 Report.pdf.

Pielke, R., Prins, G., Rayner, S., & Sarewitz, D. 2007, 'Climate change 2007: lifting the taboo on adaptation', *Nature*, 445(7128), 597–8.

Piepenbrock, T.F. 2010, *Toward a Theory of the Evolution of Business Ecosystems*, MIT Press, Cambridge, MA.

Pinstrup-Andersen, P. & Hazell, P.B.R. 1985, 'The impact of the Green Revolution and prospects for the future', *Food Reviews International*, 1(1), 1–25.

Podmore, S. 2009, *Global sustainability challenge*, Global Sustainability Challenge, London.

Polanyi, K. 1944, *The great transformation*, Farrar & Rinehart, Inc., New York, NY.

Porritt, J. 2005, *Capitalism: As if the world matters*, Earthscan, London.

Porter, M.E. 1980, *Competitive strategy: techniques for analyzing industries and competitors*, Free Press, New York, NY.

Porter, M.E. 1990, *The competitive advantage of nations*, Free Press, New York, NY.

Porter, M.E. & Kramer, M. 2011, 'The big idea: creating shared value', *Harvard Business Review*, 89, 1–2.

Prahalad, C.K. & Hart, S.L. 2002, 'The fortune at the bottom of the pyramid', *Strategy + Business* 26, 2–14.

Prince of Wales Corporate Leaders Group on Climate Change 2009, *Copenhagen Comminque on Climate Change*, University of Cambridge Programme for Sustainability Leadership, Cambridge.

Princen, T. 2005, *The logic of sufficiency*, MIT Press, Cambridge, MA.

Prins, G. & Rayner, S. 2007, *Wrong trousers: Radically rethinking climate policy*, Institute for Science, Innovation and Society, Oxford.

Prins, G., Galiana, I., Green, C., Grundman, R., Hulme, M., Korhola, A., Laird, F., Nordhaus, T., Pilke, R., Rayner, S., Sarewitz, D., Shellenberger, M., Stehr, N., & Tezuka, H. 2010, *The Hartwell Paper: A new direction for climate policy after the crash of 2009*, University of Oxford and London School of Economics, Oxford.

Putnam, R.D. 2000, *Bowling alone: The collapse and revival of American community*, Simon & Schuster, New York, NY.

PwC 2011, *Counting the cost of carbon: Low carbon economy index 2011*, PricewaterhouseCoopers LLC, London.

Rajak, D. 2008, "Uplift and empower': The market, the gift and corporate social responsibility on South Africa's platinum belt', *Research in Economic Anthropology*, 28, 297–324.

Ramírez, R., Selsky, J.W., & Van der Heijden, K. 2008, *Business planning in turbulent times: New methods for applying scenarios*, Earthscan, London.

Ramirez, R., Selsky, J.W., & Van der Heijden, K.E. 2010, *Business planning for turbulent times: New methods for applying scenarios*, 2nd edn, Earthscan, London.

Rand, A. 1966, *Capitalism, the unknown ideal*, New American Library, New York, NY.

Rands, G. & Starik, M. 2009, 'The short and glorious history of sustainability in North American management education', in C. Wankel & A. F. Stoner (Eds), *Management education for global sustainability*, pp. 19–50, IAP, New York, NY.

Rao, M.S. 2008, 'Empowering farmers through ICT: Lessons from ITC e-choupal', *National Conference on e-Governance–2008*, Panchkula, February.

Rasche, A. & Esser, D.E. 2006, 'From stakeholder management to stakeholder accountability: applying Habermasian discourse ethics to accountability research', *Journal of Corporate Citizenship*, 65, 251–67.

Rawls, J. 1971, *A theory of justice*, Belknap Press of Harvard University Press, Cambridge, MA.

Rayner, S. 2003, 'Democracy in the age of assessment: reflections on the roles of expertise and democracy in public-sector decision making', *Science and Public Policy*, 30(3), 163–70.

Republic of Rwanda 2011, *Green growth and climate resilience: National strategy for climate change and low carbon development*, Republic of Rwanda, Kigali.

Ries, A. & Trout, J. 2001, *Positioning: The battle for your mind*, 20th anniversary edn, McGraw-Hill, New York, NY.

Rifkin, J. 2002, *The hydrogen economy: The creation of the worldwide energy web and the redistribution of power on earth*, Polity, Oxford.

Robert, M. 1995, *Product innovation strategy pure and simple: How winning companies outpace their competitors*, McGraw-Hill, New York, NY.

Roberts, P. 2008, *The end of food*, Houghton Mifflin Company, Boston, MA.

Robins, N. 2008, 'The emergence of sustainable investing' in C. Krosinsky & N. Robins (Eds), *Sustainable investing: The art of long-term performance*, pp. 3–17, Earthscan, London.

Romm, J.J. 2004, *The hype about hydrogen: Fact and fiction in the race to save the climate*, Island Press, Washington, DC.

Rossi, M., Charon, S., Wing, G., & Ewell, J. 2006, 'Design for the next generation: incorporating cradle-to-cradle design into Herman Miller Products', *Journal of Industrial Ecology*, 10(4), 193–210.

Rouse, W.B. 2006, *Enterprise transformation: Understanding and enabling fundamental change*, Wiley-Interscience, Hoboken, NJ.

Royal Society 2009, *Geoengineering the climate: Science, governance and uncertainty*, The Royal Society, London.

Sadri, S. & Sadri, J. 2011, 'Excellence, sustainability and the bottom of the pyramid paradigm', *Journal of Economics and Sustainable Development*, 2(4), 175–92.

Salamon, L.M. 2003, *The resilient sector: The state of nonprofit America*, Brookings Institution, Washington, DC.

Sandberg, P., Khan, N., & Leong, L. 2010, *Vision 2050. The new agenda for business*, World Business Council for Sustainable Development, Geneva.

Savitz, A.W. 2006, *The triple bottom line: How today's best-run companies are achieving economic, social, and environmental success-and how you can too*, 1st edn, Jossey-Bass, San Francisco, CA.

Schaltegger, S. 2003, *An introduction to corporate environmental management: Striving for sustainability*, Greenleaf, Sheffield.

Scharmer, C.O. 2009, *Theory U: Learning from the Future as it Emerges*, Berrett-Koehler Publishers.

Scherer, A.G., Palazzo, G., & Baumann, D. 2006, 'Global rules and private actors: Toward a new role of the transnational corporation in global governance', *Business Ethics Quarterly*, 16(4), 505–32.

Schiller, P.L. Bruun, E.C., & Kenworthy, J.R. 2010, *An introduction to sustainable transportation: Policy, planning and implementation*, Earthscan, London.

Scholte, J.A. 2000, *Globalization: A critical introduction*, St. Martin's Press, New York, NY.

Schor, J. 2010, *Plenitude: The new economics of true wealth*, Penguin Press, New York, NY.

Schouten, G. & Glasbergen, P. 2011, 'Creating legitimacy in global private governance: The case of the Roundtable on Sustainable Palm Oil', *Ecological Economics*, 70, 1891–9.

Schröder, M. 2007, 'Is there a difference? The performance characteristics of SRI equity indices', *Journal of Business Finance & Accounting*, 34(1–2), 331–48.

Schumacher, E.F. 1973, *Small is beautiful: A study of economics as if people mattered*, Blond and Briggs, London.

Schumpeter, J.A. 1939/1982, *Business cycles: A theoretical, historical, and statistical analysis of the capitalist process*, Porcupine Press, Philadelphia, PA.

Schumpeter, J.A. 1943, *Capitalism, Socialism, and Democracy*, George Allen & Unwin Ltd, London.

Schumpeter, J.A. 1947, *Capitalism, socialism, and democracy*, 2d edn, Harper & brothers, New York, NY.

Scoones, I. 1998, *Sustainable rural livelihoods: A framework for analysis*, Institute of Development Studies, Brighton.

Seitanidi, M.M. 2010, *The politics of partnerships: A critical examination of nonprofit-business partnerships*, Springer, Dordrecht.

Sen, A.K. 2000, *Development as freedom*, Anchor books, New York, NY.

Senge, P., Smith, B., & Kruschwitz, N. 2008, 'The next industrial imperative', *Strategy and Business*, 51, 44–55.

Senge, P.M. 1999, *The dance of change: The challenges of sustaining momentum in learning organizations*, Nicholas Brealey, London.

Senge, P.M. 2008, *The necessary revolution: How individuals and organizations are working together to create a sustainable world*, Nicholas Brealey, London.

Sharfman, M.P., Shaft, T.M., & Anex Jr, R.P. 2009, 'The road to cooperative supply-chain environmental management: trust and uncertainty among pro-active firms', *Business Strategy and the Environment*, 18(1), 1–13.

Shen, X., Downing, T.E., Hamza, M., United Nations University Institute for Environment and Human Security & Stiftung, M.R. 2010, *Tipping Points in Humanitarian Crisis: From Hot Spots to Hot Systems*, United Nations University, Institute for Environment and Human Security.

Shiva, V. 2002, *Water wars: Privatization, pollution and profit*, Pluto Press, London.

Shleifer, A. & Vishny, R.W. 1996, *A survey of corporate governance*, NBER Working Papers 5554, National Bureau of Economic Research, Inc., Cambridge, MA.

Shove, E. 2010, 'Beyond the ABC: climate change policy and theories of social change', *Environment and Planning A*, 42(6), 1273–85.

Shrivastava, P. 2010, 'Pedagogy of passion for sustainability', *Academy of Management Learning & Education*, 9(3), 443–55.

Simon, H.A. 1955, 'A behavioral model of rational choice', *The Quarterly Journal of Economics*, 69(1), 99–118.

Singer, P. 1972, 'Famine, affluence, and morality', *Philosophy and Public Affairs*, 1(3), 229–43.

Sitkin, A. 2010, *International business: Challenges and choices*, Oxford University Press, Oxford.

Sjaastad, E. & Bromley, D.W. 2000, 'The prejudices of property rights: On individualism, specificity, and security in property regimes', *Development Policy Review*, 18(4), 365–89.

Skea, J., Ekins, P., & Winskel, M. (Eds) 2011, *Energy 2050: Making the transition to a secure low carbon energy system*, Earthscan, London.

Slater, D.J. & Dixon-Fowler, H. 2010, 'The future of the planet in the hands of MBAs: An examination of CEO MBA education and corporate environmental performance', *Academy of Management Learning & Education*, 9(3), 429–41.

Slavin, T. & Jha, A. 2009, 'Not under our backyard, say Germans, in blow to CO_2 plans', *The Guardian*, 29 July. Accessed 3 June 2011 at http://www.guardian.co.uk/environment/2009/jul/29/germany-carbon-capture.

Smith, A. 1776, *An inquiry into the nature and causes of the wealth of nations*, Whitestone, Dublin.

Smith, P.F. 2010, *Building for a changing climate: the challenge for construction, planning and energy*, Earthscan, London.

Smith, R. & Carlton, J. 2007, *Environmentalist groups feud over terms of the TXU buyout, Wall Street Journal*, 3 March, p. A1.

Snowden, D.J. 2001, 'Narrative patterns', *Knowledge Management, Ark Group*, 4(10).

Soper, K., Ryle, M.H., & Thomas, L.E. 2009, *The politics and pleasures of consuming differently*, Palgrave Macmillan, Basingstoke.

Sparkes, R. 2002, *Socially responsible investment: A global revolution*, J. Wiley, New York, NY.

SSEE 2009, *Future of mobility roadmap: Ways to reduce emissions while keeping mobile*, Smith School of Enterprise and the Environment, Oxford.

SSEE 2011, *International climate change negotiations: Key lessons and next steps*, Smith School of Enterprise and the Environment, Oxford University, Oxford.

Starik, M., Rands, G., Marcus, A.A., & Clark, T.S. 2010, 'From the guest editors: In search of sustainability in management education', *The Academy of Management Learning and Education (AMLE)*, 9(3), 377–83.

Stasinopoulos, P. (Ed) 2009, *Whole system design: An integrated approach to sustainable engineering*, Earthscan, London.

Steger, U. 2009, *Sustainability partnerships: The manager's handbook*, Palgrave Macmillan, Basingstoke.

Sterk, W., Ott, H.E., Watanabe, R., & Wittneben, B. 2007, 'The Nairobi Climate Change Summit (COP 12-MOP 2): Taking a Deep Breath before Negotiating Post-2012 Targets?', *Journal for European Environmental & Planning Law*, 4(2), 139–48.

Stern, N.H. 2008, *The economics of climate change: The Stern review*, Cambridge University Press, Cambridge.

Stern, P.C. 2011, 'Contributions of psychology to limiting climate change', *American Psychologist*, 66(4), 303–14.

Stewart, T.A. & Immelt, J. 2006, 'Growth as a process', *Harvard Business Review*, June, 60–70.

Stibbe, A. 2009, *The handbook of sustainability literacy: Skills for a changing world*, Green, Totnes.

Sullivan, R. & MacKenzie, C. (Eds) 2006, *Responsible investment*, Greenleaf Publishing, Sheffield.

Sullivan, R. 2011, *Valuing corporate responsibility: How do investors really use corporate responsibility information?* Greenleaf Publishing, Sheffield.

Sunstein, C.R. & Thaler, R. 2008, *Nudge: Improving decisions about health, wealth, and happiness*, Yale University Press, New Haven, CT.

Sustainability & GlobeScan 2010, *Survey on sustainability leadership 2010*, Sustainability and GlobeScan, Washington, DC.

Sustainable Consumption Roundtable 2006, *I will if you will: Towards sustainable consumption*, Sustainable Development Commission, London.

Svendsen, A. & Laberge, M. 2005, 'Convening stakeholder networks: a new way of thinking, being and engaging', *Journal of Corporate Citizenship*, 19, 91–4.

Thaler, R.H. & Sunstein, C.R. 2003, 'Libertarian paternalism', *The American Economic Review*, 93(2), 175–9.

The Economist 2007, 'Eco-warriors at the gate', *The Economist*, 1 March.

Thomas, S. 2010, *The EPR in crisis*, Greenwich Business School [Online]. Accessed 3 June 2011 at http://www.nuclearconsult.com/docs/information/economics/eprcrisis31110.pdf.

Thomas, S., Repetto, R., & Dias, D. 2007, 'Integrated environmental and financial performance metrics for investment analysis and portfolio management', *Corporate Governance: An International Review*, 15(3), 421–6.

Thompson, K. 2010, *Do We Need Pandas?: The Uncomfortable Truth about Biodiversity*, Green Books, Totnes.

Thrift, N. 2002, '"Think and act like revolutionaries": episodes from the global triumph of management discourse', *Critical Quarterly*, 44(3), 19–26.

Tilman, D., Socolow, R., Foley, J.A., Hill, J., Larson, E., Lynd, L., Pacala, S., Reilly, J., Searchinger, T., & Somerville, C. 2009, 'Beneficial biofuels—the food, energy, and environment trilemma', *Science*, 325(5938), 270–1.

Tischner, U.E. 2010, *Case studies in sustainable consumption and production: Food and agriculture*, Greenleaf, Sheffield.

Tol, R.S.J. 2009, 'The economic effects of climate change', *The Journal of Economic Perspectives*, 23(2), 29–51.

Treacy, M. 1995, *The discipline of market leaders: Choose your customers, narrow your focus, dominate your market*, HarperCollins, London.

Trentmann, F. 2012, 'The *Oxford handbook of the history of consumption*', Oxford University Press, Oxford.

Turner, R.K. 1994, *Environmental economics: An elementary introduction*, Harvester Wheatsheaf, New York, NY.

Turney, J. 2010, *The rough guide to the future*, Rough Guides, London.

UN Global Compact undated, *Blueprint for corporate sustainability leadership* [Online]. Accessed 30 July 2011 at http://www.unglobalcompact.org/docs/news_events/8.1/Blueprint.pdf.

United Nations Global Compact & Accenture 2010, *A New Era of Sustainability*, Accenture, London.

United Nations Population Division 2009, *World Population Policies 2009*. Accessed 6 May 2011 at http://www.un.org/esa/population/publications/wpp2009/Introduction.htm.

van der Heijden, K., Ramírez, R., Selsky, J.W., & Wilkinson, A. 2010, 'Turbulence, business planning and the unfolding financial crisis', in R. Ramirez, J. Selsky, & K. van der Heijden (Eds), *Business Planning for Turbulent Times: New Methods for Applying Scenarios*, pp. 261–82. Earthscan, London.

Vermeulen, W.J.V. & Seuring, S. 2009, 'Sustainability through the market–the impacts of sustainable supply chain management: introduction', *Sustainable Development*, 17(5), 269–73.

Vogel, D. 2005, *The market for virtue: The potential and limits of corporate social responsibility*, Brookings Institution Press, Washington, DC.

von Hayek, F.A. 1944, *The road to serfdom*, G. Routledge & Sons, London.

Wagner, H. 2009, *Introduction to wind energy systems: Basics, technology and operation*, Springer, Berlin.

Wajcman, J. 2010, 'Feminist theories of technology', *Cambridge Journal of Economics*, 34(1), 143–52.

Walker, G. & King, D.A. 2008, *The hot topic: How to tackle global warming and still keep the lights on*, Bloomsbury, London.

Walsh, J. 2004, 'Taking stock of stakeholder management', *Academy of Management Review*, 30, 426–38.

Wankel, C. & Stoner, J.A.F. 2009, *Management education for global sustainability*, Information Age Publishing, Charlotte, NC.

Ward, H. 2009, *Resource nationalism and sustainable development: A primer and key issues*, IIED, London.

Warner, M. & Sullivan, R. 2004, *Putting partnerships to work: Strategic alliances for development between government, the private sector and civil society*, Greenleaf Publishing, Sheffield.

WEF & Accenture 2012, *More with less: Scaling sustainable consumption and efficiency*, World Economic Forum, Geneva.

WEF & Deloitte 2011, *Consumption dilemma: Leverage points for accelerating sustainable growth*, World Economic Forum, Geneva.

Weick, K.E. & Sutcliffe, K.M. 2001, *Managing the unexpected*, Jossey-Bass San Francisco, CA.

Weitzman, M.L. 2007, 'A review of the Stern Review on the economics of climate change', *Journal of Economic Literature*, 45(3), 703–24.

Weitzman, M.L. 2011, 'Fat-tailed uncertainty in the economics of catastrophic climate change', *Review of Environmental Economics and Policy*, 5(2), 275–92.

Wenham, S.R. (Ed) 2007, *Applied photovoltaics*, 2nd edn, Earthscan, London.

Werbach, A. 1997, *Act now, apologize later*, 1st edn, Cliff Street Books, New York, NY.

Werbach, A. 2009, *Strategy for sustainability: A business manifesto*, Harvard Business School Press, Boston, MA.

Werther, W.B. & Chandler, D. 2011, *Strategic corporate social responsibility: Stakeholders in a global environment*, 2nd edn, Sage Publications, Thousand Oaks, CA.

Weybrecht, G. 2009, *The sustainable MBA: The manager's guide to green business*, Wiley, Hoboken, NJ.

Wheeler, D. 1997, *The stakeholder corporation: A blueprint for maximizing stakeholder value*, Pitman, London.

White, P. 2009, 'Building a sustainability strategy into the business', *Corporate Governance*, 9(4), 386–94.

Whitmarsh, L., O'Neill, S., & Lorenzoni, I. 2011, 'Climate change or social change? Debate within, amongst, and beyond disciplines', *Environment and Planning A*, 43(2), 258–61.

WHO 2008, *Safe water, better health*, WHO, Geneva. Accessed 26 May 2011 at http://whqlibdoc.who.int/publications/2008/9789241596435_eng.pdf.

Wicks, A. & Goodstein, J. 2009, 'Stakeholder responsibility and stakeholder commitment', *Notizie di Politeia*, 93, 9–24.

Wilkinson, R.G. 2010, *The spirit level: Why equality is better for everyone*, Penguin, London.

Wissenschaftlicher Beirat der Bundesregierung Globale Umweltveränderungen (Germany) 2010, *Future bioenergy and sustainable land use*, Earthscan, London.

Wittneben, B., Sterk, W., Ott, H.E., & Brouns, D. 2006, 'The Montreal climate summit: starting the Kyoto business and preparing for post-2012', *Journal for European Environmental & Planning Law*, 3(2), 90–100.

Wittneben, B.B.F. 2007, 'Institutional change in the transfer of climate-friendly technology', *Business and Society*, 46(1), 117–24.

Wood, D. undated, *Handbook on climate-related investing across asset classes*, Institute for Responsible Investment, Boston, MA.

World Bank 2003, *Poverty and climate change: Reducing the vulnerability of the poor through adaptation*, World Bank, Washington DC.

World Bank 2010, *World development report 2010: Development and climate change*, World Bank, Washington DC.

World Commission on Environment and Development & Brundtland, G.H. 1987, *Our common future*, Oxford University Press, Oxford.

Worldwatch Institute 2010, *State of the world 2010: Transforming cultures from consumerism to sustainability*, Earthscan, London.

Wright, T. 2007, 'Indonesian proposal: Pay us not to chop down our trees', *The Wall Street Journal*, August 10, p. A1.

WWF 2010, *WWF – Living Planet Report* [Online]. Accessed 6 April 2011 at http://wwf.panda.org/about_our_earth/all_publications/living_planet_report/.

Yasuhara, K., Komine, H., Yokoki, H., Suzuki, T., Mimura, N., Tamura, M., & Chen, G. 2011, 'Effects of climate change on coastal disasters: new methodologies and recent results', *Sustainability Science*, 6(2), 219–32.

You, Y. & Howe, B. 2011, 'Turning submarine telecommunications cables into a real-time multi-purpose global climate change monitoring network', in J. Martin, J. Ellul, L. Gomez, & Y. Reddy (Eds) *SENSORCOMM 2011, The Fifth International Conference on Sensor Technologies and Applications*, pp. 184–90, IARIA.

Zadek, S., Lingayah, S., Murphy, S., & New Economics Foundation 1998, *Purchasing power: Civil action for sustainable consumption*, New Economics Foundation, London.

Zadek, S., Pruzan, P.M., & Evans, R. 1997, *Building corporate accountability: Emerging practices in social and ethical accounting, auditing and reporting*, Earthscan, London.

Zakhem, A.J., Palmer, D.E., & Stoll, M.L. 2007, *Stakeholder theory: Essential readings in ethical leadership and management*, Prometheus Books, Amherst, NY.

Index